After the boats were lowered, the officers were setting the topmast and large gaff flag. The flags were sparkling clean, flapping in the wind one last time above the old, seasoned steel warrior. A stiff breeze was moving them so that they were clearly and mightily standing out against the grey Nordland sky. Nobody will ever forget that view.

Lt Cdr von Reiche, SMS *Prinzregent Luitpold*

CAROLINE & ANDREW

SCAPA 1919

The Archaeology of a Scuttled Fleet

Innes McCartney

OSPREY PUBLISHING
Bloomsbury Publishing Plc
Kemp House, Chawley Park, Oxford OX2 9PH, UK
1385 Broadway, 5th Floor, New York, NY 10018, USA
29 Earlsfort Terrace, Dublin 2, Ireland
www.ospreypublishing.com – Email: info@ospreypublishing.com

OSPREY is a trademark of Osprey Publishing, a division of Bloomsbury Publishing Plc

First published in Great Britain in 2019.

ISBN: HB 9781472828903; eBook 9781472828958; ePDF 9781472828965; XML 9781472828972

21 22 23 24 25   10 9 8 7 6 5 4 3 2

Index by Kate Inskip
Printed and bound in India by Replika Press Private Ltd.
Front cover: The sinking of SMS *Bayern* during the scuttle of the German High Seas fleet at Scapa Flow, 21 June 1919 (Ullstein Bild via Getty Images).
Bottom left: The stern anchor of SMS *Brummer* (Gavin Anderson).
Bottom centre: DTM model of the wreck of SMS *Cöln*, January 2017 (Sea War Museum Jutland).
Bottom right: The auxiliary steering wheel from SMS *Cöln* (Gavin Anderson).

Osprey Publishing supports the Woodland Trust, the UK's leading woodland conservation charity.

To find out more about our authors and books visit **www.ospreypublishing.com**. Here you will find extracts, author interviews, details of forthcoming events and the option to sign up for our newsletter.

CONTENTS

PREFACE

I first visited Scapa Flow in 2001 as a guest of the UK Ministry of Defence. We flew up to Kirkwall from RAF Northolt on a BAe 146 of No. 32 (The Royal) Squadron. On our arrival at the Harbour Authority Offices at Scapa Flow, the Junior Minister of Defence, Dr Lewis Moonie, read a statement declaring that the UK would be bringing the 1986 Protection of Military Remains Act into force – something I had championed. We then lunched at the British Legion with some of Orkney's naval veterans and visited the HMS *Royal Oak* memorial in St Magnus Cathedral before flying back to London.

This memorable but all too short visit was a reminder of the importance of Scapa Flow and its naval past and I vowed I would return in the future to examine the shipwrecks. Years passed, taking me on numerous shipwreck investigations including the Battle of Jutland, the first and second U-boat campaigns and Operation *Deadlight*, so it was not until 2013 that I was able to begin to dive on and survey the Scapa wrecks from John Thornton's dive boat MV *Karin*.

Within a few days of arriving I came to regret not having dived up in Scapa Flow many years previously as it was evident that the wrecks and, importantly, the outlying and often overlooked salvage sites had a very special tale to tell. Although it was possible to write a detailed account of the

Figure i. The author on board MV *Karin* after a survey dive on SMS *Brummer* in November 2017. (Patricia McCartney)

Grand Scuttle (a phrase I have shamelessly borrowed from the title of Dan van der Vat's book) and its archaeology based on archival research and underwater images, I felt more was needed.

Working on the Battle of Jutland wrecks had demonstrated the value of marine geophysics, especially multibeam bathymetry. When it came to studying the shipwrecks this technology offered so much that diving could not on its own. The Jutland survey had been laid on by Gert Normann Andersen who was in the process of establishing the Sea War Museum Jutland at the time.

In 2017, with the excellent museum now open to the public and the centenary celebrations having passed, it was time to look for a new survey project. In this case our mutual interests coincided again and I was delighted to be working with the Sea War Museum Jutland once more. The survey of Scapa Flow took place in January over a 10-day period. As he had been throughout our Jutland survey, Nick Jellicoe was an enthusiastic and knowledgeable participant.

Within the survey data is the old German anchorage where the Grand Scuttle took place but also the areas where salvaged ships were partially broken up. When combined with detailed archival work and my diving surveys, it becomes clear that there is a lot more remaining on the bottom of Scapa Flow than many may presume, and I hope this book contributes to furthering knowledge of these remains.

I wish to personally acknowledge the following for contributing in myriad ways to this project: Gert Normann Andersen, Rasmus Normann Andersen, Mogens Dam and all the team at the Sea War Museum Jutland and JD-Contractor A/S; David Mackie, Andrea Massey and Sarah Maclean at Orkney Library & Archives; Ian Killick and Anthony Roy at the UK Hydrographic Office; Dr Jann Witt at the Deutscher Marine Bund; Dr Stephan Huck at the German Navy Museum; Matt Skelhorn at MOD Salvage & Marine; Dr John Bevan at the Historical Diving Society; Jonathon Clay and Pam Alexander at SOCOTEC; Mark Lawrence at ADUS/Deepocean; Gabriel Walton at Ultrabeam; Prof Ian Buxton and Dr Brian Newman at Newcastle University Special Collections; Dr Richard Osborne and Prof Aidan Dodson at the World Ship Society; Steve Allen at York Archaeological Trust; Tony Lovell at The Dreadnought Project; Andrew Choong at the Ship's Plans Department of the National Maritime Museum; Gary Fabian at Bathymetric Research; John Thornton of John's Diving Charters MV *Karin*; Linda Thornton of the Polrudden Guesthouse; The Leverhulme Trust; Bournemouth University; Orkney Harbour Authority; UK National Archives; Institute of Engineering and Shipbuilding in Scotland; National Library of Scotland; Caird Library; Brotherton Library; EIVA A/S; Dr James Delgado; the late Gary Staff; Marsden Samuel; the late Gavin Anderson; Ian Murray Taylor; Amy Cromarty; Ivan Houston; Fiona Houston; Naomi Watson; Nick Jellicoe; Annette Heubner; Dougal Campbell; Tommy Clark; Barry Jackson; Oliver Lörscher; and lastly but mostly, Patricia McCartney.

Figure ii. With Gert Normann Andersen aboard MV *Vina* at Scapa Flow in 2017 on the Sea War Museum multibeam survey. Great to be working with him again. (Sea War Museum Jutland)

INTRODUCTION

Section 1 "All the News That's Fit to Print."

The New York Times.

THE WEATHER
Fair Sunday and Monday; northwest and north winds.

VOL. LXVIII...NO. 22,429.   ....   NEW YORK, SUNDAY, JUNE 22, 1919. 114 PAGES. In Nine Parts.   FIVE CENTS

GERMAN CREWS SINK MOST OF GREAT SCAPA FLOW FLEET; SHIPS, WITH SEACOCKS OPEN, GO DOWN UNDER GERMAN FLAG; BAUER IS NAMED AT WEIMAR TO HEAD PEACE CABINET

Figure i. *The New York Times* headline of 22 June 1919, the day after the Grand Scuttle. (New York Times)

On 21 June 1919 the world witnessed a German admiral order the 74 most modern warships of his fleet to deliberately sink themselves. The Grand Scuttle took place at Scapa Flow in the Orkney Islands of Scotland. It remains a unique event in the annals of naval history. The following years of salvage of that fleet were equally unprecedented. A century later the remains of scuttle and salvage represent a unique underwater landscape with a rich cultural history of its own.

Scapa Flow and the archaeology of the Grand Scuttle

The Grand Scuttle transformed the undersea landscape of Scapa Flow in a way which is completely unique. Historical landscapes have been compared to a palimpsest where each layer of use and reuse leaves archaeological traces behind. In reality it was not just the scuttling which did this, but also the decades of salvage which followed. This created an underwater industrial landscape and, off the small island of Rysa Little, a scrapyard of the remains of partially dismantled battleships; it has also created a globally unique legacy of that momentous day in June 1919.

The scuttling of the German Fleet at Scapa Flow also remains the most globally notable event to have taken place in the Orkney Islands. It placed Scapa Flow on the world map. As shown in Figure i, the *New York Times* reported on 22 June: 'GERMAN CREWS SINK MOST OF GREAT SCAPA FLOW FLEET; SHIPS, WITH SEACOCKS OPEN, GO DOWN UNDER GERMAN FLAG'.[1] Within months, tourists from America began to enquire as to how they might visit the remains of the sunken and beached ships.[2]

The salvage of all but eight of the 74-ship scuttle was also worldwide news. During the salvage years, the LZ 127 *Graf Zeppelin* was on occasion seen buzzing curiously over the salvage sites of the German battleships. Since the 1960s the world's curiosity concerning the remaining wrecks has continued to grow. Today, Scapa Flow represents one of the world's great recreational diving destinations and Orkney welcomes thousands of divers yearly to explore the wrecks. A report in 2001 showed that the numbers of visiting divers had grown steadily since 1981 and that in 2000 over 3,500 divers had made over 11,100 individual dives on the German wrecks.[3]

The 2001 UNESCO Convention on the Protection of the Underwater Cultural Heritage states that 'underwater cultural heritage' means all traces of human existence having a cultural, historical or archaeological character which have been partially or totally under water, periodically or continuously, for at least 100 years.[4] On the centenary of the Grand Scuttle in 2019, therefore, the wrecks would become recognized as a globally important cultural asset.

In reality, however, the historical and cultural significance of the remains of the Grand Scuttle had already been officially recognized several years previously. In 2002, seven of the nine surviving wrecks were protected as monuments under the Ancient Monuments and Archaeological Areas Act 1979. This put them on an equal footing with the world-famous archaeological sites on land in Orkney, such as Skara Brae, the Ring of Brodgar and the Standing Stones of Stenness, which too receive large numbers of visitors annually.

The German ships of 1919 have passed from weapons of war to economic resources to cultural artefacts. The centenary of the Grand Scuttle is an opportune time to compile a comprehensive new study based on original data of the Grand Scuttle and the salvage years, and highlighting how this seamlessly interfaces with surveys of the extant archaeology we see today. In order to do this, the entire project has been based on original research, from the archive to the fieldwork.

Historical sources

A significant body of published sources covering the Grand Scuttle, the salvage years and beyond exists. However, as the more assiduous researchers who have worked in this field in the past have shown, much of this material is notable for a number of factual errors often repeated from book to book.[5] Particularly inconsistent are dates and timings relating to the salvage and the disposal of the German Fleet after 1919.[6]

In order to attempt to provide the reader with an accurate narrative it was decided early on that, wherever possible, primary source documentation from archival records would form the basis of the research underpinning the project. This entailed visits to a number of archives in the UK and the ordering of documents from Germany and the USA.

Notable archival sources were found in the National Archives, the Brotherton Library, the Naval Historical Branch, the UK Hydrographic Office, the Orkney Archive, the Imperial War Museum, the National Maritime Museum, National Archives and Records Administration (NARA) in the United States and the Bundesarchiv in Germany. In total, the archival research from 2014 to 2018 examined 139 individual file boxes and photographed 13,455 pages of text and images. The most important sources were sorted into databases so that they could be accessed by specific date. This was particularly important with the Admiralty sales and disposals data, and with the records of the *Orkney Herald* and the *Orcadian*, where it was noted that dates of specific events differed even between these two contemporary newspapers.

Within the archival data were some notably important documents which the reader will inevitably discern – namely, from the archive, the Admiralty disposals ledger, Admiralty reports of the scuttle, Royal Navy reports of the salvage of the beached warships, German officers' reports of the scuttling of their ships while they were being held as prisoners, the *Orkney Herald* and the *Orcadian*, the Harry Murray Taylor diaries, the 1919 hydrographic survey of each shipwreck and the company records of Metal Industries.

The published sources which proved of great value were those written by participants in the scuttle and salvage operations. These included classic accounts of the scuttle by von Reuter and Friedrich Ruge and accounts of the salvage years by Ernest Cox, Thomas McKenzie and Harry Grosset. Books which proved particularly useful included Ian Buxton's history of Metal Industries,[7] Campbell's analysis of the Battle of Jutland[8] and Friedman's compilation of British intelligence records of the ships of the High Seas Fleet.[9]

The photographic record of the Grand Scuttle and salvage years

A significant number of photographs of the events of the scuttle were published in 1919 and more have come to light in subsequent years. A hundred years on, it is not possible to directly attribute some of them to specific photographers present at the time, so establishing provenance is a challenge. There is also a problem with the German ships being misidentified in captions. All of these issues needed addressing when analyzing the photographs of the interned fleet and the Grand Scuttle.

Some photographs look suspiciously composed or enhanced. An example which raises suspicion can be seen in Figure ii. This photograph appeared in *The Sphere* on 5 July 1919. It is captioned: 'A British Destroyer Endeavouring to Force a Sinking German Destroyer Up an Island Beach'. It looks as if it could be a composite image, almost too good to be real. Certainly it was unique among the photographs uncovered during the research. Would not such a dynamic photograph have seen wider circulation at the time?

However, the photograph cannot be ruled out as a fake. This is because of the following mention of the destroyer HMS *Vega* in the Admiralty report of the Grand Scuttle: 'owing to a mistake in the engine-room she was in a collision with

Figure ii. A photograph apparently showing a British destroyer forcing a German torpedo boat into shallow water, as published in 1919. It seems almost too good to be true. But is it? (*The Sphere*)

a German destroyer and sustained serious damage forward'.[10] HMS *Vega*'s pennant number at that time was F09, the same as seen in the photograph. So it may be genuine, but in this instance caution prevails and until additional evidence is found, such as proof of its original provenance, it remains unverified.

Images accepted as genuine taken by local photographer J. Omond, Lt Peploe of HMS *Westcott* and paymaster C. W. Burrows from HMS *Victorious* show events from the time the British learned that the German ships were being deliberately sunk by their crews. These are particularly useful because we know where the photographers were when the photographs were taken. Others whose credibility seems not to be in doubt have also been used. Together, these photographs represent the best I have found, and they are placed together for the first time in Chapter Two, to provide a chronology of the events of the day.

There is a plentiful supply of photographs depicting the salvage of the vessels in the 1920s and 1930s, many of which can be found in the Orkney Archive. Metal Industries also kept photo albums of the ships it broke up. Both sources have been used in this publication. It was much more challenging to find photos of the later low-scale salvage years of the 1960s and 1970s.

Archaeology and historical text

Archaeological studies focused on the modern era quite often involve a complex interface with the historical record. This is particularly true of the wrecks of the Grand Scuttle and the subsequent salvage years. These events were well documented at the time and, as a result, the locations of the wreckage that remained have always been known. It was the role of archaeology to study the remaining objects in detail and to critically assess what they actually represent.

This meant analyzing the extant remains of nine shipwrecks and interpreting what has happened, and is happening, to them. The site formation processes taking place on each wreck have been analyzed in as much detail as possible, greatly aided by having access to the 2006 ADUS multibeam survey of the wrecks. This allowed for comparisons to be made on seven of them with our own detailed multibeam survey of 2017. It is unusual to have such detailed datasets a decade apart, and the analysis clearly shows how the wrecks have degraded through this period.

There was a notable absence of detailed records concerning the preparation of the larger warships for towing south, as well as of the piecemeal salvage activity which took place on the wrecks after the Second World War. In these cases, archaeological surveys have been able to identify some of the processes at work and specifically identify the sites where the wrecks were processed.

Figure iii. The Sea War Museum Jutland's two survey vessels used to survey Scapa Flow in 2017. Left, MV *Vina*, and right, the *Limbo* being deployed from *Vina* during the survey.

The Sea War Museum Jutland multibeam survey, 2017

The Sea War Museum Jutland carried out a multibeam survey of Scapa Flow over a 10-day period in January 2017. As the museum's affiliated archaeologist, I was present throughout and was involved in the planning of the project and the subsequent processing and presentation of all of the multibeam data shown in this book.

Due to their relatively shallow depth, the nine remaining wrecks are ideal shipwreck targets for a multibeam survey. Aside from the wrecks, we also wanted to use the multibeam to search and map as much of the former German anchorage, as well as the salvage areas around it, as we could in the time allocated. We also wanted to scan a number of other very shallow areas. To acquire the data needed we employed two survey vessels: the 2,065-tonne survey ship *Vina*, our base of operations, and *Limbo*, a small day boat which can operate in very shallow water.

Both vessels are equipped with identical Reson 7125 multibeam systems and they use EIVA Navisuite software. The two vessels can be seen in Figure ii. As it was, *Limbo* proved exceptionally useful because a number of areas were simply too shallow or enclosed for *Vina* to work in. Full credit goes to the team who worked on *Limbo* every day in sometimes choppy conditions. It was not a task for those who get seasick. The data *Limbo* gathered on the shallow sites, such as SMS *S36*, are unrivalled in detail.

The survey ended up covering an area of around 40km². The data were readied for archaeological analysis as shown in Figure iv, with the greatest care being taken to acquire the highest resolution possible on each specific shipwreck site.

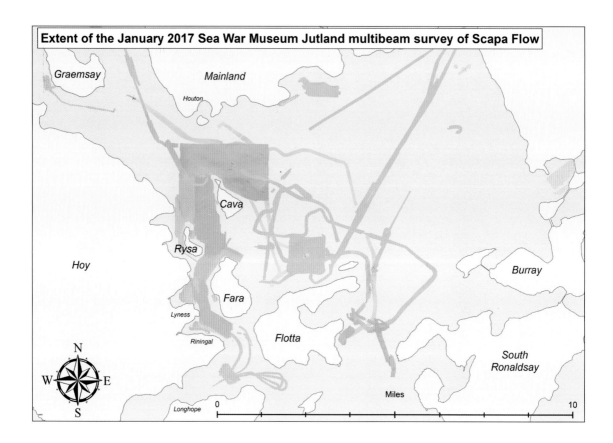

Extent of the January 2017 Sea War Museum Jutland multibeam survey of Scapa Flow

Graemsay

Mainland

Houton

Cava

Rysa

Hoy

Burray

Fara

Lyness

Riningal

Flotta

South Ronaldsay

Miles

Longhope

0   10

N
W   E
S

Figure iv. The full extent of the area of coverage of the 2017 multibeam survey. The focus was on the German anchorage, but all the other major shipwrecks were also scanned.

Multibeam systems create a sound pulse in a fan of up to 512 individual beams from an echosounder under the hull. The returning soundwave is picked by an antenna array and the directional information is processed to produce a swath of depth readings in three dimensions. Multibeam is primarily used by hydrographic surveyors to acquire data relating to depth of water and type of seabed. Its ability to record objects on the seabed in three dimensions makes it a useful tool for surveying shipwrecks. This is particularly the case when the wrecks are very large or when there is low visibility or marine growth that make surveys by more traditional diving methods challenging.

The shipwreck survey data we acquired came in the form of a point cloud, made up of millions of individual depth readings. A point cloud can be processed in several different ways to maximize its potential archaeological value. The means by which the shipwreck data from the Scapa survey were processed is given in Figure v, which uses the example of the battleship wreck of SMS *Markgraf*.

Starting at the top, Image A shows the original point cloud once it is drawn out from the original survey data. It has been coloured to give height

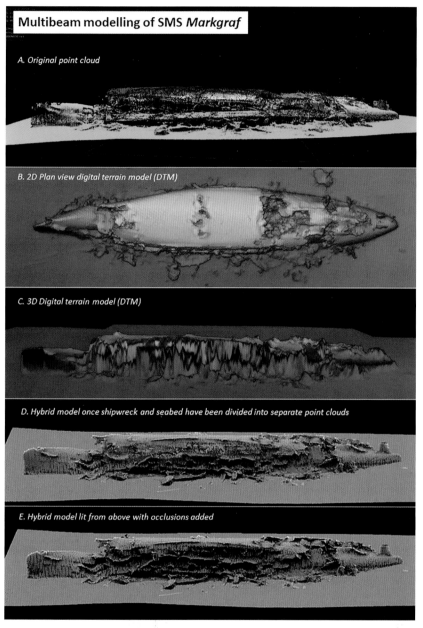

Multibeam modelling of SMS *Markgraf*

A. Original point cloud

B. 2D Plan view digital terrain model (DTM)

C. 3D Digital terrain model (DTM)

D. Hybrid model once shipwreck and seabed have been divided into separate point clouds

E. Hybrid model lit from above with occlusions added

Figure v. The original point cloud gathered over SMS *Markgraf* and how it was processed to produce the survey results.

readings from the seabed. It shows every depth point recorded over the entire shipwreck. The challenge for surveyors on objects which stand up off the seabed, such as this, is to get point readings from the vertical aspects of the object. In a hull-mounted multibeam system, the 'top-down' nature of the soundings means that points generally accumulate on horizontal surfaces, as can be clearly seen.

In Image B the point cloud has been processed into a 'Digital Terrain Model' (DTM), shown from above in plan view and coloured to show height range. The DTM plan view is usually used for seabed mapping, and it creates excellent site maps which are used to depict every wreck site. Accurate measurements can be made from them and, as with all the data, it can be georeferenced into the maps of the survey. Its limitations are evident when covering larger upstanding objects, when a curtaining effect is seen in three dimensions, as shown in Image C.

In order to avoid this effect and study the wreck in three dimensions the point cloud is processed in another way to create a 'hybrid model'. The point cloud is manually cut into sections which separate the seabed from the wreckage. These separate point clouds are then coloured differently. In Image D the initial result is shown, with artificial 'illumination' from directly above. This is suitable for most applications, but in the case of large solid objects the absence of points on some vertical surfaces creates the false impression that the wreck is see-through and hollow inside.

Finally, to give a more accurate visual impression, occlusion objects are added to the interior of the point cloud. The final solid-looking model can be seen in Image E. I first came across the use of occlusion objects in the 2006 ADUS survey of the wrecks, which produced excellent results. Our hybrid models were prepared in the same way in order to analyse how the wrecks have deteriorated in the 11 years between surveys. Image E clearly shows how the edges of decks can be seen poking out of the side of the wreck from areas where the original outer armour of the ship has been removed by salvage.

The diving surveys of the wrecks

The diving on the wrecks all took place from John Thornton's MV *Karin*, a live-aboard dive charter vessel based in Stromness. John Thornton has been diving at Scapa since 1981 and is the longest-serving dive operator in Orkney, with an unrivalled knowledge of the wrecks and how they have altered over the last 40 years. The dives took place in two-week periods in 2013, 2014, 2016 and 2017.

I recorded the wrecks using video and photographs. Where necessary, objects were measured conventionally with a tape. Several other divers acknowledged in the preface also contributed their own material to the project, helping to create detailed datasets on each site visited. Many hours of video were reviewed to create the sets of images presented, and in all cases the video surveys were reconciled to the multibeam data, so that the exact location of each object recorded on video has been established.

Times and measurements

Imperial measurements have been used to describe the ships and events in a historical context (except where the metric system was already in common use [e.g. 88mm gun]). The displaced tonnage of the German ships is given as 'design displacement' based on the German convention in use from 1882 to 1927.

The metric system has been used to discuss the archaeology of the wrecks. This convention was the simplest to apply as Britain migrated to the metric system after the scuttling and salvage of the ships.

During the Grand Scuttle the German navy used Central European Time (GMT+1hr) which, during the summer of 1919, coincided with British Summer Time (BST) (also GMT+1hr). To the extent that time zones recorded during the Grand Scuttle are known, they have been corrected to BST.

1   *The New York Times*, 22 June 1919, p. 1.

2   Orkney Archives (various dates), microfilmed records of the *Orkney Herald*, 1919–1931. Kirkwall, 21 May 1921.

3   ScapaMAP 2000–2002, Report Compiled for Historic Scotland on the Mapping and Management of the Submerged Archaeological Resource in Scapa Flow. Orkney: Scapa Flow Marine Archaeology Project, 2003, pp. 14–16.

4   UNESCO, 2001. Definitions of the 2001 Convention, http://portal.unesco.org/en/ev.php-URL_ID=13520&URL_DO=DO_TOPIC&URL_SECTION=201.html (accessed June 2018).

5   D. van der Vat (1982), *The Grand Scuttle: The Sinking of the German Fleet at Scapa Flow in 1919* (London: Hodder & Stoughton), p. 233.

6   I. Buxton (1992), *Metal Industries: Shipbreaking at Rosyth and Charlestown* (Kendal: World Ship Society), p. 12.

7   I. Buxton (1992), *Metal Industries: Shipbreaking at Rosyth and Charlestown* (Kendal: World Ship Society).

8   N. J. M. Campbell (1986), *Jutland: An Analysis of the Fighting* (London: Conway).

9   N. Friedman (ed.) (1992) *German Warships of World War I: The Royal Navy's Official Guide to the Capital Ships, Cruisers, Destroyers, Submarines and Small Craft, 1914–1918* (London: Greenhill).

10 National Archives (various dates), Sinking of German Fleet at Scapa Flow. ADM 116/2074. London.

PART ONE
THE GRAND SCUTTLE 1919

The largest battleship to be successfully
scuttled, SMS *Bayern* rolls over and sinks, as
immortalised in this famous C. W. Burrows
photograph. (Orkney Archive)

CHAPTER 1
ARMISTICE AND INTERNMENT AT SCAPA FLOW

Figure 1.1. In preparation for internment, the German ships had to unload all ammunition. The hundreds of brass cordite cases of a Kaiser-class battleship are seen here coming ashore at Wilhelmshaven. Their seemingly disorderly state on the quay gives an indication of the social upheaval under way and of the haste with which the ships had to be disarmed. (Archiv Deutscher Marinebund)

The German High Seas Fleet, which had been the source of tension between Britain and Germany in the years up to World War I, fell under British control in 1918. Its internment in Scapa Flow while the negotiations at Versailles dragged on was a difficult affair, with the Germans justifiably feeling they were little more than prisoners. The publishing in May 1919 of the terms of the Armistice offered to Germany set in motion the events that led to the Grand Scuttle in June.

The German naval mutiny and the Armistice

On 5 October 1918 the German government formally offered an armistice under the terms of the Fourteen Points devised by the American President Woodrow Wilson. Negotiations would take time to be completed, but it meant that World War I was drawing to a close. However, although the German army had been forced into a general retreat on the Western Front, the German navy and its powerful High Seas Fleet was still a potent, undefeated force.

In order to influence the armistice negotiations in favour of Germany, the naval high command planned a major fleet operation in the southern North Sea. In the simplest of terms, destroyer raids in the Thames estuary would force the British Grand Fleet from its Scottish bases into the area, which by then would have been sowed with minefields. The German battlefleet would then appear to attack the disrupted formations of the Grand Fleet when at their weakest and force a result in favour of Germany at whatever cost.

Operational planning went ahead and by 29 October the High Seas Fleet began to muster at Schillig Roads. But the plan was already beginning to unravel from within. There had been growing discontent in the High Seas Fleet since 1916 and now mutiny broke out on a number of the larger capital ships. Despite attempts to round up the ringleaders, the plan had to be abandoned and the force returned to its bases.

The simmering anger of the lower deck could not be easily contained. As the battleships were dispersed they took the mutiny with them to Kiel, where it soon spread ashore, and as workers' councils (copied from the model of the Russian Revolution the previous year) took over control of the ports of Wilhelmshaven and Hamburg, several regions and major cities of Germany also descended into the chaos of revolution under the banner of the red flag. There would be no final battle with the Grand Fleet, and Germany's navy was to go on to suffer an even greater humiliation than that of mutiny: internment at Scapa Flow.

What remained of the German government attempted to assuage the anger of the mutineers by decreeing on 4 November that the German fleet would not be sacrificed, but by then it hardly mattered. The High Seas Fleet, once such a potent symbol of national prestige, had effectively defeated itself, never to fight again. Kaiser Wilhelm II, the German navy's arch progenitor, fled into exile on 9 November and two days later the guns of World War I finally fell silent.

Article XXI of the Armistice Agreement called for the immediate surrender at Harwich of Germany's large U-boat force. Article XXIII, dealing with the German surface fleet, was subject to considerable wrangling. In the end the 74 ships deemed Germany's most powerful were to be interned in a neutral

Figure 1.2. In front of the world's media the internment fleet arrives at Rosyth. In this image a Kaiser class battleship passes a British ship with news cameras recording the greatest naval capitulation in history. The British press called it 'surrender', but the ships were not handed over and retained German crews until the end. (Getty)

or Allied port, pending the outcome of the final peace treaty which was to be negotiated in Versailles in the coming months.

After failed attempts to find a suitable custodian of the German ships, the role of jailer fell upon the Royal Navy. A light cruiser, SMS *Königsberg*, was sent to Rosyth to make arrangements and arrived back in Wilhelmshaven on 18 November with the terms by which the internment would take place. The interned fleet had to have its gun breech doors removed and be de-ammunitioned. It had to be ready to sail for arrival at Rosyth in 24 hours. The unenviable task of command was offered to Admiral von Reuter, who was to remain in post until the fleet was no more.

In order to comply with instructions, von Reuter needed the mutinous men to work as one in order to get the ships ready and sail them to Rosyth. His reputation as a fair officer undoubtedly helped, and he was able to reach an accord with the workers' councils whereby he alone would be in charge when the ships were at sea and individual orders must be complied with. There was to be no end of trouble with the revolutionaries, but as they wanted the fleet interned too, they cooperated to the extent that it was readied in time to meet the strict British timetable. Three ships required additional work, however, and they were left behind to sail later.

On the afternoon of 19 November the fleet passed out of the Jade Bight for the final time. As it went through the swept channels, the torpedo boat SMS *V30* wandered off course, struck a mine and sank. Other ships developed mechanical problems, but von Reuter brought 70 ships in a 19-mile long procession to within 50 miles of Rosyth in time for the 21 November rendezvous. Waiting for him was what appeared to be the entire Grand Fleet. In fact the British force, together with some Allied vessels, amounted to over 250 warships of every kind – a curious backhanded compliment to the undefeated, some of the Germans thought. But in reality the entire ritual had been carefully choreographed for the world's press to make sure that nobody missed the point that victory at sea does not always have to come by force of arms.

As the Germans proceeded to their anchorage for two days of detailed searches and inspections, Admiral Beatty issued the following order by radio: 'The German flag will be hauled down at 3.57 in the afternoon and it is not to be re-hoisted without permission.' This humiliation was felt profoundly by officers and men alike, and despite von Reuter's protests that it was unprecedented to make such an order, it was never rescinded.[1] The German flag was not to fly again until the day of the Grand Scuttle.

It was only after the Germans had anchored for inspection in the Firth of Forth that they were then told they would be transferred to Scapa Flow. The torpedo boats left in flotillas between 22 and 24 November, and the battleships and light cruisers followed suit. Each transfer was matched by an equal number of British warships. Berths had been allocated in advance, so that by 27 November the entire interned fleet, aside from the stragglers, had moored up for the last time, although they did not realize it.

The final vessels to arrive were those which had departed for Scapa Flow directly from Germany. The battleship SMS *König* and the light cruiser SMS *Dresden* arrived in December, as did *V30*'s replacement, *V129*. Finally, in January, the powerful new battleship *Baden* took her place as the 74th and final ship. Only now did the Germans come to realize that Scapa Flow was to be their place of internment. The German authorities complained, but to no avail. Scapa Flow was to be the prison of the High Seas Fleet. The final make-up of the interned fleet is listed in Appendix 1.

Internment at Scapa Flow

The British had been planning for the internment in Scapa Flow longer than von Reuter had guessed. The standing orders under which his British captors operated were strict and detailed. Although they changed during the internment, they can be summarised broadly. Under the Orkney & Shetland command, nine trawlers were to watch the interned fleet, three at a time, one to make rounds in each patrol section (see Figure 1.4) on a rolling three-day basis, with another in reserve. A further group of Canadian-built drifters (the CDs) were to operate as communication vessels. The fleet was to maintain two guard destroyers in Gutter Sound at all times, with a further pair on two hours' notice.

Figure 1.3. German torpedo boats being transferred to Scapa Flow. They were escorted by similar numbers of British ships as well as, it seems from this German image, airships. (Archiv Deutscher Marinebund)

Figure 1.4. (Opposite) The interned High Seas Fleet in Scapa Flow as arranged the day before the Grand Scuttle, showing the buoyage and anchorage scheme, drifter patrol zones, guard destroyers and depot ships.

A nominated capital ship was to provide armed men at the ready. Any fraternization beyond the business at hand was forbidden. Sailors were reminded of their duties by wartime propaganda concerning Germany's supposed criminality at sea.[2]

Even before von Reuter knew his fleet was to be transferred to Scapa Flow the British had requested transports from Germany to go there to pick up the surplus German crews. Once the ships were interred, skeleton crews only were to man them. Around 20,000 German sailors had brought the fleet over. After three separate trips by six transports, the German personnel were reduced to around 5,000–6,000 by the year's end.

There is some debate as to the exact numbers of Germans present after each wave of repatriation. However, von Reuter was able to ship home troublemakers and others on compassionate grounds throughout the internment, so that by May 1919 the number of German sailors present was around 4,400.[3]

The Germans were not prisoners of war but internees. But from the outset it was a distinction that would not be recognizable to most. For the Germans the rules of internment, like those for the Royal Navy, were laid down in written instructions which altered in only minor details during the internment.[4] Broadly, there was to be no direct radio communication with Germany whatsoever, in either direction. Any communication would be made on von Reuter's behalf via the British fleet. There would be no shore leave, no use of boats to communicate with other ships and no other movement of personnel without permission in advance, with the exception of the chaplains.

The banning of shore leave, even to perambulate on an uninhabited islet, seems unnecessarily harsh. Despite von Reuter's requests, dutifully relayed to the Admiralty in London, the ban, like the one covering the use of the German naval ensign, was never lifted.[5] As others have observed, 'magnanimity in victory was not Beatty's strong suit'.[6]

The Royal Navy underwent significant restructuring and downsizing after World War I. This led to no fewer than four changes in command in respect of the Admiral in immediate charge of supervising the German fleet. Admirals Packenham, Oliver, Keyes and Leveson, and finally Vice-Admiral Sydney Fremantle, all took up the role and each had slightly differing views as to how to treat their captives. They all had to refer to Sir Charles Madden, the Admiral in Charge of the Atlantic Fleet (the Grand Fleet no longer existed in name), and he took his orders from the Admiralty.

Outgoing and later incoming mails were censored, as were the German newspapers. All supplies except coal, diesel fuel and water had to come from Germany, where they were loaded on board the battleship SMS *Friedrich der Grosse* and, on their arrival, distributed by the patrolling drifters. There were

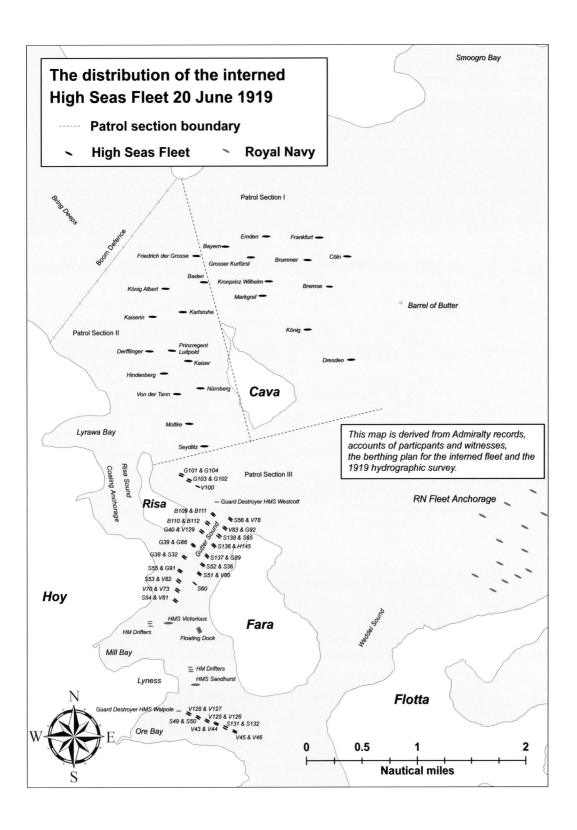

The distribution of the interned High Seas Fleet 20 June 1919

- - - - - **Patrol section boundary**

➘ **High Seas Fleet**   ➘ **Royal Navy**

Smoogro Bay

Bring Deeps

Boom Defence

Patrol Section I

Emden   Frankfurt

Bayern

Friedrich der Grosse   Brummer   Cöln

Grosser Kurfürst

Baden   Kronprinz Wilhelm

König Albert   Bremse

Markgraf

Kaiserin   Karlsruhe

Barrel of Butter

König

Patrol Section II

Prinzregent
Derfflinger   Luitpold

Kaiser   Dresden

Hindenberg

Von der Tann   Nürnberg   **Cava**

Lyrawa Bay   Moltke

Seydlitz

This map is derived from Admiralty records,
accounts of particpants and witnesses,
the berthing plan for the interned fleet and the
1919 hydrographic survey.

Risa Sound

Coaling Anchorage

G101 & G104
G103 & G102   Patrol Section III
V100

Risa   Guard Destroyer HMS Westcott   **RN Fleet Anchorage**

B109 & B111
B110 & B112   S56 & V78
G40 & V129   V83 & G92
Gutter Sound   S138 & S65
G39 & G86   S136 & H145
G38 & S32   S137 & G89
S55 & G91   S52 & S36
S53 & V82   S51 & V80
V70 & V73   S60
S54 & V81

Hoy   HMS Victorious

HM Drifters   Floating Dock   **Fara**

Mill Bay   Weddel Sound

HM Drifters

Lyness   HMS Sandhurst

Flotta

Guard Destroyer HMS Walpole   V128 & V127
S49 & S50   V125 & V126
V43 & V44   S131 & S132
Ore Bay   V45 & V46

N
W   E
S

| 0 | 0.5 | 1 | 2 |

Nautical miles

THE GERMAN FLEET IN

Figure 1.5. The German fleet interned in Scapa Flow, looking south from Houton. The island to the centre left is Cava. The battleships and light cruisers are in the foreground, with the battlecruisers in front of Gutter Sound and the torpedo boats beyond. On the right the boom defence vessels guarding Bring Deeps can be seen. (Orkney Archive)

always shortages of soap, writing paper and other essentials, including a dentist. But there seems to have been a surfeit of brandy and beer. When fishing could no longer help pass the time, music and drunkenness became the frequent accompaniments of boredom.

Despite the rules in place, fraternization between captor and captive did go on. The more open transactions took place at night. As the photographs show, it was but a short row out to the German vessels, and as has been the custom with naval ratings since time immemorial, a black market soon developed. Brandy, schnapps, Iron Crosses (including some finely made fake medals), binoculars, cameras and even pieces of ship went one way; soap, newspapers, chocolate, tobacco and other luxuries the other.[7]

Even on the torpedo boats fraternization was difficult to deter. Cdr Cordes, the Head of Torpedo Boats, was forced to officially complain that his men were openly bartering German government property for 'smoking requisites' from a British picket boat in broad daylight as it made its way from boat to boat.[8] Lt Ruge noted that from early on, the torpedo boats were compelled to place a night-time guard to deter souvenir hunters.[9]

In fact, it bordered on impossible to maintain any semblance of discipline on board the German ships. The larger the ships, the more fractious the relationship seems to have been between officers and men. Since they were not at sea, the workers' councils regarded themselves as being in joint command. Routine maintenance was not carried out and the fetid conditions gave rise to rats and cockroaches. The battleship *Grosser Kurfürst* was held to be the most disgusting, while discipline on the battlecruiser *Derfflinger* (von Reuter's old command) and on *Von der Tann* was said to have been 'hair-raising'. Aboard the light cruiser *Bremse*, a plot to murder the captain was uncovered.[10]

OW. 28th NOV., 1918.

The torpedo boats were notably more loyal, the connection between officers and men always closer in these smaller communities where each man relied on the next for survival. So, in contrast to the capital ships, Lt Friedrich Ruge in command of the torpedo boat SMS *B112* was able to later write humorously that he observed the 3rd Flotilla painting ship on a Sunday,

Figure 1.6. SMS *Karlsruhe* seen early on during the internment with a drifter alongside. Behind her is probably SS *Sierra Ventana*, which took home some of the first wave of repatriated sailors. (Orkney Archive)

Figure 1.7. The 2nd Torpedo Boat Flotilla, 3rd Division was moored to the east of Rysa. In the background are the battlecruisers *Seydlitz* and *Moltke*. Most of these small vessels were tied to buoys in pairs. Morale and discipline was notably higher in these small craft. (Orkney Archive)

Scapa-Flow
v.d.Tann, Kaiser, Moltke, Nürnberg, Seydlitz u. Torpedoboote

Figure 1.8. An atmospheric shot looking southwest from Cava. In the centre is the battleship SMS *Kaiser* bracketed by the battlecruisers *Von der Tann* and *Moltke*. The light cruiser *Nürnberg* is to the left. The view down Gutter Sound shows the torpedo boat moorings. The large ship in the centre distance is possibly HMS *Victorious*, which was moored in that area in April 1919. (Archiv Deutscher Marinebund)

presumably to pass the time. His ship soon followed suit.[11]

Von Reuter's command was originally aboard the flagship SMS *Friedrich der Grosse*, which experienced its share of difficulties. Rebellious elements took to 'stomping over his head to prevent him sleeping'.[12]

Trouble with the agitators reached a peak in March when two individuals were found trying to slip aboard a supply ship to foment unrest. Von Reuter ordered them to be returned to Germany. When they resisted, the entire ship went on strike. The British got involved and requested the pair be turned over to them. Von Reuter's refusal to do so helped defuse the situation, but it flared up again on 24 March when the troublesome duo refused to board SMS *B98* for repatriation. On this occasion the British went further and approached with a destroyer armed with guns and torpedoes, finally compelling the pair to depart.

By this time von Reuter had been invited to transfer his flag to the happier environs of the light cruiser SMS *Emden*. An accompanying party of British marines ensured his safe transfer as he took residence in his new ship. From this point, things calmed down somewhat, but von Reuter knew he could not trust the lower deck. This had a significant influence on the way in which the plans to scuttle the fleet had to be made.

In March 1919 Rear-Admiral Robert Prendergast was made head of the entire Orkney & Shetland Command, having previously been in command of Scapa Flow. His flag was the old pre-dreadnought battleship HMS *Victorious*, now a depot ship. In April 1919 the naval base at Scapa Flow was moved from Long Hope to its newly built headquarters at Lyness. This brought the depot ships into Gutter Sound in close proximity to the torpedo boats.[13]

The possibility that scuttling might be inevitable was on von Reuter's mind from the moment he took command.[14] He was well aware that no naval officer surrenders his ship under any circumstances, and after all, this was the Kaiser's decree and he had taken an oath. That his captors might resort to force was always a consideration, especially when his men were at their most unruly. Since resisting armed takeover by the British was not a feasible option, scuttling was the only recourse if the armistice negotiations failed satisfactorily to resolve the fate of his fleet.

On 11 May the peace terms as handed to Germany at Versailles reached von Reuter. The interned fleet was to be handed over. The decision as to whether to scuttle now only hinged on whether Germany would accept the terms of the treaty. If it did not, it would mean a resumption of hostilities.

Figure 1.9. A rare photo taken on board the interned flagship SMS *Friedrich der Grosse*. To the right is the last arrival at Scapa Flow, SMS *Baden*. This brand new 15-inch gunned battleship was saved from sinking during the Grand Scuttle and later sunk as a target in the English Channel. (Archiv Deutscher Marinebund)

Despite urgent requests, von Reuter received no specific instructions and it is generally accepted, as he always insisted, that he acted alone in deciding on the final fate of his interned ships.[15] The only question remaining to be settled was one of timing.

Planning the seizure and planning the scuttle

From the outset of the armistice negotiations, the British had been aware that the Germans might scuttle their ships if the peace treaty required that they hand them over. In order to ensure that this did not happen, plans had been drawn up by Oliver to seize the ships with armed force, and Madden had approved them. As with von Reuter's plans, the only question now concerned timing. Anticipating that the handover of the fleet might require a show of force, and knowing that the deadline for the Armistice had been extended until 23 June, Fremantle had plans in hand to seize the German ships on the night of 21–22 June. The plan was approved on 19 June and the orders were drawn up.[16]

As the negotiations dragged on and the deadline was repeatedly extended, a fraught atmosphere developed in the German ships. On the key matter of timing, the British naturally held the advantage of receiving regular updates from Versailles. Von Reuter had to rely on four-day-old copies of British newspapers to work out the deadline for German acquiescence or rejection. His officers and men were restless.

On 31 May, the anniversary of their victory at the Battle of Jutland, as they saw it, the German fleet celebrated. The British did not. Despite orders to downplay the event, banners flew and flares were fired. The torpedo boats in particular put on a show of defiant bravado. Afterwards, Cdr Cordes, head of the torpedo boats, began to make his own scuttling arrangements. Von Reuter had to curb his enthusiasm.[17]

Figure 1.10. These small images were taken by Midshipman J. S. C. Salter of HMS *Ramilles* on 31 May 1919. They show the German torpedo boats with their superstructures supposedly draped in banners to celebrate the German victory at Jutland. In the picture on the right the large ship in the background may be the depot ship HMS *Sandhurst*, which had recently been moved to Lyness. (Salter Papers, Brotherton Library)

Concern over the unpredictable discipline of his men was always at the forefront of his mind. The feverish atmosphere in May led him to fear a general strike breaking out in the fleet, which would have been an excuse for the British to implement a seizure. In March, the British had asked him to reduce the size of the crews aboard the German ships down to the size of the maintenance crews on the mothballed British ships of comparable size. Von Reuter had stalled, smelling a rat, but by May the time was opportune to reduce his men to minimum numbers. This would allow him to get rid of elements that could not be trusted, and it might also save lives in the end.[18]

So finally, on 18 June, the last transport departed for Germany, repatriating 2,700 sailors, leaving 1,860 officers and men behind.[19] As a number of British drifters took the men out to the ship home, others went about distributing mails, including, ironically, von Reuter's orders to scuttle the interned fleet which he had drafted the previous day and which had been sent on the British mail ships, instead of on his own barge, so as not to raise suspicion.[20] The Germans were now ready, awaiting only a signal from SMS *Emden* to sink 856 million marks' worth of warships in a single momentous event. Von Reuter's famous order is provided in full in Appendix Two.

On the ships now only crewed by small numbers of men, it was inevitable that word would get out. On 20 June von Reuter learned that the lower deck on two capital ships knew what was planned. He had no choice but to order the captains to use their own discretion to decide which men to bring into the growing coterie of those in the know. This order, too, was dutifully sent around on British drifters. That evening, as usual, a four-day-old copy of *The Times* reached von Reuter. It revealed to him that a final ultimatum to Germany to accept the terms or face the consequences of a resumption of war was set to be delivered at noon on 21 June. The time to act had come. The historic signal denoting 'Paragraph Eleven, Confirm' would fly from SMS *Emden*'s halyard the next morning.

1   D. van der Vat (1982), The Grand Scuttle: The Sinking of the German Fleet at Scapa Flow in 1919 (London: Hodder & Stoughton), p. 123.

2   National Archives (various dates), Internment of German Warships at
      Scapa Flow. ADM 116/1825. London. National Archives (various dates),
      Sinking of German Fleet at Scapa Flow. ADM 116/2074. London.

3   D. van der Vat (1982), *The Grand Scuttle: The Sinking of the German Fleet
      at Scapa Flow in 1919* (London: Hodder & Stoughton), p. 136.

4   National Archives (various dates), Internment of German Warships at
      Scapa Flow. ADM 116/1825. London. National Archives (various dates),
      Sinking of German Fleet at Scapa Flow. ADM 116/2074. London.

5   L. von Reuter (1940), *Scapa Flow: The Account of the Greatest Scuttling of all
      Time* (London: Hurst & Blackett), p. 66–67.

6   D. van der Vat (1982), *The Grand Scuttle: The Sinking of the German Fleet
      at Scapa Flow in 1919* (London: Hodder & Stoughton), p. 106.

7   A. J. Marder (1970), *From the Dreadnought to Scapa Flow: The Royal Navy in the
      Fisher Era, 1904–1919. Volume V: Victory and Aftermath* (London: OUP), p. 272.

8   M. Brown & P. Meehan (1968), *Scapa Flow: The Story of Britain's Greatest
      Naval Anchorage in Two World Wars* (London: Allen Lane, Penguin),
      pp. 129–130.

9   F. Ruge (1973), *Scapa Flow 1919* (London: Ian Allen), p. 64.

10   D. van der Vat (1982), *The Grand Scuttle: The Sinking of the German Fleet
      at Scapa Flow in 1919* (London: Hodder & Stoughton), p. 147.

11   F. Ruge (1973), *Scapa Flow 1919* (London: Ian Allen).

12   A. J. Marder (1970), *From the Dreadnought to Scapa Flow: The Royal Navy
      in the Fisher Era, 1904–1919. Volume V: Victory and Aftermath* (London:
      OUP), p. 273.

13   C. W. Burrows (2007), *Scapa and a Camera* (Penzance: Periscope), p. 10.

14   D. van der Vat (1982), *The Grand Scuttle: The Sinking of the German Fleet at
      Scapa Flow in 1919* (London: Hodder & Stoughton), p. 163.

15   A. J. Marder (1970), *From the Dreadnought to Scapa Flow: The Royal Navy
      in the Fisher Era, 1904–1919. Volume V: Victory and Aftermath* (London:
      OUP), p. 278.

16   National Archives (various dates), Sinking of German Fleet at Scapa Flow.
      ADM 116/2074. London.

17   L. von Reuter (1940), *Scapa Flow: The Account of the Greatest Scuttling of all
      Time* (London: Hurst & Blackett), p. 97.

18   L. von Reuter (1940), *Scapa Flow: The Account of the Greatest Scuttling of all
      Time* (London: Hurst & Blackett), pp. 93–97.

19   H. H. Herwig (1980), *'Luxury' Fleet: The Imperial German Navy 1888–1918*
      (London: George Allen & Unwin), p. 257.

20   L. von Reuter (1940), *Scapa Flow: The Account of the Greatest Scuttling of all
      Time* (London: Hurst & Blackett), p. 100.

CHAPTER 2
THE GRAND SCUTTLE

Figure 2.1.a Peploe's first photographs show *B109* and *B111* beginning to list. Steam is emitting from the foundering boats. *B111* did not sink until 1600hrs, but alongside, other torpedo boats were also beginning to founder. (National Maritime Museum)

The scuttle was straightforward on some German ships and more challenging on others. As the British response unfolded, it was the German ships that were delayed in sinking that became targets for beaching and their men who paid with their lives. The chaotic scenes of the scuttling of the interned fleet had many eyewitnesses, not least a party of schoolchildren from Orkney. Several British participants had cameras, leaving a dramatic photographic record of the day.

An admiral's luck

As well as being the prison of the German fleet, Scapa Flow was also a busy navy base, from which there were always the comings and goings of ships of all sizes on myriad duties. Gutter Sound in particular was a busy place, especially since April, when Lyness had become the naval shore headquarters and the depot ships *Victorious* and *Sandhurst* had been moved there. For example, several photographs taken on 21 June show that there was a coaster with its fenders lowered moored in close proximity to the torpedo boats at the north end of Gutter Sound, probably waiting on the coaling station on Hoy. Also present was the German store ship SS *Dollart* from which the drifter *Nellie Laud* and others were retrieving baggage for return to Germany.[1] A party of school children aboard the tug *Flying Kestrel*, usually set aside to distribute water, was touring the interned fleet, and those children were about to get a grandstand view of events.

In addition to the routine of port life there were also the planned exercises of the Atlantic Fleet. A long-planned practice of a mass destroyer attack against a battle line had been postponed twice due to bad weather. But in fair conditions Admiral Fremantle took the fleet to sea on the morning of 21 June. He planned a return on 23 June, in time to seize the interned German ships. For von Reuter, this was a fortunate coincidence, nothing more. Inevitably it gave the German ships a better opportunity to sink before they could be boarded. As the events of the day show, the longer a ship stayed afloat, the greater the chance that it might be saved from sinking.

Figure 2.1.b The first torpedo boats begin to sink as Ruge's *B112* rolls to port, crashing into *B110* and sending both to the seabed. The time is around 1315hrs. The boats around them are in varying states of sinking. (National Maritime Museum)

Paragraph eleven, confirm

At 1000hrs, SMS *Emden* flew the signal for every ship to watch the flagship for further orders. The signal to scuttle was sent by semaphore, by signal lamp and, finally, by hoisting the seemingly innocuous message 'Paragraph eleven, confirm'. The message seems to have got around the interned fleet quickly, although not all seemed to respond immediately. For example, the written accounts of the scuttle from various ships' commanders show that SMS *Markgraf* received the signal at 1110hrs, *Frankfurt* at 1125hrs and *Dresden* at 1130hrs. Aboard *Prinzregent Luitpold* there was a difficulty decoding its meaning, leading to a delay in response of around 20 minutes.[2] In Gutter Sound, the head of torpedo boats on *S138* had arranged to fly a red pennant 'Z' (meaning 'engage the enemy') upon receipt of the scuttle order. On board *B112*, the commander, Lt Ruge, noted that the pennant was flying at the same time that the order relay from *Emden* could be seen from the nearest battlecruiser, SMS *Seydlitz*.[3] There seems to have been an understandable delay in von Reuter's message reaching the sixth flotilla, moored furthest away, south of Lyness.

1200hrs

The evidence that a general scuttle was under way began to emerge when heightened activity started being noticed on the German ships. Not long after this was observed, the battleship *Friedrich der Grosse* began to founder. The time was around midday. She was sunk by 1216hrs. Also around midday a sub-lieutenant on watch on the guard ship HMS *Westcott* sighted the first destroyers beginning to settle, the German flag being hoisted, ladders being deployed and boats lowered.[4] HMS *Westcott* immediately signalled to Admiral Prendergast aboard HMS *Victorious*. All boats were initially ordered to him and then distributed, some to await the returning fleet and some to prevent the scuttling. With the start of the British response begins the photographic record of the day's events.

1300 hrs

On HMS *Westcott* a petty officer in the ship's skiff was detailed to try to force the torpedo boats ashore. Lt Peploe, in command of HMS *Westcott*, had a camera and took some of the most remarkable photographs of the Grand Scuttle. Probably the first photographs to show it under way were taken from the bridge at around 1315hrs. They can be seen in Figure 2.1a and b. Figure 2.1a shows steam emitting from several torpedo boats as they settle. In the centre the pair of torpedo boats moored alongside each other, *B109* and *B112*, can be seen to be leaning to port. Figure 2.1b may be first to show sinking ships. In it, Lt Ruge's *B112* can be seen to roll over to port, colliding

with the neighbouring *B110*. This caused both of the ships to sink. By this time 58 men from both vessels had got away on a cutter and a raft.

Figure 2.2. Peploe's photograph of SMS *Kaiser* sinking at 1325hrs. (National Maritime Museum)

By this time *Brummer* (1305hrs), *Moltke* (1310hrs) and *Kronprinz Wilhelm* (1315hrs) had already sunk and *Kaiser* was foundering, sinking at 1325hrs. With its boat sent to prevent the torpedo boats from sinking, *Westcott* headed up towards the main anchorage of the interned fleet, passing the already sunk *Moltke*, and arriving at SMS *Hindenburg* as it was being abandoned.

Few could kill unarmed men while trying to coerce them back to their ships, and *Westcott* did not. Peploe tried instead to force the men of the *Hindenburg* back on board, spattering the side with machine-gun fire, but to no avail. In a letter penned the week after the scuttle he wrote:

> '*I put the wind up some Huns with a Lewis Gun as they wouldn't stop. However they had done their duty too thoroughly to stop the sinking & there was no object in slaying them. I could have slain hundreds, so we let them go & get assisted by trawlers.*'[5]

Midshipman McCall, also serving on *Westcott* at the time, drily observed:

> '*Short of shooting to wound or kill there was nothing else we could do; and I guess we looked pretty silly.*'[6]

Peploe put a party of men on board *Hindenburg*, and they succeeded in reaching the engine room before the lights failed and then had to retreat to the upper deck, having shut some hatches. Charges were then used to blast away the ship's cables, and this is when *Hindenburg* began to drift, with *Westcott* attempting a tow to shallow water to beach her. While this was happening, other ships nearby were sinking and Peploe was able capture some historic images. The battleship *Kaiser* was photographed as it sank, as seen in Figure 2.2.

Peploe captioned this photograph as SMS *Kaiserin* sinking. But it is not that ship because the position with Cava in the background is not right for *Kaiserin*, which was anchored further to the north. Furthermore, *Kaiser* was fitted with the thicker foremast in 1918, as seen in the photo. This was a modification her sister ship *Kaiserin* did not receive. In the background is the island of Cava, with the little 'Calf of Cava' to the left. Behind the island can be seen two battleships yet to sink, possibly *Markgraf* and *König*. Sinking by the stern, *Kaiser* can be seen to be flying some flags, but not in the number seen on *Prinzregent Luitpold*, which sank only five minutes later and was also immortalised in Peploe's photographs in Figure 2.3.

The remarkable sequence of three photos shows that the ship went down with all flags flying. She had sunk fast enough (despite an abortive start) to avoid having her flags torn down before she foundered. As Lt Cdr von Reiche recalled in his report:

> *'After the boats were lowered, the officers were setting the topmast and large gaff flag. The flags were sparkling clean, flapping in the wind one last time above the old, seasoned steel warrior. A stiff breeze was moving them so that they were clearly and mightily standing out against the grey Nordland sky. Nobody will ever forget that view.'*[7]

At the time *Prinzregent Luitpold* sank, so did the light cruiser *Dresden* and the battleship *Grosser Kurfürst*.

Meanwhile, in Gutter Sound, Admiral Prendergast headed out to see for himself what could be done. He later reported an incident with Lt Steiner of *S54* in which Prendergast personally tore down the ship's flag.[8] According to cashier C. W. Burrows of HMS *Victorious*, he was present during Prendergast's excursion and therefore must have taken the photo in Figure 2.4 at this time.[9] It seems to show an initial encounter with a torpedo boat of the V25 class, possibly even *S54* itself. The German crew can be seen to be wearing lifebelts. The officer is on the right.

Burrows then boarded a picket boat with another photographer, Lt Grant, and followed the route north taken by *Westcott*. Orders from Prendergast

Figure 2.3. With all flags flying, *Prinzregent Luitpold* heads to the deep at 1330hrs in a boiling sea, captured by Lt Peploe on HMS *Westcott*. *Karlsruhe* is behind. (National Maritime Museum)

were to 'haul down their ensigns and to take such steps as necessary to save life'. Arriving first at the foundering battlecruiser *Seydlitz*, the flag was taken down, but the cables could not be freed. The upper photo in Figure 2.5 was seemingly taken by Lt Peploe prior to the flags being taken down by Burrows' party. The lower image shows her sunk and how she looked at low tide until she was salvaged by Cox & Danks in 1929.

1400hrs

As well as Burrows, Grant and Peploe, there were other photographers present during the scuttle, although they have not been easy to specifically identify. Grant's photographs, too, do not seem to have been credited specifically to him. When von Reuter stepped off SMS *Emden* into the British drifter *CD1* that he had at his disposal, he headed for the nearest land at Houton to inform the British of what he had done. Briefly ashore, he was met by an unnamed young officer in tennis whites who quickly headed off to the action in a speedboat, taking a camera with him.[10] The image in Figure 2.6 supposedly showing the battleship SMS *König* sinking at 1400hrs on its port side is one such unattributed photograph.

At 1400hrs the light cruiser *Cöln* also sank, as did the battleship *Kaiserin*. HMS *Westcott* was still attending *Hindenburg* at 1415hrs and Peploe captured the precise moment the nearby battlecruiser *Von der Tann* sank, as shown in Figure 2.7.

Meanwhile, *Hindenburg* had been briefly boarded by men on Burrows' picket boat, but was listing heavily. They had then continued north until they reached the battleship *König Albert*, where the drifter *CD1* with von Reuter on board was spotted asking for aid to pick up the crew of *Bayern* who were in the water. So Burrows' little vessel closed on the rapidly sinking battleship. It was during the sinking of this battleship, that Burrows took perhaps the most iconic and famous photographs of the Grand Scuttle. Figure 2.8 shows *Bayern* seen side on, sinking from the stern at around 1400hrs. She finally sank at 1430hrs. This photograph and the other showing her leaning heavily have been commonly used by the souvenir shops, breweries and T-shirt sellers of Orkney for 100 years, but they still have a powerful resonance.

At this time, the destroyers which had been exercising with the fleet had begun to return to the main anchorage. HMS *Venetia*, along with two of Prendergast's tugs, had taken the light cruiser *Bremse* in tow and seemed successfully to beach her at Smoogro Bay, only to see her roll over and sink at 1430hrs.

Both Peploe's and Burrows' final photographs of a sinking ship were of the famous battlecruiser SMS *Derfflinger*, which foundered by the bow at

Figure 2.4. C. W. Burrows accompanied Admiral Prendergast on his initial inspection of the sinking torpedo boats. This photo shows one of these encounters which took place early in the British response to the Grand Scuttle. (C. W. Burrows)

Figure 2.5. *Seydlitz* foundered at 1350hrs. She is seen in Peploe's photograph sinking by the stern, and in the later photograph as sunk, lying on her starboard side. The coaster behind can be seen in a number of photos taken during the day. (National Maritime Museum)

Figure 2.6. SMS *König* turning turtle as she sinks at around 1400hrs. (Archiv Deutscher Marinebund)

Figure 2.7. Peploe took three photos of *Von der Tann* sinking at 1415hrs. *Nürnberg* is to the left. (National Maritime Museum)

1445hrs. When seen together as a group in Figure 2.9 they show how the ship sank, with her stern rising into the air. She turned completely upside down before sinking.[11] The photographers' vessels must have been very close together at this time. Photographs of ships that sank after 1500 remain largely unattributed.

Figure 2.8. The famous photograph of SMS *Bayern* sinking. She foundered at around 1430hrs. (C. W. Burrows)

1500hrs

In Gutter Sound, the fight to save as many torpedo boats as possible was still going on. Only two flotillas, the 1st and the 4th Half Flotillas, were sunk entirely. The scuttling attempts of the other flotillas met with mixed success. Ruge thought that in some cases the sinking process seemed to come to a halt, as if the inlet valves had become fouled.[12] This was possible as the boats were by this time carrying heavy beards of marine growth on their undersides. The same delay seemed to happen during the sinking of the light cruisers, and in both cases the British were able to beach the ones sinking slowest.

The unattributed photographs in Figure 2.10 published in the *Illustrated London News* a week after the Grand Scuttle show the half-painted *B111* lying on top of *B109*, before she slid off into the depths. The boats of the 3rd Half Flotilla can be seen sinking to the left. In the lower photograph is probably *G103*, which can be seen sinking on her mooring at around 1500hrs. Behind is the hull of *Seydlitz* on her side, and behind her is *Nürnberg*, which was in the process of drifting to Cava after the cables were cleared by the guard destroyer HMS *Walpole*. She took to this task after deploying her boats to assist in beaching the torpedo boats in Gutter Sound.[13] In the centre is the light cruiser *Karlsruhe*, which was to founder at around 1550hrs. To the left *Hindenburg* is now adrift, with HMS *Westcott* attempting to tow her ashore.

There are fewer photographs of events to the east of where *Baden* sank as the known photographers' duties did not take them into that area. However, there is a collection of four photographs taken from high up on the hill above Houton air station from 1500hrs onwards which dramatically depict the sinking and beaching taking place at that time. They appear to have been published as souvenirs by J. Omond in the weeks after the scuttle. They are shown as an annotated group in Figure 2.11. Omond was an Orkney-based photographer. He is thought to have personally taken this sequence after sighting the scuttling of the ships while out cycling.[14]

The top three photos look south towards Gutter Sound and show the battleship *Baden* being kept afloat and *Hindenburg* with *Westcott* in attendance. At 1545hrs the light cruiser *Karlsruhe* takes her final plunge to the bottom. *Nürnberg* can be seen drifting towards Cava, and in the last shot she has beached. The camera has turned south-eastward and captures the moment at around 1630hrs when the battleship *Markgraf* rolled over to port before sinking.

Figure 2.9. *Derfflinger* sinks at 1445hrs, as captured by Peploe in the top two images and by Burrows in the bottom one. Their two vessels must have been quite close at this time. Burrows was on a picket boat out of shot in Peploe's photographs. (National Maritime Museum & C. W. Burrows [bottom image])

Figure 2.10. Torpedo boats at the top of Gutter Sound sinking in the afternoon. The half-painted *B111* is shown lying on top of the already sunk *B109* in the top image. She later slid off and sank. A torpedo boat of the 3rd Half Flotilla (probably *G103*) is shown sinking on her mooring in the bottom image. The time must have been around 1500hrs. (*Illustrated London News*)

1600hrs

At least two other postcards credited to Omond are known to exist (there are probably more) which show *Markgraf* sinking at 1645hrs. One is shown in Figure 2.12. However, these could not have been taken by Omond, as he was taking the images in Figure 2.11 at the time. The actual photographer is unknown. On the left image in Figure 2.12, drifters are next to the ship, but by the time she sank they had wisely departed. During the deliberately slow sinking of *Markgraf*, her captain and a petty officer were killed by gunfire. A detailed analysis of *Markgraf*'s sinking is given in Chapter 11, and the account by the senior surviving officer can be found in Appendix 3.

1700hrs and after

SMS *Markgraf* was the last major warship to sink still anchored, although a towline had been attached to her. A quarter of an hour later the last major warship sank when *Hindenburg* finally settled upright in shallow water on the east side of Cava. A pair of unattributed photographs showing her settling by the bow before she came to rest on the shallow seabed uniquely upright were published in the *Illustrated London News*. As the only ship to settle upright during the Grand Scuttle, *Hindenburg* was much photographed as a wreck and during the subsequent lifting operations (see Chapter 7).

By the time *Hindenburg* sank, the Grand Scuttle was almost at an end. In Gutter Sound the torpedo boats had either sunk or been towed or drifted onto beaches. Figure 2.14 shows three of a clutch of eight beached off Fara. No fewer than 20 of the 50 torpedo boats scuttled had been pulled into the shallows, and 19 of these would be recovered by the Royal Navy in the

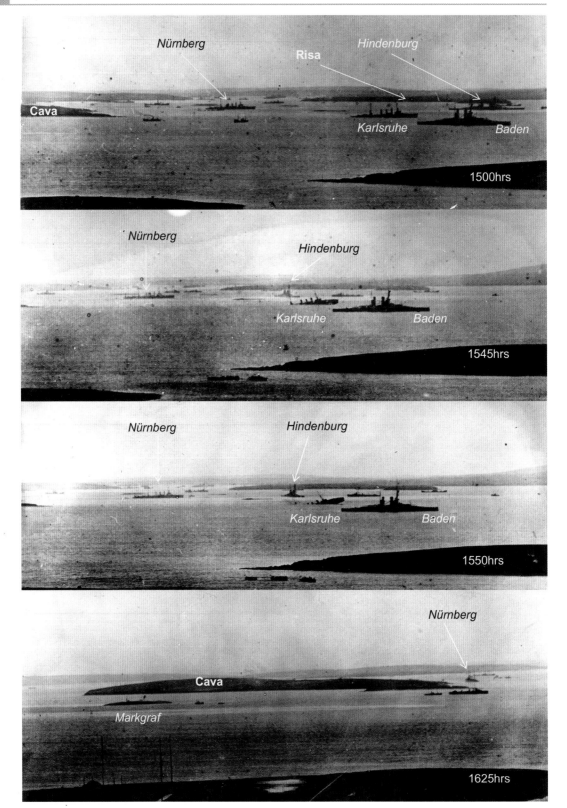

following weeks. In the last cases, pumps had been brought on board by the British to try to keep them afloat.

Only one ship failed to sink in any way. The unlucky torpedo boat *S132* was still floating on its mooring that evening. The last torpedo boat to be ditched was *G102*, which had been dragged into Mill Bay. But at 2300hrs, despite pumps working to keep her up, she had to be left to settle. She became the last ship to sink on the day.[15]

Aftermath

Figure 2.16 shows the final result of the Grand Scuttle in the evening of 21 June 1919. Aside from *Hindenburg* and *Bremse*, all of the large warships had sunk on their anchorages. Attempts had been made to tow *Markgraf* and *Dresden*, but they sank where they were anchored. The light cruisers *Frankfurt*, *Emden* and *Nürnberg* had been successfully beached. In the evening the battleship *Baden* was being kept afloat on her anchorage by a team from HMS *Ramillies*, but on 23 June she was towed to Smoogro Bay, where she flooded and settled on the bottom next to *Frankfurt* and *Emden*.[16] During the scuttle one British destroyer, HMS *Vega*, was badly damaged in a collision with a sinking torpedo boat caused by a mistake in the engine room, as possibly shown in the photograph described in the introduction.

When the fleet had returned to Scapa Flow at around 1430hrs there were eight larger warships still afloat. Half of these were saved from sinking.[17] This shows that delays in sinking by whatever cause did in fact increase the

Figure 2.11. (Opposite) Photos taken by J. Omond from the hill behind Houton between 1500hrs and 1625hrs. These remarkable shots show the last hour of the Grand Scuttle. *Baden* is not sinking, while *Karlsruhe* is seen to sink by the stern. Behind her are the upturned hulls of two already departed ships. *Hindenburg* can be seen drifting with *Westcott* in pursuit. At 1625hrs the camera turns southeast to *Markgraf* as she founders. *Nürnberg* can be seen beached off Cava. (Orkney Archive)

Four stages in the sinking of the German Battleship *Markgraf* in Scapa Flow on June 21st 1919.   J. Omond M.A.

Figure 2.12. SMS *Markgraf* rolls over onto her port side as she sinks at around 1645hrs. She was the last warship to sink on her mooring, the sinking delayed by the humane actions of her captain, who was later killed by gunfire from a drifter. (Orkney Archive)

chances of the vessel in question being boarded and stopped from sinking. In the four larger warships which were beached, there are known reasons why their sinking took longer, preventing the complete success of the procedure.

The scuttling process of *Baden* had been hindered by the fact that the drifter *Cachosin*, with the artist Bernard Gribble RA on board, was standing off her at around 1200hrs. *Cachosin* was able to prevent the crew from evacuating the ship until a boarding party from the battleship HMS *Ramilles* went on board.[18] The party from *Ramilles* was able to stem the flow of encroaching seawater. The generators on board were still functioning and the lights were on, which inevitably helped.

Midshipman Salter, serving on HMS *Ramilles*, collected an album of photographs taken when the fleet had taken control of the recovery of the German sailors. In Figure 2.17, some can be seen being towed to *Ramilles* and posing for a photo on her quarterdeck. Figure 2.18 shows, on the left, *Baden*'s captain, Cdr Zirzow, in conversation with Captain Luce of *Ramilles*. Luce is rumoured to have warned Admiral Fremantle that the Germans might scuttle if the fleet put to sea.[19]

On the right in Figure 2.18, in the centre of the image and seen disembarking, is Lt Horstmann, who was found hiding on board *Baden* by a boarding party while trying to finish the job of scuttling. According to a recently found letter, the boarding party dragged him to the upper deck, where he was told 'he would be shot at sunset if he did not immediately take us below and show us how to shut off the valves. His only reply was, "you can shoot me now".'[20]

Figure 2.13. SMS *Hindenburg* sank at 1700hrs and was the last of the major warships to founder. The ship was unique in foundering upright, which ultimately made it a difficult task to salvage. In the left hand image, *Nürnberg* can be seen beached behind. (*Illustrated London News*)

The drifter *CD2* was alongside von Reuter's flagship *Emden*, recovering officers' stores to be taken to the German storeship SS *Dollart*, as was a water boat, filling *Emden*'s tanks. The communication drifter *CD1* was also present. Von Reuter did not begin the scuttling her until *Friedrich der Grosse* began to sink, distracting British attention. The crew disembarked onto the drifters and von Reuter did so too, to *CD1*. At around 1415hrs the destroyer HMS *Shakespeare* arrived on the scene, its crew boarding *Emden* and stemming the flow of water by shutting valves and watertight doors. The ship was then towed to Smoogro Bay and beached.[21] Undoubtedly the late start to the scuttle gave the British ample opportunity to save this ship.

Nürnberg was saved from sinking by the guard destroyer HMS *Walpole*, which had proceeded up Gutter Sound. She had lowered boats and boarded six torpedo boats before boarding *Nürnberg*. Cables were parted and the ship

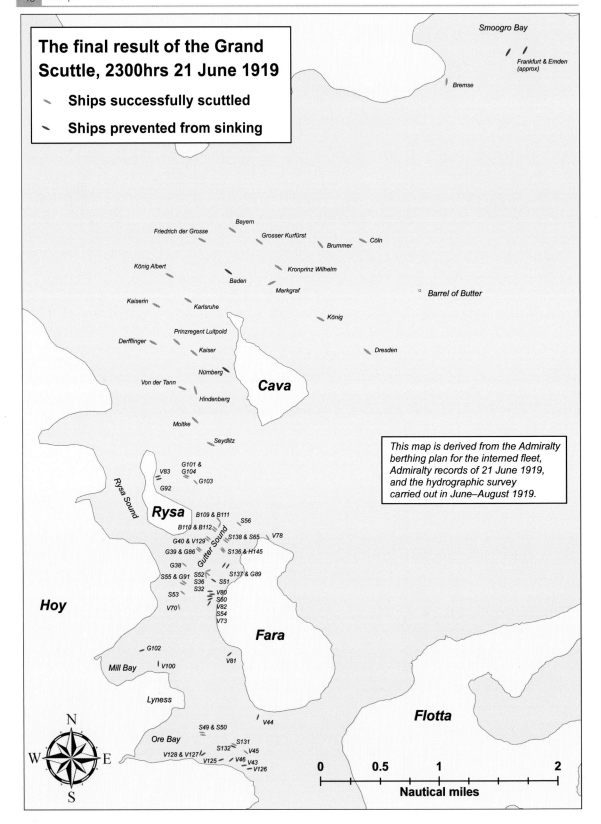

The final result of the Grand Scuttle, 2300hrs 21 June 1919

- Ships successfully scuttled
- Ships prevented from sinking

Smoogro Bay

Frankfurt & Emden (approx)

Bremse

Bayern

Friedrich der Grosse

Grosser Kurfürst

Brummer

Cöln

König Albert

Kronprinz Wilhelm

Baden

Markgraf

Barrel of Butter

Kaiserin

Karlsruhe

König

Prinzregent Luitpold

Derfflinger

Kaiser

Dresden

Nürnberg

Von der Tann

Cava

Hindenberg

Moltke

Seydlitz

G101 & G104

V83

G103

G92

Rysa Sound

Rysa

B109 & B111

S56

B110 & B112

G40 & V129

S138 & S65

V78

G39 & G86

Gutter Sound

S136 & H145

G38

S52

S137 & G89

S55 & G91

S36

S51

S53

S32

V80

V60

V70

V82

S54

V73

Hoy

Fara

G102

V81

Mill Bay

V100

Lyness

V44

Flotta

S49 & S50

Ore Bay

S131

S132

V45

V128 & V127

V125

V46

V43

V126

This map is derived from the Admiralty berthing plan for the interned fleet, Admiralty records of 21 June 1919, and the hydrographic survey carried out in June–August 1919.

N
W   E
S

| 0 | 0.5 | 1 | 2 |

Nautical miles

was allowed to drift ashore. In this case, as with the torpedo boats, the ship's proximity to nearby British vessels, coupled with the light cruisers' propensity to sink slowly, prevented the scuttle being completed.

The disembarked crew from *Frankfurt* were towed back to their ship by the drifter *Cachosin* and their boat was cut adrift. When the destroyer HMS *Wessex* arrived, 14 Germans were found on board. The cables were cut and the ship was towed to Smoogro Bay, where she bottomed in shallow water. The account written by Lt Cdr Beesel in command of *Frankfurt* reveals that one condenser lid could not be opened, even though it had been prepared previously to open easily, which may have had the effect of slowing the sinking process.[22]

The fact that 21 torpedo boats out of a total of 50 were prevented from sinking entirely was due to a combination of factors. Importantly, they were the nearest vessels to HMS *Victorious* and quickly became the centre of attention in terms of Prendergast's effort. Boats from the guard destroyers and from the Orkney command were quickly on hand. It is also clear that some of the torpedo boats sank quite slowly due to blockages. But another factor was the use of deadly force by the crews of the destroyers of the British fleet.

The German casualties

Nine German sailors were shot dead as a result of the Grand Scuttle. They were the last casualties of World War I and are buried in Lyness cemetery. A further 16 (some reports say 21) received wounds by fist, bayonet and bullet. There were standing orders which stated that force would be used if boats were lowered. In the initial confusion and panic of the day, some British boats fired haphazardly at the disembarking Germans to try to drive them back on board their ships. Most were probably warning shots, similar to the type described by Peploe and McCall, explaining why the casualties were so low. As Peploe stated, he could have killed many with his Lewis gun but did not, choosing to 'put the wind up' them instead.

Figure 2.17. The rounding up of German crews. Left, the drifter *Cudowsin* is seen towing boats probably from *König Albert* to HMS *Ramilles*. Right, seemingly unconcerned German sailors pose for a photograph on HMS *Ramilles'* quarterdeck. (Salter Papers, Brotherton Library)

Figure 2.16. (*Opposite*) The final result of the Grand Scuttle as seen on the evening of 21 June 1919, showing the distribution of the scuttled and beached ships.

Figure 2.18. Captain Luce of *Ramilles* in conversation *Baden's* Cdr Zirzow (left). Lt Horstmann of *Baden*, who had stayed on board the sinking ship to try to finish her off (right). (Salter Papers, Brotherton Library)

The fact remains that some of those who did die appear to have been deliberately targeted. In the main anchorage, two died on *Markgraf* – Cdr Schumann and PO Dittman. Dittman was unluckily hit in the head from a drifter which was '150–250' metres away; clearly random.[23] But the shot which killed Schumann was fired by a Lt Turner in a drifter when Schuman appeared to 'argue the point'; 'a very good shot too' was how the matter was later related.[24] The German version of events was that with a white flag flying he was trying to stop his men being shot at. The third time he emerged from cover he was killed instantly.[25] The drifter appears to have been *Cabalsin*, manned from HMS *Royal Oak*. She fired at the boats of other ships, including *Bayern*, but later reported that it had no effect as the ships were already sinking.[26] Turner 'was held to have acted justifiably under the circumstances'.[27]

The ships and men from the returning fleet were responsible for all of the killings. Prendergast's orders, given before the fleet returned, give no hint that he stipulated the use of deadly force to save the sinking ships. While firing was heavy at times, there were no deaths. Head of Torpedo Boats Cdr Cordes saw him as 'an officer of the old school, kind and humane'.[28]

However, Admiral Fremantle's report clearly states that boarding parties were ordered to use 'all possible means' to prevent German ships sinking.

His criticism in his report of Peploe and *Westcott* for not being more willing to use small-arms fire to drive the Germans back onto *Hindenburg* reveals much.[29]

In the case of the torpedo boats being scuttled in Gutter Sound, his orders to the flotilla leader HMS *Spenser*, leading six others, were 'that the German destroyers were to be required to surrender, being boarded and fired upon if necessary'. These orders were seemingly followed. Most of the deaths occurred at the south end of Gutter Sound, where the 6th Torpedo Boat Flotilla, having belatedly received the signal, had scuttled last and their ships had not reached the point of no return when *Spenser* arrived on the scene.

The officers were rounded up on the deck of *S132* (which, it will be remembered, was the only ship still perfectly afloat in the evening) while the British attempted to save the sinking ships. The officers were told they would be shot if their vessels sank. At this time a German lieutenant survived death when the gun held at his temple slipped when fired.[30] The shooting appears to have been sporadic, but the fact remains that three were shot dead in *V126*'s boat and others were killed and wounded while in the water.

In this light, Cdr Cordes' view that some killing was unnecessary seems justified.[31] But equally, this was no premeditated slaughter. In the chaos of the day, with emotions high and guns drawn, the casualties seem notably light. The last to die was Kuno Evertsberg of SMS *Frankfurt*, shot dead aboard HMS *Resolution* on 23 June. At the subsequent trial, after 50 minutes' deliberation, the jury found the case 'not proved'.[32]

1   National Archives (various dates). Sinking of German Fleet at Scapa Flow. ADM 116/2074. London.
2   National Archives and Records Administration (various dates), microfilmed records of the German Navy, PG64939, Roll T1022-1629. Washington, DC.
3   F. Ruge (1973), *Scapa Flow 1919* (London: Ian Allen), p. 111.
4   Imperial War Museum (various dates), private papers of Admiral Sir Henry McCall. London.
5   Caird Library (various dates), Charles Peploe letters, AGC 10/21. London.
6   Imperial War Museum (various dates), private papers of Admiral Sir Henry McCall. London.
7   National Archives and Records Administration (various dates), microfilmed records of the German Navy, PG64939, Roll T1022-1629. Washington, DC.
8   National Archives (various dates), Sinking of German Fleet at Scapa Flow. ADM 116/2074. London.
9   C. W. Burrows (2007), *Scapa and a Camera* (Penzance: Periscope), pp. 105–109.

10   L. von Reuter (1940), *Scapa Flow: The Account of the Greatest Scuttling of all Time* (London: Hurst & Blackett), p. 109.

11   National Archives (various dates), Sinking of German Fleet at Scapa Flow. ADM 116/2074. London.

12   F. Ruge (1973), *Scapa Flow 1919* (London: Ian Allen), p. 115.

13   National Archives (various dates), Sinking of German Fleet at Scapa Flow. ADM 116/2074. London.

14   In email correspondence with David Mackie of Orkney Archives.

15   National Archives (various dates), Sinking of German Fleet at Scapa Flow. ADM 116/2074. London.

16   National Archives (various dates), Scuttling of German Ships at Scapa Flow and instructions for the internment of such ships. ADM 137/3816. London.

17   National Archives (various dates), Sinking of German Fleet at Scapa Flow. ADM 116/2074. London.

18   National Archives (various dates), Sinking of German Fleet at Scapa Flow. ADM 116/2074. London.

19   University of California Irvine (various dates), Arthur J. Marder Papers MS.F.002. Correspondence with Cmdr. W. M. Phipps Hornby. Irvine, CA.

20   BBC (2015), Letter from Sub Lt Markham of HMS *Revenge* to his mother, 26 June 1919. http://www.bbc.co.uk/news/magazine-33152438.

21   National Archives (various dates), Sinking of German Fleet at Scapa Flow. ADM 116/2074. London.

22   National Archives and Records Administration, (various dates), microfilmed records of the German Navy, PG64939, Roll T1022-1629. Washington, DC.

23   National Archives and Records Administration (various dates), microfilmed records of the German Navy, PG64939, Roll T1022-1629. Washington, DC.

24   University of California Irvine (various dates), Arthur J. Marder Papers MS.F.002. Correspondence with Cmdr. W. M. Phipps Hornby. Irvine, CA.

25   National Archives and Records Administration (various dates), microfilmed records of the German Navy, PG64939, Roll T1022-1629. Washington.

26   National Archives (various dates), Sinking of German Fleet at Scapa Flow. ADM 116/2074. London.

27   University of California Irvine (various dates), Arthur J. Marder Papers MS.F.002. Correspondence with Cmdr. W. M. Phipps Hornby. Irvine, CA.

28   L. von Reuter (1940), *Scapa Flow: The Account of the Greatest Scuttling of All Time* (London: Hurst & Blackett), pp. 141–144.

29 National Archives (various dates), Sinking of German Fleet at Scapa Flow.
    ADM 116/2074. London.

30 F. Ruge (1973), *Scapa Flow 1919* (London: Ian Allen), p. 117.

31 L. von Reuter (1940), *Scapa Flow: The Account of the Greatest Scuttling
    of All Time* (London: Hurst & Blackett), pp. 141–144.

32 Orkney Archives (various dates), microfilmed records of the *Orcadian*
    1919–1938. Kirkwall, 12 February 1920.

CHAPTER 3
REACTION AND DISPOSAL OF THE GERMAN NAVY

Figure 3.1. The scene where most of the killing occurred, as seen at the end of 21 June looking northwest up Gutter Sound. In the foreground are (L to R) *V125*, *V46*, *V43* and *V126*, the last of which saw three of her crew shot. Afloat behind is *S132*, with the depot ship HMS *Sandhurst* and British destroyers. (Maingay Papers, Brotherton Library)

The Grand Scuttle caused admiration and outrage in equal measure. Britain tried to blame the German state for it but could produce no evidence in the end. Admiral von Reuter and his men were to remain in Britain until January 1920, while the wrangling over the spoils of the German navy was resolved.

World reaction

The schoolchildren from Kirkwall aboard the *Flying Kestrel* had seen a great deal of the action. Ships had sunk and, anecdotally at least, one German sailor had been shot in front of them. The youngest became very frightened, panicked and were placed below deck. The eldest watched everything. In 1972 Miss Kitty Watt recalled that 'it was pretty exciting at the time'.[1] On her return home, her brother, serving in the Royal Navy and home on leave, drily remarked that 'if they had been British you would have said "What brave men"'.[2]

Ironically, the following morning at Cromarty Firth, on the quarterdeck of HMS *Revenge*, von Reuter was saying the same. A furious and clearly embarrassed Fremantle had made a ceremony of publicly (there were journalists present) dressing down the German admiral. In an intemperate diatribe, von Reuter was accused of dishonourably violating naval honour: 'The honour-loving seamen of all nations will be unable to comprehend this act, with the exception perhaps, of yours.' Through an interpreter von Reuter calmly replied:

> *Tell your admiral that I am unable to agree with the purport of his speech and that our comprehension of the subject differs. I alone carry the responsibility. I am convinced that any English officer, placed as I was, would have acted in the same way.*

As Dan van der Vat has noted, Fremantle will have known well that the admiral in charge of the original HMS *Revenge*, Sir Richard Grenville, has passed into legend as ordering his ship to be blown up with him in her lest she fell into the hands of the Spanish; irony indeed.[3] One has to wonder where in the code of honour the shooting of unarmed sailors in boats was permitted.

At Versailles, where the future of the German fleet had caused considerable contention between nations, its removal by von Reuter's action eased the way forward to a final settlement. In short, the problem had been that the French and the Italians wanted the German ships for their navies, while America was indifferent and Britain wanted them scrapped.

The nations which publicly professed outrage at the Grand Scuttle were in private, in the main, quietly relieved. The British long sought, by public and secretive means, proof that von Reuter was ordered to scuttle. They found nothing to assuage the sense of embarrassment a jailer feels when his charge escapes. Germany protested its innocence but inwardly beamed with pride.[4]

The chatter in London and elsewhere at the time seemed to revolve around the view that von Reuter had been put up to it by the British. Hints had been dropped that 'we would sympathise with a gallant enemy who preferred naval hara-kiri [*sic*] to the humiliation of being surrendered as

Figure 3.2. Admiral von Reuter seen on board HMS *Revenge* on 22 June (left) and on 31 January 1920 on his return to Germany (right). The pale coat he wears was given to him in captivity. His admiral's cloak had been looted from his baggage after the Grand Scuttle. (Left, *Illustrated London News;* right, Ruge)

prize to the two Latin navies they had never met in battle'.[5] This is a nice idea, but there has never been any evidence to support it. In the meantime, the German sailors, now prisoners, were held to ransom until Germany made reparation for violating the Armistice.

Captivity and return

The 1,774 German officers and men were shipped to Cromarty Firth, departing on 22 June.[6] Von Reuter was among the earliest, arriving on 23 June. At the same time in Scapa Flow the unlucky German torpedo boat SMS *B98* arrived at its North Sea rendezvous with the mails from Germany for the interned fleet. Her commander was blithely unaware of what had unfolded the previous day. None other than Lt Peploe's HMS *Westcott* escorted her into captivity. *B98* was looted and then retained as reparation, although her captive crew were quickly repatriated. The men of the interned fleet could not have known that it would be seven long months before they too would return home. The arrangements for their reception at Cromarty were already in place because of the plans made to seize the ships on 23 June. Von Reuter ended up incarcerated at the camp at Donnington Hall after brief stays at Nigg and Oswestry.

On 2 September the Allies formally presented their demands for reparations for the lost war booty the Grand Scuttle represented to them. Until such time as the terms were adhered to, the German sailors of the interned fleet were to remain in Britain. The treatment they received varied from kindliness to cruelty, although the Seaforth Highlanders who guarded their transit south were regarded with respect. The main grievance from German accounts concerns the extent to which their luggage was looted.

Lt Cdr Fabricius of *Dresden* observed a British perspective which was held by many in the post-war years:

It was interesting to hear the opinions of the British people at the train station in Perth who had been talking to the guarding squads. The prevailing mood was that the British would have done the same or maybe would have scuttled the ships even earlier prior to the transfer. The transport leader, Lieutenant Inness from the 2nd Battalion of the Seaforth Highlanders, explained to us that he was looking forward to tell[ing] his army comrades the great trick we had played on the British Navy. The Navy that claimed sole recognition and had not done anything.

The protocol on reparations was finally accepted and signed by Germany on 10 January 1920. This paved the way for the sailors of the interned fleet to be repatriated. Von Reuter left Donnington Hall on 29 January and, aboard the 1,800-ton German steamship *Lisboa*, arrived at Wilhelmshaven on 31 January to a memorable homecoming, with bands playing and crowds cheering. His career ended abruptly when post-war austerity saw him retired early five months later. The only admiral to scuttle an entire fleet died in 1943.

The disposal of the German navy

The Grand Scuttle may have removed the most powerful ships of the German navy from the international chessboard, but it was far from all of them. In fact, at least nine battleships, 12 cruisers and over 100 torpedo boats remained. There was also the U-boat arm, being disposed of at Harwich. The Austro-Hungarian fleet added to the numbers to be divided up.

The vexed question of what to do with it all still remained, despite the scuttling at Scapa. To make up for the deficit the British felt due from the Grand Scuttle, Germany was forced to hand over to Britain 400,000 tons of lifting capacity in the form of her floating docks on which the German navy had depended, and 42,000 tons of harbour craft.[8]

In relation to the U-boats, it was agreed in autumn 1919 that all would be scrapped by 1921 by the powers which received them. Only France was allowed to retain ten in service. This was broadly adhered to, although Japan actually commissioned its allocation and later copied elements of the German designs. France and Britain ended up dumping ten U-boats in the English Channel in June–July 1921.[9]

The haggling over the surface fleet continued into December 1919. Ultimately, like the U-boats, most of the fleet was handed over to the victorious powers, with shares worked out in proportion to war effort and losses. Nearly all of the High Seas Fleet was to be scrapped or disposed of by experimental means by 1921. In total, the Central Powers navies yielded 15 battleships, nine light cruisers and 107 torpedo boats and destroyers for

Figure 3.3. The German light cruiser and veteran of the Battle of Jutland SMS *Frankfurt*, seen as a bombing target in July 1921. She had been refloated by the Royal Navy after the Grand Scuttle. (US Navy National Museum of Aviation)

distribution for the purposes of disposal by the victors and their allies.[10]

Notably, these included warships the Royal Navy saved from the Grand Scuttle and were later able to salvage (see Chapter 4); *Baden* was sunk in gunnery trials, raised and then scuttled in 1921 in the Hurd Deep, and *Nürnberg* was sunk by gunfire in the English Channel the following year. The hulks of *V44* and *V82* still appear at low tide in Portsmouth harbour. In the United States the light cruiser *Frankfurt* and the torpedo boat *G102* were sunk off the Virginia Capes in bombing experiments involving the pioneering champion of naval air power Colonel Billy Mitchell in July 1921. The United States also received SMS *V43* and *S132*, which were sunk as gunnery targets off Cape Henry at the same time.

A few elements of the High Seas Fleet survived afloat. France and Italy received light cruisers and torpedo boats for commissioning into their navies.[11] Poland and Brazil also received torpedo boats. They were mostly sunk or stricken by the end of World War II, although at Scapa Flow the interned fleet remained on the bottom. The salvage operations over the next two decades saw 66 ships recovered.

1   Brotherton Library (various dates), Liddle Collection, transcript of tape 60, by Peter Liddle. Interview with Miss K. Watt, August 1972, Leeds.
2   D. M. Ferguson (1985), *The Wrecks of Scapa Flow* (Stromness: Orkney Press), p. 75. This was transcribed from *Scapa Flow 1919: With All Flags Flying* (1986), documentary film (London: Channel Four).

3   D. van der Vat (1982), *The Grand Scuttle: The Sinking of the German Fleet at Scapa Flow in 1919* (London: Hodder & Stoughton), p. 182.

4   D. van der Vat (1982), *The Grand Scuttle: The Sinking of the German Fleet at Scapa Flow in 1919* (London: Hodder & Stoughton), p. 182.

5   J. M. Kenworthy (1933), *Sailors, Statesmen – and Others: An Autobiography* (London: Rich & Cowan), pp. 146–147.

6   National Archives (various dates), Sinking of German ships at Scapa Flow. Salvage of German ships. ADM 137/2486. London.

7   National Archives and Records Administration (various dates), microfilmed records of the German Navy, PG64939, Roll T1022-1629. Washington, DC.

8   A. Davidson Baker (1993), 'Disposing of the Kaiser's Navy 1918-1920', in J. Sweetman (ed.) *New Interpretations in Naval History* (Annapolis: Naval Institute Press), pp. 78–80.

9   I. McCartney (2002), *Lost Patrols: Submarine Wrecks of the English Channel* (Penzance: Periscope).

10   A. Davidson Baker (1993), 'Disposing of the Kaiser's Navy 1918-1920', in J. Sweetman (ed.) *New Interpretations in Naval History* (Annapolis: Naval Institute Press), pp. 78–80.

11   A. Dodson (2017), 'After the Kaiser: The Imperial German Navy's Light Cruisers after 1918', *Warship*, 2017, pp. 140-160.

CHAPTER 4
SURVEY AND SALVAGE BY THE ROYAL NAVY

Figure 4.1. The drifter *Ramna* aground on the wreck of SMS *Moltke* on 23 June 1919. It was floated off shortly afterwards. (C. W. Burrows)

Scapa Flow had to be made safe for navigation after the scuttle and the new navigational hazards needed to be surveyed to update the Admiralty charts. This work provides the first accurate mapping of the scuttled fleet. The Royal Navy recovered all but two of the beached vessels of the scuttle. This had been achieved by mid-August 1919. The salvaged vessels then awaited their disposal as was being agreed among the Allies.

Surveying the scuttled fleet

The Grand Scuttle introduced a number of dangerous new navigational hazards to Scapa Flow which in the immediate days and months afterwards led to a number of accidents. In particular, lying as they were in shallow water off Cava, the battlecruisers would disappear at high tide to lurk just under the surface. One victim of these new underwater reefs was the drifter *Ramna*, which ran aground on 23 June on the wreck of the battlecruiser *Moltke*, as shown in Figure 4.1. Doubtless this would have amused Lt Ruge of *B112*, who two days previously had witnessed the naval and civilian crew, including 'apparently the senior engineer' of this vessel, directing rifle fire at him.[1] Other incidents followed. The trawler *Raltia* of Grimsby ran hard onto the wreck of *Kaiser* in 1923. The master did not know the wreck was there as the hull only showed awash at low tide.[2]

In reality the entire area of the Grand Scuttle had to be made safe to shipping and the wrecks surveyed and their positions fixed. This task fell to Cdr C. W. Tinson of the Hydrographic Department of the Admiralty. The work was carried out from August to October 1919, during the same period in which the Royal Navy was clearing up the beached ships.

Initially a safe channel had to be marked out so that the depot ships at Lyness could be reached. The torpedo boat wrecks of *G89*, *S53*, *V70*, *G38*, *G91*, *G39*, *G86*, *V83* and *V78* were inspected by divers during this time, confirming the identities of several of them.[3] After the channels had been marked out, the task turned to surveying the larger warships.

Each wreck was located and then thoroughly surveyed using lead soundings, corrected to Chart Datum. These were the first surveys of the wrecks and are of great value today in helping ascertain the degree to which the surviving wrecks have collapsed.[4] The charts from this survey were digitized and incorporated into the mapping used to plan our January 2017 multibeam survey of the scuttled fleet, and the accuracy of this work is unsurpassed. New chart corrections covering the entire area of the Grand Scuttle were issued in November 1919.

Figure 4.2. Von Reuter's SMS *Emden* during salvage operation in Smoogro Bay. She was the simplest to recover. (Orkney Archive)

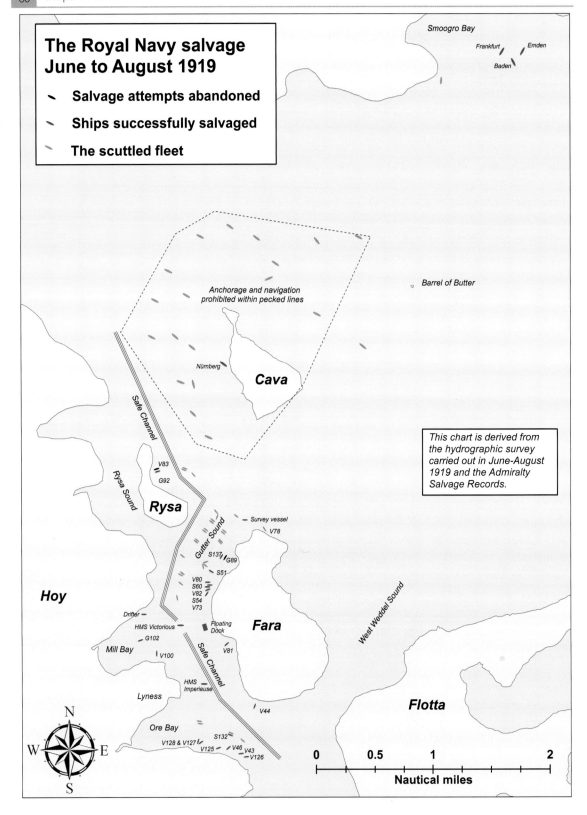

The Royal Navy salvage June to August 1919

- Salvage attempts abandoned
- Ships successfully salvaged
- The scuttled fleet

Smoogro Bay

Frankfurt   Emden

Baden

Barrel of Butter

Anchorage and navigation prohibited within pecked lines

Nürnberg

Cava

Safe Channel

This chart is derived from the hydrographic survey carried out in June-August 1919 and the Admiralty Salvage Records.

Rysa Sound

V83

G92

Rysa

Gutter Sound

Survey vessel

V78

S137 G89

S51

V80
S60
V82
S54
V73

Hoy

Drifter

HMS Victorious

G102

Floating Dock

Fara

West Weddel Sound

Mill Bay   V100

V81

HMS Imperieuse

Lyness

Safe Channel

V44

Flotta

Ore Bay

V128 & V127   S132

V125   V46   V43

V126

N

W   E

S

0   0.5   1   2

Nautical miles

The salvage of SMS *Baden, Emden, Frankfurt* and *Nürnberg*

The day after the Grand Scuttle the Royal Navy went to work on recovering the beached vessels. The ease with which they were recovered varied from case to case. Plans found on board the ships proved of great help in locating the hatches, doors and valves that been opened to the sea to sink the ships. The few German engineers retained at Scapa as prisoners from whom to extract knowledge proved less helpful. The major warships were all afloat by 12 July. *Frankfurt* and *Baden* proved the hardest to recover.

Von Reuter's flag SMS *Emden* was never fully flooded and her own diesel generator power was ultimately used to salvage her. She was partially awash and totally grounded in Smoogro Bay, but the salvage operations quickly got her afloat. A boiler was lit on 24 June and pumping had dried the ship out in four days. On 28 June she was successfully floated off and found to be watertight. She was then prepared for towing.[5]

As with *Emden*, SMS *Nürnberg* was salvaged using her diesel generator. She was partially awash and 75% of her was flooded to within two feet of the upper deck at the highest tides. Her own generator drove the pumps which reduced the water levels, allowing some valves to be shut. Divers plugged other inlets and were deployed inside to reach valves in the flooded boiler rooms. Even when compartments were secured, the ship was kept flooded to keep her on the bottom to avoid the risk of running her hard aground. On 3 July she was floated and moored alongside HMS *Royal Oak*. By 6 July she was declared seaworthy.[6]

The battleship SMS *Baden* was still anchored at her original position at the end of 21 June. Water could not be kept out, so the following day she was shifted to Smoogro Bay and anchored next to *Frankfurt*. She was slowly sinking, and despite continual pumping she finally sat on the bottom, fully flooded by 25 June. Bad weather ultimately caused her anchor to drag, so that by 28 June she had sunk in deeper water, with much of her upper deck submerged, as seen in Figure 4.5. The sinking had been effected by three

Figure 4.3. (*Opposite*) Map showing the remains of the scuttled fleet as the beached vessels were recovered and the area resurveyed during the summer of 1919.

Figure 4.4. *Nürnberg* ashore at Cava as beached (with the sunk *Hindenburg* behind), and as she was raised on 3 July. (Above: Orkney Archive; below: C. W. Burrows)

Figure 4.5. Salvage on *Frankfurt* and *Baden* in Smoogro Bay in June 1919. *Baden* can be seen to be sitting on the bottom (above). Pumps working on *Baden*, with the sea level with the upper deck (below). (Above: Orkney Archive; below: C. W. Burrows)

opened valves, and these had to be located and shut before *Baden* would float again without pumping. Submerged pumps were used to dry out compartments, and divers working in the flooded spaces finally located the valves and got them shut, so that by 11 July *Baden* was pumped out and watertight and moved to a mooring buoy in preparation for towing. She was the first ship to be towed south.[7]

SMS *Frankfurt* had been beached in Smoogro Bay, but she was full of water, which covered all but her bows at high water. As with *Baden*, pumping her out required external power. Priority went to *Baden*, so that it was not until additional equipment arrived in Scapa after 27 June that salvage work on *Frankfurt* really got under way. This was a difficult case because it was necessary to make the upper deck watertight to stop her being flooded from above at each high tide.

Moreover, she was sitting on the condenser discharge, which the divers could not plug from the outside. However, the opened torpedo tube could be plugged by the divers. With the torpedo tube shut, a large amount of pumping power was employed in the engine rooms to finally expose the condensers, which were ultimately made tight from the inside. After the leaks had been arrested, she was pumped dry and was floated off on 12 July.[8]

The salvage of the torpedo boats

Twenty torpedo boats were beached on 21 June and initially they were all considered viable for recovery. Salvage work was commenced at once by the 2nd Destroyer Flotilla with support from the depot ship *Sandhurst*. The work was difficult primarily because fuel oil covered all surfaces, making movement around and on the ships dangerous. Far worse were the conditions on board for the maintenance crews once the boats had been raised and moored to await reconditioning in the floating dock.

There was also a shortage of pumps, but the ones found on the torpedo boats were brought into service. The boats in the shallowest of water at low tide could be patched by hand and were the first to be refloated. Divers from *Sandhurst* were used on the deeper boats to do the same, so that a process of floating a boat a day was quickly developed.[9] Two tugs were used to help pull the boats off once they were watertight, so that by 1 July nine had been floated off and a further eight were being worked on. By 6 July, 13 were afloat and five more were in hand.[10]

Figure 4.6. The Royal Navy at work during the salvage operations. Above, a salvage party working on SMS *Frankfurt*. A diver is on the ladder of the tender preparing to inspect the hull. Below, ratings are pumping out a torpedo boat. Note the slope of the oil-soaked deck. (Above: Orkney Archive; below: C. W. Burrows)

In most cases the process went as smoothly as could have been anticipated, but some boats proved to be tricky to recover. *S137* had to be beached in Mill Bay for remedial work. When floated a second time it was found that collision with a tug had damaged her and the tug had to remain alongside pumping her out until she could be brought into the floating dock.[11] There is a possibility that this is in fact the torpedo boat that was actually damaged by HMS *Vega*'s collision, described in the introduction.

G92 also proved difficult to recover, and work continued into August. Divers had to be used to plug extensive holes and she was not successfully recovered to the floating dock until 15 August, the last vessel from the Grand Scuttle to be successfully salvaged by the Royal Navy.[12]

Two torpedo boats were not recovered in the end as they were considered beyond saving. *G89* was resting on rocks off Fara and was damaged in the gales which swept through Scapa on 28 June. This holed her underneath and made salvage seemingly impossible, so that attempts to recover her were abandoned.[13] Lying next to *G92* was *V83*. Attempts to raise her encountered the same difficulties. Diving efforts to plug the holes were finally ordered to be suspended in August.[14] In October *V83* is listed as requiring a maintenance crew, but plans to recover her seem to have been abandoned thereafter.[15]

Figure 4.7. Two images of the only ship not to sink during the Grand Scuttle: SMS *S132* can be seen being prepared for (above) and being towed (below) from Scapa Flow. (Salter Papers, Brotherton Library)

Dispersal

Under the terms of the Armistice protocol the salved ships were to be distributed among the Allies. SMS *Baden* was moved to Invergordon for analysis, but the rest of the German ships remained in Scapa for the rest of the year. In November, requests to the Admiralty to improve the conditions for the maintenance crews on the torpedo boats were still being made. Their living conditions were in fact far worse than the Germans had experienced during internment.[16] In 1920 the torpedo boats were towed south, many to Grangemouth, to be used for experimentation and to be sold. A full list of the fates of all the ships from the Grand Scuttle is given in Appendix 4. The Admiralty now looked to others to carry out salvage on the rest of the wrecks of the Grand Scuttle. The first to try their luck were local enterprises. Big business was to follow later.

1   F. Ruge (1973), *Scapa Flow 1919* (London: Ian Allen), p. 113.

2   Orkney Archives (various dates), microfilmed records of the *Orkney Herald*, 1919–1931. Kirkwall, 7 November 1923.

3   Hydrographic Office Archive (various dates), Chart No. C7953 Press 14 H, surveyed positions of the sunken German Fleet 1919. Taunton.

4   Hydrographic Office Archive (various dates), Chart No. C7953 Shelf Oq., S.W. portion of Scapa Flow posns of & depths over wrecks of sunken German warships and soundings N.W. of Cava I. Taunton.

5   National Archives (various dates), sinking of German ships at Scapa Flow. Salvage of German ships. ADM 137/2486, pp. 129–178. London.

6   National Archives (various dates), sinking of German ships at Scapa Flow. Salvage of German ships. ADM 137/2486, pp. 129–178. London.

7   National Archives (various dates), sinking of German ships at Scapa Flow. Salvage of German ships. ADM 137/2486, pp. 129–178. London.

8   National Archives (various dates), sinking of German ships at Scapa Flow. Salvage of German ships. ADM 137/2486, pp. 129–178. London.

9   National Archives (various dates), sinking of German ships at Scapa Flow. Salvage of German ships. ADM 137/2486, pp. 178–180. London.

10   National Archives (various dates), sinking of German ships at Scapa Flow. Salvage of German ships. ADM 137/2486, pp. 129–136. London.

11   National Archives (various dates), sinking of German ships at Scapa Flow. Salvage of German ships. ADM 137/2486, pp. 184–185. London.

12   National Archives (various dates), sinking of German ships at Scapa Flow. Salvage of German ships. ADM 137/2486, p. 191. London.

13   National Archives (various dates), sinking of German ships at Scapa Flow. Salvage of German ships. ADM 137/2486, p. 185. London.

14   National Archives (various dates), sinking of German ships at Scapa Flow. Salvage of German ships. ADM 137/2486, p. 191. London.

15   National Archives (various dates), sinking of German ships at Scapa Flow. Salvage of German ships. ADM 137/2486, p. 230. London.

16   National Archives (various dates), sinking of German ships at Scapa Flow. Salvage of German ships. ADM 137/2486, p. 242. London.

CHAPTER 5
LOOTING THE WRECKS AND THE FIRST COMMERCIAL SALVAGE OPERATIONS, 1919–1924

Figure 5.1. A rare photograph captioned 'looting parties on *Seydlitz*' taken by a Royal Navy midshipman, date not stated. From the condition of the wreck it seems this was most likely taken shortly after the Grand Scuttle. (Woodhouse Papers, Brotherton Library)

After the Royal Navy had recovered as many of the beached ships as it could, a period of official inactivity followed. Salvage of the rest of the German fleet did not begin until 1922 and was small scale, being carried out by local firms, until the arrival of Cox & Danks in 1924. But during this time a considerable degree of opportunistic looting appears to have been carried out by locals, used as they were to the bounty of myriad shipwrecks coming ashore throughout history.

Looting the wrecks

The collection of German navy souvenirs by locals and naval personnel had been going on from the moment the internment began. This was a demand the Germans had been happy to supply in return for conveniences they could not get from Germany. The hunting for souvenirs turns to looting when the ships have been abandoned and sunk. Even on the day of the Grand Scuttle, the collection of items from the German ships seemingly went on unchecked.

Notably, the boarding party from HMS *Westcott* which attempted to save SMS *Hindenburg* from sinking also liberated her typewriter 'though the character of its lettering betrayed its origin'.[1] The Germans' luggage stacked on the quarterdecks of the British battleships was naturally searched. But the main German grievance was that their personal possessions were stolen at this time, including Admiral von Reuter's cloak.

Once the ships had sunk, the illicit removal of items from them seems to have continued. The target of this activity shifted from trinkets to the valuable non-ferrous metals the ships contained. To this day many island communities regard shipwrecks as a bonanza of wealth to be freely acquired, and it seems this happened in the immediate months after the scuttle, aided by the fact that the beached wrecks were easily accessible at low tide or by small boat. It was observed that 'some of the islanders have made fortunes'.[2] But of course all shipwrecks have owners, and ultimately this free-for-all had to end.

In 1927 the *Daily Record and Mail* ran a slightly tongue-in-cheek piece which showed the extent to which the easily accessible wrecks had been looted:

> Intelligent islanders – sick of the sight of the Seydlitz – proceeded to do the scavenging for themselves. The official salvagers now busy at a job too long delayed in Scapa Flow find the ship stripped of all its removable marketable metal above the waterline and not a single button left of the Admiral's trousers! In the vicinity of the Admiralty Arch London, Orcadian innocence had been too highly estimated. It seems that those hardy, storm stiffened sons of Ultima Thule have been stripping the Seydlitz with hammer hacksaw and spanner for months when the fishing was slack. For the next fifty years the visitor to Orkney will probably find German port-holes the salient feature of native architecture.[3]

In fact evidence had already shown that the illicit removal of metals was far more organized than the simple opportunistic picking up of flotsam. For example, when the extensive salvage of the German fleet began in 1924, the firm of Cox & Danks was astonished to find that the torpedo tubes had already been taken off the ships it was lifting from the seabed. In October 1924 Cox & Danks offered an award of £50 for information on the whereabouts of the torpedo tubes from *S53*, *S55* and *G91*.[4] These ships had been fully scuttled and were on the bottom of Gutter Sound. To have recovered the torpedo tubes would have taken the use of divers and heavy lifting equipment.

A booklet published by Cox & Danks in 1931 describes what it had seen of the looting of the wrecks:

> They (torpedo tubes) were not the only things to vanish, for every bit of brass and gun-metal was stripped from above water in the Hindenburg. As for the Seydlitz, some of the island robbers put off to her in a boat, which they sank alongside so that it would not betray their presence aboard. Then they set to work and stripped every scrap of valuable metal from all those parts of the ship lying above the water-line. They lived in the ship for days and got their booty away to the smelters by packing it in herring barrels.[5]

The theft of metals from the German ships even continued as they were being towed away to be broken up. In September 1926, eight persons were subjected to fine or imprisonment at Kirkwall Sheriff Court for the theft of metals from a salvaged torpedo boat owned by Cox & Danks.[6] The following December another person received two months' imprisonment for a similar offence.[7] Both of these incidents occurred during the transit to the breaker's yard.

Small-scale salvage operations

During the early years of the salvaging of the scuttled fleet a number of smaller firms were involved in the recovery and salvage work on at least seven of the torpedo boat wrecks and also on the unfortunate *B98*, which was boarded when she arrived in Scapa Flow on 22 June, the day after the Grand Scuttle.

East Coast Wrecking Company of Dundee

The Royal Navy abandoned its attempts to recover two of the beached torpedo boats, *G89* and *V83*. Both wrecks were sold independently of the usual Admiralty process, managed from London. *V83* was sold on an unspecified date in 1920 by Commander in Chief Rosyth for £150 to the East Coast Wrecking Company.[8] This firm seems to have specialized in recovering metals from wrecks, not in wreck recovery. It also purchased for £700 the hapless *B98*, which had been wrecked off Sanday, Orkney while being towed for disposal in 1920, and for £500 an Admiralty trawler wrecked of the island

Figure 5.2. The abandoned *G89* looking weed-covered and desolate. This photo was probably taken shortly before she was recovered by A. Young of Stromness. It was the first of the German wrecks to be privately salvaged. (Orkney Archive)

of Inchkeith. The firm worked on its wrecks in Scapa in 1920 and in December it was reported that four of its vessels carried the recovered metals to Tayport. It was still working on the wrecks the following year.[9] *V83* was later sold on to P. Kerr of Aberdeen (see below).

A. Young of Stromness

In the same unconventional fashion as above, the abandoned and still beached *G89* was sold to A. Young of the Stromness Wrecking Company on an unspecified date in 1920 by Commander in Chief Rosyth for £500. This locally based firm planned to recover the beached wreck and break it up in the nearby town of Stromness. Salvage operations got under way in the summer of 1922. The approach used was to patch the hull and pump her out. The first lift attempt failed when the pump broke down.[10]

In November 1922 the company entered into a contract with the firm of J. W. Robertson of Lerwick (see below). With its better equipment, the wreck was successfully raised by pumping on 10 December, the first of the 50 wrecks of the Grand Scuttle left behind by the Royal Navy to be salvaged whole. *G89* was towed into Stromness, where a large crowd gathered hoping to see her come in. Darkness fell before she arrived and it was a few more days before the wreck was beached at the point where the breaking could begin. This was reported as being in full operation in the spring of 1923.[11] According to local folklore, her boiler tubes were reused and sold as curtain rails.

It seems that the more valuable non-ferrous metals were removed and then the breaking process was suspended. The hulk was moved to a new location in Stromness Harbour for works to resume in March 1927. The partially stripped wreck was finally sold to Cox & Danks in August 1928 and floated off and towed away to Lyness for breaking up a month later.[12]

Figure 5.3. The partially stripped wreckage of *G89* photographed in Stromness, date unknown. In 1928 she was purchased from the Stromness Wrecking Company by Cox & Danks and towed to Lyness for breaking up. (Orkney Archive)

Scapa Flow Salvage & Shipbreaking

This company was controlled by J. W. Robertson of Lerwick with the United Kingdom Salvage Company, Glasgow as a partner. Possibly driven by its success in recovering *G89*, it seemed to have ambitions to be a major player in the salvage of the German fleet, announcing that it intended to create local employment by breaking up the wrecks in Orkney and Shetland.[13] Initially it purchased the torpedo boats *S49*, *S50*, *S131* and *V45* by private tender on 26 April 1923 for £400, plus an additional £57 for their moorings.[14]

In 1923 metals were recovered from the wrecks, but in the following year lifting of the wrecks began. The first such successful recovery was that of *S131*, which was raised on 29 August 1924 using two concrete lifting barges joined together by a span of iron beams.[15] This wreck too appears to have suffered from earlier unauthorized pilfering of metals.[16]

One unique aspect of the lifting operations of this company is the employment of what it referred to as 'tide balloons'. These were used in conjunction with the lifting barges to raise the wrecks from the seabed. They were in effect large lifting pillows, resembling small airships, with an H girder keel. Two pairs were used with 100- and 150-ton lifting capacity. They have left a unique photographic record of the four torpedo boats raised in this way (see Figure 5.4).[17]

The lifting operations were generally uneventful, and *V45* was lifted in mid-October 1924, *S50* in early November and *S49* in December.[18] The plans

Figure 5.4. The unique lifting system used by Scapa Salvage & Shipbreaking involved the use of 'tide balloons' alongside the concrete lifting barges. The recovery of *S131* can be seen in the upper image with the barges and balloons being used. The lower image shows the overgrown bows of an unknown torpedo boat with the balloons in place. (Orkney Archive)

to break the wrecks up locally seem to have been changed in favour of selling them whole and then towing them to shipbreakers further south. This required Admiralty permission to do so. The first pair sold was *S131* and *V45* in December 1924. On 23 January 1925 *S131* was towed away by the company's tug *Trustee* for scrapping at Granton Shipbreaking. *V45* shortly followed, going to J. J. King & Sons of Garston.[19]

During negotiations for the sale of the second batch, gales threatened to damage the wrecks on their moorings. *S49* had to be sunk to protect her. She was raised again in February 1925.[20] The final pair were sold and shipped south in March 1925. *S49* was towed to Granton Shipbreaking and *S50* was towed to the Multilocular Company, Stranraer and arrived at Luce Bay on 23 March.[21]

The moorings the company had purchased were raised in June 1925 and the original concrete barges laid up at Stromness were floated off and towed away in the same year.[22] So ended the Scapa Flow & Shipbreaking Company's involvement in the raising of the German fleet. It was the only serious competition to face Cox & Danks, which was already working on its lifting of torpedo boats when *S131* was recovered, as described in the next chapter.

P. Kerr of Aberdeen

Mr P. Kerr of Aberdeen purchased *V83* from the East Coast Wrecking Company on 25 September 1925. Salvage operations on the wreck ended in failure when the trawler *Energy*, which was being used as a salvage vessel, sank beside the wreck on 17 October. According to the Admiralty disposals ledger, further salvage operations took place in 1928. *V83* was surveyed by multibeam and diving (see Chapter 17).

J. W. Mowatt of Stromness, 1937

Two of the torpedo boats recovered by the Royal Navy were lost while being towed south for sale or reallocation. *V81* was lost on tow, ran aground and sank in Sinclair's Bay, Wick, Caithness on 13 February 1920.[23] *S54* foundered off Flotta in the same month and her partially salvaged remains were surveyed by multibeam and diving (see Chapter 17).

The wreckage of *V81* was sold to J. W. Mowatt of Stromness (possibly the same person known as Johnny Mowatt, a mechanic who worked for Cox & Danks) on 23 September 1937 for £60. It was the last of the scuttled torpedo boats to be sold. By then, most of the others had been salvaged and broken up. Mowatt worked on the wreck site until August 1938. By that time he had raised 23 tons of non-ferrous and 30 tons of ferrous metal from the wreck.[24] The remaining dispersed wreckage was reported as being found in 1995.[25]

1   Imperial War Museum (various dates), private papers of Admiral Sir Henry McCall. London.

2   G. Cousins (1965), *The Story of Scapa Flow* (London: Muller), p. 128.

3   Orkney Archives (various dates), microfilmed records of the *Orkney Herald*, 1919–1931. Kirkwall, 29 June 1927.

4   Orkney Archives (various dates), microfilmed records of the *Orkney Herald*, 1919–1931. Kirkwall, 22 October 1924.

5   D. Masters (1931), *Salvage Work at Scapa Flow* (London: Cox & Danks).

6   Orkney Archives (various dates), microfilmed records of the *Orkney Herald*, 1919–1931. Kirkwall, 8 September 1926.

7   Orkney Archives (various dates), microfilmed records of the *Orkney Herald*, 1919–1931. Kirkwall, 8 December 1926.

8   Naval Historical Branch (various dates), *CP 8a Sale Book*, p. 20. Portsmouth.

9   Orkney Archives (various dates), microfilmed records of the *Orkney Herald*, 1919–1931. Kirkwall, 15 December 1920 and 12 January 1921.

10 Orkney Archives (various dates), microfilmed records of the *Orkney Herald*, 1919–1931. Kirkwall, 30 August 1922.

11 Orkney Archives (various dates), microfilmed records of the *Orkney Herald*, 1919–1931. Kirkwall, 13 December 1922 and 4 April 1923.

12 Orkney Archives (various dates), microfilmed records of the *Orkney Herald*, 1919–1931. Kirkwall, 9 March 1927.

13 Orkney Archives (various dates), microfilmed records of the *Orkney Herald*, 1919–1931. Kirkwall, 6 June 1923.

14 Naval Historical Branch (various dates), *CP 8a Sale Book*, p. 64. Portsmouth.

15 Orkney Archives (various dates), microfilmed records of the *Orkney Herald*, 1919–1931. Kirkwall, 10 September 1924.

16 Orkney Archives (various dates), microfilmed records of the *Orkney Herald*, 1919–1931. Kirkwall, 11 November 1924.

17 Orkney Archives (various dates), microfilmed records of the *Orkney Herald*, 1919–1931. Kirkwall, 10 September 1924.

18 Orkney Archives (various dates), microfilmed records of the *Orkney Herald*, 1919–1931. Kirkwall, 22 October 1924, 12 November 1924 and 24 December 1924.

19 Orkney Archives (various dates), microfilmed records of the *Orkney Herald*, 1919–1931. Kirkwall, 28 January 1925. Naval Historical Branch (various dates), *CP 8a Sale Book*, p. 64, Portsmouth.

20 Orkney Archives (various dates), microfilmed records of the *Orkney Herald*, 1919–1931. Kirkwall, 2 February 1925.

21 Orkney Archives (various dates), microfilmed records of the *Orkney Herald*, 1919–1931. Kirkwall, 1 April 1925. Naval Historical Branch (various dates), *CP 8a Sale Book*, p. 64, Portsmouth.

22 Orkney Archives (various dates), microfilmed records of the *Orkney Herald*, 1919–1931. Kirkwall, 29 April 1925, 13 May 1925 and 27 May 1925.

23 Canmore National Record of the Historic Environment Scotland (various dates), https://canmore.org.uk/site/101973/sms-v81-final-location-sinclairs-bay-north-sea

24 Naval Historical Branch (various dates), *CP 8a Sale Book*, p. 144. Portsmouth.

25 Hydrographic Department of the Admiralty (2017), Record of Wreck No. 916 SMS *SV81* (Taunton: Hydrographic Office).

PART TWO

THE INDUSTRIAL SALVAGE YEARS, 1924–1939

Cox & Danks workers on a salvaged torpedo
boat in the floating dock, circa 1924.
(Orkney Archive)

CHAPTER 6
COX & DANKS' SALVAGE OF THE TORPEDO BOATS

Figure 6.1. The converted floating dock at work with a salvaged destroyer on the surface. During lifting operations the deck was a hive of activity. The two distinctive L-shaped halves contained not only the winches, but offices, powerhouses and workshops. (*The Engineer*)

Cox & Danks earned worldwide fame for its pioneering work on the salvage of the German fleet. This work began with the raising of 25 torpedo boats from the bottom of Gutter Sound in 1924–1926. The method used was as unique as it was successful, utilizing an ex-German floating dock. The archaeological remains from the salvage days can be seen in the few portions left in Scapa Flow today.

The coming of Cox & Danks to Scapa Flow

The appearance in Scapa Flow of Cox & Danks in 1924 marks the point where the recovery of the wrecks shifted from the largely piecemeal to the industrial scale. Ernest Cox was a self-made engineer who had become rich making munitions during World War I and had turned his hand to shipbreaking at his facility in Essex. A forcible character and a natural engineer, he seemed to relish the type of challenge represented by the wrecks of the High Seas Fleet. He and his chief salvage officer Thomas McKenzie made a successful salvage team. These two important figures in the history of Scapa Flow can be seen in Figure 6.2.

Admiralty disposals records show the scale of Cox's ambition. In May 1924 he finalized payments on the battlecruiser *Hindenburg* and four torpedo boats. In September he bought a further 21. The following month he acquired the battlecruiser *Seydlitz*. He bought the light cruiser *Bremse* in 1925, the battlecruiser *Moltke* in 1926, the torpedo boat *S54* in 1927, the battleship *Kaiser* in 1928 and the battlecruiser *Von der Tann* and the battleship *Prinzregent Luitpold* in 1929.[1] All of these ships he would go on to salvage, leaving few remains in most cases.

The old Admiralty depot at Lyness was to serve as the land base for Cox & Danks, and later for Metal Industries. Here all of the facilities for working on the recovered ships were set up, along with the necessary offices, catering and accommodation. While much of the area was changed during World War II and after, it retains its character and is the location of the Scapa Flow Visitor Centre and Museum, which has many fascinating exhibits from the wrecks and the salvage era.

In 1922 Cox & Danks had purchased and then profitably broken up the old Grand Fleet battleships HMS *Orion* and HMS *Erin*. Subsequently it acquired the ex-German 'floating submarine testing dock'. This had been purchased from the Admiralty for £8,500 in April 1923, presumably to be broken up as well.[2] Anecdotally, it is related that a Danish customer suggested it would make a fine lifting barge to work on the scuttled German ships, leading Cox to begin his world-renowned salvage years at Scapa Flow.[3]

Figure 6.2. Mr Ernest Ralph Guelph Cox (seated) and Mr Thomas McKenzie seen together during the Cox & Danks period of salvage at Scapa Flow. McKenzie went on to work for Metal Industries on the salvage of the battleships up to the start of World War II, when he became Principal Salvage Officer, reaching the rank of Commodore RNVR. (Orkney Archive)

Figure 6.3. The ex-German floating dock as converted to recover the torpedo boats. The two halves lifted the wrecks by tide and hand winches. The system allowed for the recovered vessels to be 'rolled' into the upright position for beaching.

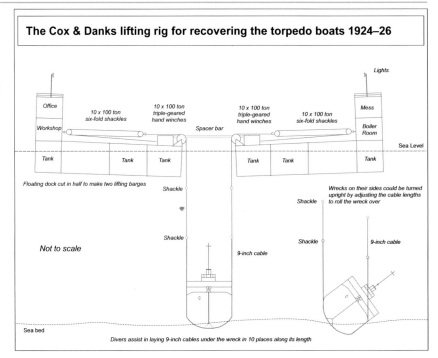

The Cox & Danks lifting rig for recovering the torpedo boats 1924–26

The lifting of the torpedo boats

The floating dock and two ex-Admiralty tugs, named *Ferrodanks* and *Sidonian*, arrived in Scapa in late May 1924.[4] The news that Cox was to work on the wrecks had been circulating in advance. The floating dock was designed for lifting and testing submarine hulls. Its employment on salvage work required a number of modifications, not least cutting it in half lengthwise to make two L-shaped barges.

The converted floating dock was innovative in the fact that it made use of mechanical lifting as well as the tide. The use of twenty 100-ton hand winches, ten on each barge, provided the means, and the men provided the muscle, with anything up to six men cranking on each winch. Trial and error refined the system over time. Initially chains were planned to be used for the lifts. However, on their first use on the salvage of the torpedo boat SMS *V70* they failed in succession, sending shattered pieces in all directions. Incredibly nobody was killed. They were then replaced by 9-inch-diameter cables which proved perfectly suitable for the job.[5]

In practice each dock was moored above the wreck to be salvaged in line with its orientation. Divers were mainly used to pass the lifting wires under each of the wrecks. This was done in a number of ways, including by tunnelling and by using water jets. Once the wires were secured, the wreck was lifted clear of the seabed by men working on the winches. At that time it could then be 'rolled' into the upright position by winding the cables on either dock to achieve the desired result.

Figure 6.4. Images showing the salvage of the torpedo boats under way. The industrial scale of the process is evident from the number of recovered torpedo boats seen beached in the upper image. The lower image shows a torpedo boat being beached and gives a good view of the pulleys of the hand winches used in the lifting process. (Orkney Archive)

It was important to get the wreck upright before it was beached. Then it could be moved progressively to Lyness with the use of both winch and tide. The manual winding usually took place at low tide to get the best assistance from it. It was exhausting work, carried out in groups of 20 turns, but it doubled the amount of lifting height achieved per tide, compared with using tide alone. The barge would then be towed towards Lyness until the salvaged ship touched bottom at high tide. The lifting wires were then shortened and at low tide the whole process would recommence until the salvaged vessel was laid up at Lyness or Mill Bay.

Figure 6.3 shows the lifting system used to recover the torpedo boats. The entire arrangement can be seen in Figure 6.1, with the L-shaped barges either side of a recovered torpedo boat which has been winched right up to the level of the barges' decks. This image gives a good impression of the sheer size and scale of the operations.

Figure 6.5. (Opposite) The clearing of the torpedo boats from Gutter Sound. Initially the Royal Navy removed the beached wrecks, then local salvors and Cox & Danks cleared the rest. The large torpedo boats lifted last were late-war examples that had been scuttled off Rysa. The full extent of the work of Cox & Danks can be seen from the wrecks marked in blue.

Cox was very much a front-line general, and by force of character and the employment of experts such as McKenzie, he made the salvage efforts successful when many said it could not be done. But of course, not everything worked. There was a fire on the floating dock in April 1925 which almost proved disastrous. A second larger floating dock brought to Scapa to recover the torpedo boats was found to be unsuitable for the work and nearly tipped over. It was relegated to a workshop while the lifting continued with the older one.

Figure 6.4 shows closer views taken during the ongoing salvage work. The upper image shows the recovered torpedo boats with the barge in the foreground. The corroded and overgrown state of the recovered wrecks is evident. The lower image shows a torpedo boat being beached. The spacer bar to keep the two halves of the dock apart is in place and the large number of hand winches on either barge can be seen. This was a unique innovation which aided in the successful recovery of these smaller wrecks.

Cox provided employment for many locals at at time when life was difficult. The going rate for winchmen was ten shillings a tide and it seems the workers (including the Lyness postman) would drop all other work when the call came.[6] When the harvest called winchmen away, the men of the Lyness lifeboat willingly took over. Even newsmen covering the salvage could get ordered in to assist.

Each salvage case provided its own challenges. Whereas the first wreck recovered, *V70*, had been alone on the seabed, most had been sunk in pairs, moored together. On the seabed they were often entangled and occasionally lying partially on top of each other. Moreover, they had often dragged their large steel mooring buoys down with them. When freed, they shot to the surface 'as if they had been fired from a gun'.[7]

The diving work could be hazardous, and there were several dangerous incidents involving trapped divers. In one incident Harry Grosset was head-down under a torpedo boat passing a wire through when the cables supporting her slipped slightly and caused the ship to come down and crush his helmet into the soft seabed, denting it. A harder seabed would have resulted in his death.[8] On another occasion when work was being carried out on the wreck of *G91*, the collapsing funnel trapped a diver on the bottom. He was only freed when the errant item was cleared by other divers.

Through the use of floating docks, Cox & Danks recovered no less than 25 torpedo boats in less than three years, between August 1924 and May 1926. This lifting system was ultimately entirely successful in its mission. The fastest lifting time, from the positioning of the barges over the wreck to its successful beaching in Mill Bay, was four days, for SMS *S65*. Periods of bad weather proved to be the most difficult hindrance to operations.

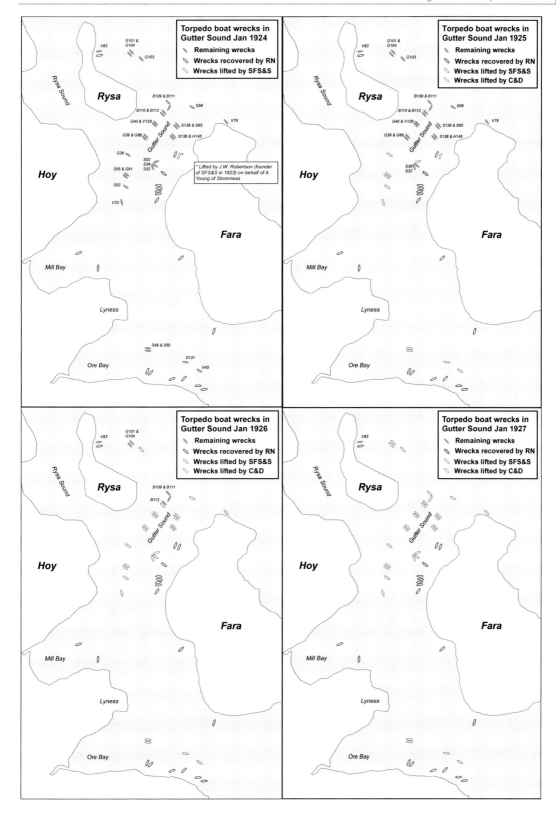

Torpedo boat wrecks in Gutter Sound Jan 1924
- Remaining wrecks
- Wrecks recovered by RN
- Wrecks lifted by SFS&S

* Lifted by J.W. Robertson (founder of SFS&S in 1923) on behalf of A. Young of Stromness

Torpedo boat wrecks in Gutter Sound Jan 1925
- Remaining wrecks
- Wrecks recovered by RN
- Wrecks lifted by SFS&S
- Wrecks lifted by C&D

Torpedo boat wrecks in Gutter Sound Jan 1926
- Remaining wrecks
- Wrecks recovered by RN
- Wrecks lifted by SFS&S
- Wrecks lifted by C&D

Torpedo boat wrecks in Gutter Sound Jan 1927
- Remaining wrecks
- Wrecks recovered by RN
- Wrecks lifted by SFS&S
- Wrecks lifted by C&D

Figure 6.6. The salvaged torpedo boats were broken up in Lyness and in a number of other shipbreakers. The wrecks had to be made dry before they could be towed away. The upper image shows a torpedo boat alongside at Lyness in the process of being stripped. The lower image shows the last boats in Mill Bay awaiting their fates. At least two were later re-sunk to assist in the recovery of the troublesome *Hindenburg*. (Orkney Archive)

Figure 6.5 shows how the clearance of the torpedo boats from Gutter Sound proceeded during this time. The larger ones, which were of destroyer size, were left to last, with SMS *G103* being the first recovered in September 1925. SMS *G104* was the last to be recovered, during the following April.

Cox was not a salvage man. He was a scrap-metal dealer, and metals from wrecks are the prime motive behind the salvage of most ships. One of the great challenges of salvage at Scapa Flow was the remoteness of the location. The logistical costs of importing cutting and breaking equipment to Orkney and of exporting the metal had to be weighed against the risk of losing entire wrecks if a tow went awry for any reason. This did happen on occasion, as the Royal Navy experienced.

Cox & Danks adopted both policies, cutting up some wrecks at Lyness but also selling entire ships which had to be towed to breakers in the south. Of the 25 torpedo boats lifted, Granton Shipbreaking bought nine of the wrecks. It broke up eight of them in Granton. The ninth, *G103*, became stranded on tow off Lochielair in November 1925, but was subsequently broken up too, although it is not clear whether she was towed off to Granton or was salvaged

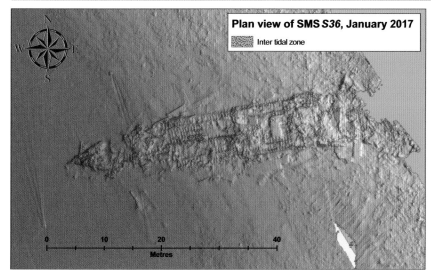

Plan view of SMS *S36*, January 2017

Inter tidal zone

0   10   20   40

Metres

Figure 6.7. Plan view DTM of the wreck of SMS *S36* as sunk to assist in the raising of SMS *Hindenburg*. She was later broken up in situ but this multibeam scan reveals just how much of the ship remains on the mud and rock bottom off the west of Cava.

in situ as a wreck. The former seems more likely.[9] The famous shipbreaking firm of T. W. Ward bought and broke up a further five and Alloa Shipbreaking (later Metal Industries) three more. The balance of eight remained in Scapa Flow, where they were gradually reduced to scrap by Cox & Danks. Photos showing the last torpedo boats are shown in Figure 6.6. At least two of the last eight wrecks remaining in Scapa Flow gave further service, aiding in the salvage of the battlecruiser SMS *Hindenburg*, as will be described below.

Surviving torpedo boat wreckage from the Cox & Danks era

During the multibeam survey of January 2017, aided by the supporting ground truthing carried out by divers, the supposed sites of a number of torpedo boats were examined. The results show that in fact few sites remain now. It is clear from the descriptions of the salvage works that there would have been some degree of dispersed debris from the Cox era left behind in Gutter Sound when he finished, but by now it is largely long gone. What was left appears to have been cleared away, possibly during the time it was a busy naval base during World War II.

SMS *V78*

This wreck proved a difficult challenge for Cox & Danks as it had sunk completely upside down. It had to be lifted and then sunk again in deep water before it could be gradually recovered.[10] A section of bridge (identified by a telegraph), a funnel and dispersed wreckage were reported found in 1998.[11] The area north of Fara where *V78* was scuttled was scanned by multibeam in 2017 and dispersed pieces of wreckage were found over a wide area. The site has not been further examined.

SMS *S36*

Portions of at least two torpedo boats salvaged by Cox & Danks were re-sunk to aid in the salvage of SMS *Hindenburg*. SMS *S36* is stated to have been sunk by Cox on the west side of Cava (see Figure 7.1 for her position).[12] This was done to provide an anchor point for a cable attached to *Hindenburg*'s foremast in an attempt to keep the battlecruiser upright while it was being lifted. The initial attempt in 1926 failed as the cables snapped under the strain.[13] The wreck of *S36* was then broken up in situ.

S36 may have been selected for this task as she was being lifted when fire broke out on the drydock. This was attributed to an oil slick which had leaked from *S36*. The reason became clear when she was beached. The wreck had twisted when she sank (she was one of three moored to the same buoy which were tangled together on the bottom) and had two large tears in the hull from which fuel leaked out.[14] The site has been known of for many years and occasionally gets visited by divers. *S36* is described as being barely visible among the mud and rock seabed, with only the prop shafts showing.[15]

However, the multibeam scan of the site made by *Limbo* in January 2017 shows for the first time just how much of this wreck still remains. The results of the scan can be seen in Figure 6.7. It shows that at least 60 metres of the keel of the ship is still present, with the watertight framing clearly visible. The stern can be seen to have been broken away slightly, possibly as a result of the salvage works aimed at removing the propellers. One of the real benefits of multibeam is that the wrecks are revealed in great detail, as opposed to diving through the kelp, which may not reveal nearly as much. It seems that *S36* was deliberately driven hard into the beach to make it as secure as possible. This is probably why she was broken up where she lay.

SMS *Hindenburg* torpedo boat sections

As described in the next chapter, *Hindenburg* caused great trouble during the salvage attempts. Part of the problem was the fact that she lay upright on a very hard rock seabed, which meant that the rounded profile of the stern, sitting on hard rock, became unstable when the bow section began to rise. Initially *S36* had been sunk to provide an anchor point for a stabilizing cable to the wreck. When this failed to work, first one wedge and then another were made out of the two sections of an unknown torpedo boat (or boats) and placed under the propellers. The strongly built engine room areas were chosen for this purpose. The wedges were placed *in situ* and filled with jute bags of fast-setting concrete (known as Ciment Fondu), then lowered to the seabed and fitted in place by divers. Each wedge is said to have cost Cox £2,000 to make. But since he already

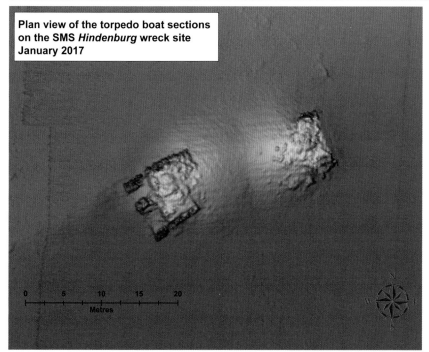

Plan view of the torpedo boat sections on the SMS *Hindenburg* wreck site January 2017

Figure 6.8. Plan view DTM of the two wedges made of sections of torpedo boat used to stabilise *Hindenburg* during her salvage. These were filled with bags of Ciment Fondu by divers to provide a cushion under the wreck to prevent her rolling when she began to rise.

had over £40,000 invested in the recovery and nothing to show for it, it was a risk he had to take.[16]

Of no practical use or recoverable value after *Hindenburg* was raised, the wedges remained in place and are still present today. The site has been surveyed by multibeam and diving and the results show that, surprisingly, the wedges seem to have survived in much the same condition as they would have been in when the divers made them in 1930. Figure 6.8 shows the plan view of the wedges as seen by multibeam in January 2017. The detail is good and the shape of the ship sections can be easily discerned, as can the piling of cement inside their structures. The port-side wedge appears to be in the better condition.

The wedges were surveyed by diving in November 2016, as shown in Figure 6.9. In excellent visibility, they were studied in detail. They are of course unique 'shipwrecks' and were in great condition for their age, clearly showing what they were built to do. The sections of torpedo boat are degrading but could still be clearly discerned, with the close framing seen also on the multibeam of *S36*. The jute of the bags of concrete is no longer present, and each 'bag' now resembles a large rock. They can be seen to have been methodically piled up inside the carcasses of the two wedges and are held in place with chains. Some of them appear to have been reduced to rubble, either by time or by the forces involved in raising the ship.

On the starboard-side wedge a section of the ship's hull still contained its timber filling within the watertight spaces. This is commonly seen on

Figure 6.9. Images of the *Hindenburg* wedges. Top, a diver is examining the port side of the wedge. The outer skin has corroded away, leaving mainly the frames present. Below, a section of the framing shows the layered sections of cork as cut and stacked inside this compartment. To the right can be seen some of the squashed concrete bags which filled the two wedges.

German-built ships of this period. It can be seen inside watertight sections of hull on the German shipwrecks at Jutland, such as SMS *Frauenlob*, and is a filling material routinely seen on U-boat wrecks as well. The *U1* on display in Munich shows this feature quite clearly.

A small section of this material was sent for analysis to the York Archaeological Trust, where timber specialist Steve Allen confirmed that it was cork. A naturally light (hence buoyant) material, it was clearly used to insulate hulls but also to pad watertight sections to prevent them being crushed by water pressure. Figure 6.9 depicts the two wedges as seen in 2016. The metal framing for the ships is deteriorating, but the cork slabs, neatly cut and stacked inside one watertight section, can still be clearly seen, as can the cement 'bags' used to fill the wedges.

Conclusions

The salvage of the torpedo boats from Gutter Sound was a brilliant success for Cox & Danks. Little now remains of these operations, except the examples shown. Two torpedo boats survive in much better condition, and they are described in detail in Chapter 17. The salvage of the High Seas Fleet is an important part of Scapa Flow's cultural heritage and the remains of the torpedo boats used to recover the *Hindenburg* need to be seen in that regard. The wedges in particular are a curiously unique cultural artefact with nothing similar for comparison, as far as is known.

1   Naval Historical Branch (various dates), *CP 8a Sale Book*. Portsmouth.

2   Naval Historical Branch (various dates), *CP 8a Sale Book*. Portsmouth.

3   G. Bowman (1964), *The Man Who Bought a Navy* (London: Harrap), p. 57.

4   Orkney Archives (various dates), microfilmed records of the *Orkney Herald*, 1919–1931. Kirkwall.

5   H. Murray Taylor (2013), 'The Salvaging of the Ex-German High Seas Fleet at Scapa Flow (1924–1930)', *22nd Proceedings of the Annual Conference 2012* (Gosport: Historical Diving Society), p. 10.

6   H. Grosset (1953), *Down to the Ships in the Sea* (London: Hutchinson), p. 134.

7   H. Grosset (1953), *Down to the Ships in the Sea* (London: Hutchinson), p. 130.

8   H. Grosset (1953), *Down to the Ships in the Sea* (London: Hutchinson), p. 135.

9   Naval Historical Branch (various dates), *CP 8a Sale Book*. Portsmouth.

10   Orkney Archives (various dates), microfilmed records of the *Orkney Herald* 1919–1931. Kirkwall.

11   Hydrographic Department of the Admiralty (2017), Record of Wreck No. 1034 SMS *V78* (part) (Taunton: Hydrographic Office).

12   I. G. Whittaker (1998), *Off Scotland: A Comprehensive Record of Maritime and Aviation Losses in Scottish Waters* (Berwick upon Tweed: C-Anne), p. 81. Hydrographic Department of the Admiralty (2017), Record of Wreck No. 1073 SMS *S36 (Bow Section)* (Taunton: Hydrographic Office).

13   G. Bowman (1964), *The Man Who Bought a Navy* (London: Harrap), pp. 124–126.

14   T. Booth (2011), *Cox's Navy: Salvaging the German High Seas Fleet at Scapa Flow 1924–1931* (Barnsley: Pen & Sword), pp. 53–54.

15   L. Wood (2008), *Scapa Flow Dive Guide* (Southend-on-Sea: Aquapress), p. 65.

16   G. Bowman (1964), *The Man Who Bought a Navy* (London: Harrap), pp. 208–213.

CHAPTER 7
COX & DANKS' SALVAGE OF THE WARSHIPS

Figure 7.1. (Above and opposite) SMS *Moltke* being lightened, with SMS *Hindenburg* still wrecked in the background (above), and *Moltke* as she arrived in Rosyth after the tow south in May 1928. The airlocks can be seen on her hull, along with the accommodation hut for the transfer crew (opposite). (Orkney Archive)

Following his successful raising of 25 torpedo boats, Cox turned to the remaining large warships. The results were technically a stunning success, but not a profitable one. Seydlitz and Hindenburg proved especially difficult. With a fall in metal prices in 1931, after seven successful cases, Cox & Danks wound up its salvage operations. Significant remains of some of the salvaged ships can still be found where the wrecks were recovered.

The salvage of the large warships, 1927–1939

For Cox & Danks, the recovery of 25 torpedo boats had brought 23,000 tons of salvaged warships to the scrapyard. Cox's initial investment of £40,000 had been repaid and he now believed he had the experience and hardware to begin to recover the larger warships. In the end he recovered seven of them – two battleships, four battlecruisers and the light cruiser SMS *Bremse*. Ironically, the larger wrecks lying in the shallowest water, *Hindenburg* and *Seydlitz*, proved the most difficult to recover. The lesson learned was that the wrecks that were upside down came up the easiest, but all were difficult and dangerous to work on.

Cox & Danks bowed out in 1931 and in 1934 Metal Industries took over, with Thomas McKenzie now in charge. From deeper water, they recovered another five battleships and a battlecruiser before the outbreak of World War II. Figure 7.2 shows the location, depth and year of salvage of the 12 battleships and battlecruisers recovered between 1927 and 1939. They range from 19 metres to 43 metres in depth.

The map in Figure 7.2 features the 2017 multibeam survey and also shows the seven wrecks which still lie in the old German anchorage. The deep impressions made in the softer seabed in the western and northern areas still remain as ghostly reminders of where the ships sank. Archaeological remains can be found on all of the sites where the large warships were recovered and in some sites where they were worked on after raising, as the next three chapters will show.

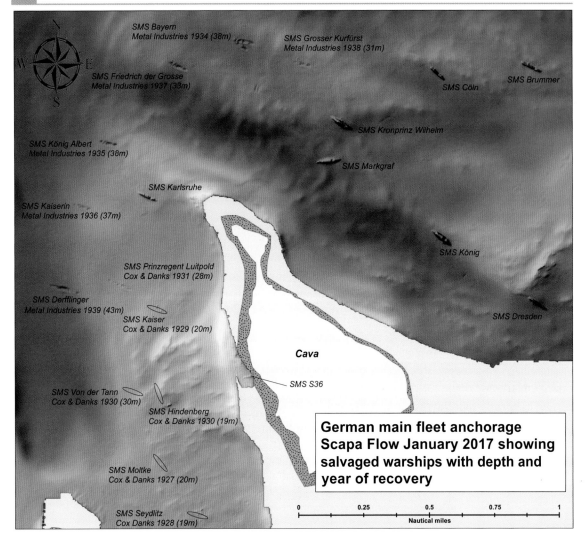

SMS Bayern
Metal Industries 1934 (38m)

SMS Grosser Kurfürst
Metal Industries 1938 (31m)

SMS Friedrich der Grosse
Metal Industries 1937 (33m)

SMS Cöln

SMS Brummer

SMS Kronprinz Wilhelm

SMS König Albert
Metal Industries 1935 (38m)

SMS Markgraf

SMS Karlsruhe

SMS Kaiserin
Metal Industries 1936 (37m)

SMS König

SMS Prinzregent Luitpold
Cox & Danks 1931 (28m)

SMS Derfflinger
Metal Industries 1939 (43m)

SMS Kaiser
Cox & Danks 1929 (20m)

SMS Dresden

Cava

SMS S36

SMS Von der Tann
Cox & Danks 1930 (30m)

SMS Hindenberg
Cox & Danks 1930 (19m)

**German main fleet anchorage
Scapa Flow January 2017 showing
salvaged warships with depth and
year of recovery**

SMS Moltke
Cox & Danks 1927 (20m)

SMS Seydlitz
Cox Danks 1928 (19m)

0   0.25   0.5   0.75   1

Nautical miles

Figure 7.2. The remains of the battleships and battlecruisers of the scuttled fleet today, as seen on multibeam. Seven warships remain in situ. Archaeological remains of a further 12, salvaged between 1927 and 1939, with date and depth shown, have been found on each of the sites as they have been investigated.

Salvage using airlocks to work inside the wrecks, 1927–1939

One common aspect of the salvage work across the Cox & Danks and Metal Industries years was the use of airlocks. This system gave access to the interiors of the wrecks while they still lay on the bottom and it became more advanced as the years progressed and as necessity demanded. Compressed air was used to drive water out of the hulls of the wrecks through the deck openings (when upside down) and the airlocks, by using a series of doors which, when shut, prevented the air escaping while workers entered and left the wreck. The earliest examples, such as those used on *Moltke*, were made from old boiler cylinders, but in the Metal Industries years they were custom fabricated to suit each job being undertaken.

In the Metal Industries years the airlocks were fabricated and refurbished at Lyness and then shipped in one piece to the sites. Cox & Danks assembled them in sections once the base had been fitted to the wrecks. The airlocks were fitted by divers. This was extremely arduous and difficult work. The larger examples, such as that seen in Figure 7.3, weighed up to 30 tons. Great care had to be taken in securing them in place. Once they were bolted down and secured with guys, a manhole was cut into the wreck and work could begin. The wrecks were subdivided into several airtight compartments, so that the flow of air through the wreck could be controlled and the lift carefully coordinated. Workers made each subdivision airtight by plugging and patching all openings through which air could escape from the dry areas or to which it could migrate through the subdivisions. See Figure 8.6 for a diagram of the lifting process in practice.

Conditions inside the wrecks could be extremely unpleasant, with surfaces covered in oil, coal dust, rust, marine growth and rotting, fetid organic material. This could lead to the build-up of poisonous and explosive gasses, resulting in the need on the deeper sites for a chemist, Charles F. Cowan, to test the air quality daily. Subdivisions had to be periodically flushed with clean air, and a spray was developed to combat gas build-up. The deeper locks had to be able to allow a change of shifts through the day. If bad weather developed, workers would have to wait inside the airlock until it was safe to leave, sometimes for many hours.

Workers also ran the risk of decompression sickness (the bends), and cases of this were not uncommon.[1] The deeper the wreck and the longer the time exposed to pressure, the greater the risk. Haldane's tables were used for decompression schedules on the deep wrecks and there were recompression chambers to treat cases as they occurred, but decompression science was not advanced. By the time Metal Industries worked on *Derfflinger*, working time had been reduced to one hour and decompression in the airlock took 90 minutes. But of the 7,635 man shifts worked, 266 cases of the bends were recorded; workers ran a 3.5% chance of injury on each shift.[2]

SMS *Moltke*, raised 9 June 1927

Prior to *Moltke*, the raising of upside-down warships had been successfully carried out on the wrecks of the monitor HMS *Glatton* and the cruiser HMS *Vindictive*, but the 22,616-ton *Moltke* was over four times the size of these. The wreck lay on uneven ground with a 17-degree list to port, her bows being slightly higher. Much of her showed at low water and she was a

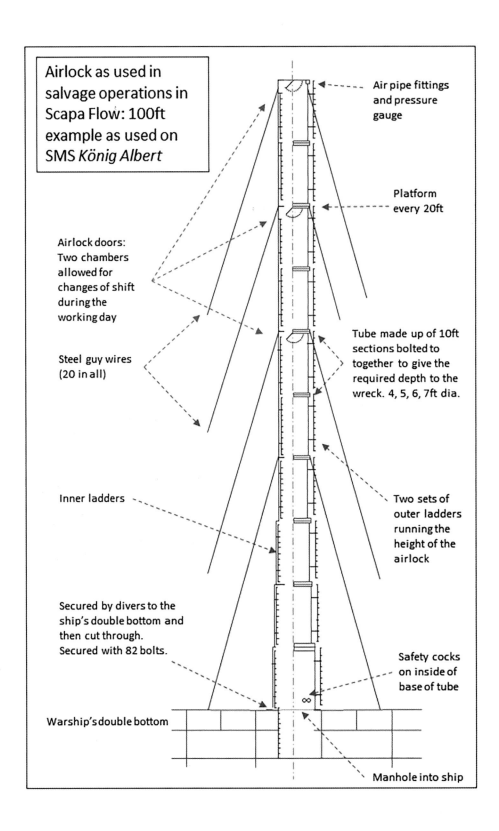

Airlock as used in salvage operations in Scapa Flow: 100ft example as used on SMS *König Albert*

Air pipe fittings and pressure gauge

Platform every 20ft

Airlock doors: Two chambers allowed for changes of shift during the working day

Tube made up of 10ft sections bolted to together to give the required depth to the wreck. 4, 5, 6, 7ft dia.

Steel guy wires (20 in all)

Inner ladders

Two sets of outer ladders running the height of the airlock

Secured by divers to the ship's double bottom and then cut through. Secured with 82 bolts.

Safety cocks on inside of base of tube

Warship's double bottom

Manhole into ship

notable navigation hazard. In her prime she had been one of the most famous warships in the world and briefly von Hipper's flagship during the night at Jutland.

The first airlock was fitted forward and another further aft. During the salvage, compressed air continued to flow forward, despite efforts to make the subdivisions airtight. Initial attempts to correct the list by using the floating dock to add lift and a sunken section of the salvaged torpedo boat *G38* to push down on the upper side of the stern were not on their own successful.[3] Ultimately, compressed air had to be introduced into the lower port-side bunker and the upper starboard bunker was filled with water.[4] With compressors forcing air into the stern, the wreck rose stern first on 9 June 1927. It was only once she was clear of the bottom that the flow of air could be controlled longitudinally by making the bulkheads airtight and the wreck could be stabilized.[5]

Once sufficiently clear of the seabed, *Moltke* was gradually winched by cables anchored on Cava and by tug to the shoreside at Cava, so that by 30 June she was parallel to the shore 200 metres off the beach. At that point the wreck was cut into and the process of lightening her began.[6] The photograph in Figure 7.1 shows this under way. In the background the sunken *Hindenburg* can be clearly seen. *Moltke* is sitting on a projection of shallower seabed off Cava, which can be seen in Figure 7.2. It was in this area that Cox & Danks worked on several of the wrecks it recovered.

Operations off Cava continued until early September, when *Moltke* was towed to Lyness. There, around 3,000 tons of metals were removed, some of which were sold to the USA later that year.[7] Once the wreck was readied for towing, Cox had to insure her. On 18 May she left under tow for Rosyth. An accident almost caused a collision with the Forth Bridge, but ultimately she was berthed in the Admiralty drydock at Rosyth, where Metal Industries (known as Alloa Shipbreaking at the time) broke her up. She was gone by March 1929.[8]

The multibeam survey of the salvage site reveals that it was clear of large pieces of wreckage. Some small pieces of wreck could be discerned (see Figure 7.4), but to date these have not been examined by diving, as priority was given to more obvious archaeological features.

SMS *Seydlitz*, raised 2 November 1928

As previously described, the famous battlecruiser SMS *Seydlitz*, which had shipped 5,000 tons of water at Jutland but still got home, was lying on her side with her upper port side visible above the water. This created a challenge which in retrospect was made a lot more difficult by partially salvaging

Figure 7.3. (Opposite) An example of the advanced system of airlock used on the deeper wrecks in Scapa Flow. In this instance the airlock was fitted with a double chamber to allow a change of shift of workers during the day. On the deeper wrecks, working time was limited to one hour, requiring up to 90 minutes of decompression in the airlock.

Figure 7.4. The seabed where *Moltke* was salvaged, as seen in 2017. It is clear of large debris.

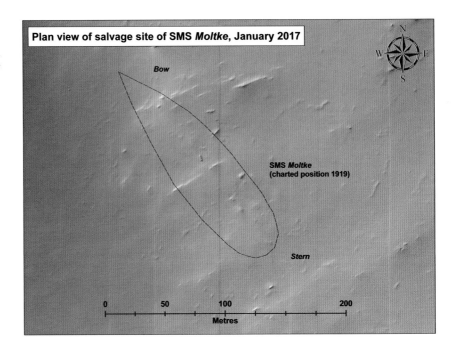

Plan view of salvage site of SMS *Moltke*, January 2017

Bow

SMS *Moltke*
(charted position 1919)

Stern

0   50   100   200
Metres

1,800 tons of armoured plate from the upper side (Cox needed cash) and attempting to lift the wreck sideways. Ultimately the lost weight had to be made good by shovelling in 1,800 tons of gravel by hand.

Using eight airlocks, the wreck was subdivided into eight compartments. The upper side required the use of custom-made patches, increasing the cost of recovery. Work had begun in 1926. During that year she had also been mined for coal during the General Strike.[9] The first attempt to raise her proved fruitless in June 1927 because forward compartments failed under pressure, forcing the bows upwards and causing the wreck to roll over and sink at a 48-degree angle. As she was prevented from rolling over completely by her upper works, divers now had to cut them clear, while workers made the compartments airtight again.

The wreck remained unstable and several test lifts failed to find a means of bringing her up safely. Ultimately an unknown number of scrap boiler casings were lowered to the seabed and filled with rapid-setting Ciment Fondu. The lower side of the wreck was then lowered onto them, providing a stabilizing platform from which to lift the ship evenly. On the upper side a section of torpedo boat was lashed to her as a counterbalance; this can be seen in Figure 7.5. The cables attaching her to the floating dock started to break during the successful lift of 2 November 1928, but this time she remained afloat and stable. She was immediately towed to Lyness, with a short grounding at low tide off Fara.[10] At Lyness she was lightened.

This included the removal of her fore turret. She was towed to Rosyth on 3 May 1929. Despite a brief grounding at Crockness and a later gale, she was berthed in Rosyth and completely broken up by December 1931.

The *Seydlitz* wreck site has been enjoyed by recreational divers for many years. As shown in Figure 7.5, it is crowded with features. Each dive reveals more details. I have dived on this site a number of times, and some of the more notable items recorded are shown in Figure 7.7, with their locations marked on Figure 7.6. The feature which usually has a line tied to it is an 88mm gun in its original shield, as seen in Images A and B. This is an anti-aircraft gun, and it is a rare survivor at Scapa. Another gun lies nearby (C) with its muzzle buried. The base of the crow's nest, probably from the foremast, can be seen in Image D.

The southern side of the wreck site seems to be the area which contains items remaining from the salvage operations. Image E shows one of the unknown number of concrete boiler ends Cox used to stabilize the wreck. Interestingly, Image F shows a portion of wreckage which will require more analysis to be certain as to what it is. It looks to be either a portion of the torpedo boat Cox used to stabilize the wreck or a portion of the ship's double bottom, which was discarded during operations to open her up to recover coal and steel and ultimately to salvage her. The torpedo boat may have been *G38*, which had previously been used to stabilize *Moltke*.[11]

Figure 7.5. SMS *Seydlitz* finally afloat in 1928; note the airlocks and the remains of a torpedo boat lashed to the side as a counterbalance (above). *Seydlitz* in the dry dock awaiting breaking (below). (Orkney Archive)

SMS *Kaiser*, raised 20 March 1929

The wreck of the *Kaiser* lay at an angle of 8 degrees. It has been said that she was one of the easier wrecks to recover, but in salvage that is a relative term. The wreck was fitted with four airlocks, and patching and making compartments airtight took the usual several months. The wreck was raised entirely on 20 March 1929. She remained at her sinking position until 23 March, while divers cleared away hanging debris, and then towing began. The following day she was grounded off Cava.[12] Work to clear the superstructure went on for several days, so that by 4 April she had been brought to a point between the *Hindenburg* wreck and Cava.

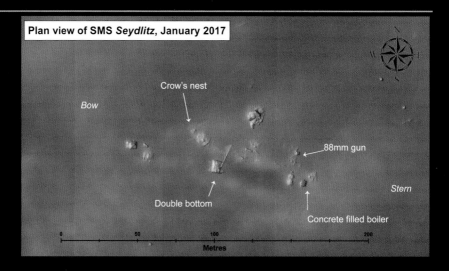

Plan view of SMS *Seydlitz*, January 2017

Bow

Crow's nest

88mm gun

Double bottom

Stern

Concrete filled boiler

0   50   100   200

Metres

Figure 7.6. Plan view of the *Seydlitz* wreck and salvage site. The site is characterized by much dispersed wreckage from the ship's superstructure and salvage operations.

Figure 7.7. Notable features recorded on the *Seydlitz* salvage site as described in the text.

The armoured conning tower was the tough and stubborn obstacle preventing further progress until it could be cut loose, a procedure which was done from inside the ship. The *Kaiser* was deflated and allowed to sink so that the conning tower rested on the hard seabed off Cava and was slowly crushed up inside the ship. At this point, it was chained up, with the chains attached to steel shafts which had been brought out to the wreck for this purpose. The position reported for the crushing was between Cava and the wreck of *Hindenburg*, or approximately in the same area where *Moltke* had been previously worked upon. It was done by

Figure 7.8. Probably Ernest Cox in the hat posing by the propellers of the salvaged *Kaiser* (above); *Kaiser's* iron bell seen with some of Cox's men in 1929 (below). (Orkney Archive)

mid-April, and then she was moved to Lyness. Thence she was towed to Rosyth, arriving on 24 July. Breaking commenced in September and her book was closed in December 1931.[13]

This site was surveyed by video on four occasions during 2013–2017 and it is now well understood. Some of the key features are shown on the multibeam site plan in Figure 7.9 and in the underwater images. The seabed is of hard gravel and the wreck left little impression on the bottom. But a range of fascinating objects were left behind after the salvage. Figure 7.10 shows the remains of the heavy armoured spotting and control top. This is probably the best-preserved example of this feature in the world. Images A and B show the triangular shape of the upper platform seen from underside and the top. The rangefinder was removed prior to the internment. Image C shows the drum-shaped lower platform with the access door from the mast. Image D shows the well-preserved features and floor inside.

Figure 7.9. The heavy armoured spotting top on the cigar mast as seen on the *Kaiser* wreck site.

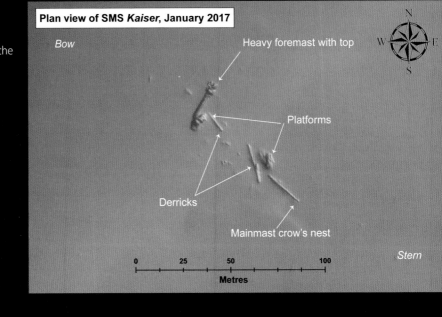

Figure 7.9. The heavy armoured spotting top on the cigar mast as seen on the *Kaiser* wreck site.

Figure 7.11 shows some of the features to the east of the foremast. In Image A, a crushed searchlight is seen underneath the platform it was once mounted upon. Image B shows the remains of the crow's nest at the top of the mainmast. Only the platform with the access hatch remains *in situ* now. Image C shows one of at least two boat cradles lying between the derricks. In Image D

Figure 7.10. The well-preserved armoured control and spotting top on the SMS *Kaiser* site.

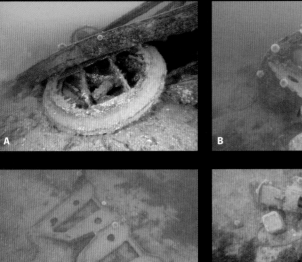

Figure 7.11. Searchlight platforms, a crow's nest, a boat rest and coal winches as seen on the *Kaiser* wreck site.

a collection of three coal winches is shown. These appear to have been roped together with a plastic container, perhaps to be salvaged at some point.

SMS *Bremse*, raised 27 November 1929

During the Grand Scuttle, the light cruiser SMS *Bremse* was beached in shallow water at the westerly edge of Smoogro Bay, where she capsized. Cox & Danks began work on her in May 1929. The bow was clear but the stern lay deeper. The superstructure was cut off and the wreck made upside down, only to topple over and require the process to begin again from the other side.[14] This caused a major oil leak which had to be burned off. Leaking oil also caused a fire inside the wreck during the works. Airlocks were fitted, and once secure, she was blown to a floating condition. She was then towed directly to Lyness and broken up there, having been entirely disposed of by May 1931.[15]

Figure 7.12. SMS *Bremse* as seen during the salvage process (note the airlocks), showing that the fore part of her upper deck has been cut away (Orkney Archive). This included her forward gun, which has been salvaged and is now on display at the Scapa Flow Visitor Centre at Lyness.

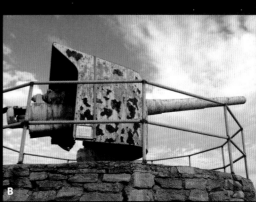

Figure 7.13. The wreck and salvage site of SMS *Bremse* as seen on multibeam in 2017. Oddly, she seems to lie just to the east of the position where the wreck was surveyed in 1919.

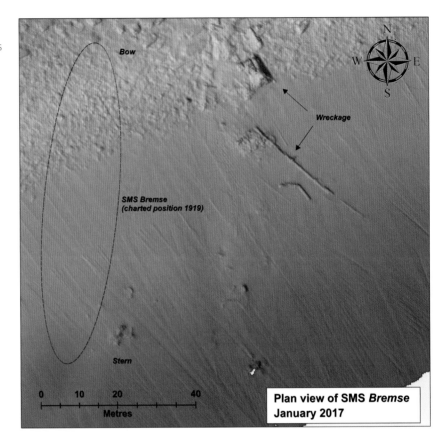

The site where *Bremse* was salvaged was located during the multibeam survey in January 2017 and it can be seen in Figure 7.13. A very shallow impression is left in the seabed. But at the shallower end to the north of the wreck site, it seems some of the fore section of the ship remains. It is known from photographs (see Figure 7.12) that some of her forward upper deck was cut away during the salvage operations. Her forward gun was found on the wreck site as reported in 1982.[16] It was subsequently recovered and is on display outside the Scapa Flow Visitor Centre at Lyness.

SMS *Hindenburg*, raised 22 July 1930

Due to her sinking upright, the battlecruiser *Hindenburg* became the iconic image of both the scuttled fleet and the salvage years. She was the sister ship of SMS *Lützow* (sunk at Jutland) and SMS *Derfflinger*, the flushed deck design making them visually impressive, but they were also among the finest warships ever built. *Hindenburg* was the largest ship ever recovered from the sea at the time. The recovery process was fraught with difficulties and was, until brought to success, a major financial drain on Cox & Danks.

Figure 7.14. SMS *Hindenburg* during the abortive early salvage attempts, with 'Cox & Danks' confidently emblazoned on the 'B' turret (left), and as finally raised and delivered upright to Metal Industries in 1930, in one of the salvage years' most iconic photographs (right). (Left: Orkney Archive; right: Marine Technology Special Collection, Newcastle University)

Work actually began on the wreck in the weeks after the recovery of the last destroyer, *G104*, in April 1926. Her upright condition meant that there were myriad locations from which air could escape, and all had to be patched. In the end some 800 custom-made patches (one costing £500 alone) had to be individually fitted. Saithe fish ate the tallow on the patches, requiring resetting with concrete mixed in. In no less than four attempts that year *Hindenburg* could not be recovered.[17] Bad luck and bad weather played their part. At one point a gale caused a section of the torpedo boat *G38* to punch a hole in the large floating dock. Ultimately the wreck was abandoned in September and returned to only in 1930 after experience had been gained on other sites, not least *Seydlitz*.

A key element in the challenges faced was that this specific class of battlecruiser contained a 'leak pump' system which could transfer water around the ship through large-bore pipes.[18] These were situated in and just above her double bottom, in the most inaccessible part of the wreck.[19] Cox acknowledged in 1932 that these pipes had been a major problem. When the bow was raised, an unstoppable flow of water ran aft, causing instability and the need for constant pumping out.[20] The fact that the wreck lay on solid rock meant that the stern would simply roll where it wanted and the wreck would topple over as a consequence.

In 1930, once 300 of the patches had been replaced, attempts to raise her were resumed and the instability challenge addressed. As related in the previous chapter, in 1926 this had initially involved sinking a torpedo boat

Figure 7.15. Salvage operations on SMS *Hindenburg* in 1926 (above). Broken cables can be seen hanging down from the foremast. There is another image in this sequence, showing them under load. The lower photo shows that the masts were removed before she was successfully lifted. (Orkney Archive)

(*S36*) off Cava and wiring the foremast to it, which ended in failure. On its own it could not solve the problem, so the concrete pillows were made, as seen in Figures 6.8 and 6.9. These resolved the stability issue and enabled the wreck to be raised without toppling over. Figure 7.15 shows snapped cables affixed to the tripod mast from the floating dock during the earlier phase of salvage, and also that prior to the wreck being successfully lifted in 1930 the forward tripod mast had been cut off her, presumably to aid in stability. She was finally successfully raised on 22 July 1930 and was made fast in Mill Bay the following evening.[21] She was towed to Rosyth in August and was completely broken up by the end of the following year.[22]

The *Hindenburg* salvage site and the nearby *Von der Tann* site are shown on multibeam in Figure 7.16. Apart from the wedges previously described, both sites are devoid of any substantial wreckage.

SMS *Von der Tann*, raised 7 December 1930

Work immediately began on the upside-down wreck of Germany's first battlecruiser, the famous *Von der Tann*, nemesis of HMS *Indefatigable* at the Battle of Jutland. A long airlock system, similar to that used on *Kaiser*, was employed, but this time the wreck was ten metres deeper and ten airlocks were used to help subdivide the wreck. Foul air was encountered during the salvage operations, leading to the use of the even fouler-smelling spray to dampen the dangerous fumes. Nevertheless, towards the end of operations a pipe full of dangerous gas was cut into, causing an explosion which injured four workers, including McKenzie, who fully recovered after a spell in hospital. SMS *Von der Tann* was successfully raised on 7 December 1930 after four months of work.[23]

Upon raising, she was gradually pulled towards Cava. It took several days to get her to within half a mile of the shore, where she was moored with her bows to the island. As reported in the *Orcadian*, it was at this time that the superstructure which was hanging down from the wreck was blasted off, including her masts, the derricks and a portion of the bridge.[24] She was towed

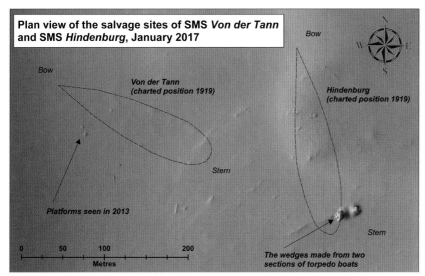

Figure 7.16. The salvage site of SMS *Hindenburg* and SMS *Von der Tann*, as seen during the January 2017 multibeam survey. The sites are seen to be clear of any substantial wreckage, aside from the wedges described in the previous chapter. The small anomalies are pieces of wreckage and natural geology.

to Lyness on 8 February 1931. Interestingly, such a location would have placed her in close proximity to the *Hindenburg* site, raising the important issue that the wreckage from the different sites off Cava could be mixed up. This is complicated even further by the fact that as described above, both *Moltke* and *Kaiser* were also both extensively worked on in this area as well. Certainly no heavy wreckage was detected in this area by our survey. It might lie further inshore, but it could be that, like so much other debris from the scuttle and salvage, it was removed in subsequent years.

Due to a fall in metal prices, *Von der Tann* was not sold to Metal Industries until March 1933, long after Cox & Danks had ceased operations at Scapa Flow. She arrived in Rosyth in July 1933 and was broken up over the next ten months. [25] In 2013 we looked at the *Von der Tann* area for some wreckage to dive.

Figure 7.17. SMS *Von der Tann* as delivered to Rosyth. Note the cut-down airlocks and the hut for the transfer crew. (Orkney Archive)

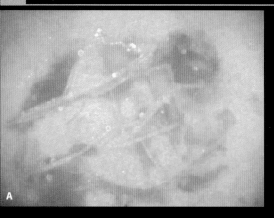

Figure 7.18. A small platform, probably from the upper bridge area of SMS *Von der Tann*, as seen in 2013.

Unsurprisingly, we found very little. But we did examine one target which turned out to be a pair of small platforms. The more intact one was seen to be largely circular in shape and is shown in Figure 7.18. This was probably situated in the region of the upper bridge.

SMS *Prinzregent Luitpold*, raised 9 July 1931

This battleship, a hotbed of mutiny in 1917, was the last ship Cox & Danks recovered. She lay in 28 metres with a 20-degree list. In total, 14 airlocks were fitted and the interior of the wreck was subdivided into 13 airtight compartments, including the outer bunkers used to correct the list (see Figure 8.6 for a diagram of a broadly similar system employed on *König Albert*).[26] The compartments were made watertight down to the level of the armoured deck.

In a similar depth to *Von der Tann*, the same fetid and explosive gases were encountered, especially forward. Conditions were so bad at times that smoke helmets had to be used. Despite the precautions taken in the use of sprays, regular venting, electric lighting and so on, an explosion did occur, and in this case it claimed the life of carpenter William Tait. He had been knocked unconscious and drowned. The subsequent coroner's enquiry placed no blame on the firm. It was just bad luck.[27]

There is a surviving Admiralty file on the lifting and towing of SMS *Prinzregent Luitpold* written by Cmdr P. Ruck Keene RN, who was a witness to the process. He went on to pioneer submarine safety systems as a member of the post–World War II Ruck Keene Committee. The file shows that the process used to clear and remove the wreck was similar to that used for *Kaiser*, her sister ship which had already been successfully recovered. After an abortive attempt to raise her in June, SMS *Prinzregent Luitpold* was raised on 9 July 1931, whereupon her divers blasted off the remains of her funnels and her top hamper. She was then moved to the rocky seabed off Cava.

The turrets remained in the ship, as did the conning tower. This armoured structure hung too low in the water to allow for docking in Rosyth and, as with *Kaiser*, it had to be crushed into the hull, using a similar system of supports to hold it up. This was accomplished by 16 July, when she was towed to Lyness.[28] Low scrap prices meant that Cox retained her in Scapa until 1933, when she was sold to Metal Industries, arriving in Rosyth

Figure 7.19. SMS *Prinzregent Luitpold* as delivered to Rosyth. Note the forward torpedo tube door and the high number of airlocks. (Marine Technology Special Collection, Newcastle University)

in May (see Figure 7.19) and being completely demolished by March 1934.[29]

I have examined the remaining wreckage of this once-mighty battleship since 2013. In 2017 the multibeam survey provided a detailed plan of all the features on the site. This can be seen in Figure 7.20. This wreck sits on a soft seabed and the impression the wreck made 100 years ago is still visible. The noticeable double impression at the easterly end may have been made by the abortive attempt to raise her. The photographs in Figure 2.3 show she sank by stern, rolling to starboard.

In 2013 the easterly section of wreckage had been recorded on video and was seen to include a large round armoured top with slot windows. Following its mast to the point it broke off led to a searchlight platform in the vertical position with the degraded remains of the light still in place. The top can be seen in Figure 7.21, from the southwest in Image A and from the northwest in Image B. At the time it was not clear whether this was the foremast or the mainmast.

The appearance of a further large area of wreckage seen on the multibeam survey in 2017 prompted a survey dive on this area later that year. The results were particularly noteworthy and images are shown in Figures 7.22 and 7.23. The northern end of the wreckage contains the degraded remains of the foremast and its crow's nest (Figure 7.22, Images A & B). This resembles the bucket-type nest seen elsewhere, notably on the mainmast of *Derfflinger* (see the next chapter). The casing has separated from the base and mast, and the base with its access hatch lies close by. Just to the south of the crow's nest is a pair of platforms which lie on top of each other with the crushed remains of a searchlight sandwiched between them (Image C).

Most marked was the southerly structure which appeared to have been made almost entirely of bronze. It was made up of the remains of a walled platform which seems to have been partially salvaged. This can be seen in

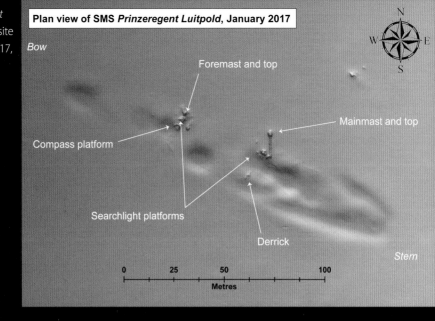

Figure 7.20. SMS *Prinzregent Luitpold* wreck and salvage site as seen on multibeam in 2017, with features observed on dives 2013–2017.

Plan view of SMS *Prinzeregent Luitpold*, January 2017

Bow

Foremast and top

Mainmast and top

Compass platform

Searchlight platforms

Derrick

Stern

0   25   50   100

Metres

Image D, with a portion of the now heavily distorted structure of the platform and what looks like a ladder, both made of quality non-ferrous metal. The conclusion is that this was probably where a magnetic compass was stationed. That entire bridges themselves were made of bronze is not uncommon, as visitors to the World War I–era British monitor HMS *M33* on display at the National Museum of the Royal Navy will know. Its entire bridge was seemingly so built so as to mitigate compass deviation, a feature also seen on the entire conning towers of British submarines of the same period.

Beside this bronze structure was the unmistakable sight of a partially buried German navy compass stand of the High Seas Fleet era. This can be seen in Figure 7.23, with the shaft leading to its base leading off to the top right and with the gimbal in the bottom left. A similar example can be seen at the Waterside Café in Finstown, Orkney, which is alleged to have come from

Figure 7.21. SMS *Prinzregent Luitpold*'s armoured top on its mainmast, as filmed in 2013.

A

B

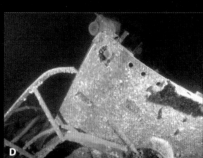

Figure 7.22. The foremast crow's nest and surrounding features on SMS *Prinzregent Luitpold*, as described in the text.

the salvage of SMS *Grosser Kurfürst*.[30] Items such as this are now increasingly rare, after so many years of salvage and recreational souvenir hunting, and this was a notable discovery in 2017.

The end of the Cox & Danks era

The salvage of *Prinzregent Luitpold* led the *Orcadian* newspaper to dub Ernest Cox 'Britain's brainiest bulldog'.[31] Certainly his drive and sheer force of will overcame many obstacles deemed insurmountable during the salvage of 32 ships of the scuttled fleet. But despite his undoubted qualities, anyone can fall victim to the economic cycle. A booklet produced by Cox & Danks afterwards states that for all its efforts and an investment of £450,000, it made a profit of £10,000.[32] Others have concluded that in fact the £10,000 was a loss. In either

Figure 7.23. A compass stand buried beside its bronze platform on the wreck of the *Prinzregent Luitpold* (left), and a similar example on display in a café on Orkney which comes from a German battleship during the salvage years (right). (Ivan Houston)

case, the returns seem unimportant compared with the achievement, and it is said that Cox's scrap-metal business, neglected by him throughout the salvage years, had quietly made him a millionaire during this time anyhow.[33]

With metal prices at a low in 1931, it was time to call it a day. *Von der Tann* and *Prinzregent Luitpold* lay in Mill Bay and two years were to pass before Cox's entire salvage operation was purchased by Metal Industries. The company's records show that alongside the last warships, Cox's salvage vessel *Ferrodanks* and the floating dock were broken up in 1934, going the same way as the mighty warships they had done so much to help recover.

William Tait's death had in fact been the fourth among Cox's employees. Deckhands Henderson and Taylor had been killed in accidents on deck in 1925 and Herbert Hall had died in a diving accident in 1929. An unknown number had been injured in burns, falls, and so on. Marine salvage was dangerous work, at a time long before Health & Safety entered the language of the workshop.

1   T. McKenzie (1949), 'Marine Salvage in Peace and War', *Institution of Engineers and Shipbuilders in Scotland*, 93, paper 1122, pp. 123–161, p. 127.

2   Orkney Archives (various dates), Diaries of H. Murray Taylor: Notes on *Derfflinger* Salvage, D1/59. Kirkwall.

3   Naval Historical Branch (various dates), *CP 8a Sale Book*, p. 74. Portsmouth. Telegram received from the King's Harbour Master on 22 May 1927.

4   Anon. (1927), 'The Salving of the Ex-German Battle-Cruisers "Moltke" and "Seydlitz", *The Engineer*, 7 July, pp. 741–745. London.

5   A. Gowans Whyte & R. L. Hadfield (1933), *Deep-Sea Salvage* (London: Sampson Low, Marston & Co.), pp. 115–120.\

6   Orkney Archives (various dates), microfilmed records of the *Orkney Herald*, 1919–1931. Kirkwall.

7   Orkney Archives (various dates), microfilmed records of the *Orkney Herald*, 1919–1931. Kirkwall.

8   Newcastle University Special Collections (various dates), Accounts and Minutes of Metal Industries Shipbreaking. Newcastle.

9   T. Booth (2011), *Cox's Navy: Salvaging the German High Seas Fleet at Scapa Flow 1924–1931* (Barnsley: Pen & Sword), p. 68.

10   Orkney Archives (various dates), microfilmed records of the *Orkney Herald*, 1919–1931. Kirkwall.

11   Hydrographic Department of the Admiralty (2017), Record of Wreck No. 1013 SMS *G38* (Taunton: Hydrographic Office).

12   Orkney Archives (various dates), Microfilmed records of the *Orcadian*, 1919–1938. Kirkwall.

13   Newcastle University Special Collections (various dates), Accounts and Minutes of Metal Industries Shipbreaking. Newcastle.

14   Orkney Archives (various dates), Microfilmed records of the *Orcadian*, 1919–1938. Kirkwall.

15   Naval Historical Branch (various dates), *CP 8a Sale Book*. Portsmouth.

16   Hydrographic Department of the Admiralty (2017), Record of Wreck No. 1120 SMS *Bremse* (Taunton: Hydrographic Office).

17   Orkney Archives (various dates), Microfilmed records of the *Orkney Herald*, 1919–1931. Kirkwall. 15 September 1926.

18   G. Staff (2014), *German Battlecruisers of World War One: Their Design, Construction and Operations* (Barnsley: Seaforth), p. 290.

19   National Maritime Museum (various dates), 'Pumpenplan' SMS *Lützow*. London.

20   E. Cox (1932), 'Eight Years Salvage Work at Scapa Flow', *Proceedings* (London: Institute of Mechanical Engineers).

21   Orkney Archives (various dates), Microfilmed records of the *Orkney Herald*, 1919–1931. Kirkwall, 30 July 1930.

22   Newcastle University Special Collections (various dates), Accounts and Minutes of Metal Industries Shipbreaking. Newcastle.

23   Orkney Archives (various dates), microfilmed records of the *Orcadian*, 1919–1938. Kirkwall, 11 December 1930.24 Orkney Archives (various dates), microfilmed records of the *Orcadian*, 1919–1938. Kirkwall, 18 December 1930.

25   Newcastle University Special Collections (various dates), Accounts and Minutes of Metal Industries Shipbreaking. Newcastle.

26   National Archives (various dates), account of the salvage and towing to Rosyth of the ex-German battleship *Prinz Regent Luitpold*, ADM 1/8766/77. London.

27   Orkney Archives (various dates), coroner's verdicts of the deaths at work of Cox workers, SC11/7/2/21 to 27. Kirkwall.

28   Orkney Archives (various dates), microfilmed records of the *Orcadian*, 1919–1938. Kirkwall, 16 July 1931.

29   Newcastle University Special Collections (various dates), Accounts and Minutes of Metal Industries Shipbreaking. Newcastle.

30   S. Henry, K. Heath & M. Littlewood (2018), *High Sea Fleet Salvage Sites Report* (Edinburgh: Historic Environment Scotland), p. 21.

31   Orkney Archives (various dates), microfilmed records of the *Orcadian*, 1919–1938. Kirkwall, 16 July 1931.

32   D. Masters (1931), *Salvage Work at Scapa Flow* (London: Cox & Danks).

33   J. N. Gores (1971), *Marine Salvage* (Newton Abbot: David & Charles), p. 228.

CHAPTER 8
METAL INDUSTRIES' SALVAGE OF THE WARSHIPS

Figure 8.1. Left, an elderly Robert McCrone photographed by Ian Buxton in 1981 in his garden with the large bell from SMS *König Albert* (Ian Buxton). Right, Metal Industries diver Arthur Nundy working on SMS *Bayern* in 1934. Nundy Marine Metals was to continue piecemeal salvage works at Scapa Flow after World War II. (Orkney Archive)

Unlike Cox & Danks, Metal Industries made good profits from the German wrecks. It bought well and was excellently managed. Thomas McKenzie brought the expertise which successfully raised five more battleships and a battlecruiser from Scapa Flow. Work ended when World War II broke out. Derfflinger was not brought south until late 1946.

The Metal Industries years at Scapa Flow

If Admiral von Reuter had been the reluctant hero and Ernest Cox the salvage pioneer, then Robert McCrone was the business genius who founded Britain's greatest shipbreaking company. It began as Alloa Shipbreaking in 1922, although the company never operated from Alloa. Among several innovations was the early investment in oxygen-manufacturing plant, drastically lowering the costs of cutting up metal. Cannily, one of the company's earliest investors was well connected at the Admiralty, giving the firm an advantage on the purchasing of ships coming up for sale. For example, where Cox & Danks had paid £1,000 each for *Kaiser* and *Prinzregent Luitpold*, McCrone paid £750 each for the three other ships of the same class, *Friedrich der Grosse*, *Kaiserin* and *König Albert*.[1]

McCrone had originally demurred from purchasing the wrecks of the High Seas Fleet *in situ*, but began buying the salvaged ships from Cox in 1926. In that year he paid £600 each for *G101*, *G104* and *B109*. The metals recovered sold for more than £20,000. By contrast, Cox & Danks had originally bought the three destroyers for £200 each and had had to salvage them before making any profit. Cox took the risks and McCrone made the money.[2] Connections at the Admiralty also smoothed rental access to Admiralty drydock space at Rosyth, opening the way for Metal Industries to buy the battleships and battlecruisers Cox began recovering in 1927. Naturally the terms were paid on delivery, with Cox footing the insurance bill each time.

Cox finally sold his salvage business to Metal Industries in 1933 for £3,500, at a time when metal prices were beginning to recover. Thomas McKenzie convinced McCrone that with better plant and a more professional approach, more of the battleships could be profitably raised. To prove the point, he accepted a low wage based on commission. Better equipment was purchased, along with the vessel *Bertha* (*Metinda* followed in 1934), and the Admiralty site at Lyness was leased. With the 41-year-old McKenzie in sole charge, work commenced in 1934.

SMS *Bayern*, raised 1 September 1934

After surveying several of the remaining wrecks, the new company selected the 15-inch-gun, 28,079-ton SMS *Bayern* as its first target, probably due to the minimal 9-degree list seen by the divers. During the Grand Scuttle, *Bayern*, the largest and most modern battleship class to be scuttled (*Baden* was saved from sinking), had provided the most iconic photographs of the day, as seen in Chapter 2. Work began in October 1933. Deeper than any of the wrecks Cox recovered, the new cases required custom-made airlocks. Seven were fitted to the wreck and the work of making each of the seven compartments airtight progressed well.

Figure 8.2. Left: *Bayern*, as successfully raised in September 1934, with probably Thomas McKenzie on the stern. Note the 90ft airlocks. (Orkney Archive). Right: *Bayern* being broken up in July 1935 at Rosyth. The forward part of the ship has been cut down to the upper deck. Note the remains of the hawse holes and the shafts from her three windlass engines. (Marine Technology Special Collection, Newcastle University)

But salvage work is never entirely predictable, and on 18 July 1934 *Bayern* unintentionally rose to the surface after a drainage pipe burst, allowing compressed air to rush into the fore part of the wreck. It rose to the surface, with the rapidly expanding air then forcing the stern up as well until the air escaped and the stern plunged to the bottom again. The rising *Bayern* fortunately missed *Bertha*, moored nearby.

This uncontrolled rise also separated the body of the ship from its four massive gun turrets, which remain to this day on the bottom. They were intended to act as a keel and their unplanned loss made the upside-down wreck unstable and she listed to 29 degrees to port. For two weeks she lay bow up while air was shifted into the starboard-side bunker to correct the list. This had been achieved by 2 August, but then the great ship listed to 42 degrees to port and had to be sunk to prevent it rolling right over.[3] On 30 July worker John Bee died in the upper section of an airlock. The coroner's inquiry concluded his death was due to heart failure.[4]

Work started again to correct the list. This time it was particularly arduous due to the angle at which the ship was lying; as McKenzie remarked, 'the men had to literally slide to their work'.[5] It was not until 1 September that, after a successful test lift, *Bayern* was finally brought to the surface. The following day she was towed to a sandbank less than a mile from Lyness and short airlocks were fitted. On 11 September she was towed to Lyness. She was then subject to crushing, similar to the work Cox had carried out off Cava, so that her conning tower was pressed inside the wreck. [6] She was towed to Rosyth on 26 April 1935 and completely demolished by March 1936.[7]

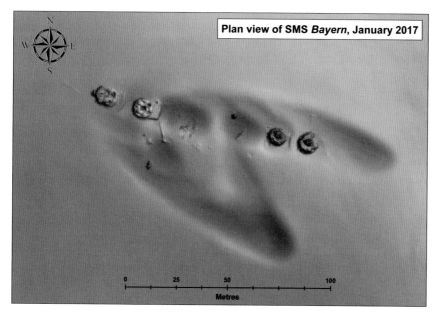

Plan view of SMS *Bayern*, January 2017

Figure 8.3. The plan view DTM of SMS *Bayern*, showing her four turrets. The double impression in the seabed was caused by the accidental lifting of the ship in July 1934, two months before she was finally raised.

The remains of SMS *Bayern* represent some of the most impressive wreckage from the High Seas Fleet to be found in Scapa Flow. The huge 15-inch gun turrets remain much as they were in 1934. The multibeam plan view can be seen in Figure 8.3. The four turrets are easily recognizable. There are also other sections of dispersed wreckage on the site.

The DTM in plan does not show the height by which the turrets themselves rise above the level of the seabed. This requires further processing of the point cloud to create a three-dimensional hybrid model of the wreck site. This can be seen in two images in Figure 8.4. The easterly pair of turrets ('C' and 'D') are more intact and rise an impressive 13 metres from the seabed. 'A' turret is quite well buried forward and has much collapsed debris from the turret's inner structure lying on top it. For some unexplained reason, the top of the 'B' turret is a lot cleaner.

It is clear that when the bow section of the ship had to be re-sunk in August 1934, it landed upon 'A' and 'B' turrets and crushed the shell hoists and inner platforms. This is why they look different from the easterly pair of turrets, which are largely intact, with their uppermost points representing the bottoms of the hoists used to lift cordite charges up into the gun house. Interestingly, unlike the smaller-calibre turrets in the other warships, which remained inside the hulls, these turrets do not appear to have been vertically restrained, or else simply broke away under their own weight. The circular platforms (a pair on 'C' and a single on 'D') housed within the armoured barbettes of the ship can be clearly seen on the hybrid model.

Figure 8.4. Hybrid model of the *Bayern* turrets reveals the different condition of the two pairs. 'A' and 'B' were crushed when *Bayern's* bows were resunk in August 1934.

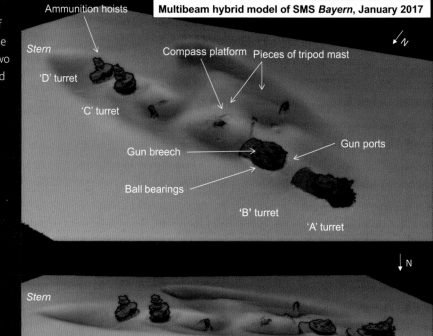

Ammunition hoists

Stern

'D' turret

'C' turret

Compass platform   Pieces of tripod mast

Gun breech

Ball bearings

Gun ports

'B' turret

'A' turret

N

Stern

N

The upper image in Figure 8.4 has been labelled to show the locations of the images taken of features of the wreck during survey dives in 2013. These are shown in Figure 8.5. Images A to C were taken around 'B' turret and show, in Image A, the armoured plate on the front of the turret with the base of curved gun port for the starboard-side gun. This is as close as one can get to the 15-inch guns, which were not seen on the dives. Image B shows the ball bearings upon which the turrets rotated when sitting in their barbettes. Interestingly, British systems used rollers, which look markedly different.[8] From the top of the turret one can look down into the gun house and see the partially dismantled massive breeches of the 15-inch guns, as shown in Image C.

Moving astern, there is an area of wreckage which, when investigated, turned out to be a large section of the tripod mast. Although it is very broken up, a platform can be seen attached to a mast leg in Image D, with railings to the right. Investigating this in more detail led to the discovery of what appeared to be a docking telegraph, replete with intact glass, as seen in Image E. Consulting the plans of this ship reveals that a platform with this feature was attached to each of the legs of the tripod mast.[9] During the ascent at the end of a dive, Image F was captured, showing the outline of the twin ammunition hoists at the highest point of the 'D' turret. It is clear that the entire turret assembly from the viewports at the top to the hoists at the bottom fell out of the ship in one piece in 1934.

The *Bayern* turrets are a unique example of Germany's attempt to build powerful battleships comparable to Britain's Queen Elizabeth class. They are an impressive spectacle to see and remain a popular alternative dive site to the seven surviving large wrecks.

SMS *König Albert*, raised 31 July 1935

Metal Industries commenced work in October on its next target, the battleship SMS *König Albert*. The first of eight 100ft airlocks was fitted by early December. To maintain stability as the compartments were filling, they were made airtight all the way down to the upper deck. The recovery of this particular

Figure 8.5. Images of the features seen on the *Bayern* site in 2013.

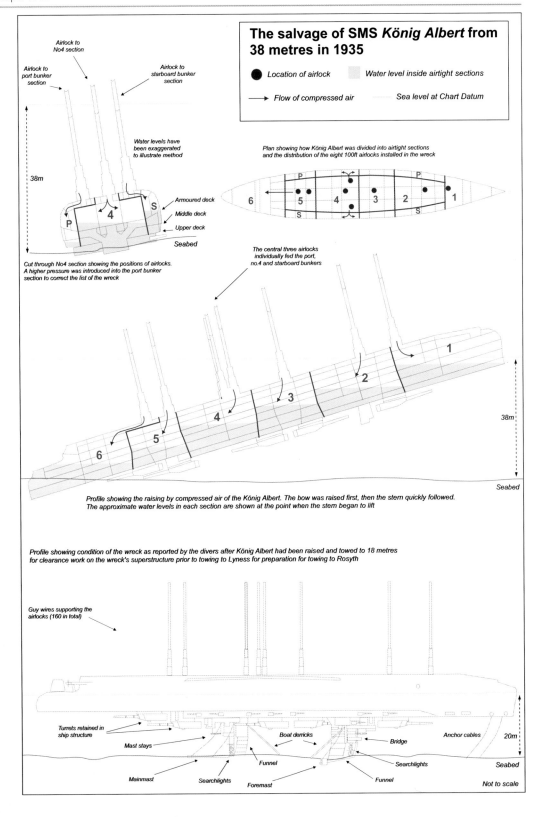

The salvage of SMS *König Albert* from 38 metres in 1935

● Location of airlock ▢ Water level inside airtight sections

→ Flow of compressed air ⎯ Sea level at Chart Datum

Airlock to No4 section

Airlock to port bunker section

Airlock to starboard bunker section

Water levels have been exaggerated to illustrate method

38m

Armoured deck
Middle deck
Upper deck
Seabed

Cut through No4 section showing the positions of airlocks. A higher pressure was introduced into the port bunker section to correct the list of the wreck

Plan showing how König Albert was divided into airtight sections and the distribution of the eight 100ft airlocks installed in the wreck

The central three airlocks individually fed the port, no.4 and starboard bunkers

38m

Seabed

Profile showing the raising by compressed air of the König Albert. The bow was raised first, then the stern quickly followed. The approximate water levels in each section are shown at the point when the stern began to lift

Profile showing condition of the wreck as reported by the divers after König Albert had been raised and towed to 18 metres for clearance work on the wreck's superstructure prior to towing to Lyness for preparation for towing to Rosyth

Guy wires supporting the airlocks (160 in total)

Turrets retained in ship structure

Mast stays

Boat derricks

Bridge

Anchor cables

20m

Mainmast

Searchlights

Foremast

Funnel

Searchlights

Funnel

Seabed

Not to scale

ship is a good example of how the ten upside-down warships were recovered using compressed air. Figure 8.6, based on a number of McKenzie's drawings, shows the distribution of the airlocks, how they worked in practice and the way in which the wreck was segmented into airtight compartments.

There were minor differences in each case, but the principle is the same. The ships were far longer than the water depth, meaning that when they were recovered bow first, the stern would dig into the seabed prior to lifting from the bottom. This is partly why, where the seabed was soft, the impressions left behind and seen on multibeam in 2017 always seem to be more marked at the stern. As well as granting a degree of control over the lift, the reason why they were lifted in this way was to assist in breaking the suction holding the ship. McKenzie always stressed that suction was one aspect of the salvage operations which could not be accurately calculated.

Figure 8.6 also shows how some of the wrecks were cleared of overhanging debris by being brought into shallower water in order to have derricks, samson posts, masts and so on blasted off by divers. This was done prior to towing to Lyness, where final preparations were made before the tow south.

The reality of working on making the compartments airtight was that it was far from a simple task. All the descriptions given by McKenzie and others who took part, including some very interesting oral accounts, stress how complex and difficult the work could be.[10] Wading dresses were provided, and working up to the neck in water was not uncommon. McKenzie described some of the duties: 'Doors had to be strongbacked, heavy pipes had to be broken and blanked, hundreds of cables, ventilators etc. had to be cut and the apertures sealed up before the bulkheads could be made airtight.'[11]

On 31 July, when she was successfully lifted, around 3,500 tons of extra buoyancy were required to break König Albert out of the mud and for the bow to race to the surface. This caused a massive upheaval of water which briefly completely obscured the airlocks from view. She was allowed to settle out overnight before the stern was raised in the morning. She was towed to shallower water, where she lay apparently with her

Figure 8.6. (Opposite) Diagrams showing the salvage process using compressed air on the König Albert. This method was similar to that used in nine other cases.

Figure 8.7. SMS König Albert as delivered to Rosyth in May 1936. (Marine Technology Special Collection, Newcastle University)

Figure 8.8. Plan view DTMs of the *König Albert* salvage site showing the impressions made in the seabed by the upside-down battleship. The deepest areas were formed by 'Q' turret and the forward superstructure. This is a consistent feature across the wrecks sunk on softer seabed.

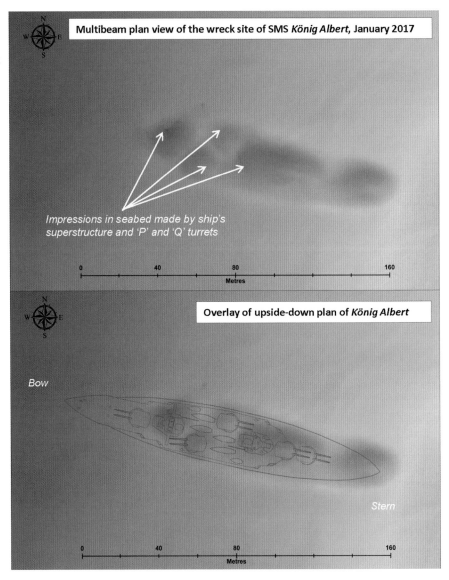

Multibeam plan view of the wreck site of SMS *König Albert*, January 2017

Impressions in seabed made by ship's superstructure and 'P' and 'Q' turrets

0   40   80   160

Metres

Overlay of upside-down plan of *König Albert*

Bow

Stern

0   40   80   160

Metres

turrets and superstructure on the bottom, as shown in Figure 8.6. There she had all the underhanging superstructure blasted off. On 27 August she was towed to Lyness.[12] She arrived in Rosyth in May 1936 and was broken up by the end of 1937.[13]

The sinking and salvage site of SMS *König Albert* was surveyed by multibeam in January 2017. It revealed a fine example of the impressions left in the soft seabed by the upper structures of the upside-down battleship as she rested on the bottom for 16 years. This is shown in Figure 8.8 with an overlay of an upside-down plan drawing of the Kaiser-class battleship.

The deepest craters in the seabed were in this case caused by 'Q' turret and the forward and aft superstructures. The stern has also left a deep impression, to which the salvage method certainly contributed. Similar phenomena can be seen on the DTMs of all the wrecks lifted by Metal Industries and also on *Prinzregent Luitpold*, Cox & Danks' last battleship.

Figure 8.8 also shows that almost no wreckage can be seen on the site, although some was reported present in the past. This confirmed the view that we took in 2014 and 2016 when we scanned the area in *Karin* with her bottom sounder and found nothing of sufficient consequence to be worth using up a valuable survey dive on. The conclusion must be that the ship was towed off the site still carrying nearly all of her upper works. The lingering question was whether they could be found by searching for the site she was moved to or whether this material had later been salvaged.

SMS *Kaiserin*, raised 14 May 1936

McKenzie stated that the wreck of the battleship *Kaiserin* was found under the surface within an hour of commencing the search for her and that divers made a thorough survey of the wreck. It was found to be listing at an 11-degree angle with the upper works quite buried in the seabed.[14] Before the days of underwater cameras, diver surveys were critically important to the salvage operations. Divers were required to have a high degree of technical knowledge and to be able to accurately relate what they had seen on dives. Much of this was done using sketches, and it is surprising how few seem to have survived. The sketch seen in Figure 8.9 is now a rare example. It was drawn by the Salvage Officer Harry Murray Taylor (McKenzie's son-in-law) during the salvage operations and it shows the orientation of the wreck and the way in which the masts broke away during the sinking process. The wreck was lying on soft seabed, a consistent feature of the wrecks raised by Metal Industries.

Figure 8.9. Salvage Officer Harry Murray Taylor's brief sketch of the orientation of *Kaiserin* on the bottom as derived from diver surveys of the wreck in December 1935. This is a rare depiction of the actual condition of the wrecks as found. (Orkney Archive)

The salvage process used was identical to that employed on *König Albert*, which was a sister ship. In fact McKenzie was involved in recovering all of the five Kaiser-class battleships built, gaining greater experience with each one lifted. SMS *Kaiser*, *Prinzregent Luitpold* and *König Albert* were already salvaged

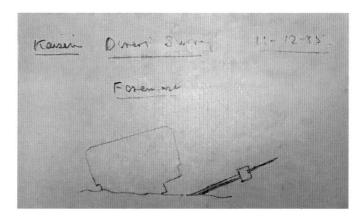

Figure 8.10. Plan view DTM of the *Kaiserin* site showing the ship's impression in the seabed and dispersed wreckage.

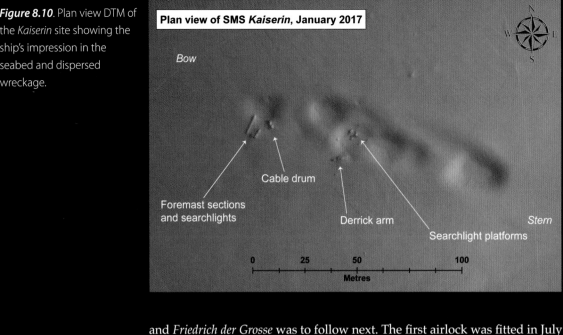

Plan view of SMS *Kaiserin*, January 2017

Bow

Cable drum

Foremast sections and searchlights

Derrick arm

Searchlight platforms

Stern

0   25   50   100

Metres

and *Friedrich der Grosse* was to follow next. The first airlock was fitted in July 1935, the last in October.

After six months of patching and sealing of bulkheads, *Kaiserin* was lifted by the bow in the now-familiar pattern on 14 May 1935. Her airlocks were replaced with short ones and she was moved to 12 fathoms off Rysa on 18 May. There her underhanging superstructure was blasted off, including the two prominent samson posts of the Kaiser class of battleship. On 22 May she was transferred to Lyness, where crushing took place to the armoured conning tower.[15] She arrived in Rosyth in August. Breaking began in November and was completed within 12 months.[16]

The multibeam DTM from the January 2017 survey can be seen in Figure 8.10. It shows the impressions of the wreck's superstructure as she lay on the seabed, with the deep stern impression made by the salvage operations. It also shows that there are two distinct patches of wreckage present.

Both of these areas were surveyed by diving in November 2017. The western section was characterized by two sections of what was probably the foremast. Like *Prinzregent Luitpold*, *Kaiserin* was not modified during the war to take the thicker cigar mast with its armoured spotting and control top. The sections present appeared to be from the slim original type. The impression was that material on this site had become buried over time. There were also the corroded remains of at least a pair of searchlights and a large cable drum.

The eastern section of wreckage contains similar type material, as seen in Figure 8.11. Image A shows what was probably a derrick arm. It is deeply

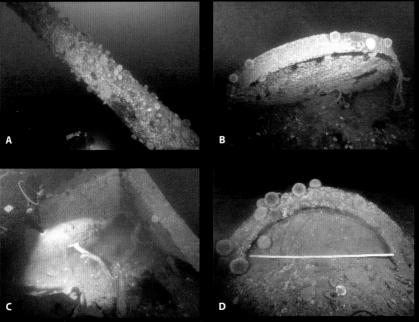

Figure 8.11. Wreckage seen on the eastern section of debris on the *Kaiserin* sinking and salvage site.

A

B

C

D

buried and stands around four metres clear of the seabed. The flattened termination at the top suggests that it snapped off after being bent. To the north of it are a pair of semi-circular searchlight platforms, one lying on top of the other. They are partially buried, as seen in Image B, and one has been broken in two, as diver Naomi Watson is illuminating with her torch. Image D shows an entire and intact searchlight iris assembly. This is one of the best-preserved examples to have been found during the surveys. The one-metre ruler gives a good indication of their large size.

Figure 8.12. The Metal Industries vessel *Bertha* hurriedly leaves the salvage site of *Friedrich der Grosse* in a storm. Note the airlocks (left). (Orkney Archive). Right: One of *Friedrich der Grosse's* bells on display at Stromness Museum. German naval bells were sometimes made of iron.

Figure 8.13. The DTM of the *Friedrich der Grosse* sinking and salvage site, showing a clear imprint of the ship and her armoured foremast.

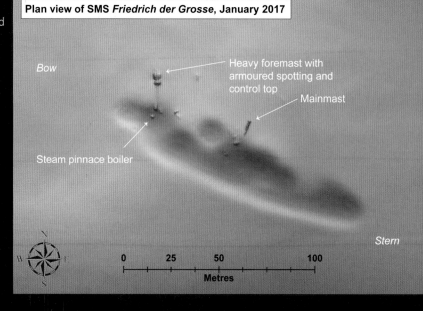

Plan view of SMS *Friedrich der Grosse*, January 2017

Bow

Heavy foremast with armoured spotting and control top

Mainmast

Steam pinnace boiler

Stern

0   25   50   100

Metres

SMS *Friedrich der Grosse*, raised 29 April 1937

As soon as *Kaiserin* was at Lyness, work began on the last remaining Kaiser-class battleship, von Reuter's flagship during most of the internment, SMS *Friedrich der Grosse*. This case was trickier than the last two because the wreck was lying with a 16-degree list and was four degrees down at the stern. In all, ten airlocks had to be fitted, with an additional pair to the wing bunkers, which were now divided into pairs. This was designed to give better control and stability during lifting. The bow was duly lifted on 28 April 1937 after nine months of preparatory work. The following day the compressors ran again and the stern was brought to the surface.[17] Then on 30 April she was towed to Rysa, where divers reported she was sitting on her funnels with the Samson posts buried in the seabed at low water. The derrick arms and masts were not present. The underhanging parts were blasted off and short airlocks fitted, and on 10 May she was towed to Lyness.[18] She was then towed to Rosyth in August, scrapped immediately and gone completely by May 1938.[19]

Figure 8.12 shows how conditions in Scapa Flow can be far from benign at times. The tender *Bertha* can be seen as she let go of her moorings and pipes and moved clear of the airlocks, which can be seen to the right. When bad weather come in quickly the men would have to wait in the airlocks to be picked up. This was not an experience for the faint-hearted. On the right in Figure 8.12 is a photo of one of *Friedrich der Grosse*'s iron bells with its top broken off, recovered in 1984. It is on display at Stromness Museum.

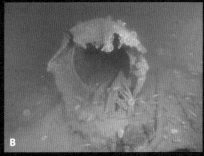

The results of the multibeam survey are shown in Figure 8.13. The orientation at which the wreck lay can still be clearly discerned from the impression in the seabed. The wreck was lying heavily over on her starboard side, with the stern being the deepest point. The depth of the stern was probably accentuated by the lifting operation. The imprint of both 'P' and 'Q' turrets can be seen, along with the remains of some wreckage.

It is quite clear from this image that the main piece of wreckage on the site is the large cigar mast (as termed by British naval intelligence during World War I) with its armoured spotting and control platforms on split levels. Of the five Kaiser-class battleships, only *Friedrich der Grosse* and *Kaiser* were retrofitted with this heavy mast and top. In the previous chapter the example on *Kaiser* looks remarkably similar on the DTM. They were identical designs. Other examples can be seen on the König-class battleships which follow. The area around what is probably the mainmast was not dived, but the point cloud shows that it is pointing upwards and clear of the seabed.

This area of the wreck around the foremast was subject to a dive survey in November 2017, and the results can be seen in Figure 8.14. Image A shows the forward end of the top. It is now half-buried in the seabed, but it retains its roof and its interior appears to be largely unmolested. The lower platform shares similar features to the one recorded on the *Kaiser* wreck site (see Figure 7.10.). Image B shows the base of the cigar mast at the point at which it broke away from the wreck. The remains of its internal ladder, wiring and large pieces of coal are present.

Nearby (as shown on Figure 8.12 and in Image C) is a small boiler sitting isolated on the seabed. This is a boiler which powered one of the ship's steam pinnaces. These wooden tenders were used to ferry the men. Clearly in this case it was not used to evacuate the crew as the small number of men on board did not need to use all of the ship's boats. The pinnace has rotted away over time, leaving just the boiler. There is a similar example on the wreck of the light cruiser *Karlsruhe* (see Chapter 14.)

Figure 8.14. The remains of the armoured control top and a boiler as seen on the *Friedrich der Grosse* wreck and salvage site in November 2017.

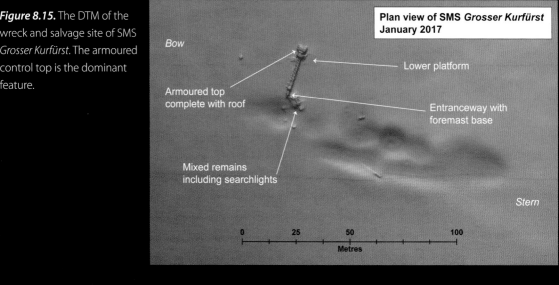

Figure 8.15. The DTM of the wreck and salvage site of SMS *Grosser Kurfürst*. The armoured control top is the dominant feature.

Plan view of SMS *Grosser Kurfürst* January 2017

Bow

Lower platform

Armoured top complete with roof

Entranceway with foremast base

Mixed remains including searchlights

Stern

0   25   50   100
Metres

SMS *Grosser Kurfürst*, raised 26 April 1938

Of the four König-class battleships built by the Germans, all were scuttled at Scapa Flow, but only *Grosser Kurfürst* was salvaged. The others are described in Part 3. She was initially surveyed by diving in the spring of 1937. Work began in May, as soon as *Friedrich der Grosse* was secured. This wreck presented a greater challenge, perhaps the greatest undertaken in all marine salvage at that time. This was because she lay at the extreme angle of 23 degrees with her

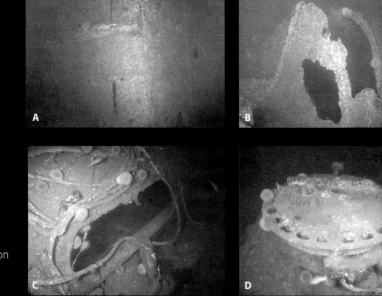

Figure 8.16. Features recorded on video in the area around the foremast on the wreck and salvage site of SMS *Grosser Kurfürst*.

starboard side in the seabed. Again, ten airlocks were employed and the work of sealing took nearly a year. The wreck was raised using the well-practised two-stage process. The bow came up on Monday 25 April and the stern followed a day later. The list was corrected to a manageable 5 degrees by differential pumping in the bunker sections during the raising of the bow.[20]

On 27 April she was towed to Rysa, where divers reported that only her derricks were touching the bottom and the rest of the wreck was clear. Blasting commenced the following day, clearing the aft upper superstructure, the funnels, the derricks and the forward upper-bridge structure. The ship's anchors were salvaged by *Bertha*. On 15 May she was towed to Lyness, where diver inspection showed she was resting on the conning tower at half tide. Crushing and blasting continued until preparations for towing were complete.[21] In July she arrived at Rosyth. Metal Industries closed the book on her in January 1940.[22] It is said that some of her metals ended up being reused in the building of the great Cunard liner, RMS *Queen Mary*.[23]

The DTM of the wreck as surveyed in January 2017 is shown in Figure 8.15. The impression in the seabed, heavier at the stern, matched the description of the wreck's orientation and method of salvage by raising the bow first. The main area of wreckage can be seen to be focused around the heavy foremast and its armoured spotting and control top. Dispersed wreckage lies at its base. This feature was known to be present on the site after a dive there in 2013 when the area was recorded on video. Highlights of the features seen are shown in Figure 8.16.

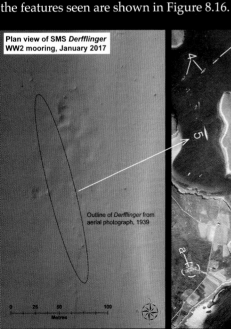

Plan view of SMS *Derfflinger*
WW2 mooring, January 2017

Outline of *Derfflinger* from aerial photograph, 1939

0 25 50 100
Metres

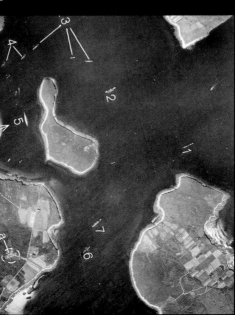

Figure 8.17. The DTM of *Derfflinger's* wartime berth as scanned in 2017 (left), and *Derfflinger* seen at that location on a Luftwaffe reconnaissance photograph in October 1939 (right). (Library of Contemporary History, Stuttgart)

Figure 8.18. The DTM of
Derfflinger's sinking and
salvage site showing
dispersed wreckage from both
masts. A deep impression can
be seen at the stern, probably
caused by the salvage
method.

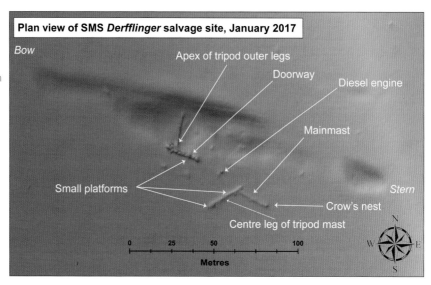

The armoured top is seen in Image A with its roof in place. It is only slightly buried and remains intact. Image B shows that the roof over the lower spotting platform has corroded through and will inevitably disappear entirely. The length of mast present is measured at 24 metres long. Its lower termination is very neat, suggesting that it was cleanly removed. The entrance door at the base of the mast can be seen in Image C. This is surrounded by the very broken remains of a platform and at least one searchlight. The rotating base of a searchlight was found sitting on a plate on the seabed, as seen in Image D. The remains of the base of the yoke which held the light can be seen on its top.

SMS *Derfflinger*, raised 25 July 1939

Survey work began on what was to be the final ship of the High Seas Fleet raised from the seabed of Scapa Flow in May 1938. The famous battlecruiser SMS *Derfflinger* was a sister to *Hindenburg*, which had been raised with much difficulty by Cox & Danks. *Derfflinger* presented her own challenges, not least the great depth at which she lay, the deepest recovered wreck, in 43 metres of water. She also had a list of 20.5 degrees, with her port side buried in the seabed. Nine airlocks were fitted, feeding seven sections and the two outer bunkers, which all had to be made airtight. Prior to her final lift, differential pumping had taken off most of the list.[24]

The bow was raised on 24 July 1939 and the stern the following day. On 26 July her forward tripod mast and mainmast were blasted off and she was towed to a site in ten fathoms of water off Rysa. At that position further blasting took place and short airlocks were fitted. With war impending, plans to move her south had to be suspended as dockyard space was now at a premium.[25]

Therefore on 25 August, she was moved to 'inside Rysa', where the last underhanging pieces were removed. Three days after war was declared she was pulled closer to the shore and rested on the bottom. Accommodation and compressors were set up and then, re-inflated and on a ten-anchor mooring, she waited out the war with a maintenance crew on board.[26]

Both the sinking site and the wartime site of *Derfflinger* were located and scanned by multibeam. In Figure 8.17, the wartime site is shown next to a Luftwaffe aerial photograph from October 1939. From this we were able work out the position where the wreck was moored. There is clearly some disturbance of the seabed under where the ship was, but the site had not been subject to diving as of 2018.

Figure 8.18 shows the original sinking and salvage site. The way the wreck was lying can be discerned, as well as the presence of the masts and

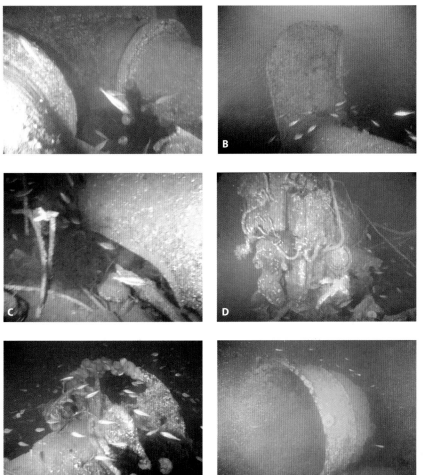

Figure 8.19. Features recorded on the *Derfflinger* sinking and salvage site in October 2013.

other small pieces of wreckage. I had a good idea of what would be found on this site from the data gathered during a survey dive of the site in October 2013. The positions of the features recorded are shown on the DTM.

The diving commenced at the west end of the area of wreckage and in Figure 8.19 Image A the junction point of the two outer legs of the tripod mast can be seen. The top itself appears either to have been removed from the site or to be buried now, as it was not seen. Moving east, the southerly leg led to a small platform pointing upwards. This once held a searchlight (Image B). At seabed level was the access doorway to the mast, as shown in Image C.

Moving on to the seabed between the two areas of masts, a diesel engine was located, as shown in Image D. These were used to power some of the ships' boats. This boat must have gone down with the ship during the Grand Scuttle. There was little remaining of the boat itself. Reaching the linear features to the east, it was discerned that the western one is probably the central leg of the tripod mast, as it was found to have a small platform at each end. The central leg of *Derfflinger*'s foremast had two platforms, as can be seen in the photographs of her sinking in Chapter 2. In fact the central leg was her original foremast, to which the legs were added in 1917. The other leg which points southeast turned out to be the ship's mainmast. This was made up of an open platform (Image E) and a crow's nest (Image F). Photographs of the ship throughout her career seem to hint that it is possible that the crow's nest seen was originally fitted to the foremast before it was modified.

Derfflinger remained in Scapa until 1946. She spent more of her life upside down on the surface than upright. Rosyth was not available, so a surplus 30,000-ton floating dock was purchased from the Admiralty and *Derfflinger* was prepared to be transported in it. This required the removal of the 'B' and 'C' turrets and the all underhanging wreckage down to the level of their barbettes. She was then docked on 12 October and towed to the Metal Industries' new facility at Faslane on the Clyde. She was the only large German warship not scrapped on the Forth. She had been dismantled completely by June 1948.[27]

The end of the Metal Industries years

The breaking up of *Derfflinger* ended the phase of entire-ship recovery at Scapa Flow, but it did not bring to an end the salvage of metals from the larger ships. Seven remained – three König-class battleships and four light cruisers. They were to be subject to varying degrees of salvage over the following three decades, as described in Part 3. The first post-war salvage operator was Arthur Nundy, who had worked as a diver for Cox & Danks and Metal Industries (see Figure 8.1). The metals of the old battleships now

also had the attraction of being radiation-free; such metals came to fetch premium prices in the space age.

1   Naval Historical Branch (various dates), *CP 8a Sale Book*. Portsmouth.

2   I. Buxton (1992), *Metal Industries: Shipbreaking at Rosyth and Charlestown* (Kendal: World Ship Society), pp. 12–18.

3   T. McKenzie (1934), 'How the "Bayern" was Raised', *Shipbuilding and Shipping Record*, 1 November.

4   Orkney Archives (various dates), microfilmed records of the *Orcadian*, 1919–1938. Kirkwall, 6 May 1937 and 20 September 1934.

5   T. McKenzie (1934), 'How the "Bayern" was Raised', *Shipbuilding and Shipping Record*, 1 November, p. 6.

6   Orkney Archives (various dates), Diaries of H. Murray Taylor: Notes on Bayern Salvage 1934–1935, D1/59/5, Kirkwall. T. McKenzie, 'How the "Bayern" was Raised', *Shipbuilding and Shipping Record*, 1 November 1934.

7   Newcastle University Special Collections (various dates), Accounts and Minutes of Metal Industries Shipbreaking. Newcastle.

8   I. McCartney (2016), *Jutland 1916: The Archaeology of a Naval Battlefield* (London: Bloomsbury), p. 118.\

9   G. Koop & K.-P. Schmolke (1995), *Vom Original zum Modell: Die Linienschiffe der BAYERN-Klasse* (Bonn: Bernard & Graefe Verlag).

10   Orkney Archives hold sound recordings by Sandy Robertson, Murray Taylor and John Rosie, who all, in addition to other duties, took tours inside the airlocks for work.

11   T. McKenzie, (1935) 'How the "König Albert" was Raised at Scapa Flow', *Shipbuilding and Shipping Record*, 17 October, p. 434.

12   Orkney Archives (various dates), Diaries of H. Murray Taylor: Salvage Logs for König Albert and Kaiserin, 1935, D1/59/7. Kirkwall.

13   Naval Historical Branch (various dates), *CP 8a Sale Book*. Portsmouth.

14   T. McKenzie (1936), 'How the "Kaiserin" was Raised at Scapa Flow', *Shipbuilding and Shipping Record*, 16 July, p. 71.

15   Orkney Archives (various dates), Diaries of H. Murray Taylor: Kaiserin 1935–1936. D1/59/1. Notes in D1/59/5, Kirkwall.

16   Newcastle University Special Collections (various dates), Accounts and Minutes of Metal Industries Shipbreaking. Newcastle.

17   Orkney Archives (various dates), microfilmed records of the *Orcadian*, 1919–1938. Kirkwall, 6 May 1937.

18   Orkney Archives (various dates), Diaries of H. Murray Taylor: Friedrich Der Grosse 1936–1937, D1/59/2. Kirkwall.

19   Newcastle University Special Collections (various dates), Accounts and Minutes of Metal Industries Shipbreaking. Newcastle.

20   Orkney Archives (various dates), microfilmed records of the *Orcadian*, 1919–1938. Kirkwall, 6 May 1937 and 28 April 1937.

21   Orkney Archives (various dates), Diaries of H. Murray Taylor: Grosser Kurfürst 1937–1938, D1/59/3. Kirkwall.

22   Newcastle University Special Collections (various dates), Accounts and Minutes of Metal Industries Shipbreaking. Newcastle.

23   S. C. George (1973), *Jutland to Junkyard: The Raising of the Scuttled German High Seas Fleet from Scapa Flow – the greatest salvage operation of all time* (Cambridge: Patrick Stephens), p. 150.

24   T. McKenzie (1949), 'Marine Salvage in Peace and War', *Institution of Engineers and Shipbuilders in Scotland*, 93, paper 1122, pp. 123–161.

25   T. McKenzie (1949), 'Marine Salvage in Peace and War', *Institution of Engineers and Shipbuilders in Scotland*, 93, paper 1122, pp. 123–161.

26   Orkney Archives (various dates), Diaries of H. Murray Taylor: Derfflinger 1938–1939, D1/59. Kirkwall. The interpretation of 'inside Rysa' is open to question.

27   Newcastle University Special Collections (various dates), Accounts and Minutes of Metal Industries Shipbreaking. Newcastle.

CHAPTER 9
METAL INDUSTRIES' BATTLESHIP CLEARANCE SITES AT RYSA

Figure 9.1. Fiona Houston shines her torch into the doorway on the eastern side of Rysa site A.

Wreckage relating to the clearing of the underhanging structures of the battleships raised by Metal Industries has been known to exist off Rysa for many years. This is a globally unique undersea scrapyard which is only now receiving recognition of its importance. By combining the results of careful survey dives and archival research with the multibeam survey, the remains of three of the five ships worked on in this area have been identified, along with the suggested locations of the other two.

Metal Industries' post-salvage movement of battleships

One of the key research targets during the 2017 multibeam survey was to examine the seabed in the area to the north and east of the island of Rysa Little (or simply Rysa, sometimes spelled 'Risa'). This area has long been known to contain dispersed wreckage of High Seas Fleet origin. The first references to wreckage being present are recorded in the UK Hydrographic database in 1939 as foul anchorage.[1] In more recent years the area has been extensively visited by recreational divers. I began recording sites in this area in 2013 and it quickly became apparent that the only way to begin to understand what the wide range of wreckage represented was to get an appreciation of its extent.

The area surveyed in 2017 threw up a number of significant targets, and their locations are shown in Figure 9.2. The seabed outside the areas shown contains a distribution of small anomalies one would expect to see on the bottom of a long-serving anchorage. But the sites grouped A–H were clearly different and the wreckage seen was expected to be related in some way. Sites A–D were already known to be German.

Running concurrently, the archival research indicated clearly that the wreckage present was likely to have come from the Metal Industries years. It was off Rysa that it carried out the clearance of underhanging debris from the recently salvaged battleships. Cox & Danks tended to do this off Cava, where little wreckage remains now.

Therefore, one of the research targets was to establish the locations and extent of the sites used in the Rysa area by Metal Industries. The most useful source was the Murray Taylor diaries which, in conjunction with other sources, reveal that four battleships and the battlecruiser

Figure 9.2. Map showing the locations of the eight areas of notable groupings of wreckage as detected during the 2017 survey.

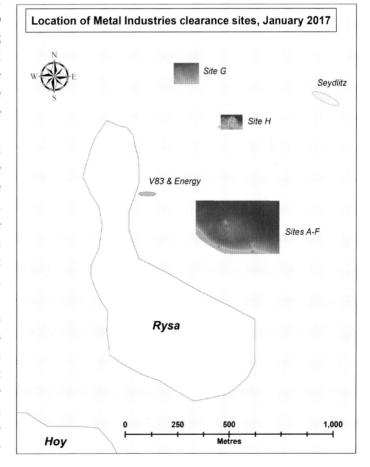

Figure 9.3. Plan view DTM of Rysa G site, showing the remains consistent with a Kaiser-class battleship.

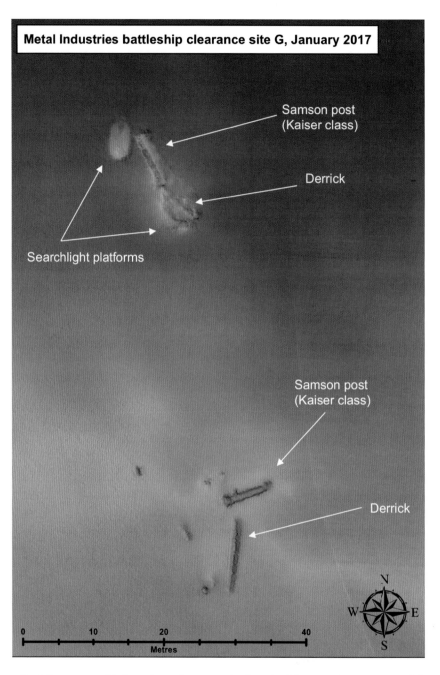

Metal Industries battleship clearance site G, January 2017

Samson post (Kaiser class)

Derrick

Searchlight platforms

Samson post (Kaiser class)

Derrick

Derfflinger were likely to have been worked on in this area. A summary of the evidence found for the known movements of the salvaged ships is given below.

SMS *Bayern* (named class of battleship), raised 1 September 1934

Murray Taylor notes that *Bayern* was 'towed into sandbank' on 2 September and nine days later was towed to Lyness.[2] According to McKenzie's published work, the supposed sandbank was 'less than one mile from the base at Lyness'[3]. This probably places her in Gutter Sound, following the Cox & Danks method, and suggests she was not worked on off Rysa.

SMS *König Albert* (Kaiser-class battleship), raised 31 July 1935
The Murray Taylor diaries state that on 16 August blasting was being carried out on the superstructure. At the same time, he was overseeing the fitting of No. 2 airlock to the wreck of SMS *Kaiserin* which, he notes, was one mile away. During the following week he notes that the forward mast, bridge and both funnels had been blasted off and the samson posts were to follow. The next entry states that she was moved to Lyness on 28 August.[4] No evidence has been found to place her further inshore at Rysa.

SMS *Kaiserin* (Kaiser-class battleship), raised 11 May 1936
The diaries state that she was moved to Rysa on Monday 18 May.[5] During that week the samson posts and the remains of the bridge, mainmast and aft superstructure were blasted off. On Friday 22 May she was towed to a bank (probably at Gutter Sound) until high tide and then towed to Lyness in the evening.[6]

SMS *Friedrich der Grosse* (Kaiser-class battleship), raised 29 April 1937
The diaries state that she was towed to Rysa on 30 April. Diver survey showed hat she was sitting on her funnels with the samson posts buried in the seabed at low water. Blasting removed all wreckage to a level above the line of the forward and aft conning towers. This was completed by 7 May. On 10 May she was towed to Lyness, clearing the bank in Gutter Sound.[7]

SMS *Grosser Kurfürst* (König-class battleship), raised 26 April 1938
The diaries state that she was towed to Rysa on 27 April. The towing log states that she was grounded in 12 fathoms (around 20m) at low water. The following day divers found that her derricks were on the bottom. Blasting cleared her to the level of her armoured conning towers by 10 May. On 15 May she was towed to Lyness and moored in Ore Bay.[8]

SMS *Derfflinger* (named class of battlecruiser), raised 25 July 1939
The diaries state that she was towed to Rysa and was aground on 27 July. Blasting continued periodically through to 25 August, when she was shifted to her wartime position.[9]

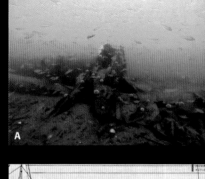

Figure 9.4. Features seen on Rysa site G.

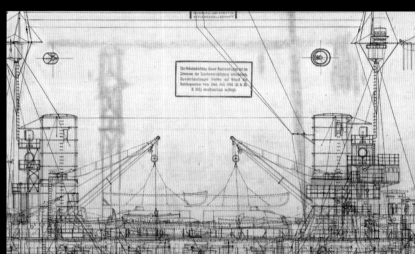

Figure 9.5. Section of the plans of SMS *Friedrich der Grosse*, showing locations and types of cranes, masts and searchlight platforms. (The Dreadnought Project)

In each case, apart from *Bayern*, it is clear that the underhanging superstructure from these ships, if still present on the seabed, should be found in the waters off Rysa. Both Cox & Danks and Metal Industries stated in newspaper interviews that they planned to recover metals cleared from the salvaged ships, but no evidence has so far been found to confirm whether they ever did. But it is quite possible that wreckage has been salvaged in the past from the clearance sites, so that what we see now is only a part of what Metal Industries left behind. No accurate positions have so far been found to show where each vessel was worked on. Moreover, it is not clear whether the ships were periodically moved during the clearance process. There is no clear evidence of this in the Murray Taylor diaries, but it remains a possibility. So although we have sites containing wreckage, the challenge has been to attempt to work out what it represents. This required survey by diving and analysis of the remains that were found. Sites E and F were quickly discounted as probably being unrelated, so there were six remaining sites to study in more detail. They are described from north to south.

Rysa site G: Kaiser-class battleship

Ground truthing site G by means of diving identified the site as being that of a Kaiser-class battleship. The samson posts on the cranes of the Kaiser class were of a design which differed from the type seen on the Derfflinger and König classes. The differences can be seen on the remains of these features. The location of the features seen is shown in Figure 9.3.

Figure 9.4 shows, in Image A, a samson post of the Kaiser-class type, and in Image B, the more northerly of the pair of searchlight platforms present. The circular feature represents the base on which the lights were situated. They have now completely corroded away.

Figure 9.5 shows the area around the funnels on the Kaiser-class SMS

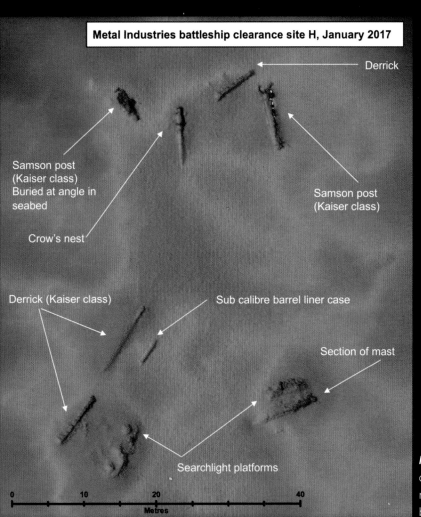

Metal Industries battleship clearance site H, January 2017

Derrick

Samson post
(Kaiser class)
Buried at angle in
seabed

Samson post
(Kaiser class)

Crow's nest

Derrick (Kaiser class)

Sub calibre barrel liner case

Section of mast

Searchlight platforms

0   10   20   40

Metres

Figure 9.6. Plan view DTM of Rysa site H, showing the remains of a Kaiser-class battleship.

Friedrich der Grosse. It shows how the cranes were oriented, and the type of pulleys used match that seen in Image A of Figure 9.4. The distance between these features on the seabed suggests that a Kaiser-class battleship was worked on at this location. The question is, which one?

Rysa site H: Kaiser-class battleship (possibly SMS *König Albert*)

The distribution of wreckage on site H can be seen in Figure 9.6. When surveyed by diving, it too was revealed to be Kaiser class by the design of the samson posts. Features seen in the wreckage at the north of the site included a crow's nest (the only one seen off Rysa), as shown in Images A and B of Figure 9.7. Images C and D show the other Samson post partially buried in the seabed, being examined by a diver. At its upper point it can be seen to have been neatly cut off. At its lower end the crushed remains of the control platform lie underneath it.

The cluster of wreckage to the southwest of site H includes an entire searchlight platform lying curiously upright on the seabed, as shown from above, with diver Conrad Mason for scale. On the DTM it is measured at 8.5 metres long, indicating that it was the lower of the pair of searchlight platforms that would have been seen on the forward and aft superstructure, as depicted in Figure 9.5. The upper platform was shorter and similar to the type seen in Figure 9.9 (Image B).

Figure 9.7. Images of features in the northern portion of Rysa site H.

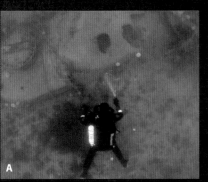

The base of the searchlight on the left of Image A in Figure 9.8 is shown in close-up in Image B. Image C shows one end of a case which held a sub-calibre barrel lining for one of the main guns. These 88mm-calibre liners could be inserted into the breeches of the main guns and used to shoot 88mm rounds in firing practice, extending the life of the 12-inch gun barrels. The ship's plans show that a pair were carried in cases on deck for each main turret. The example shown is complete, with the case in excellent condition. It is upside down with the feet pointing upwards.

Figure 9.8. Images of features seen in the southwestern portion of site H.

Figure 9.9 shows the features seen in the cluster of wreckage to the southeast of site H. The area is dominated by the smaller-sized searchlight platform. It is upside down, with the controls on the seabed underneath, as seen in Image A. Image B was taken a few metres above it and shows the mast section it lies next to, as seen on the DTM. The framing which characterizes the underside of the platforms is clearly visible. On the DTM it measures approximately 5.5 metres long.

The samson posts are clustered at the north end of the wreck, which can only be explained by some movement of the floating ship over the site during blasting operations. The features are all consistent with this site being Kaiser class – but which specific battleship? There is a clue in the Murray Taylor diaries. On 16 August 1935 he notes that he is working on the salvaged *König Albert* and also carrying out preparatory work for the future salvage of the *Kaiserin*. Crucially, he notes that the two sites are one mile apart.[10]

Site G is around one mile from the *Kaiserin* wreck site, and site H around 1.2 miles from it. So one of these two sites is likely to be *König Albert*, but it is currently not possible to say with certainty which one. However, the presence of considerably more wreckage on site H suggests it may be *König Albert*, but only because her salvage site seems to have no wreckage present. Site G would therefore be either *Friedrich der Grosse* or *Kaiserin*. This is currently a working theory and may need revising in the future.

Rysa sites A and B: SMS *Grosser Kurfürst*

There is much stronger evidence for the identity of the wreckage at sites A and B. Unique features on both sections of wreckage suggest that they are likely to be from the only König-class battleship salvaged by Metal Industries, SMS *Grosser Kurfürst*. The distribution of sites A to F is shown in plan view in Figure 9.10. Sites E and F are not attributable to the High Seas Fleet, but sites A to D definitely are.

The initial diving surveys on these sites were carried out before the multibeam survey but could identify the wreckage as German, but it could not easily discern the spatial relationship between the sites. One of the myriad benefits of marine geophysics is its ability to look at sites from a distance and show how they may be related.

Figure 9.11 shows a close-up DTM of sites A and B and highlights some of the features observed in the years these sites were surveyed by diving. Site A can be seen to be a square-shaped feature with outlying wreckage. The northerly side of the square feature appears to be curved. Site B shows linear features consistent with samson posts, derricks and general wreckage.

The dive survey of site A in 2016 took place on a day with good light and visibility and the entire feature could be caught on camera. Looking at it from a distance helped to discern exactly what it was, and this was later confirmed by examinations of ships' plans. In Figure 9.1 the square shape of the feature can be seen, with a doorway visible in the centre. In the foreground a circular window can be seen, partially buried in the seabed. Above are the blasted remains of a cigar mast.

Figure 9.12 shows the feature as seen from each side. The east and west sides have doorways and circular windows. The south side is plain. Image D shows diver Naomi Watson under the decking. Above her is the curved section of deck, which can be discerned on the DTM. Behind her the cigar mast continues down into the seabed and there is a square window each side of it.

When I examined this area and looked inside the east side window, lying

Figure 9.9. Images of features in the south eastern portion of Rysa site H.

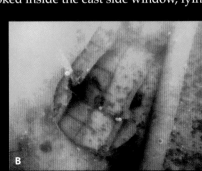

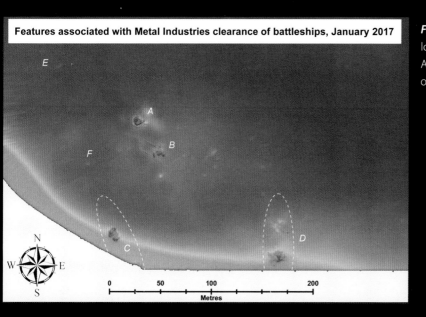

Figure 9.10. Map showing the locations of Rysa sites A–F. A–D are related to battleships of the High Seas Fleet.

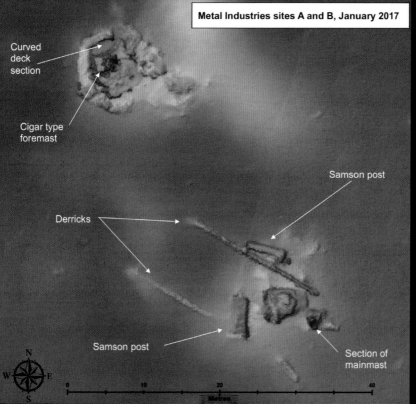

Figure 9.11. Close-up plan view DTM of Rysa sites A and B. They are revealed to be parts of the same ship.

on the sediment were a number of what appeared to be Inglefield clips, as shown in Figure 9.13. The one on the right was recovered and is shown in the inset. These clips were used for attaching a flag quickly and securely to a halyard so that the flag could be hoisted. This clearly indicated that the room was probably associated with command and signalling.

The exact location of this feature was found when examining plans of the König-class battleship. As shown in Figure 9.14, the structure between the forefunnel and the foremast is a box-like room with the correct shape, configuration and size to be site A. Moreover, it is labelled as the charthouse for the ship and is situated on the level to where the signal halyards run down. The deck extends forwards and around the armoured conning tower, explaining why it was curved at the northerly end. In fact, the entire deck surrounding the tower is present on site A, with most of it on the seabed. The tower was retained within the ship and crushed inside once it had been transferred to Lyness.

In 2016 it was confirmed by diving that site B had to be from either SMS *Grosser Kurfürst* or SMS *Derfflinger* by the type of samson posts present. The more northerly of the pair on the site can be seen in Image A of Figure 9.15. It clearly has a large pulley wheel still attached to its top. This can be seen on the ship's plan in Figure 9.14, and it is evident how it differed from the earlier type seen in Figure 9.5. Image B of Figure 9.15 shows the structure at the southeast end of the site with the blasted-off remains of the mainmast at the highest point.

With site A known to have come from *Grosser Kurfürst* and the possibility that site B could have done, the spatial relationship between both parts was analyzed and it became clear that it was most likely that they were related. The distance between the mainmast and the foremast is consistent with plans of the ship, leading to the conclusion that both sections of wreckage were blasted off the upside-down SMS *Grosser Kurfürst* at this location during early May 1938. When the plan drawing of the battleship was overlaid on the DTM, it fitted exactly with the distribution of wreckage in sites A and B, as shown in Figure 9.16.

Rysa sites C and D: unidentified

Site C is made up of a pair of distinct areas of wreckage, with the more northerly one lying in slightly deeper water. Only the edge of the second area to the southeast was captured on the multibeam survey. The area was getting too shallow for *Vina*, and when we scanned this area *Limbo* was busy on the wreck of SMS *V83*. Both sites were recorded by diving and they show mixed battleship wreckage, as shown in Figure 9.17.

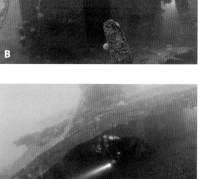

Figure 9.12. Rysa site A seen from south (A) east (B), west (C) and north (D).

Images A and B show the wreckage from the southeast and the curved end of a bridge platform. Image A was taken in 2014 when the platform was upright. By 2016 it had collapsed so that it lay on top of a winch on the seabed. It shows that even these small, seemingly innocuous sites are breaking up and are potentially dangerous for divers.

Images C and D of Figure 9.17 show a gun which lies on the seabed isolated from its shield and mounting. Its muzzle was measured as 88mm. In Image C the breech and recoil cylinders are in the foreground. Image D shows the maker's plate, reading 'Fried Krupp', the manufacturer. The gun is located in the area between the two sections of wreckage. The fact that its mount and shield are not present anywhere near it is difficult to explain.

Figure 9.13. View of sediment build-up inside the starboard window next to the foremast on Rysa site A. The features shown are Inglefield clips.

Figure 9.18 shows images from the large piece of wreckage at site D. This is a pile of broken wreckage which contains a short section of mast. It is very broken down and has few distinguishable features. One item of interest was the case of a sub-calibre barrel liner, identical to the type seen on site H (see Figure 9.7). In this instance it has been forcibly opened to see what is inside, with the case lid lying next to it. The barrel liner itself can be seen inside.

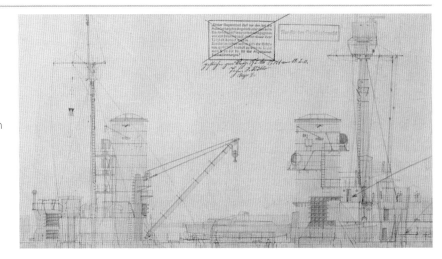

Figure 9.14. Section of the plans of the König-class battleship SMS *Kronprinz Wilhelm*, showing the design of features including cranes, lights and the forward bridge. (Bundesarchiv)

Figure 9.15. Features seen on Rysa site B.

Conclusions

The eight sites examined contain the remains of up to five German warships. Sites A and B turned out to be from the same ship, and E and F are probably not German. Five is the same as the number of warships which archival research has shown to have been worked on in the area off Rysa. Three of the five sites have been identified down to class level, and one of them is most probably *Grosser Kurfürst*. If site H is in fact related to *König Albert* it would mean that possibly C, D and G could be *Friedrich der Grosse*, *Kaiserin* and *Derfflinger*, but this is only speculation and much more research would be needed before any definite conclusions could be reached.

Although the Murray Taylor diaries have been useful in describing some of what happened on each ship after it was salvaged, they do not tell the whole story. While they seem to suggest that each raised ship was not moved after being anchored off Rysa, the possibility that they were needs to be considered. If this was the case, sites C and D could potentially be related to *Grosser Kurfürst* as well. This would lead to the question as to where the other clearance sites might be.

There is also the question of how much of the wreckage deposited on each site still remains and how much has been salvaged in the intervening years. Both Cox & Danks and Metal Industries claimed in newspaper interviews that they would be picking up wreckage from the clearance of the raised ships after the event, but no evidence has yet been found to show that they

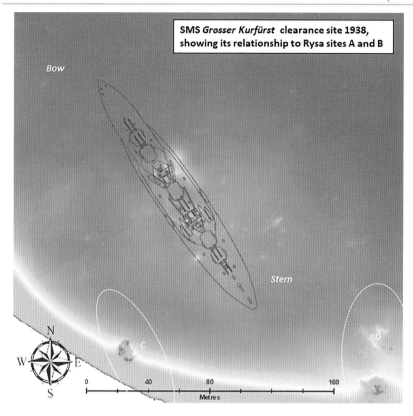

Figure 9.16. Plan view DTM showing how sites A & B are related to the wreck of SMS *Grosser Kurfürst*, which was cleared for towing at this location in 1938.

did, the *Bayern* turrets being a case in point. However, the recovery of metals from these sites by local enterprise cannot be ruled out. The lack of any debris from funnels on sites A and B is suggestive of this having happened. Was it

Figure 9.17. Searchlight platform and gun seen on Rysa site C.

Figure 9.18. Features seen on Rysa site D.

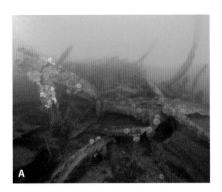

salvaged, or cut off elsewhere – maybe at sites C and D, which seem to contain funnel remains? This shows just how much we still don't know.

There is certainly more wreckage to the south of sites C and D, and a survey in that area would do much to increase our knowledge of this unique industrial undersea scrapyard. Nowhere else in the world can one go and study such a range of details of German battleship design from World War I. Every wreck site that can be identified brings the story of the salvage years to a more accurate conclusion.

1   Hydrographic Department of the Admiralty (2017), Record of Wreck No 1051 SMS *G101* (Taunton: Hydrographic Office).

2   Orkney Archives (various dates), Diaries of H. Murray Taylor: Notes on Bayern Salvage 1934–1935, D1/59/5. Kirkwall.

3   T. McKenzie (1934), 'How the "Bayern" was Raised', *Shipbuilding and Shipping Record*, 1 November.

4   Orkney Archives (various dates), Diaries of H. Murray Taylor: Salvage Logs for König Albert and Kaiserin 1935, D1/59/7. Kirkwall.

5   Orkney Archives (various dates), Diaries of H. Murray Taylor: Derfflinger 1938–1939, D1/59. Kirkwall.

6   Orkney Archives (various dates), Diaries of H. Murray Taylor: Kaiserin 1935–1936, D1/59/1. Kirkwall.

7   Orkney Archives (various dates), Diaries of H. Murray Taylor: Friedrich Der Grosse 1936–1937, D1/59/2. Kirkwall.

8   Orkney Archives (various dates), Diaries of H. Murray Taylor: Grosser Kurfürst 1937–1938, D1/59/3. Kirkwall.

9   Orkney Archives (various dates), Diaries of H. Murray Taylor: Derfflinger 1938–1939, D1/59. Kirkwall.

10   Orkney Archives (various dates), Diaries of H. Murray Taylor: Salvage Logs for König Albert and Kaiserin 1935, D1/59/7. Kirkwall.

PART THREE

THE SURVIVING WRECKS

Auxiliary helm on SMS *Cöln*. (Gavin Anderson)

CHAPTER 10
SMS *KÖNIG*

Figure 10.1. SMS *König*, launched 1 March 1913, as seen before the Battle of Jutland. She still carries anti-torpedo netting and the light foremast with small spotting top. Design displacement 25,389 tons, length 175m, ten 12-inch guns, fourteen 5.9-inch guns. (Orkney Archive)

The battleship SMS König bore the brunt of the fighting at the Battle of Jutland. Today, of the extant High Seas Fleet battleships, her partially salvaged wreckage is the least visited by divers. Yet the wreck site has much to offer, and as the geophysical and diving surveys show, it is a fascinating wreck site, made all the more special by its historical and cultural significance.

SMS *König* was the lead ship of the König class of battleship. In that regard, she is broadly similar to the wrecks of SMS *Kronprinz Wilhelm* and SMS *Markgraf* and to the salvage site of SMS *Grosser Kurfürst*. This battleship class saw more action during World War I than any other. These ships consistently demonstrated that they were robustly built and of sound design, which partly explains why the wrecks still look impressive today. This chapter, as well as looking at SMS *König* in particular, will also examine the entire class details. The minor differences between each of the other ships in the class will be described in their own chapters.

Design and history of the König class

The König class was the fourth and last class of German dreadnought battleship to be built before the outset of World War I. Only *Bayern* and *Baden* superseded them. In that way, the class represents the furthest extent of German battleship-building capability at the outset of the war. The class was in effect an upgrade of the previous Kaiser class (of which all examples were salvaged), with all of the turrets fitted along the centreline, with superfiring turrets forward and aft and one mounted amidships at the same level as the aft superfiring turret. All guns could now be fired in broadside on a wide arc. They were considered good sea boats which provided a stable gun platform with even roll in a swell. The gun layout can be seen in Figure 10.1.

The German battleship designers of the World War I era had to consider that their ships would be fighting an enemy which outnumbered them and sought victory through overwhelming firepower. Consequently, protection took precedence in the design of German dreadnoughts. They were extremely tough ships. Such quality comes at a premium cost and the Königs are considered to have been 50–60% more expensive than their British or American equivalents.[1] Their combat record seems to attest to their relatively high cost being good value for money.

The main battery consisted of ten 12-inch guns mounted in five turrets. The superfiring turrets fore and aft meant that the class could fire four guns in a bow or stern chase. Each turret was supplied by its own magazine fitted directly below it. In normal service, each magazine could hold 180 rounds. Propellant was stored in the lowest deck with shells above, the opposite way round from the British system. The propellant came in a two-part system encased in brass, of which the main cartridge was reusable. The guns' range was limited by the C/11 mounting to around 18,500m. This was modified in 1916 to increase maximum range to around 20,000m.

Additional armament consisted of 14 5.9-inch guns, with 2,240 rounds normally stowed. As with the main armament, the ranges of these guns were

Figure 10.2. The König-class ships were exceptionally well protected, as can be seen in this section through frame no.74 in the centre of the ship. Of particular note is the 40mm torpedo bulkhead 5m inboard of the hull below the waterline and extending from the armoured deck to the keel. This was not a feature incorporated into British battleships.

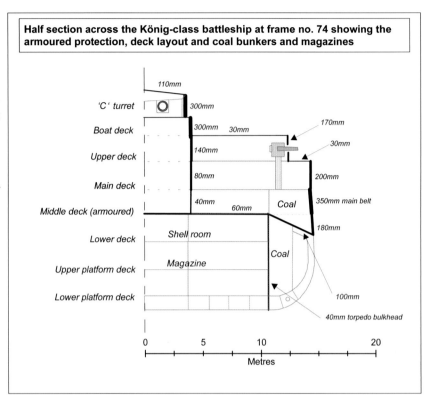

Half section across the König-class battleship at frame no. 74 showing the armoured protection, deck layout and coal bunkers and magazines

extended as well, from 13,500m to 17,000m. This was achieved by cutting back the deck over their casemates.[2] Additionally, the Königs were fitted with four 88mm flak guns in anticipation of the need to ward off aircraft and airships. All of the class were also fitted with five torpedo tubes. One was fitted in the bow and two in broadside on each side. Up to four torpedoes per tube were carried.

The class was designed to have 18 watertight compartments and was double-bottomed. These ships were also exceptionally well protected by following the citadel system, protecting in measure the entire hull except the bow and stern where they extended beyond the 'A' and 'E' turret barbettes and beyond the forward (150mm) and aft (180mm) side armoured belts. The main belt was 350mm thick, with a 180mm belt extending below. Above the main belt the citadel and casemates were protected with a minimum of 170mm. As with other German dreadnoughts of the period, the Königs were also given the exemplary protection of 40mm-thick armoured torpedo bulkheads which extended along each side of the ship below the main belt from armoured deck to keel. Turret and barbette walls were fitted with 300mm of plate. The armoured deck was 60mm thick.[3] The success of the plating system is attested to by the number of hits the ships withstood in battle. In all, over 10,000 tons of Ridel (Krupp low carbon alloy steel) armour was fitted.[4] The plating layout as seen at frame no. 74 across the centre of the 'C' turret can be seen in Figure 10.2.

The class was powered by three shafts with 3.8m-wide screws. They were coupled to three sets of turbines powered by three oil-fired and 12 coal-fired boilers. The oil-fired boilers were situated in the foremost boiler room. Top speed was designed to be 21 knots, but they proved to be faster in action, with SMS *König* exceeding 24 knots at the Battle of Jutland.

Night-time illumination was extensive in comparison with British dreadnoughts. The Königs were fitted with searchlight platforms around each turret. The platforms featured four 120-amp 110cm-diameter lights. They were controlled from armoured positions and were intended as much to blind an opponent as to illuminate him. During the Battle of Jutland they proved of great utility during the night phase when the German line came under attack from British destroyers.

SMS *König* in service

SMS *König* was laid down in October 1911, launched on 1 March 1913 and commissioned into the High Seas Fleet on 9 August 1914, just as World War I commenced. She was the first of her class. As the others, *Grosser Kurfürst*, *Markgraf* and *Kronprinz* (later *Kronprinz Wilhelm*), were completed they were formed into the 3rd Squadron (5th Division) so that by early 1915 *König* was the squadron flag.[5] The 3rd Squadron was subdivided into two divisions; the other (the 6th) was comprised of the earlier Kaiser-class battleships.

In January 1915 the 3rd Squadron was sent to the Baltic for training. As a consequence, it missed taking part in the Battle of Dogger Bank. Duties which included screening minelaying missions and carrying out training manoeuvres followed over the next year. In April 1916 *König* was part of the support force during the raid on Great Yarmouth and Lowestoft. The following month *König* led the 3rd Squadron at the Battle of Jutland.

The 5th Division (led by *König*) was the most powerful unit and as a consequence was at the van of the entire German battle fleet as the battle commenced. She was heavily engaged in pursuing the British battlecruiser fleet and the Fifth Battle Squadron, firing at several ships, including HMS *Lion* and HMS *Barham*. At around 1800hrs (BST) *König* received a blow from a portion of a 15-inch round which made a hole in the sheer strake near the bows. Several other hits from 4- to 6-inch guns were kept out by her armour.[6]

With the arrival of the British battle fleet, the wider fleet action developed and the 5th Division was again heavily engaged. It was at this time, around 1835hrs, that *König* received most of the damage she sustained during the battle. Eight hits from heavy shell were registered, seven of which were credited to Admiral Jellicoe's flagship HMS *Iron Duke*. Most hit the forepart of the ship up to the first funnel, causing varying degrees of damage, the most severe being a hit on the join between the main armoured belt and the finer 180mm lower belt (see Figure 10.2). This round penetrated and burst inside the ship, causing extensive damage, knocking out two 5.9-inch batteries and leading to flooding to the port side by the ingression of around 500 tons of water.[7] It has been suggested that had *König* been using British-style propellant charges in the 5.9-inch batteries, this hit would have caused the ship to blow up.[8]

When the German fleet executed the final turn to the west to evade the larger British fleet which was holding the easterly track at that time, *König* was the sternmost ship of the German battle line. It was during this manoeuvre that she was hit on 'C' turret, causing suffocating smoke to enter the ship.[9] After the British were finally shaken off and dusk turned to night, the High Seas Fleet headed for safely. This last period of the battle saw *König* at the back of the German line largely unengaged because the actions against HMS *Black Prince* and British destroyers which occurred during this phase took place ahead of her.

All in all, at Jutland *König* saw 45 of her crew killed and 27 wounded (including Konteradmiral Behncke) – more than any other German battleship which survived the battle. Only the casualties in the surviving battlecruisers *Seydlitz* and *Derfflinger* were higher.[10] During the battle *König* fired 167 12-inch rounds and around 137 5.9-inch rounds. She had been hit by heavy shell on ten occasions and on four occasions by 6-inch rounds.[11] The ship was repaired by 21 July 1916.

König took part in the August 1916 sortie of the High Seas Fleet. Training in the Baltic and guard duties followed. In June 1917 she was taken into Wilhelmshaven for overhaul. It was at this time that the torpedo nets were removed and better splinter shielding was added to her bridges. But the most noticeable alteration to the ship was the replacement of the foremast with a heavy single-pole battle mast (which the British referred to as the cigar mast) with a splinter-proof

Figure 10.3. SMS *König* as interned in Scapa Flow in 1919. The heavy foremast fitted in 1917 can be seen with its two-tiered foretop. The rangefinder which would have sat on top has been removed as part of the surrender terms. The torpedo nets have been removed. The secondary 5.9-inch guns can be seen, along with the large searchlights and the fore and aft armoured bridges. To the right of the foremost 5.9-inch gun, two slits in the armour can be seen. These can be found on the shipwreck today, as described later in the chapter. (May Papers, Brotherton Library)

spotting and control top, which incorporated an additional rangefinder on the top (see Figure 10.3). This coincided with the incorporation of a director firing system.[12]

In October 1917 *König* took part in Operation *Albion* to drive Russian forces from the Baltic islands. On 17 October, at the Battle of Moon Sound, *König* and *Kronprinz* engaged the Russian pre-dreadnought battleship *Slava*. They were initially outranged, and minesweepers had to clear a path to close the distance to the target. *König* hit *Slava* seven times and forced her to scuttle when she grounded.[13]

As well as from training, guard and covering duties, *König* took part in the abortive advance along the Norwegian coast in April 1918. She was being prepared for the proposed November operation in the North Sea when the naval mutiny broke out.

Mutiny, internment and scuttling

The 1918 uprising began when the fleet was gathering at Schillig Roads. On 29 October 1918 ships of the 3rd Squadron were among the first to turn to widespread insubordination. Admiral Hipper ordered the mutinous squadrons to be dispersed and the 3rd was ordered to Kiel, arriving on 1 November. SMS *König* was ordered into drydock. The mutiny was sweeping through the city, so that by 5 November the red flag was flying all over Kiel. When a rating tried to tear down the Imperial Navy Flag still flying aboard *König* he was shot dead by Captain Weniger. A bloody firefight then ensued in which two officers were killed and Weniger was hit five times, but survived.[14] The Armistice was signed six days later.

On 19 November the larger portion of the High Seas Fleet sailed for Rosyth and ultimately internment in Scapa Flow. *König* was still in drydock and only arrived at Scapa Flow in concert with the light cruiser SMS *Dresden* in early December 1918. They were allocated the most easterly berths of any of the German fleet, off Cava. On 21 June 1919 she was scuttled with the rest of the interned fleet. Her sinking time was recorded as 1400hrs.[15] Her final plunge was seemingly captured in a photograph showing the ship rolling to port with the Calf of Cava and Hoy in the distance (see Figure 2.6).

History as a wreck

The wreck of SMS *König* was sold to Metal Industries on 20 April 1936, along with her two surviving sisters, *Kronprinz Wilhelm* and *Markgraf*, and the battlecruiser *Derfflinger*. She cost £750, which was the price Metal Industries paid for each of the battleships it raised.[16] This was cheaper than the prices paid by Cox & Danks.[17] Nevertheless, buying the sunken battleships at a good price was one thing, but salvaging them was another.

As described in Chapter Eight, *Derfflinger* was salvaged prior to World War II but broken up post-war. But the battleships purchased at the same time remained on the bottom and were not raised. Metal Industries shut its depot in Lyness in 1947 and wrote off the last of the wrecks it owned.[18] This appears to have been due to a number of factors, including the low scrap-metal prices in the immediate post-war years and a switch of business focus by Metal Industries, which was becoming increasingly diversified.

Some publications state that *König* and the other six surviving Scapa Flow wrecks were sold to the UK (presumably by the German State) in 1962.[19] This is difficult to reconcile with the fact that by then the Admiralty had already sold four of them for scrap. In fact, in 1956 one of the divers who had worked for Metal Industries, Arthur Nundy, acquired the last four wrecks that Metal Industries then owned and formed Nundy Marine Metals Ltd, acquiring the salvage rights to the three other surviving light cruisers around 1962. He worked them periodically until the end of 1970, by which time he had removed most of the armour plate from the wrecks.[20]

In that year Scapa Flow Salvage Ltd acquired all of the assets of Nundy Marine Metals. It worked the seven surviving wrecks for armour plate and non-ferrous metals until 1978, when it sold out to Undersea Associates of Aberdeen, which rapidly went bankrupt in late 1979. The official receiver then put the wrecks up for sale in 1981.

Orkney Island Council was urged to buy them as a tourist attraction, but the salvage rights passed to Clark's Diving Services of Lerwick through a combination of the purchase of four of the wrecks, *König*, *Kronprinz Wilhelm*, *Markgraf* and *Karlsruhe*, and the leasing of the other three, *Dresden*, *Brummer* and *Cöln*. The leases expired in 1985 and ownership then reverted to the Ministry of Defence, from which Orkney Islands Council acquired ownership of the three wrecks on 3 November 1986. This was the current state of ownership of the wrecks in 2018. In 2002, seven of the nine surviving wrecks were designated under the Ancient Monuments and Archaeological Areas Act. The torpedo boats SMS *V83* and *S54* were unprotected as of 2018.

The salvage activity on *König* was aimed at removing its main armoured belt and its armoured bulkheads, which contained 4% nickel. Non-ferrous metals in the form of bronze, brass, gunmetal and copper were also removed. Access was gained to the areas of the ship which yielded them by the use of explosives. When Scapa Flow Salvage Ltd acquired the wreck, it observed that most of these valuable metals had already been recovered

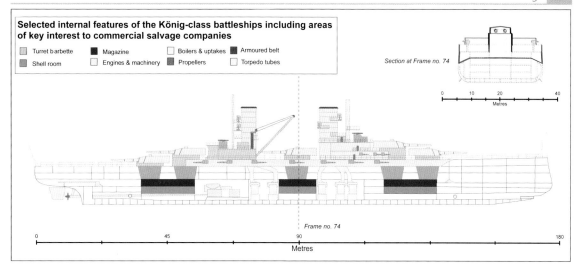

Selected internal features of the König-class battleships including areas of key interest to commercial salvage companies

- Turret barbette
- Shell room
- Magazine
- Engines & machinery
- Boilers & uptakes
- Propellers
- Armoured belt
- Torpedo tubes

Section at Frame no. 74

0   10   20   40
Metres

Frame no. 74

0   45   90   180
Metres

from *König* by Nundy Marine Metals, so the former worked primarily on *Markgraf*, which was the least salvaged of the battleships at that time.[21]

SMS *König* today

A plan view of the DTM can be seen in Figure 10.5. The wreck points to the northwest and is almost completely upside down, with a list to the port side. It is immediately obvious that it has been subjected to extensive salvage operations. The bow and stern areas are much degraded and the entire area of the engine rooms has been blasted open.

The hybrid model of the wreck is shown in Figures 10.6 and 10.7. They enhance the details seen on the DTM and allow the wreck to be viewed from any angle. Figure 10.6 shows that the fore and aft sections of the wreck are very collapsed. At the stern only the port-side rudder is recognizable, as can be observed when diving on the wreck. The bow is very broken down and its exact point is not easy to initially discern when diving. The overall depth is 40m and the maximum height of the wreck during the survey was 19m from the surface. So the wreck stands up an impressive 21m from the bottom. The highest point is amidships close to the area where some salvage work has taken place.

The model shows that most of the debris which has fallen out of the wreck lies on its starboard side. The photographic evidence shows that the ship rolled over to port when it sank, so one would expect to see more debris on this side. However, much of the debris that is present is the result of salvage and the subsequent degradation of the structure of the wreck over time. As seen in Figure 10.7, the gentle lean of the wreck can be discerned clearly. The comparative lack of any remains on the seabed on the port side of the wreck is also evident.

I conducted a video survey of the wreck in 2013 and 2014, and selected assortments of the most interesting and important features recorded are

Figure 10.4. Selected key features of the König-class battleships, showing key features and valuable components such as armour, non-ferrous machinery, propellers and torpedo tubes which were targeted during the years the ships were being commercially salvaged.

Figure 10.5. Plan view DTM of SMS *König* today which shows she is upside down and has been extensively salvaged in the past.

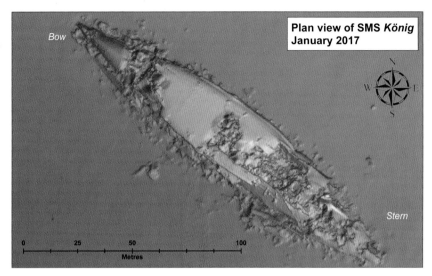

Bow

Plan view of SMS *König*
January 2017

Stern

0   25   50   100
Metres

shown in Figures 10.8–10.13, beginning at the stern end of the wreckage on the starboard side of the ship. The locations of the features shown are then depicted in Figure 10.14.

Figure 10.8 shows a portion of the ship's double bottom which now lies on the seabed. It is in line with an area where the engine-room salvage has taken place, and it must have arrived at its current location probably by being blasted off the top of the engine-room area. Examination of the class plans for this ship reveals that this piece of wreckage comes from the area where the double bottom was used to store diesel oil.

As Figure 10.9 shows, further forward at the seabed level a large piece of armoured plate was found at a 45-degree angle. It is partially buried in the seabed and is instantly recognizable by its thickness. On a dive in 2013 it was measured at 20cm thick (Image B). This is the upper, thinner portion of the main armoured belt which protected the main deck only and sat above the thicker belt which protected the middle deck above the waterline (see Figure 10.2). It must have been pulled out to its current location when the thicker main belt which would have sat above it (because the wreck is upside down) was salvaged from the wreck.

Further forward at the seabed level the foremost of the starboard-side 5.9-inch guns of the secondary armament of the ship can be seen. These guns were mounted on the upper deck. Their location at seabed level shows that the wreck has sunk into the seabed up to the level of this deck, so that the main turrets and upper superstructure are buried. The muzzle is buried but the casemate is visible, affording a small view inside. Squeezing into the tight space to the right and aft of the casemate revealed a viewing slit in the armoured belt behind. This feature can be seen clearly on the photo of

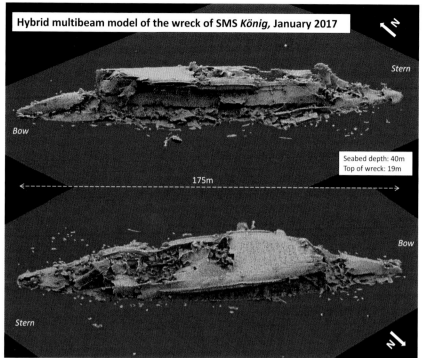

Hybrid multibeam model of the wreck of SMS *König*, January 2017

N

Stern

Bow

Seabed depth: 40m
Top of wreck: 19m

175m

Figure 10.6. Hybrid model of SMS *König* reveals many more features than the DTM. The breaks in the wreck and areas of collapse are shown in much greater detail.

Bow

Stern

N

Figure 10.7. (Below) All-round views of the hybrid model of SMS *König*. The upper images show the extensively salvaged stern portion in detail. The lower images show the way in which the bow has been broken away from the wreck. The gentle lean of the wreck to the port side can also be discerned.

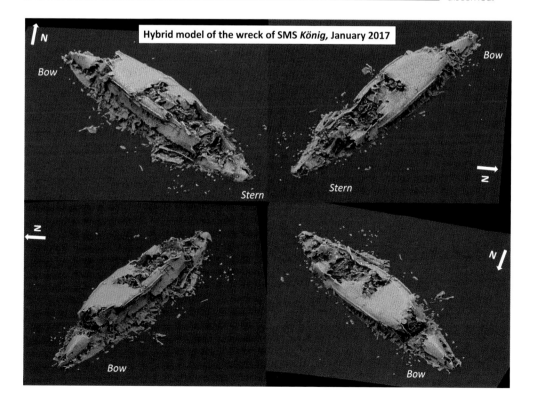

Hybrid model of the wreck of SMS *König*, January 2017

N

Bow

Bow

Stern

Stern

N

N

Bow

Bow

N

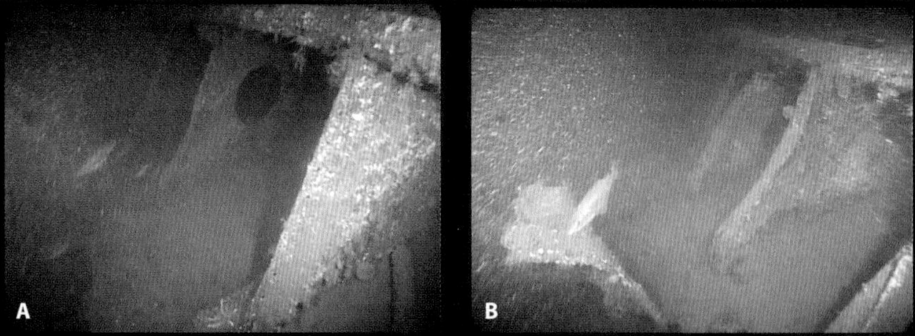

Figure 10.8. A section of SMS *König's* double bottom lies on the seabed, having been removed from the wreck during salvage operations.

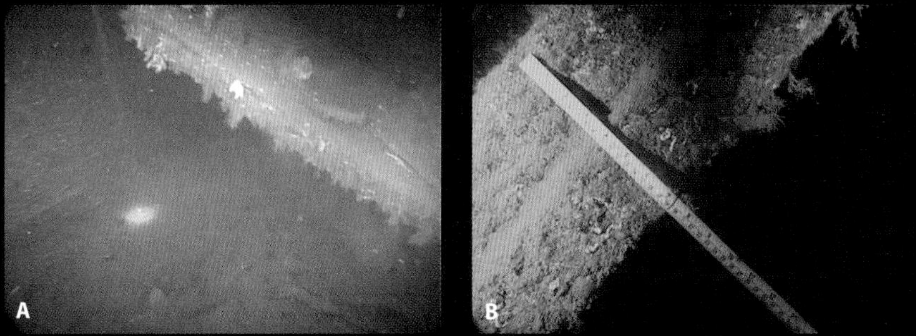

Figure 10.9. A portion of armour plate which has come off the wreck can be seen in Image A. It is 20cm thick, as shown in Image B, and is of the type used in protecting the citadel.

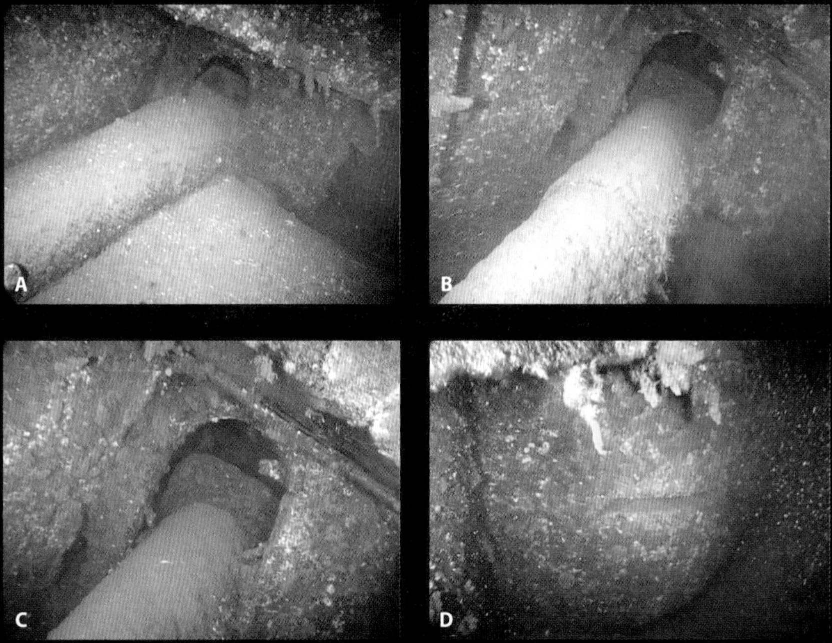

Figure 10.10. The forwardmost of the 5.9-inch guns on the starboard side of the wreck. The barrel lies partially buried in the seabed and following it aft leads to the casemate. To right behind it is a viewing slit in the protective armour, as can be seen in Figure 10.2.

SMS *König* taken in 1919 in Scapa Flow, shown in Figure 10.3, and it was the site of a secondary torpedo aiming station.[22]

Forward of this gun lie the remains of the bow section. Figure 10.11 shows a pair of features from this area. Image A shows anchor chain lying in a heap near the bow. Image B shows a portion of the deck which lies just forward of the 5.9-inch gun. By swimming under it and looking up, the deck of the ship is revealed. The circular feature is a coaling hatch, clearly identifiable on the

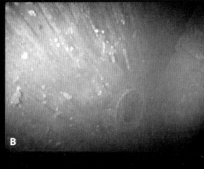

König-class ship plans.[23] Having originally most likely been made of brass (as the British ones were), the hatch has long since gone. Just to the right of it the edge of the armoured wall of the upper deck can be seen. It is quite impressive to see a nicely preserved area of deck on this famous battleship.

Turning back from the bow and ascending to near to the top of the wreck, there is the opportunity to examine the wreck within through a number of holes in its side. At roughly the same area as the 5.9-inch gun but higher up (or lower down if the wreck was upright), a way was found into the wreck at the level of the upper platform deck. The survey video of this area recorded a passageway that was three decks deep reaching from the lower platform deck to the lower deck. These three decks were the ones protected by the armoured torpedo bulkhead.

Figure 10.12 shows two images from this section of the wreck. To the left is the armoured torpedo bulkhead. At the level of the lower platform deck a doorway can be seen leading into the next compartment. It can also be seen that this passageway continued onward, with ladders attached to the torpedo bulkhead, as seen in Images A and B.

The class drawings reveal that coal was stored in the area between the outer hull and the torpedo bulkhead, as shown in Figure 10.2, so it seems that this area of the wreck was probably a coal bunker. What was particularly notable about seeing this was being able to view the torpedo bulkhead of this remarkable class of ship in place inside the wreck with the outer hull still *in situ* on the exterior side. This bulkhead gave incomparable protection from underwater damage but was not a feature on British designs, so it is very unusual to be able to view it in its original position, surrounded by the rest of

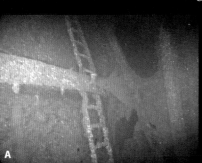

Figure 10.12. A hole in the starboard side of the wreck nearest its upper point allowed for an examination inside the wreck at this point. The area is part of the coal bunker which runs around the outside of the torpedo bulkhead. The ladder between two deck levels and the doorway into the next compartment can be seen.

Figure 10.13. Close to the highest point of the wreck there is a hole caused by salvage. Within it lie the remains of at least one of the ship's Schulz-Thorneycroft boilers. Clearly upside down, the pair of water traps are the highest points of the boiler's remains.

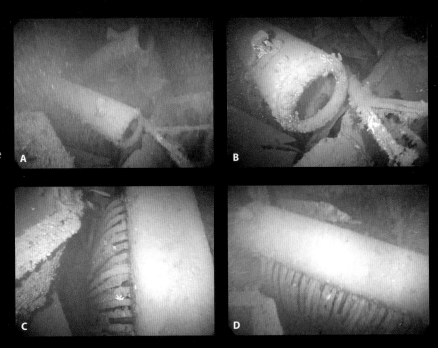

the ship's structure. This bulkhead is not a rare feature on these wrecks – as will be shown, it makes up much of the exterior of the hulls of the wrecks today, because the outer armour has been salvaged. However, to view it as it was originally built, as part of the interior of the ship, is notable.

Returning to the stern area of the wreck while traversing along the top, one first goes over an area of intact ship's keel. Then the point where the holes were blasted into the wreck during the salvage operations is found. Here the remains of at least one boiler were recorded. The German warships were built using a boiler of the Schulz-Thorneycroft type. It was a three-drum design with the steam drum at the apex and two water traps at the lower corners. This is the type of boiler most commonly found on German warships of the World War I era.[24]

Figure 10.13 shows the remains of this boiler as recorded in 2013. The highest points of the boiler shown in Images A & B are the two water traps which, interestingly, no longer seem to have their inspection covers. One feature of the Schulz-Thorneycroft design was the curved nature of the water tubes which ran between the water traps and the steam drum. Images C and D clearly show these curved water tubes. This boiler appears to be situated at the forward end of the boiler room directly under the after funnel on the starboard side (see Figure 10.4 for the exact position on the class drawing). Similar boilers can be studied on other High Seas Fleet wrecks, not least on the two surviving torpedo boats (see Chapter 17).

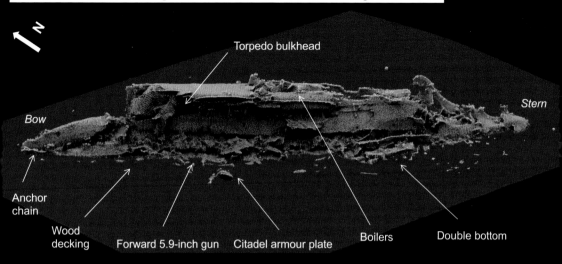

Figure 10.14. The hybrid model of SMS *König* showing the approximate locations of features observed on dives on the wreck.

Bringing together the selection of observed features on the wreck and the three-dimensional model, Figure 10.14 shows the approximate locations of the features described. As seen on the salvage sites, the detailed multibeam models can be matched to the video surveys with a high degree of confidence, so that all the items can be easily relocated in the future by those who are fortunate enough to get to interact with the wreck site. In reality, the multibeam and the video surveys complement each other, so that using both in conjunction with each other leads to a fuller understanding of the wreck in its current condition.

Structural changes observed in the wreck of SMS *König*, 2006–2017

One interesting aspect of how the wreck has changed over time is its overall height. This is recorded through time on the Hydrographic Office record of the wreck.[25] The entire scuttled German fleet was surveyed in detail by Cmdr T. W. Tinson RN during August to October 1919.[26] In this survey, *König* was originally recorded as being around 12 metres (7 fathoms) from the surface at its highest point. In fact, from 1919 until 1977 it was recorded as standing up to only 12 metres from the surface, so around 27–30m high.

Even accounting for the loss in height due to salvage, it is hard to see how the wreck could stand so high in its current orientation, and this would seem to suggest that when *König* originally sank, she was much more on her beam ends and over time has gradually rolled into a more upside-down plane

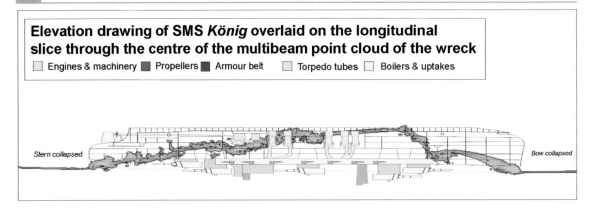

Elevation drawing of SMS *König* overlaid on the longitudinal slice through the centre of the multibeam point cloud of the wreck

☐ Engines & machinery ■ Propellers ■ Armour belt ☐ Torpedo tubes ☐ Boilers & uptakes

Stern collapsed

Bow collapsed

Figure 10.15. A slice through the entire length of the multibeam point cloud of the wreck of SMS *König* incorporated into a drawing of the ship, showing how its valuable metals have been removed in the past.

For example, it is known that in the 1980s divers could get under the main deck to see the turret sides.[27] This is now seemingly impossible, indicating that the wreck is degrading, possibly still rolling and sinking further into the seabed.

In Figure 10.15, a slice through the length of the point cloud has been combined with the drawing of the König class. Today the wreck lies with a lean to port of 20 degrees. So in order to line up both the wreck and the drawing, the slice has been rotated to the vertical plane. The result clearly shows that the collapsed areas of the wreck have been primarily caused by the salvage operations, which grew increasingly complex once the easily removable items such as the propellers had been salvaged.

The collapsed nature of both the bow and the stern has been caused by the use of explosives to blast down into the wreck to effect the removal of the transverse armoured bulkheads at the ends of the armoured citadel of the ship. This is best seen at the fore section where the area of collapse lines up

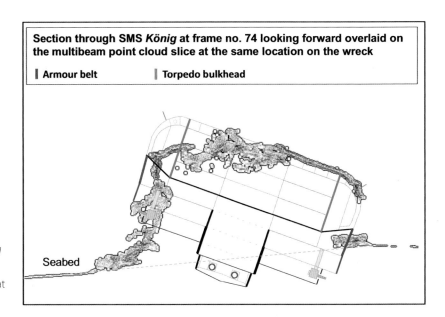

Section through SMS *König* at frame no. 74 looking forward overlaid on the multibeam point cloud slice at the same location on the wreck

▌ Armour belt ▌ Torpedo bulkhead

Seabed

Figure 10.16. Slice through the point cloud of SMS *König* at frame no. 74 overlaid on a section drawing of the ship at that location.

perfectly with where the forward bulkhead was situated. This process which degraded the fore and aft sections was exacerbated by the process of the removal of all of the ship's five torpedo tubes, which were also situated in these areas, and of the chain-winding machinery and other valuable targets of opportunity.

Figure 10.15 also the reveals the extent of the excavations in the region of the engine room, where the valuable turbines and condensers were to be found. There was no need to blast right down to the seabed, because the upside-down nature of the wreck placed the items within easy reach, just under the soft underbelly of the double bottom. The accuracy of the process of matching up the class drawing with the point cloud in order to highlight changes in the wreck is perhaps best evidenced by the exposed nature of the after set of boilers in Figure 10.15, which matches the way in which they are seen on the wreck today, as shown in Figure 10.13.

Figure 10.16 uses a similar methodology to look at the salvage of the main armoured belt which ran down the side of the ship. In this case the wreck drawing is rotated so that it lines up with the orientation of the wreck, which leans 20 degrees to the port side. It is immediately evident that on the higher

Figure 10.17. Changes in the wreck of SMS *König* through time as evidenced by multibeam surveys in 2006 and 2017.

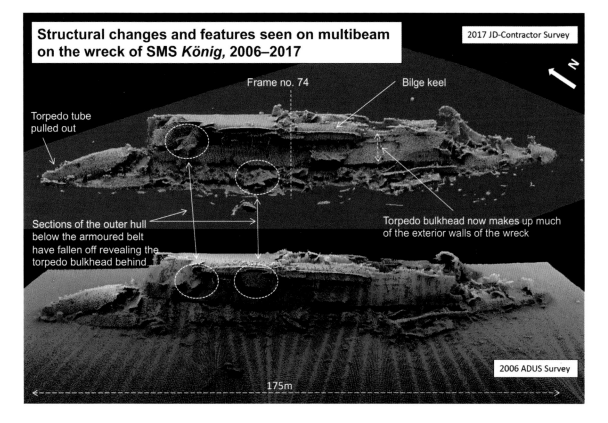

Structural changes and features seen on multibeam on the wreck of SMS *König*, 2006–2017

2017 JD-Contractor Survey

N

Frame no. 74

Bilge keel

Torpedo tube pulled out

Torpedo bulkhead now makes up much of the exterior walls of the wreck

Sections of the outer hull below the armoured belt have fallen off revealing the torpedo bulkhead behind

2006 ADUS Survey

175m

starboard side of the ship the main armour is gone. In fact, the outer walls of the entire wreck are predominantly made up of the torpedo bulkhead which was fitted inboard of the armoured belt, as shown in Figure 10.12.

The exact location of frame 74 is shown on Figure 10.17, and it can be seen that in this area the bilge keel has been cut through and the keel on the starboard side has collapsed down to the level of the upper platform deck. On both sides of the wreck, the torpedo bulkhead is now, in the absence of the armoured belt, functioning as the outer walls of the wreck's structure. Around the area of frame 74 it can be seen that portions of the overhanging keel have been falling away. This turns out to be a feature consistent on all of the battleship wrecks. Further aft, as highlighted on Figure 10.17, the overhanging keel has completely collapsed to the seabed. A portion of this area of the keel is shown in Figure 10.8.

In 2006 ADUS carried out multibeam surveys of the protected seven Scapa Flow wrecks. These data have been particularly useful in assessing how the wrecks have changed in the decade between those surveys and the 2017 ones. The comparison between the two datasets in terms of *König* can be seen in Figure 10.17. Most noticeable is the collapse to the seabed of a large portion of the outer hull in the central section of the wreck during this time. A further large portion of the outer hull at the point of the break forward is in the process of tearing itself loose and will inevitably go the same way. When this area was recorded on video in 2013 (see Figure 10.12) it looked much closer to the 2006 survey than it does today. Both of these areas are highlighted in Figure 10.17.

These changes are not insignificant. What they reveal is that increasingly the wreck is being supported solely by its multi-compartmentalized framework, held together externally by the torpedo bulkhead. It is axiomatic to observe that the ship was never designed to take such stresses. This process of collapse is broadly consistent across all three of the König-class battleships, as the following chapters will show.

Conclusions

The salvage history is now very much a feature of the archaeological remains of all of the remaining High Seas Fleet wrecks at Scapa Flow. For good or ill, it too is part of their archaeology and ultimately their cultural history. SMS *König* bears the scars of salvage. Aside from the obviously blasted areas of the wreck, one additional feature which the multibeam survey seemed to reveal is that the entirety of the main armoured belt has been removed. A very comprehensive job seems to have been done in its removal. Video surveys did not record any examples of it on the wreck, although some is reputed to survive on the port side, but probably now buried.

Comparing the 2017 survey data with the 2006 ADUS survey reveals that the outer hull is collapsing. This is natural because all wrecks degrade over time. It is not easy to discern simply by looking at the multibeam surveys how long these wrecks will remain upright. The König-class battleships were exceptionally well built, and this is the main reason they remain so extant, even after extensive salvage. Clearly their protection as a monument has also slowed their degradation, by preventing further metal recovery. It may actually be the case that the removal of the armoured belt reduced the loading on the frames, and ironically helped preserve the ship's structure.

SMS *König* is by any measure a famous and important shipwreck. However, it seems to be the least popular of the German wrecks with divers, with at least one dive guide suggesting that only the marine life is of any interest. But the surveys show that this is not the case at all. Both the multibeam survey and the video survey dives have revealed a great number of interesting features on this majestic shipwreck. Undoubtedly it will yield further fascinating results each time it is surveyed, as the wreck changes over time.

1   T. Philbin (1973), *Warship Profile 37: SMS König* (Windsor: Profile Publications), p. i.

2   H. J. Koerver (ed.) (2009), *Room 40: German Naval Warfare 1914–1918. Volume 2: The Fleet in Being* (Steinbach: LIS Reinisch), p. 19.

3   G. Koop & K.-P. Schmolke (1999), *Planmappe: Linienschiffe Ostfriesland und König* (Bonn: Bernard & Graefe Verlag).

4   T. Philbin (1973), *Warship Profile 37: SMS König* (Windsor: Profile Publications), p. 7.

5   J. E. T. Harper (1927), *Reproduction of the Record of the Battle of Jutland* (London: HMSO), p. 109.

6   N. J. M. Campbell (1986), *Jutland: An Analysis of the Fighting* (London: Conway), pp. 143–144.

7   N. J. M. Campbell (1986), *Jutland: An Analysis of the Fighting* (London: Conway), pp. 187–195.

8   N. J. M. Campbell (1986), *Jutland: An Analysis of the Fighting* (London: Conway), p. 381.

9   National Archives (various dates), O. Groos, *The Battle of Jutland: Official German Account*, Admiralty translation, 1926, ADM 186/626, p. 131. London.

10   N. J. M. Campbell (1986), *Jutland: An Analysis of the Fighting* (London: Conway), p. 341.

11   N. J. M. Campbell (1986), *Jutland: An Analysis of the Fighting* (London: Conway), pp. 348–363.

12   T. Philbin (1973), *Warship Profile 37: SMS König* (Windsor: Profile Publications), p. 18.

13   G. Staff (2010), *German Battleships 1914–18 (2)* (Oxford: Osprey), p. 31.

14   D. Woodward (1973), *The Collapse of Power: Mutiny in the High Seas Fleet* (London: Arthur Baker), pp. 147–148.

15   L. von Reuter (1940), *Scapa Flow: The Account of the Greatest Scuttling of All Time* (London: Hurst & Blackett), p. 149.

16   Naval Historical Branch (various dates), *CP 8a Sale Book*, p. 138. Portsmouth.

17   I. Buxton (1992), *Metal Industries: Shipbreaking at Rosyth and Charlestown* (Kendal: World Ship Society), p. 28.

18   D. van der Vat (1982), *The Grand Scuttle: The Sinking of the German Fleet at Scapa Flow in 1919* (London: Hodder & Stoughton), pp. 214–215

19   E. Gröner (1990), *German Warships 1815–1945. Volume One: Major Surface Vessels* (London: Conway), p. 28.

20   B. Jackson (2010), *But Not All Men Live! From Scapa to Africa and All Dives in Between. The true tale of a diver who did it all, and lived* (Fareham: Barry Jackson), pp. 46–97.

21   ScapaMAP 2000–2002 (2003), Report Compiled for Historic Scotland on the Mapping and Management of the Submerged Archaeological Resource in Scapa Flow. Orkney: Scapa Flow Marine Archaeology Project, Appendix III.

22   T. Philbin (1973), *Warship Profile 37: SMS König* (Windsor: Profile Publications), p. 19.

23   G. Koop & K.-P. Schmolke (1999), *Planmappe: Linienschiffe Ostfriesland und König* (Bonn: Bernard & Graefe Verlag).

24   I. McCartney (2016), *Jutland 1916: The Archaeology of a Naval Battlefield* (London: Bloomsbury), pp. 25–26.

25   Hydrographic Department of the Admiralty (2017), record of Wreck No. 1083 SMS *König* (Taunton: Hydrographic Office).

26   Hydrographic Office Archive (various dates), Chart No. C7953 Press 14 H, surveyed positions of the sunken German Fleet 1919. Taunton.

27   R. Macdonald (2017), *Dive Scapa Flow* (Edinburgh: Mainstream), p. 109.

CHAPTER 11
SMS *MARKGRAF*

Figure 11.1. SMS *Markgraf* as seen after her 1918 refit and prior to internment at Scapa Flow. She has been fitted with the cigar mast with splinter-proof spotting and control top. Note the rangefinder on its top. She also now has an admiral's bridge fitted aft of the forward conning tower, similar to SMS *König*. Design displacement 25,389 tons, length 175m, ten 12-inch guns, fourteen 5.9-inch guns. (Orkney Archive)

SMS Markgraf *is a König-class battleship. She fought at Jutland and Moon Sound and survived being mined. Her casualties from the Grand Scuttle included her captain, and they are all buried in Lyness cemetery. Although partially salvaged, she is the most intact of the battleship wrecks. Surveys of this site reveal a still impressive shipwreck in the process of decay.*

Design and service history

SMS *Markgraf* was the third of the König class. She was built at A. G. Weser and launched on 4 June 1913. Although she was commissioned on 1 October 1914, trials continued, so that she did not become fully operational with the 3rd Squadron until January 1915. In design terms she was practically identical to SMS *König*, with British intelligence making no distinction between them.[1]

Prior to 1917 the only minor visual difference between the two ships was the absence of an admiral's bridge on *Markgraf*. This was fitted in 1917. The 1918 refit included the fitting of the same cigar mast and splinter-proof spotting and control top as seen on *König* after her refit in 1917.[2]

SMS *Markgraf* in service

In January 1915, the 3rd Squadron missed the Battle of Dogger Bank as it was conducting training in the Baltic. During the rest of the year *Markgraf* took part in uneventful sorties and minelaying operations in the North Sea. In 1916 she was more active, being involved in further fleet advances and in providing distant support for the Lowestoft raid of 24 April.

At Jutland she was third ship in the 5th Division of the 3rd Squadron. The entire division was made up of the four König-class battleships and it formed the lead unit of the German battlefleet. At 1646hrs she opened fire, following Admiral Sheer's command. The initial target was HMS *Tiger*, which was at maximum range. Her secondary armament also briefly engaged two British destroyers, probably HMS *Nestor* and HMS *Nicator*, the former being disabled, shortly to sink.[3]

As the British battlecruisers ran north, the 5th Battle Squadron of the 15-inch-gunned Queen Elizabeth class took position astern of them. It was at this time, around 1710hrs, that *Markgraf* was hit three times by 15-inch heavy shell. One round passed through the starboard samson post and did no further damage. Another passed right through the foremast pole, which incredibly remained standing for the rest of the battle, although nearly cut in two. However, the third hit did much more damage, striking the side armour aft and creating a hole into which 400 tons of water rushed, flooding compartments and cabins.[4]

As the main fleet action unfolded, the older armoured cruiser HMS *Defence* was targeted by the lead ships of the German battlefleet. When she blew up, *Markgraf* claimed the victory, although the credit was most likely SMS *Lützow*'s. During the fleet action, which lasted until the German fleet was able to disengage, *Markgraf* was hit at 1832hrs by HMS *Orion*, knocking out a casemate and killing all but two of its crew. A near miss at 1833hrs struck and bent the port propeller shaft, overheating the bearings and causing the engine to be shut down, reducing speed to 17 knots.[5] She was hit once by HMS *Agincourt* at around 1914hrs with a 12-inch round which failed to detonate and was kept out by her armour.[6]

When the German battle line initially reversed course, despite her reduced speed *Markgraf* was able to hold her position in line, which was now third from the rear. However, on the final course reversal and the taking up of night formation, she ended up swapping places with *Kronprinz* and effectively became the lead ship of the 5th Division, placing her in the middle (13th place) of the German line of 24 major warships.[7]

During the sequence of night actions which followed it was mainly the leading battleships of the line which fought off destroyer attacks and sank HMS *Black Prince*. But at around 0200hrs on 1 June the German line was attacked by the 12th Destroyer Flotilla. This attack caused the battle line to turn sharply to starboard to avoid the oncoming torpedoes. Two aimed at *Markgraf* were spotted through the firing director telescope, and early evasive action luckily caused one to miss by only 30 yards. Even luckier, the other passed right underneath her without detonating.[8] SMS *Pommern* was not so lucky and was destroyed by a torpedo hit in a massive fireball at this time, with the loss of her entire crew.

During the battle, the exact number of hits scored by *Markgraf* is not known, although two hits on HMS *Princess Royal* are credited to her. She may well have been responsible for at least one of the uncredited hits on the 5th Battle Squadron during the run north and possibly for some of the other 57 hits British ships received from German main armament. She fired 254 rounds during the battle, the highest number fired by any German battleship. SMS *Markgraf*'s secondary armament claimed hits on HMS *Warrior*, the light cruiser HMS *Calliope* and a number of destroyers.

She was hit directly by heavy shell five times, as described, although the near miss which wrecked a propeller shaft could be classed as a sixth hit. Overall, she suffered casualties of 11 killed and 13 wounded at Jutland. Upon her return, *Markgraf* was repaired at A. G. Vulcan Hamburg and was ready for sea by 20 June, when she was ordered for training in the Baltic.

Operations recommenced in August, when *Markgraf* was temporarily assigned to the 1st Scouting Group along with *Grosser Kurfürst* and the brand-new *Bayern*. Such was the damage sustained by the battlecruisers at Jutland that only two were ready for action at that time. The August advance returned to port once it was learned that the entire British fleet had sortied. After another uneventful advance across the North Sea in September, *Markgraf* returned to the 3rd Division and its cycle of training and guard duties.

On 5 November *Markgraf* was present during the operation to recover two stranded U-boats, *U20* and *U30*. On the return leg both *Grosser Kurfürst* and *Kronprinz* were torpedoed by the British submarine HMS *J1*, requiring extensive repairs.[9] Most of 1917 was spent on picket duty or training in the Baltic. A refit took place in January. The mutinies in the summer did not affect the ship, although deserters informed British intelligence that much of the trouble had been planned aboard her.[10]

In October she took part in Operation *Albion*, directed against Russia, where she was principally used for shore bombardments at Cape Ninnast and, later, positions on Kynö Island. By 29 October she was sailing for Kiel when she stuck two mines in quick succession in the Irben Strait. This caused limited damage, with only 260 tons of water coming on board. Damage was limited by the torpedo bulkhead, one of the finest design aspects of these high-quality warships. She was repaired by 23 November.

Figure 11.2. An atmospheric photograph of SMS *Markgraf* seen from the stern on her mooring at Scapa Flow in 1919. In the distance the island of Hoy forms a backdrop for (L to R) a drifter, SMS *Kaiserin*, SMS *Karlsruhe* and SMS *Bayern*. Her port-side crane is swung out. Note the searchlight platforms. (May, Liddle Collection)

Much of 1918 was taken up with guard and picket duties and a refit in March to early May, during which the cigar mast was fitted. In October she was readied for the fleet advance planned for the end of the month when rebellion broke out on board, heralding the beginning of the naval mutiny.

Mutiny, internment and scuttling

The disobedience in the 3rd Squadron resulted in it being ordered to Kiel, where it duly arrived on 1 November, but not before 47 members of *Markgraf*'s crew had been imprisoned. That trouble that was brewing in the squadron was noticed by the light cruisers stationed at Brunsbüttel, when *Markgraf* unprecedentedly did not salute them as the 3rd Squadron made its way into the Kiel Canal. The ship seemed to have a strange air, with men milling around on the decks.[11] On 1 November, 180 of her crew were arrested and placed ashore. A further 70 arrests followed the next day. But by 4 November the crew of *Markgraf* had put its commander ashore and the ship was under the command of a soldiers' council. Some semblance of order was restored during transit and internment by a reduction in the size of the crew and by careful management of the men.

On the night before the Grand Scuttle, the ship's captain, Walter Schumann, with permission to use his discretion as to whom to tell about the plan to scuttle, informed the crew gathered in the wardroom of what was to happen. Not all were in agreement. One machinist was a US citizen, and he rejected the idea. Speaking in favour of the plan was Senior Mate Hermann Dittman, who, 'fired up by love for his country tried to explain in short words why the sinking of the ship was necessary'.[12]

On the morning of 21 June the condenser pumps were removed in preparation and Schumann and Fleet Engineer Faustman (who wrote a full report of what happened, which can be found in Appendix 3) burned all of the ship's documentation, logs and plans in the boilers. The signal was received at 1110hrs and the crew were ordered to assemble on the middle deck. There was some delay, with the crew reluctant to obey, choosing instead to pack their belongings. Some were found below by Faustman and had to be chased up on deck.

Once the boats were ready for lowering the order was given to open the bottom valves and flood the ship. Worried about the safety of his crew, Schumann later ordered the valves shut in order to get them all safely off. This short delay, along with crew's tardiness in obeying orders, was to prove tragic. As the crew continued to evacuate into the boats, the first pistol and rifle shots from a drifter (probably *Cabalsin*) hit the ship. This was probably at around 1430hrs. One of the first shots hit Dittman in the back of the head, killing him instantly. Realizing that the firing would continue, Schumann ordered the white flag to be run up the foremast.[13]

But by this time firing was being directed at the ship from both sides. It was clearly aimed at driving the crew back on board. Schumann was forced to take cover, and it was while waving a white handkerchief and trying to stop the shooting that he too was shot in the face and killed by a Lt Turner.[14] As the drifter continued circling *Markgraf*, the crew in small groups were able to get away in the launch and the two bodies were placed in the speedboat. Engineer Faustman had been below during the shooting getting his belongings but emerged only then to discover what had happened. Knowing the valves were underwater and could not be reached, he left the ship aboard the speedboat with the last of the crew, carrying the captain's bag for his wife, now a widow with four small children.[15]

The speedboat made for Cava, only to be fired on from the beach. This firing ceased when the 'outpost and civilian' – the party firing from the beach – found themselves accidentally under fire from the drifters. It was this shore party that apparently finally compelled the nearby drifters to stop shooting. Faustman and others were then picked up and taken to HMS *Ramilles*.[16] While this was happening, the destroyer HMS *Vectis* had taken *Markgraf* in tow and for half an hour tried to move her. Although the ship's cables were released, they would not run out and it seems attempts to finally cut them were too late and *Markgraf* foundered on her mooring, as photographed in Figure 2.12.[17]

SMS *Markgraf* was the last battleship to sink, foundering at 1645hrs. Fifteen minutes later the drifting SMS *Hindenburg* became the last major warship to sink during the Grand Scuttle. By then, *Markgraf*'s crew and the commander's body had been taken off. Schumann's body lay overnight in the cabin of a pinnace aboard HMS *Ramilles* before a coffin was produced.[18]

History as a wreck

Like the other surviving battleships, the wreck was sold to Metal Industries on 20 April 1936 for £750.[19] A detailed history of the surviving battleship *König* was given in the previous chapter. *Markgraf*'s history as a wreck does not differ in the details of how she was bought and sold over the following years.

One aspect of the salvage operations on her that is different is the fact that when in 1970 Scapa Flow Salvage Ltd began its tenure on the wrecks, it observed that *Markgraf* was the last of the battleships to fully retain her armoured belt. Nundy Marine Metals had focused more closely on the shallower *König* and *Kronprinz*. In its final year of operations in 1970 it had removed the torpedo tubes, but seemingly not much else.[20] It was Scapa Flow Salvage which recovered all of the armoured belt and the forward and after armoured bulkheads.[21] In comparison with the other two wrecks, the work was somewhat neater and the damage caused in its removal (especially of the bulkheads) more limited, and the wreck is consequently the most intact of the battleships. This is the main reason it is one of the most popular wrecks with divers.

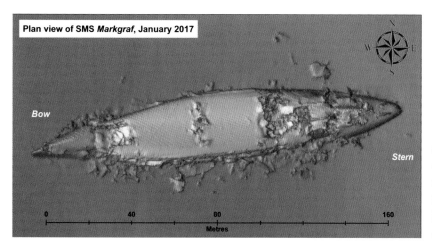

Plan view of SMS *Markgraf*, January 2017

Bow

Stern

0   40   80   160

Metres

Figure 11.3. Plan view DTM of SMS *Markgraf*. As with all the battleship wrecks in Scapa Flow, she is upside down and bears the tell-tale signatures of salvage activity.

SMS *Markgraf* today

One of the first targets of the 2017 survey was the wreck of SMS *Markgraf*. The DTM can be seen in Figure 11.3. The wreck points to the west and is the only surviving warship to not be pointing northwest. This is probably due to the abortive attempt to tow the ship as she foundered. As with the other battleships, she is upside down. There is a list to port and, like *König*, the main area of dispersed wreckage around the wreck is on the starboard side. Also, it is immediately evident that this wreck has been commercially salvaged in the past. This activity has been focused in the usual areas of the engine room and the armoured belt. The bow section appears broken in the area where the forward armoured bulkhead was removed.

The detailed point cloud built up during the survey is shown in the hybrid model seen in Figures 11.4 and 11.5. Again, similar to *König*, further details are revealed. The angle of lean of the wreck is easily discerned, as is the extent to which the bow area has collapsed as a result of salvage. The general depth of the seabed is around 45 metres and the highest point of the wreck we recorded is at a depth of 24 metres, meaning the wreck stands an impressive 21 metres high – exactly the same as *König*. The video recordings of the survey dives on this wreck over the last few years were examined in the light of the multibeam scans, and a number of key features identified on the wreck are shown in Figures 11.6–11.13. The locations of the features shown are given in Figure 11.14.

Figure 11.6 shows features recorded in the bow area of the wreck. Images A and B are from an area near the forward break. At this point a section of armour

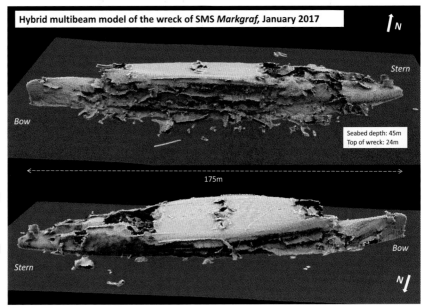

Hybrid multibeam model of the wreck of SMS *Markgraf*, January 2017

N

Stern

Bow

Seabed depth: 45m
Top of wreck: 24m

175m

Stern

Bow

N

Figure 11.4. Hybrid model of SMS *Markgraf* shows additional detail over that seen on the DTM. The areas where the armoured belt has been pulled out have left distinctive linear features running along the sides of the wreck.

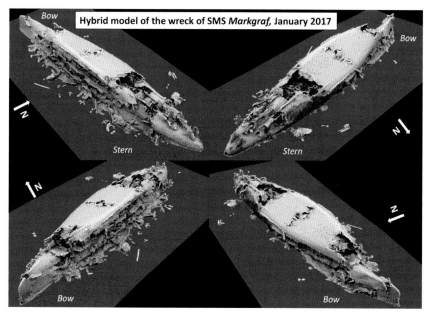

Hybrid model of the wreck of SMS *Markgraf,* January 2017

Figure 11.5. All-round views of the wreck of SMS *Markgraf*. The upper images show the wreck from the stern, showing how the wreck leans and the dispersal of debris around it. The bottom images show the wreck from the bow. In both cases the result of removing the armour is evident along the slightly higher starboard side.

has split, revealing its thickness. When measured, it was found to be 15cm. This is consistent with the thickness of the armoured belt at its foremost termination. The belt predominantly protected the middle deck at this point. This reveals that the bow section is buried to around the level of the middle deck as the area recorded was close to the seabed. Perhaps armour of this thickness was not as

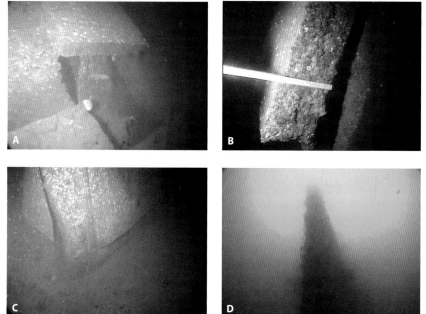

Figure 11.6. Armoured plate of 15cm thickness as seen on the bow section of the wreck in images A and B. Images C and D show the intact bow.

Figure 11.7. Features seen in the area of 'A' and 'B' turrets on SMS *Markgraf*. Images A and B show the doorway and interior of what may be the chain windless compartment. Images C and D show the side of 'B' turret and the counterbalance of 'A' turret.

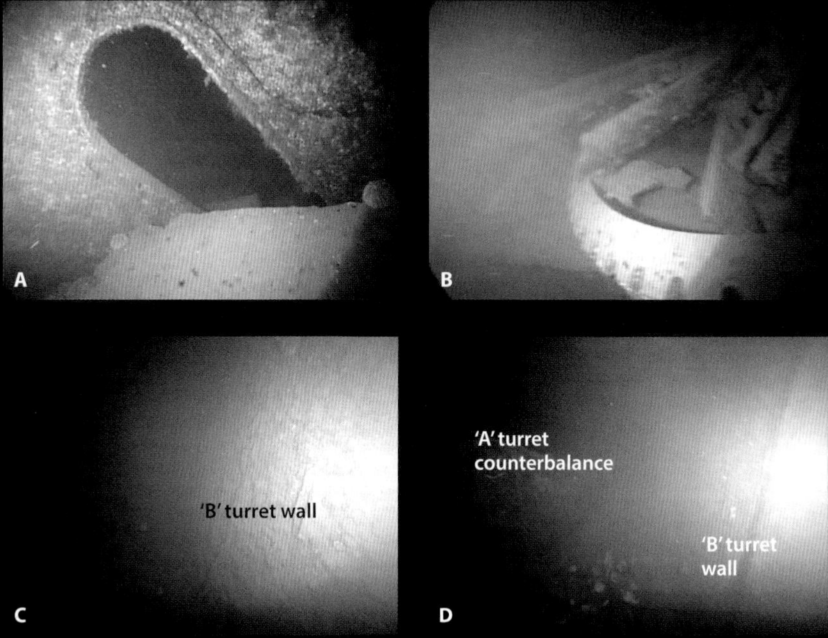

attractive to the salvors, or perhaps it was pulled out to inspect and then for whatever reason left *in situ*. But interestingly, the 17cm bulkhead armour forward was removed. Images C and D show the bow of the *Markgraf* to be intact, in contrast with that of *König*. The multibeam images reveal that the forward torpedo tube has been removed (see Figure 11.17 for exact location). The neater salvage activity on this wreck, which seems to have caused less collateral damage, is probably the reason the bow survived intact.

A little further aft at the level of the seabed a door can be found which leads into a small compartment. This can be seen in Images A and B of Figure 11.7. That a door would appear in the side of an armoured shipwreck is odd, but it is explained by the fact that what one is looking at in this area is not the original side of the ship but the internal longitudinal bulkhead inboard of the armoured belt, which at this point has been salvaged. Peering into this compartment reveals geared machinery which may be a portion of the anchor chain windlass engine.

Just aft of the doorway also at the seabed level it is possible to squeeze under the deck and observe the armoured wall of 'B' turret (Figure 11.7, Image C), and pushing further forward into a confined area, the counterbalance of 'A' turret can be reached (at the centre of Image D). In the narrow space between the two turrets it is possible to turn around in order to come out. The angle of lean of the wreck can be discerned from the angle of the counterbalance.

Another fascinating area of the ship to explore can be accessed through another doorway in the side of the ship. This one is at around 36m depth and

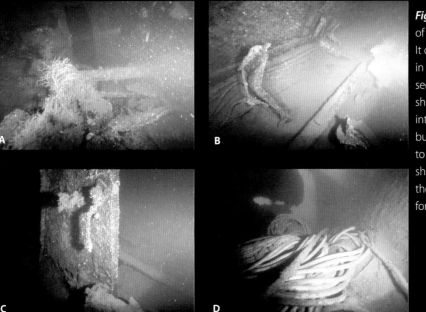

Figure 11.8. An examination of the area of the middle deck. It can be accessed via a door in the side of the wreck, as seen in image A. Image B shows the knees on the interior of the transverse bulkhead; C shows what looks to be an open hatch; and D shows a mass of hose which then leads out into the forward break in the wreck.

in line with the after end of 'B' turret, as shown in Figure 11.13. Image A in Figure 11.8 shows the door being illuminated by Amy Cromarty. It appears that this door gives access to the wreck in the space between the armoured (middle) deck and the main deck. Across the compartment the walls of

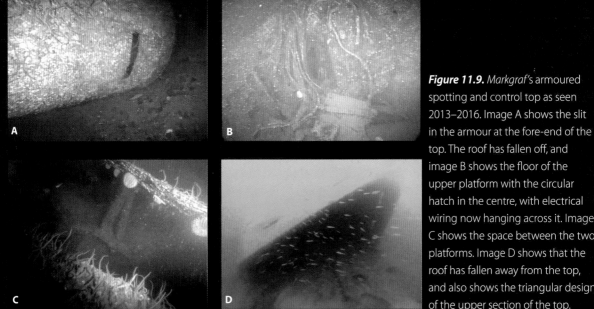

Figure 11.9. *Markgraf's* armoured spotting and control top as seen 2013–2016. Image A shows the slit in the armour at the fore-end of the top. The roof has fallen off, and image B shows the floor of the upper platform with the circular hatch in the centre, with electrical wiring now hanging across it. Image C shows the space between the two platforms. Image D shows that the roof has fallen away from the top, and also shows the triangular design of the upper section of the top.

'A' & 'B' turret barbettes can be dimly made out. Entering the door and turning left, the survey dive followed the inner side of the outer wall of the wreck. Here are what appeared to be a number of the knees supporting the main deck below (remember that the wreck is upside down), shown in Image B.

Further along, what looked like an open deck hatch was seen. One wonders whether this had been jammed in its open position to assist the ship's scuttling, a rare example of human agency on a modern shipwreck. Green light appeared quickly as the forward break came into view, as seen in Image D. This short swim through the wreck ended with looking down on what appeared to be the last unsalvaged vestiges of the forward armoured bulkhead.

Another area recorded was the armoured spotting and control top. This lies on the seabed a little way off the wreck on the starboard side. Its details can be seen in Figure 11.9. It comprises two platforms, the upper of which was triangular in design and originally held a rangefinder. The lower was circular. Both platforms were used to control the gunnery system of the ship. Image A shows the viewing slit at the front of the upper platform which now lies on its side. Swimming around to the right, it was found that the top of this platform had fallen off, so the inside could be seen. The deck and circular hatch into the heavy mast can be seen in Image B. Image C shows the gap between the two platforms and shows the support around the thick mast which supported the upper platform. Finally, on another survey dive the top was recorded with a wider-angle lens, showing how the roof has fallen away and showing its

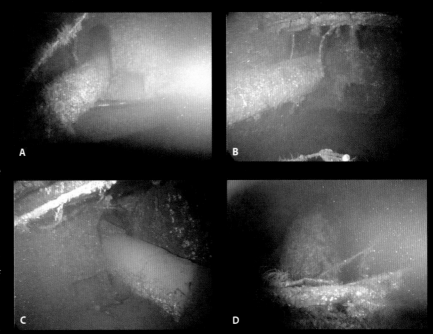

Figure 11.10. Nearly all of the row of 5.9-inch guns along the starboard side of the wreck can be seen in various spots at the seabed level, as shown in Images A–C. Image D shows the mount of one of these guns exposed because the armour at this point on the wreck has been salvaged.

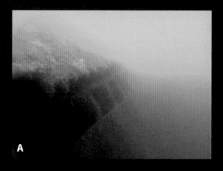

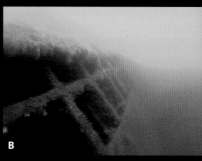

Figure 11.11. A strip of steel near the uppermost portion of the wreck appears to have been deliberately pulled out of the wreck.

A   B

triangular design. It looks as if the mast might have been twisted as the forward part is actually in the top right of the image, pointing slightly upwards.

The central area of the wreck is characterized by the row of 5.9-inch guns which run along the side of the ship. The four forward-facing ones are easier to see, and examples are shown in Images A & B in Figure 11.10. The one in Image A appears largely intact, with its protective shroud in place. Conversely, in Image B some of the casemate appears to have fallen away or been removed. Image C shows one of the aft-facing guns. Image D is particularly interesting. It is all too easy to focus on specific items of interest and miss surrounding features. Looking up from one of the forward-facing guns, the mount can be seen. This reveals that the armoured plate which ran along the main and upper decks has also been removed. These are the very guns which claimed a British destroyer at the Battle of Jutland.

Figure 11.12. The impressive twin rudders of SMS *Markgraf* seen in clear conditions, with a diver for scale. (Gavin Anderson)

Figure 11.13. Image A shows the impressive twin rudders of SMS *Markgraf* seen in somewhat gloomy conditions. Image B shows a doorway in a bulkhead near the port side 'A' frame which leads into the interior of the wreck at this point.

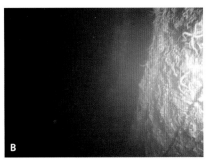

Another interesting feature on this wreck is the fact that strips of steel have been peeled away from her in various places. In Figure 11.11 a strip of the thinner steel near the top of the wreck has been removed in this fashion. This is clearly salvage activity. Perhaps it was removed for a specific reason, possibly to see inside the ship at this point in the hunt for valuable metals (the salvors of this wreck apparently did not have detailed plans). It could have also have been removed to check its chemistry. Nickel and chromium content made some of the ship's structure relatively more valuable.

The stern section of the wreck is dominated by the graceful curved stern and the impressive upright twin rudders. These can be seen in Figure 11.12. The diver in the photograph helps give an indication of the rudders' impressive size. The rudders are shown from the starboard side in Image A of Figure 11.13. They are the best example of this feature on any of the three battleships.

On the starboard side a little forward of the rudders there is a gash in the side of the hull which, with a squeeze, leads into the compartment with a door seen in Image B of Figure 11.13 on the right-hand side. It leads some way into the wreck.

Figure 11.14 highlights the locations on the hybrid model of the wreck of the features shown in the series of underwater images. It was a very useful exercise to reconcile the images from the survey video files with their locations on the wreck model. The great amount of detail on the hybrid model made the task relatively straightforward.

One interesting feature of the wreck is a heavy chain which is wrapped around her, right across the keel and down the starboard side. The level of detail on the multibeam scans means that this chain can be seen very clearly on the DTM of the wreck and also on the point cloud in the hybrid model. The orientation of the wreck, lying west to east, is out of line with the orientation of all of the other surviving warships. It shows that *Markgraf* may have been detached from one of its moorings during her scuttling, possibly in the abortive attempt by the Royal Navy to beach her. *Markgraf* appears then to have got wrapped around this chain as she foundered.

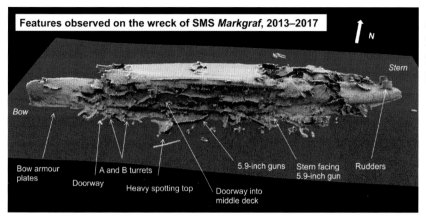

Figure 11.14. Hybrid model of SMS *Markgraf* highlighting the features depicted in the previous underwater images.

Structural changes observed in the wreck of SMS *Markgraf*, 2006–2017

The wreck was first surveyed in the weeks after she sank and was recorded as being 20 metres from the surface.[22] Today it is 4 metres deeper to the top of the wreck. So over time she seems to have gradually sunk deeper into the seabed. The wreck's highest point of 24m was reported in 1998 is still the same today, so no collapse in recent years is obvious.[23] The changes in the wreck most likely occurred during the salvage years up to 1977. As the deepest of the surviving battleship wrecks, she is also the most upside down. This could suggest that, compared with the others, she had more time as she sank to roll over to the vertical before she impacted the seabed. But, like *König*, she may have rolled more to her current orientation over her nine decades on the bottom of Scapa Flow.

As the multibeam and diving images reveal, *Markgraf* is the most intact of the three battleship wrecks. This can be observed in several ways. Figures 11.15 and 11.16 use the same methodology as was used on *König* to depict

Figure 11.15. A slice through the entire length of the multibeam point cloud of the wreck of SMS *Markgraf* incorporated into a drawing of the ship, showing how the targeting by salvors of her key economic resources has shaped the way the wreck looks today.

Elevation drawing of SMS *Markgraf* overlaid on the longitudinal slice through the centre of the multibeam point cloud of the wreck

☐ Engines & machinery ■ Propellers ■ Armour belt ☐ Torpedo tubes ☐ Boilers & uptakes

Bow collapsed

Figure 11.16. A slice through point cloud of SMS *Markgraf* at frame no. 74 overlaid on a section drawing of the ship at that location, revealing the neatly removed armoured belt from the ship's sides and 15-degree lean to port of the wreck.

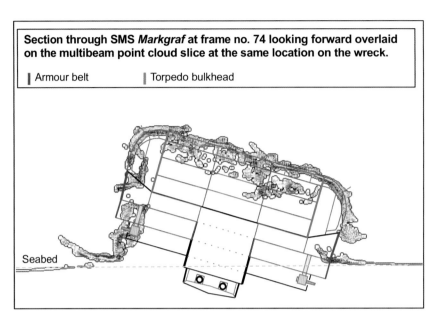

Section through SMS *Markgraf* at frame no. 74 looking forward overlaid on the multibeam point cloud slice at the same location on the wreck.

▌Armour belt   ▌Torpedo bulkhead

Seabed

what remains of the wreck today. The drawings of the wreck in both elevation and section at frame no. 74 are shown. Figure 11.15 shows the far better overall condition of the wreck when compared with *König*. Instantly recognizable is the much more intact nature of the stern area. The work carried out on the wreck by Nundy Marine Metals was limited to the removal of the torpedo tubes and portions of the engine room. The propellers had been removed by Metal Industries.

The majority of the blasting into the hull to remove the armour was carried out by Scapa Flow Salvage Ltd in the years 1972 to 1977. It initially worked on the side armour and then removed the armoured transverse bulkheads fore

Figure 11.17. Large sections of the armoured deck survived the salvage of the belt, as shown in the hybrid model of *Markgraf*. Only very minor structural changes can be observed on the multibeam scans from 2006 and 2017. These appear to be limited to the collapse of the port-side bilge keel.

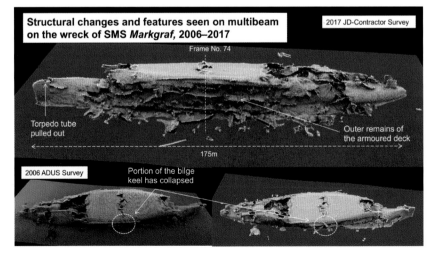

Structural changes and features seen on multibeam on the wreck of SMS *Markgraf*, 2006–2017

2017 JD-Contractor Survey

Frame No. 74

Torpedo tube pulled out

Outer remains of the armoured deck

175m

2006 ADUS Survey

Portion of the bilge keel has collapsed

and aft. The evidence clearly shows that it was a much neater worker than Nundy Marine Metals. The collateral damage appears to be far less, especially in the attempt to remove the after armoured bulkhead. On the other two battleship wrecks this has caused the stern to collapse, but on *Markgraf* this is not the case, and it appears that if it was removed then it has been very neatly lifted out of the wreck. There is more access to the forward bulkhead because the bow section has collapsed, opening the wreck at this point.

Figure 11.18. No visit to Scapa Flow is complete without the walk up the hill at Lyness to remember all those buried there. The dead from the Grand Scuttle lie in the German plot alongside Walter Schumann. They are a reminder of the chaotic and sometimes violent scenes which took place on that momentous day.

The blasting by Nundy into the engine room is clearly evident and extensive.

Figure 11.16 shows the section through the wreck at frame no. 74. It shows the angle of lean to be 15 degrees to port. It reveals that the sides of the wreck are also in better condition overall than seen on *König*. It is clear that the heavy armoured belt has been removed from the port and starboard sides. Interestingly, this process has not completely disturbed the armoured deck or the outer structure of the lower hull. It is known that the divers who removed the belt worked from inside the coal bunker behind the belt (for a section diagram of the König class, see Figure 10.2) and set charges which removed the belt in manageable pieces, blasting them outwards to be later lifted from where they fell on the seabed.[24]

This process seems to be reason the armoured deck is visible in Figure 11.16 although clearly bent downwards. It is also discernible on the hybrid model, highlighted in Figure 11.17. It also seems as if portions of the much weaker main and upper decks survived the removal of the armoured belt as well, and they too can be seen in places. The doorway which led into the area shown in Figure 11.8 was in the space between the main and armoured decks, and a good portion of the main deck could be seen on the wreck's exterior in that area in 2014.

Interestingly, comparing the ADUS multibeam survey of 2006 with the 2017 survey, practically no discernible differences of any consequence can be seen. As shown in Figure 11.17, only a portion of the keel of the ship in the region where the heavy chain crosses the bilge keel appears to have collapsed in that time. It may have been caused by the chain being snagged from above. If this was the case, it would not represent collapse at all but damage from another cause. On *König* it was surprising to see how little that wreck had changed; on *Markgraf* it is even more surprising.

Conclusions

SMS *Markgraf* is another fascinating example of the more famous warships on the seabed of Scapa Flow. Her combat record and her survival through shellfire and mine are of course historically notable. But her social history is too, with her role in the naval mutiny. Equally poignant is the sad loss of the ship's captain – a man who died doing his nation's duty in peacetime – and his senior mate during the Grand Scuttle. Captain Schumann is buried in Lyness alongside the graves of his countrymen from both world wars.

As a shipwreck, SMS *Markgraf* is one of the most popular with visiting divers. It is not hard to see why. She is an imposing wreck that is always exciting and educative to explore. Ultimately one gets a uniquely personal insight into these mighty warships by being able to interact with them. In that regard, *Markgraf* is especially generous in what she reveals.

1   H. J. Koerver (ed.) (2009), Room 40: German Naval Warfare 1914–1918. Volume 2: The Fleet in Being (Steinbach: LIS Reinisch), p. 21.

2   G. Staff (2010), *German Battleships 1914–18 (2)* (Oxford: Osprey), p. 29.

3   National Archives (various dates), O. Groos, *The Battle of Jutland: Official German Account*, Admiralty translation, 1926, ADM 186/626, pp. 74–75. London.

4   N. J. M. Campbell (1986), *Jutland: An Analysis of the Fighting* (London: Conway), pp. 144–145.

5   N. J. M. Campbell (1986), *Jutland: An Analysis of the Fighting* (London: Conway), pp. 162, 193–195.

6   N. J. M. Campbell (1986), *Jutland: An Analysis of the Fighting* (London: Conway), pp. 206, 245.

7   National Archives (various dates), O. Groos, *The Battle of Jutland: Official German Account*, Admiralty translation, 1926, ADM 186/626, Chart 34. London.

8   National Archives (various dates), O. Groos, *The Battle of Jutland: Official German Account*, Admiralty translation, 1926, ADM 186/626, p. 200. London.

9   I. McCartney (2008), *British Submarines of WW I* (Oxford: Osprey), p. 40.

10 H. J. Koerver (ed.) (2009), *Room 40: German Naval Warfare 1914–1918. Volume 2: The Fleet in Being* (Steinbach: LIS Reinisch), p. 21.

11 D. Woodward (1973), *The Collapse of Power: Mutiny in the High Seas Fleet* (London: Arthur Baker), p. 133.

12 National Archives and Records Administration (various dates), microfilmed records of the German Navy, PG64939, Roll T1022-1629. Washington, DC.

13   National Archives and Records Administration (various dates), microfilmed records of the German Navy, PG64939, Roll T1022-1629. Washington, DC.

14   University of California Irvine (various dates), Arthur J. Marder Papers MS.F.002, correspondence with Cmdr W. M. Phipps Hornby. Irvine, CA.

15   National Archives and Records Administration (various dates), microfilmed records of the German Navy, PG64939, Roll T1022-1629. Washington, DC.

16   National Archives and Records Administration (various dates), microfilmed records of the German Navy, PG64939, Roll T1022-1629. Washington, DC.

17   National Archives (various dates), sinking of German Fleet at Scapa Flow, ADM 116/2074. London.

18   A. J. Marder (1970), *From the Dreadnought to Scapa Flow: The Royal Navy in the Fisher Era, 1904–1919. Volume V: Victory and Aftermath* (OUP: London), p. 282.

19   Naval Historical Branch (various dates), *CP 8a Sale Book*, p. 138. Portsmouth.

20   B. Jackson (2010), *But Not All Men Live! From Scapa to Africa and All Dives in Between. The true tale of a diver who did it all, and lived* (Fareham: Barry Jackson), pp. 93–97.

21   ScapaMAP 2000–2002 (2003), Report Compiled for Historic Scotland on the Mapping and Management of the Submerged Archaeological Resource in Scapa Flow. Orkney: Scapa Flow Marine Archaeology Project, Appendix III.

22   Hydrographic Department of the Admiralty (2017), Record of Wreck No. 1087 SMS *Markgraf* (Taunton: Hydrographic Office).

23   R. Macdonald (1998), *Dive Scapa Flow* (Edinburgh: Mainstream), p. 80.

24   R. Macdonald (1998), *Dive Scapa Flow* (Edinburgh: Mainstream), p. 141.

CHAPTER 12
SMS *KRONPRINZ WILHELM*

Figure 12.1. SMS *Kronprinz* (as she was then) early in her career equipped with torpedo nets and the early version of the armoured spotting and control top which featured an open lower platform, later enclosed. (Orkney Archive)

This König-class battleship is the third of its type still lying in Scapa Flow. While appearing to be the wreck which has suffered the most through time, she is still fascinating. Her service history involved surviving battles and torpedo hits, and her 12-inch guns which fired at the Battle of Jutland and Moon Sound are uniquely visible among the High Seas Fleet wrecks at Scapa Flow.

Design and service history

SMS *Kronprinz* (as she was named when commissioned) was the last of the König-class battleships to be built. She was built at Germania, Kiel and entered service with the 3rd Squadron in February 1915. The squadron was divided into two divisions. Along with her three sisters *König, Markgraf* and *Grosser Kurfürst*, she made up the 5th Division. The 6th was made up of the earlier Kaiser class, whose salvaged remains have already been described.

She was in nearly all regards the same as *Grosser Kurfürst*, except that *Grosser Kurfürst* had her 88mm guns under the after funnel removed in 1918. *Kronprinz* and *Grosser Kurfürst* can be distinguished from *König* and *Markgraf* in 1918 because only the latter pair had admirals' bridges and also the later, slightly more compact two-platform armoured spotting and control tops.[1]

Both *Kronprinz* and *Grosser Kurfürst* were fitted originally with the cigar mast and a single control top, which appears to have initially had an open crow's nest on a platform underneath it. Later photographs of *Kronprinz* show that the crow's nest was enclosed at some point, so that the whole arrangement looks similar to the later design two-platform type, except for the fact that the upper top looks noticeably taller on *Kronprinz* and *Grosser Kurfürst*. Images of the control top on the wreck can be seen in Figure 12.9.

SMS *Kronprinz* in service

The service life of SMS *Kronprinz* bears many similarities to the lives of *König* and *Markgraf*. The early war was characterized by sweeps and minelaying operations in the North Sea and training in the Baltic. On 8 May 1915 the right gun of 'C' turret suffered a premature explosion. Operations in 1916 began with a North Sea sweep in March. In April she sortied as part of the long-range cover for the Lowestoft and Great Yarmouth raid and the following month she took part in the Battle of Jutland.

As previously described, the 5th Division was in the van of the German battlefleet during the battle. The division entered the fight with *Kronprinz* fourth in line, aft of her sisters. On the order to open fire *Kronprinz* was initially unsighted but within minutes was firing at the cruiser HMS *Dublin* and then at the battleship HMS *Malaya*, on which she claimed a hit at 1717hrs.

As the initial 'Run to the North' developed into the general fleet action, the disabled light cruiser SMS *Wiesbaden* became the centre of attention for passing British ships, including two destroyers. One, HMS *Onslow*, passed beyond the stricken ship to launch a torpedo attack on *Kronprinz* at 8,000 yards. Both torpedoes passed astern of her and were seen by the 6th Division in line astern. The allure of the damaged *Wiesbaden* drew in the

British 1st Cruiser Squadron, which subsequently passed far too close to the German battle line, leading directly to the destruction of HMS *Defence* and fatal damage to HMS *Warrior*. During this action, hits were claimed by the ships of the 5th Division, including *Kronprinz*.[2]

Although severely shaken by several near misses, *Kronprinz* remained unscathed during the battle, and after the German line had extracted itself from the fighting by a final reversal of course and fell into night order, the 3rd Division was in the centre of the German line. The night actions mainly affected the head of the German line, but at around 0200hrs on 1 June the 3rd Division altered course to avoid torpedoes. One was seen to explode in the wake of *Kronprinz*. This attack by destroyers led by HMS *Faulknor* sunk the old battleship SMS *Pommern* with all hands.[3] Throughout the battle *Kronprinz* fired 144 rounds from her main guns. Interestingly, her secondary armament was not used at all, and she was the only German dreadnought at Jutland not to use it. Undamaged, *Kronprinz* was ready for action the day following her return to base.

She took part in the fleet operations of July, August and September. Baltic training followed and the 3rd Squadron was passing back into the North Sea in time to take part in the operation off the Jutland coast in November to try and recover two stranded U-boats, *U20* (the nemesis of the *Lusitania*) and *U30*. *U30* had got herself free but *U20* had to be blown up where she was stuck fast.[4] *U20*'s conning tower, periscope and other items are now part of the collection on display at the Sea War Museum Jutland.

On the return leg *Kronprinz* and *Grosser Kurfürst* were torpedoed by the British submarine HMS *J1*. *Kronprinz* was struck under 'A' turret, but although she shipped 250 tons of water, she was otherwise unaffected; the torpedo bulkhead prevented anything more than superficial damage. Repairs took one month, after which the normal routine of training and patrolling continued. On training manoeuvres on 5 March 1917 *Kronprinz* was accidentally in collision with *Grosser Kurfürst*. This time the damage (in the region of 'B' turret) was more serious, with 600 tons of water entering the ship and repairs carrying on until 14 May.

In September 1917 *Kronprinz* joined the naval forces being readied for what became Operation *Albion*, the conquest of the Baltic islands. After coastal bombardment duties, on 17 October she took part in the battle of Moon Sound alongside her sister SMS *König*. *Kronprinz* engaged the Russian pre-dreadnought *Graschdanin* (ex-*Tsarevitch*) and *König* the *Slava*. Before the Russian forces withdrew, *Kronprinz* landed two hits as well as engaging the cruiser *Bayan*. Minor grounding while leaving the Baltic led to repairs in Wilhelmshaven until January 1918.[5]

Further fleet advances and picket duties followed. Then on 15 June 1918 *Kronprinz* was formally renamed SMS *Kronprinz Wilhelm* in honour of the Crown Prince, heir to the Kaiser. In October she was in Wilhelmshaven preparing for a major sortie into the North Sea when the battlefleet succumbed to mutiny.

Mutiny, internment and scuttling

The 1st Division played a major part in the refusal to sail and the consequent collapse of naval discipline. On 28 October the crew of *Kronprinz Wilhelm* and *König* became mutinous, refusing orders. Aboard *Kronprinz Wilhelm* the crew charged their officers with trying to subvert the armistice negotiations by planning a suicide mission.[6] This was the same claim made by the crew of *Markgraf* the following day. The 3rd Division was transferred to the Jade Bight, but as Admiral Scheer plaintively concluded, 'upon the hoisting of the red flag the history of the Imperial Navy came to an end'.[7]

On 19 November SMS *Kronprinz Wilhelm* departed Wilhelmshaven for Scotland and internment in Scapa Flow. On the day of the Grand Scuttle she sank beneath the waves at 1315hrs in the midst of the great wave of sinking taking place around that time. *Moltke* had sunk just before her at 1310hrs and *Kaiser* followed at 1325hrs. The rancour felt by the British took a long time to subside. Admiral Fremantle's apparent order that the German sailors were to be treated with a minimum of courtesy inevitably led to violence and robbery. A crewman from *Kronprinz Wilhelm* received a punch in the mouth which lost him his false teeth.[8]

History as a wreck

The history of this wreck is similar to that of SMS *König* and SMS *Markgraf*. She was sold to Metal Industries in 1936 and was bought and sold over the following years until finally protected as a monument in 2002. Salvage operations followed a similar pattern to *König*. Nundy Marine Metals recovered much of her armoured belt and non-ferrous components. It seems that whereas Nundy had been slowly removing metals for several years, there was a significant push to recover the last of the armour from *Kronprinz* and *König* during 1970.[9]

When Scapa Flow Salvage began work on this wreck it focused on the removal of whatever it could find that had not previously been recovered.[10] This seems to have primarily been the remaining side armour, of which some residual portions are said to remain buried in the seabed on the south side of the wreck. The wreck is the most damaged of the three battleships, but in some ways it is also the most attractive to dive due to the features which can be seen.

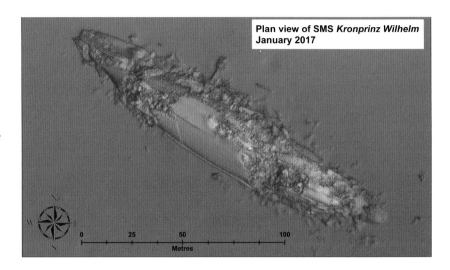

Figure 12.2. Plan view DTM of SMS *Kronprinz Wilhelm* as scanned in January 2017. The wreck is revealed to be the most damaged of the three battleships, bearing the usual marks of extensive commercial salvage in the past.

SMS *Kronprinz Wilhelm* today

The multibeam DTM of SMS *Kronprinz Wilhelm* can be seen in Figure 12.2. At first view this wreck looks appreciably different from the other two battleship wrecks, even though they are of an identical design. Whereas the central hull portions of *König* and *Markgraf* look to be upside down and largely intact, *Kronprinz Wilhelm* looks to have become somewhat flattened. Instantly recognizable are features such as the foremast and control top which lie on the north side of the wreck, having snapped as the ship sank. Almost the entire length of the starboard-side bilge keel can be seen running along the central portion of the wreck on the south side. The wreck's orientation, pointing to the northwest, is consistent with the ship sinking on her mooring on the day she was scuttled. All the surviving wrecks are orientated in this way except *Markgraf*.

The original point cloud converted into a hybrid model is shown in Figures 12.3 and 12.4. As with *König*, the wreck is clearly broken at both bow and stern, and like both of the other battleships, the area of the engine rooms has been opened by salvors using explosives. Uniquely of the three battleships, *Kronprinz Wilhelm* leans to the starboard side. Equally uniquely, the lean is extreme and probably closely represents the orientation the wreck first took when she settled on the bottom of Scapa Flow.

Figures 12.3 and 12.4 both reveal that this is the most collapsed of the three battleships. Alongside the fore and aft section, the area around the engine room is the most damaged, opened and collapsed of the three battleship wrecks. Like *König*, the wreck received much of the structural damage through the salvage works of Nundy Marine Metals, which seems to have caused wider patterns of damage than those that followed.

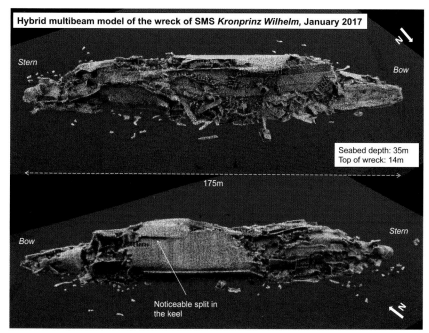

Hybrid multibeam model of the wreck of SMS *Kronprinz Wilhelm*, January 2017

Stern

Bow

Seabed depth: 35m
Top of wreck: 14m

175m

Bow

Stern

Noticeable split in
the keel

Figure 12.3. The hybrid model of SMS *Kronprinz Wilhelm* reveals the wreck to be broken in a way which is similar to SMS *König*. She has a much more pronounced lean than the other two battleship wrecks.

The overall depth of the seabed is 35 metres and the top of the wreck was recorded in 2017 at 14 metres. In 1919 the top of the wreck was recorded as being at 11 metres, so the wreck has subsided by 3 metres. This has occurred in recent years because as late as 2008 the top of the wreck was recorded by commercial survey as being a similar 11.4 metres. By 2010, when resurveyed, this had dropped to 12.25 metres.[11]

Key features of note seen during video surveys of the wreck from 2013 are shown in Figures 12.4 to 12.11 and the locations of the features depicted are given in Figure 12.13. As with the other battleships I have chosen the important features, but also those which tend to show the condition of the wreck itself.

The underwater images of the wreck start at the stern. In Figure 12.5 the mighty 12-inch guns of the 'D' and 'E' turrets are shown. In Image A it can be seen that the stern portion of the wreck has collapsed to the extent that the muzzles of the guns of the 'E' turret are now being forced into the afterdeck as it has slumped down onto them. It was a bit of squeeze getting in there, but I was able to get under the port-side gun and turn around, and Image B shows the view looking back at the glacis plate of 'E' turret with its two guns on either side. This is one of the truly iconic images one can see on the battleship wrecks, with *Kronprinz Wilhelm* alone allowing such access to her main armament.

Moving further aft, the way in which the two after turrets relate to each other becomes clear. In Image A of Figure 12.6 the port-side 12-inch gun of

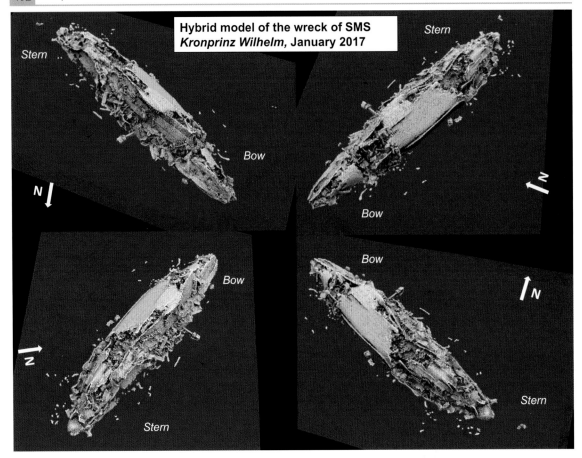

Hybrid model of the wreck of SMS *Kronprinz Wilhelm*, January 2017

Figure 12.4. All-round views of the wreck of SMS *Kronprinz Wilhelm*. The highest point of the wreck is at the surviving keel section on the starboard side. The very pronounced lean of the wreck to starboard is also clearly evident.

Figure 12.5. Both images depict features of the 'E' turret on *Kronprinz Wilhelm*. In Image A, the muzzles of the 12-inch guns are buried in the afterdeck as it has collapsed down onto them. Turning around, Image B shows the glacis plate of the 'E' turret. An opening out to the seabed can be seen on the right.

'D' turret can be seen as it lies on the seabed under the wreck. The starboard gun is buried now. The manner of the gun's construction as a series of three sleeved tubes and a jacket can be seen at its end. Unlike British versions, there was no cable winding on the barrels of German heavy naval guns. The thick inner tube is clearly visible. Only 190 of these guns were made and few can be seen now. This is a finely made weapon which the British estimated cost around six times as much as the equivalent British version.[12]

Image B shows that overhanging the gun is the roof of 'E' turret. This perfectly illustrates the overlying nature of the superfiring arrangement of

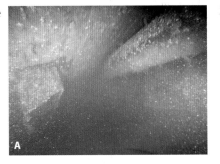

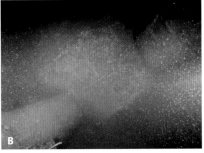

Figure 12.6. The 12-inch guns of 'D' turret on *Kronprinz Wilhelm*, showing inner sleeve in Image A. Image B shows how the same gun lies with the roof of 'E' turret above it, with the turret's officer's sighting hood above.

these turrets. The area between the two turrets is notably compact, more so than one might imagine. There is only a very narrow space between the counterbalance of 'E' turret and the armoured ring of the superfiring 'D' turret. Image B also reveals the presence of the officer's sighting hood in the roof of 'E' turret. This is how the item is labelled on British intelligence papers, and it may have been able to fulfil that role.[13] In reality, though, it is the right-hand lens of the turret's individual rangefinder, as shown in Figure 12.7. The left-hand lens (which probably was the one which could also function as the officer's sighting hood) was situated between the guns and is now buried. This rangefinder would have been used as a last resort if the wider rangefinders situated elsewhere (e.g. at the top of the foremast) had been knocked out.

Moving forward, one comes to a large piece of armour now lying on the seabed, as shown in Images A and B of Figure 12.8. In Image A, a slit can be seen in the centre. This armoured plate is curved and can be matched on wartime photographs of the König class to a position just forward of the aftermost 5.9-inch gun. This is sometimes given as the position of the after port-side torpedo control station.[14] The top (once the bottom) of the plate was slightly tricky to measure because it appeared to still be attached to remnants of the upper deck, as seen in Image B. It was measured at 20cm thickness, confirming it to be from the armoured belt surrounding the casemate guns.

The extreme angle of lean on this wreck means that the actual upper deck where the 5.9-inch guns were mounted is elevated above the level of the seabed by around 4 metres (see Figure 12.15 later in this chapter). It took a dive in better visibility to spot one of these guns in the same area when looking up from the seabed. This gun can be seen in Images C and D of Figure 12.8. It was something of a surprise and

Figure 12.7. The right-hand lens housing for the rangefinder on the 'E' turret of *Kronprinz Wilhelm*. This is situated on the port side of the turret roof, outward of the line of the port gun. A control shaft can be seen to the left of it.

Figure 12.8. The casemates on the upper deck housed 5.9-inch guns. The armour aft of 'D' turret has fallen out and is on the seabed. Further inwards and upwards, a 5.9-inch gun can still be seen clinging to the deck to which it was mounted – but for how much longer?

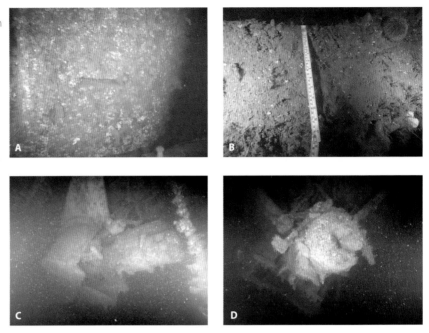

a little unnerving to see this immensely heavy gun, still retaining its shield and resolutely clinging to the deck to which it was mounted. The stresses on the bolts holding it to the 3cm-thick upper deck must be immense. Of course, inevitably it must fall off as the wreck continues to degrade. Visiting divers

Figure 12.9. Images of the control top and heavy foremast on SMS *Kronprinz Wilhelm*. Images A and D show this mast. The outer skin has mostly rotted away. The top is shown in Image B with the roof missing. Image C shows the collapsed remains on the lower platform.

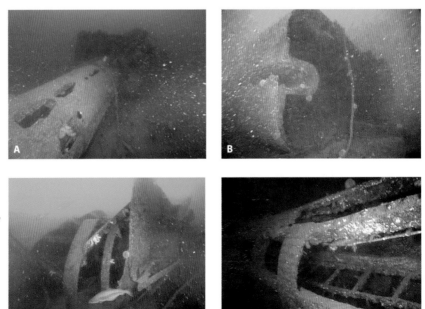

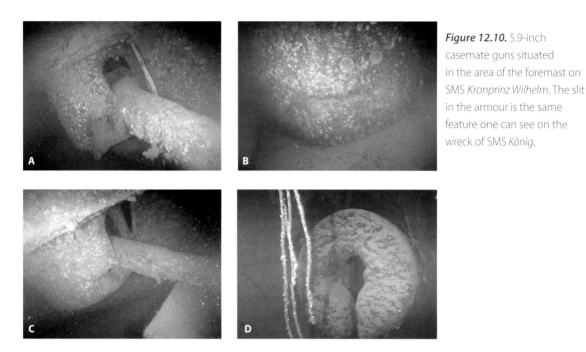

Figure 12.10. 5.9-inch casemate guns situated in the area of the foremast on SMS *Kronprinz Wilhelm*. The slit in the armour is the same feature one can see on the wreck of SMS *König*.

would be well advised to treat objects such as this with considerable caution. It is difficult to imagine any scheduled monument on land still being open to the public with such an obvious potential danger to life being present.

Moving further forward, another feature is the cigar mast and control top as shown in Figure 12.9. The mast itself is now quite rotten, with much of the outer skin gone, as seen in Images A and D. In Image D the ladder used to climb into the top can be clearly seen. The top itself has lost its roof, as shown in Image B, which also shows the slightly triangular design of the top. This structure was solidly made, being splinter proof. There was also a lower platform, as shown in Image C, marking it as a different design to the other two battleship wrecks. Time has not treated the lower platform kindly and it is now very corroded. Nevertheless, the frames and the solid base still survive.

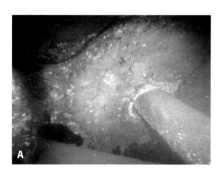
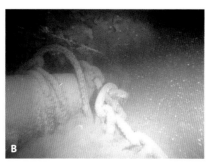

Figure 12.11. Chain windlass and port side 12-inch gun on the wreck of SMS *Kronprinz Wilhelm*.

Figure 12.12. The anchor hawse pipes and bolsters (Images A–C) and the bow (Image D) of the wreck of SMS *Kronprinz Wilhelm.*

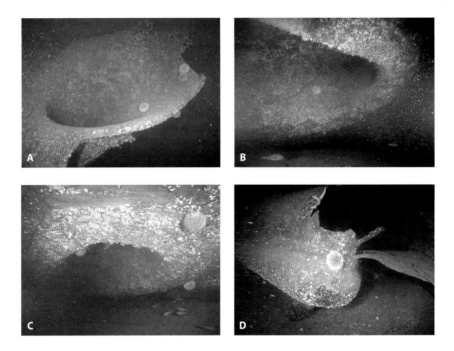

Returning to the body of the wreck itself and the site where the mast is attached leads to an area where more of the casemate guns can be seen. They are much nearer the seabed than the one seen earlier and are shown in Images A and D of Figure 12.10. In Image B a slit in the armour of the casemate belt can be seen. This is exactly the same feature as the one which can be observed on the wreck of SMS *König* (see Figures 10.3 and 10.10). It is described as the location of a torpedo control station. Image D shows a close-up of the breech of one of the 5.9-inch guns. This is a typically iconic image of the way all of the breeches of these guns look across all of the surviving wrecks of the Grand Scuttle.

Moving further forward and looking carefully in the region of the forward turrets, it is possible to just get under the foredeck in a number of places. In one area the shaft of one of the forward anchor chain windlasses can be seen to have fallen out through the upturned deck and onto the seabed. This was most probably caused by the salvage of the windlass machinery in the forward area of the ship. The shaft in its current position can be seen in Image A of Figure 12.11. Beyond the shaft, in Image B, the barrel of the port-side 12-inch gun of 'A' turret can be seen. It is partially buried in the seabed and has both heavy rope and anchor chain wrapped over it.

Heading forward, there are the unmistakable now partially broken remains of the pair of port-side hawse pipe bolsters, one of which can be seen in Figure 12.12, Image A. The foredeck is now almost touching the seabed at this point, but further glimpses of what is underneath reveal the huge hawse

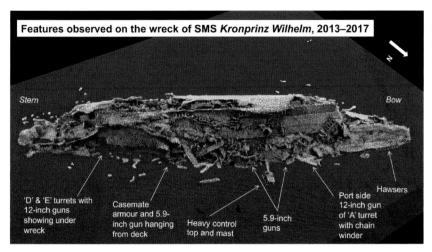

Features observed on the wreck of SMS *Kronprinz Wilhelm*, 2013–2017

Stern

Bow

N

'D' & 'E' turrets with 12-inch guns showing under wreck

Casemate armour and 5.9-inch gun hanging from deck

Heavy control top and mast

5.9-inch guns

Hawsers

Port side 12-inch gun of 'A' turret with chain winder

Figure 12.13. Key features of the wreck of SMS *Kronprinz Wilhelm* as shown in the underwater images highlighted on the hybrid model of the wreck.

pipe openings. Their sheer size when seen up close is impressive. This feature can be seen in Images C and D. Finally, the extreme point of the bow rests on the seabed, with the plating below it (now above) having been clearly torn open, probably as a result of the salvage of the forward-firing torpedo tube.

One of the first survey dives on *Kronprinz Wilhelm* took around an hour just picking through the wreckage along the port side from stern to bow. There are myriad features which can be observed on this fascinating shipwreck, of which only a few are shown here. Time spent on any of the battleship wrecks will reveal an almost endless stream of features which are unique to these very special shipwrecks. All of the features shown in Figures 12.5 to 12.12 are depicted in their locations on the hybrid model of the wreck in Figure 12.13.

Structural changes observed in the wreck, 2006–2017

As with the wrecks of *König* and *Markgraf*, in order to evaluate the current state of collapse, a slice lengthwise through the point cloud of the wreck has been incorporated into the drawing of the König class. This can be seen in Figure 12.14. The similarities to the wreck of SMS *König* are unmistakable, with both ends of the wreck now broken down. The engine room is exposed in much the same manner and the process of blasting to access the transverse bulkheads and torpedo tubes looks very similar.

The wreck's angle of lean is the most extreme of the three battleships, at 39 degrees to starboard. This is probably close to its original orientation on the day she landed on the bottom of Scapa Flow and possibly much closer to the original orientations of *König* and possibly *Markgraf* when they originally

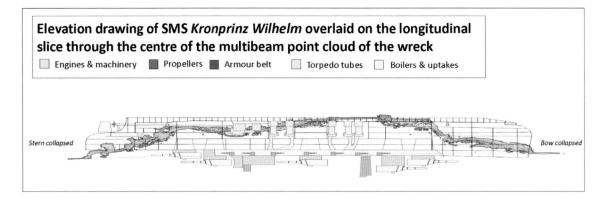

Elevation drawing of SMS *Kronprinz Wilhelm* overlaid on the longitudinal slice through the centre of the multibeam point cloud of the wreck

☐ Engines & machinery ■ Propellers ■ Armour belt ☐ Torpedo tubes ☐ Boilers & uptakes

Stern collapsed

Bow collapsed

Figure 12.14. A slice through the entire length of the multibeam point cloud of SMS *Kronprinz Wilhelm* incorporated into a drawing of the ship, showing how the commercial salvage of this wreck has affected its condition today.

sank. Quite why *Kronprinz Wilhelm* has not rolled more to the horizontal can only be guessed at. But comparing Figure 12.15 with the similar ones for *König* and *Markgraf* (Figures 10.17 and 11.16) reveals that *Kronprinz Wilhelm* is probably much more embedded into the seabed than the others, helping her to retain her steeper orientation.

Looking at Figure 12.15, it seems as if the armoured belt on the lower starboard side of the wreck is in fact buried beneath the seabed, forming a dead weight anchor. This would accord with some accounts which say that not all of the armoured belt on this side of the wreck was recovered in the 1970s.[15] It surely would have taken some effort to dig out the armoured plates from below the seabed. On the upper port side, however, the entire armoured belt was obviously removed, and similar to *König*, the outer wall of the wreck on the port side is now largely made up of the torpedo bulkhead and the collapsed remains of the stubs of the decks and the collapsing double bottom.

Figure 12.15. Slice through the point cloud of SMS *Kronprinz Wilhelm* at frame no. 74 overlaid on a section drawing of the ship at the same location. It shows how the removal of the armoured belt leaves the torpedo bulkhead to make up much of the wreck's outer surface on its port side.

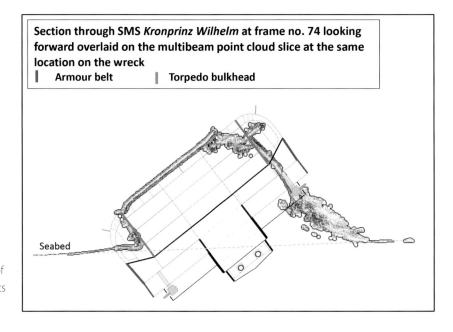

Section through SMS *Kronprinz Wilhelm* at frame no. 74 looking forward overlaid on the multibeam point cloud slice at the same location on the wreck

▌ Armour belt ▌ Torpedo bulkhead

Seabed

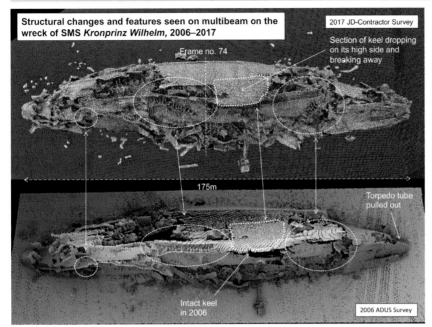

Structural changes and features seen on multibeam on the wreck of SMS *Kronprinz Wilhelm*, 2006–2017

2017 JD-Contractor Survey

Frame no. 74

Section of keel dropping on its high side and breaking away

175m

Torpedo tube pulled out

Intact keel in 2006

2006 ADUS Survey

Figure 12.16. Structural changes observed in the wreck of SMS *Kronprinz Wilhelm* through time as evidenced by multibeam surveys in 2006 and 2017.

On the hybrid model the wreck appears to be twisted somewhat, with the stern and bow sections at a more horizontal angle than the mid-section through frame no. 74 seen in Figure 12.15. This would accord with the visual confirmation that the foredeck is nearly horizontal with the seabed, as seen in Figures 12.11 and 12.12.

That the overall height of the wreck has changed since 1919 is known, as described earlier. But it seems this change in distance to the top of the wreck has occurred since the wreck was surveyed in 2008. The drop seems to be in the region of three metres or so. While it could be explained by the entire structure slipping deeper into the mud, the fact that it has occurred in recent years and has not been a consistent process through time points to another possible explanation – structural collapse. This is of particular interest because, as seen in the previous two chapters, no significant collapse in the other battleships can be observed in the multibeam scans of the wrecks taken in 2006 and 2017. This is not the case with *Kronprinz Wilhelm*. Much more obvious collapse can be seen, and it is significant.

Figure 12.16 compares the multibeam scans of 2006 with the ones made in 2017. In this case a number of changes to the wreck have occurred. By looking at both surveys it is observed that most of the changes are seen on the top and on the port side of the wreck. There is an overall degrading of the port side which can be observed from the stern through to the forward area of collapse. Most markedly this can be seen in the central section of the wreck, near the top. In this area significant changes have taken place since 2006.

These changes primarily involve the double bottom where it used to overhang the edge of the top of the wreck below which the armoured belt

Figure 12.17. Changes to the keel of the wreck of SMS *Kronprinz Wilhelm*, 2006–2017. The large section of double bottom which has shifted its orientation is highlighted and can be seen on Figure 12.16 as well.

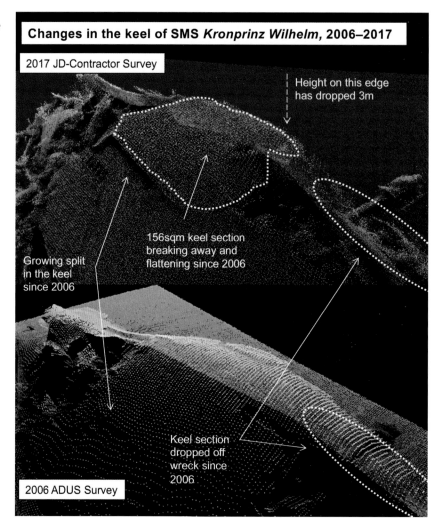

Figure 12.17. Changes to the keel of the wreck of SMS *Kronprinz Wilhelm*, 2006–2017. The large section of double bottom which has shifted its orientation is highlighted and can be seen on Figure 12.16 as well.

had been salvaged. All along this edge the double bottom has broken away and is in the process of sliding down the side of the wreck to the seabed. This process can clearly be seen in the 2017 scan shown in Figure 12.16, with the features which look like sets of stairs. These are breakaway portions of the ship's double bottom. Forward and aft of the plate highlighted in Figures 12.16 and 12.17 noticeable new voids in the top of the wreck have been created by this process. The section of the overhanging double bottom as it looked in 1997, prior to collapse, can be seen in Image A of Figure 12.18.

The partial collapse of the keel at its upper edge explains why the height of this wreck has noticeably changed in the last few years. The highest edge of the wreck has either simply fallen off or has flattened in its orientation. The large section of keel highlighted in Figures 12.16 and 12.17 is the most noticeable

Figure 12.18. Images showing the way the top of the wreck is degrading. Image A was shot in 1997 and shows a portion of the overhanging double bottom on the port side, long since collapsed (John Thornton). Image B was shot in November 2017 and shows the newer spilt in the double bottom and fracturing of the underlying frames.

feature. In fact, before 2006 it was not a discrete piece of wreckage, but still part of the overall top side of the wreck. As is shown in Figure 12.17, a large tear has opened up along the spine of the wreck, splitting the keel into two in the area shown and creating this large piece of potentially unstable wreckage. It is measured on the hybrid model at 12x13 metres (156m^2). It has flattened at its higher point, which partly explains the height drop of the wreck. As with the keel sections either side of it, this section is breaking up. This is seemingly the largest piece of wreckage to be observed to have shifted so dynamically on any of the battleship wrecks in the decades since the salvage years.

The fact that it is breaking away from the rest of the wreck was confirmed by diving in November 2017, when the area was resurveyed by video. The stern end of the split can be seen in Image B of Figure 12.18. It clearly shows how the skin of the keel has been forcibly pulled away by gravity from the double bottom and how the frames inside have fractured. It seems likely that this entire section of wreckage is will inevitably slide off the wreck.

Quite why this has happened is more difficult to say with certainly. Suffice to say, it is likely that the split in the hull has been caused by internal stresses within the wreck which, as described, is notably twisted. The area surrounding the split in the keel contains the forward boiler rooms and the fore-end of 'C' turret structure. These heavy features have been oriented at an angle where gravity was likely at some point to force them to twist into a more vertical orientation.

If in fact these features have shifted in this way it is easy to see how the keel could have split in the way that it has, but this is mere speculation. It is interesting to note that similar overhanging features to those falling off *Kronprinz Wilhelm* can clearly be observed dropping off *König* too, as shown in Chapter 10. These are sections of double bottom which have been unsupported since the armour was blasted off. The surprise is in the fact that it has taken so long for this type of degradation to occur. Divers should be aware that overhanging wreckage may not be as stable as it once was.

Conclusions

The wreck of SMS *Kronprinz Wilhelm* is the shallowest of the three battleship wrecks and the most broken up. Its unique attractions are the 12-inch guns which fired at Jutland and claimed hits on her British enemies. They are magnificent to see and help to make her one of the most popular of the German fleet with divers. In 2004 only SMS *Karlsruhe* was dived more often.[16] But there is much more to this wreck than just the main guns, as this chapter shows. As with the other battleship wrecks, something of interest awaits around every corner.

The salvage years significantly altered way the battleships look today. The armour plate was in theory part of the integral structure of the ships. Its removal could have weakened their integrity, like

Figure 12.19. A rare photograph showing a 26-ton section of armour plate from either *Kronprinz Wilhelm* or *König* on Nundy's pier at Rinnigal awaiting collection in 1970. (Barry Jackson)

taking bricks out of the wall of a house. Ironically though, it may be that the removal of so much dead weight in some way assisted in preserving the overall structures of the ships by relieving stresses on the framework. Certainly the weight of the armoured plates was considerable. It seems that each of the plates blasted off the König-class battleships weighed around 26 tons. The overall weight of armour (although not all was recovered) was around 10,000 tons. A rare photograph of one of the plates recovered, sitting on Nundy's pier at Rinnigal, is shown in Figure 12.19.

The multibeam surveys revealed that of the three battleships, this wreck is the most damaged. In the years since the 2006 ADUS survey the wreck has shown the most advanced signs of collapse of the three battleships. The weight relief aside, it is interesting to note that the way the wrecks are now beginning to degrade has been significantly affected by the prior salvage works carried out on them. The overhanging portions of double bottom can no longer support their own weight and have largely fallen off.

1   G. Staff (2010), *German Battleships 1914–18 (2)* (Oxford: Osprey), p. 29.

2   N. J. M. Campbell (1986), *Jutland: An Analysis of the Fighting* (London: Conway), p. 181.

3   N. J. M. Campbell (1986), *Jutland: An Analysis of the Fighting* (London: Conway), pp. 298–300.

4   R. H. Gibson & M. Prendergast (1931), *The German Submarine War 1914–1918* (London: Constable), p. 118.

5   G. Staff (2010), *German Battleships 1914–18 (2)* (Oxford: Osprey), p. 38.

6   D. Horn (1969), *The German Naval Mutinies of WW1* (New Brunswick: Rutgers University Press), p. 222.

7   D. Horn (1969), *The German Naval Mutinies of WW1* (New Brunswick: Rutgers University Press), p. 234.

8   D. van der Vat (1982), *The Grand Scuttle: The Sinking of the German Fleet at Scapa Flow in 1919* (London: Hodder & Stoughton), p. 179.

9   B. Jackson (2010), *But Not All Men Live! From Scapa to Africa and All Dives in Between. The true tale of a diver who did it all, and lived* (Fareham: Barry Jackson), pp. 92–97.

10 ScapaMAP 2000–2002 (2003), Report Compiled for Historic Scotland on the Mapping and Management of the Submerged Archaeological Resource in Scapa Flow. Orkney: Scapa Flow Marine Archaeology Project, Appendix IIIa.

11 Hydrographic Department of the Admiralty (2017), Record of Wreck No. 1088 SMS *Kronprinz Wilhelm* (Taunton: Hydrographic Office).

12 N. Friedman (2011), *Naval Weapons of World War One: Guns, Torpedoes, Mines and ASW Weapons of All Nations*. An Illustrated Directory (Barnsley: Seaforth), pp. 127–137.

13 N. Friedman (2011), *Naval Weapons of World War One: Guns, Torpedoes, Mines and ASW Weapons of All Nations*. An Illustrated Directory (Barnsley: Seaforth), p. 135.

14 T. Philbin (1973), *Warship Profile 37: SMS König* (Windsor: Profile Publications), p. 19.

15 R. Macdonald (2017), *Dive Scapa Flow* (Edinburgh: Mainstream), p. 125.

16 ScapaMAP (2001–2006), Marine Heritage Monitoring with High Resolution Survey Tools: Scapa Flow 2001–2006. Orkney: Scapa Flow Marine Archaeology Project, p. 4.

CHAPTER 13
SMS *BRUMMER*

Figure 13.1. SMS *Brummer*, launched 11 December 1915. Design displacement 4,316 tons, length 140m, four 5.9-inch and two 88mm guns. Two torpedo tubes and little-used minelaying capability. Note the clipper bow, designed to resemble the British style. (US Naval History & Heritage Command)

SMS Brummer *is the earliest built of the four remaining light cruisers sunk during the Grand Scuttle. Built as a minelayer but hardly used in that capacity, she is notorious for the attack on a convoy off Shetland in October 1917. Alongside* SMS Bremse, *she sank nearly every ship in the convoy, leading to strongly refuted claims of barbarity. The partially salvaged remains of this famous ship are one of jewels in the crown of the Scapa shipwrecks even though she has significantly deteriorated over the last decade.*

Design and service history

SMS *Brummer* and her sister SMS *Bremse* (salvaged by Cox & Danks; see Chapter 7) were designed as minelayer cruisers. She was laid down in 1915 at the A. G. Vulcan yard at Stettin and completed and commissioned in the summer of 1916. This was exceptionally quick, doubtless due to the exceptional nature of the times. These ships' propulsion systems were made up of four turbine sets (two per ship, in separate engine rooms, driving two screws) which had been built for the Russian battlecruiser *Navarin*, but were requisitioned at the start of World War I. The turbine and condenser rooms were situated one in front of the other, in a form also seen in German torpedo boats of this period (see Chapter 18). The layout is shown in Figure 13.2, where it is compared with that of the other light cruiser wrecks at Scapa Flow.[1]

The two cruisers were equipped with six boilers, of which only two burned coal. This is half the number fitted to the later light cruisers (see Figure 13.2). In all respects these were considered to be excellent vessels at sea. When pressed, they were capable of a very respectable 30-plus knots, easily surpassing their original design parameters.[2] They were in fact the fastest cruisers afloat at the time.

SMS *Brummer* was built using longitudinal framing with 21 watertight compartments. She was equipped with a double bottom along 44% of her length which was used to store oil which fired four of the six boilers; the remaining two, slightly smaller boilers (see Figure 13.2) were solely coal-fired. The armoured belt covered the central portion of the ship only and was 40mm thick. She also had a 15mm armoured deck and an armoured conning tower with 100mm-thick walls. The gun shields were also protected.

Originally intended for minelaying, *Brummer* carried a smaller complement of weaponry than usually seen on German light cruisers of this period. This reduced firepower saved space and weight and reduced the crew size by around 309, at least a third less than comparable light cruisers of the same period. She was equipped with four 5.9-inch guns, two situated in a superfiring arrangement aft, one amidships and one forward. She also had a pair of 88mm guns forward of the mainmast. It was observed in 1919 that the reduced number of guns did not affect its firepower in broadside because all the guns were mounted on the centreline. The only weakness was when chasing, which was unlikely if the ship was used in the minelaying role.[3]

Originally she was also equipped with two deck-mounted 20-inch torpedo tubes just aft of the foremast. Some sources say that two more were added in 1917.[4] The mines could be stowed on board, but never were for more than short periods during the war when she did lay mines. The mines were moved around the decks on specially laid rails. She had a planned mine capacity of 360.[5]

SMS *Brummer* and SMS *Bremse* had been built with an eye to making them resemble the British Caroline class of light cruiser. Their upper mast sections could be retracted to look like the shorter British arrangement and their bows were given the distinctive British clipper shape (see Figure 13.2), which was covered with sheet metal during construction to hide this feature from prying eyes.[6] This ruse was probably designed to help disguise them during fast, covert offensive minelaying operations off enemy shores, although they were never used in this capacity.[7]

SMS *Brummer* in service

Although *Brummer* was commissioned in April 1916, in time for the Battle of Jutland, she did not take part. She was involved in the abortive fleet advance towards the British north-east coast on 19–20 August in a screening role. In the afternoon of 19 August she reported being attacked by a submarine. British intelligence remarked that no British submarines were in the area, so if she was attacked, the culprit must have been a U-boat. Such is the risk taken when a ship is designed to resemble the enemy.

In September 1916 she was ordered to sea to locate Zeppelin *L21*, returning from a raid on Britain. SMS *Brummer* was at sea again the following month as part of the German fleet's sortie towards Sunderland. This time the approach was abandoned when the light cruiser SMS *München* was torpedoed by the submarine HMS *E38*.

In December 1916 *Brummer* was transferred to the Fourth Scouting Group and in the new year took part in a minelaying sortie off Holland along with SMS *Bremse* and SMS *Stralsund*, where 300 mines were laid off Norderney.[8] The rest of 1917 was a routine of uneventful guard ship duties until October, when *Brummer* and *Bremse* took part in a convoy raid, which was notable at the time for its controversy.

The October convoy raid came about as a direct result of the institution of the convoy system between Scandinavia and Britain. The convoy system began to be used earlier in the year as a means of parrying the unrestricted submarine assault on shipping unleashed by the Germans in February 1917. While convoys elsewhere, in the Atlantic, the English Channel and the Mediterranean, were successful in thwarting large-scale losses to the U-boats, the proximity of German bases to the Scandinavia run made it vulnerable to a raid.

Germany had no shortage of intelligence about shipping movements on the Scandinavia run, and while much of the fleet was in the Baltic conducting operations against Russia, it was decided to keep some pressure on the North Sea front by launching a raid with the two most capable ships available. With their high speed and endurance and their British-looking lines, *Brummer* and

Figure 13.2. (Opposite) The differing designs of the light cruiser wrecks in Scapa Flow. The smaller *Brummer* is distinct from the other three, which share many design commonalities. Note the different layout of features, including the engine rooms and torpedoes. SMS *Brummer* is shown as she was believed to have been painted for the 1917 convoy raid.

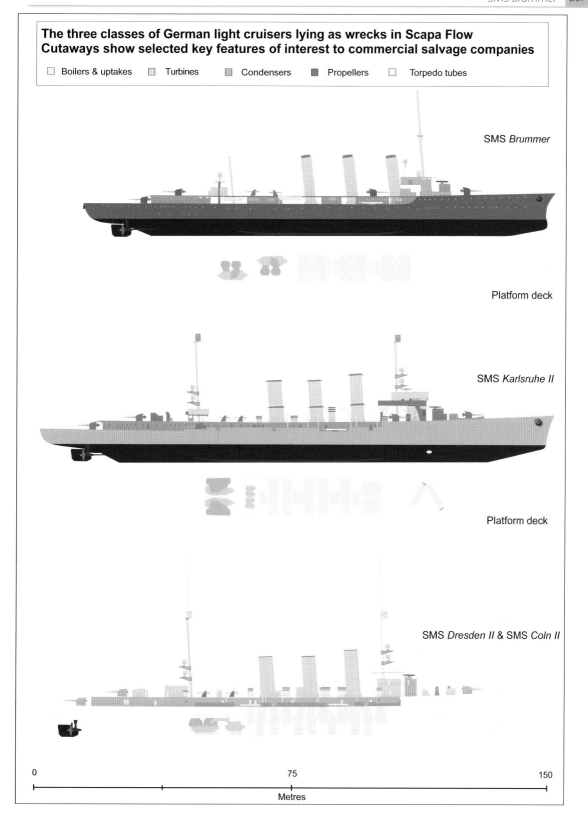

The three classes of German light cruisers lying as wrecks in Scapa Flow
Cutaways show selected key features of interest to commercial salvage companies

☐ Boilers & uptakes ☐ Turbines ☐ Condensers ◼ Propellers ☐ Torpedo tubes

SMS *Brummer*

Platform deck

SMS *Karlsruhe II*

Platform deck

SMS *Dresden II* & SMS *Coln II*

0   75   150

Metres

Bremse were selected to raid the Norway-to-Shetland convoy. As part of the plans for the raid both vessels were repainted to the darker British grey.[9] After passing up the west Denmark coast, the raiders steamed directly to intercept the convoy. Just before dawn on 17 October, 65 miles east of Lerwick, Shetland, they attacked the rear of the west-bound convoy.

The convoy was comprised of 12 merchant ships escorted by two armed trawlers and two destroyers – HMS *Mary Rose* at the head and HMS *Strongbow* at the rear. Hopelessly outmatched, both destroyers were rapidly overwhelmed and sank, along with nine of the merchant vessels. Only the trawlers and three ships escaped. One trawler returned to look for survivors. Unscathed, the German ships immediately turned for base, returning undetected despite the Royal Navy's attempts to locate them.

To the British, the attack was a crime as much as a catastrophe. The British recorded that the German ships had 'displayed a severity which is hard to distinguish from downright cruelty', firing without mercy on the neutral merchant vessels, without giving them a chance to lower boats and deliberately targeting the survivors of the hapless destroyers while they were in rafts.[10] This accusation was strongly refuted by the Germans who, in their official history, rejected the claim, stating that it stood to reason that there was no intention of deliberately firing on survivors.[11]

In February 1918 *Brummer* went into dock at Swinemünde and was there until late April. Exercises and regular duties in the North Sea continued, including a minelaying operation in May. *Brummer* was being readied to take part in the November sortie of the fleet when the naval mutiny broke out.

Mutiny, internment and scuttling

The mutiny had begun among the battleship crews at Schillig Roads. The fleet was dispersed as a result. The Fourth Scouting Group, under Admiral Karpf, initially went to Flensburg Fjord, where the mutiny soon caught up. They moved again to Swinemünde on 7 November. At this point Karpf, fearing attack by mutinous elements of the fleet, ordered the group's ships to be scuttled, apparently allowing the crews to roam the countryside fomenting rebellion.[12] Karpf was immediately replaced and some semblance of order restored. It seems that enough of the crews of *Brummer* and *Strasburg* remained loyal so that the two ships were moved to Sassnitz. A workers' council was established at this time.[13] However, within days *Brummer* had sailed with the rest of the High Seas Fleet to Rosyth for surrender, transfer and internment in Scapa Flow.

On 21 June 1919 SMS *Brummer* was scuttled alongside the rest of the interned fleet. Her plunge to the bottom of Scapa Flow took place at 1305hrs.

She was the first of the five light cruisers to be successfully scuttled. Her sister ship *Bremse* foundered at 1430hrs, despite British attempts to beach her and she became the only light cruiser to be recovered during the salvage years.

History as a wreck

SMS *Brummer* was one of the three light cruisers which were never sold outright to any salvage company. The rights to salvage her (but not own her) were first passed to Nundy Marine Metals in around 1962 for the sum of £200. The firm appears to have conducted only minor salvage operations, including relieving her of her propellers.

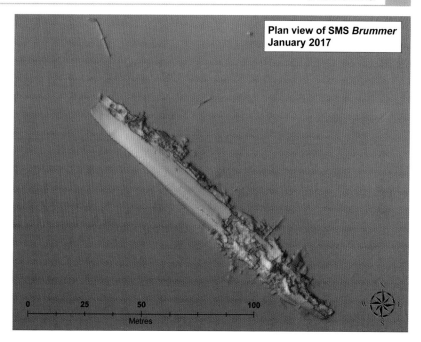

Plan view of SMS *Brummer* January 2017

Figure 13.3. Plan view DTM of SMS *Brummer* as scanned in January 2017. The wreck shows the results of commercial salvage of her engine rooms, a consistent feature of the light cruiser wrecks at Scapa Flow.

Things changed in 1971 when Scapa Flow Salvage began its tenure on the wrecks and took over the Nundy salvage rights. It was during this time that the valuable metals found within the ship's engine rooms were recovered along with her torpedo tubes.[14] As the earliest built of the surviving light cruisers, *Brummer* was the most expensively made. It was established that her non-ferrous components were more extensive than they were in the others. This was because as the war had progressed the Allied blockade of Germany had led to material shortages and the build quality of its ships consequently suffered.

The wreck was sold on in 1978 to Undersea Associates, who soon succumbed to bankruptcy. She was then leased to Clark's Diving Services Ltd, and when the lease expired in 1985, ownership transferred back to the Ministry of Defence. Finally, legal ownership passed to Orkney Islands Council on 3 November 1986. The wreck of SMS *Brummer* was designated under the Ancient Monuments and Archaeological Areas Act on 17 April 2002.[15]

SMS *Brummer* today

The DTM of the wreck of SMS *Brummer* can be seen in Figure 13.3. The wreck lies on its starboard side, as do all of the light cruiser wrecks at Scapa Flow except for SMS *Dresden*. The wreck points to the northwest along the orientation commonly seen among all of the surviving warships with the exception of SMS *Markgraf*.

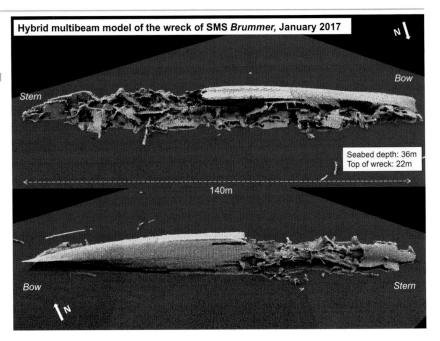

Figure 13.4. The hybrid model of the wreck of SMS *Brummer* reveals in three dimensions the extent of collapse. The stern can be seen to have rolled backwards to rest on the rudder.

Interestingly, the foremast appears to have been pulled away from the wreck at some point in the past and now lies to the north of the bow. The fore section of the wreck appears to be quite intact but the after half is broken open and in an advanced state of collapse. A number of features are readily identifiable, including the bridge with its prominent searchlight platform above, which can also be seen on the drawing of the ship in Figure 13.2.

When the survey data are converted into the hybrid model, more detail emerges, as seen in Figure 13.4 and 13.5. The bow can be seen to be clear of the seabed, with an acoustic shadow created by the multibeam showing underneath it. In fact the entire hull up to the end of the boiler rooms in still largely intact. The bridge has collapsed into the seabed, as has much of the upper superstructure. But the main area of damage coincides with the area of the engine rooms. The extreme stern is in better condition, but its orientation shows that it has twisted, rolling more to the vertical, so that the ship's single rudder is now resting on the seabed. The aftermost gun turret can also be seen.

The overall depth to the seabed is 36 metres and the top of the wreck was recorded as 22 metres, giving a height from the seabed of 14 metres. When built, SMS *Brummer* was actually 13.2 metres wide. The extra height is explained by the fact that the wreck is not completely on its side, with the upper side having a five-degree slope towards the seabed on the superstructure side. As can be seen in Figure 13.5, the highest point of the wreck is the port-side bilge keel. The depth to the top of the wreck has not changed over the last 100 years. The survey carried out immediately after the scuttling recorded the top of the wreck as being 12 fathoms (21.9m),[16] so despite the salvage works, the structure of the old ship has held together quite well.

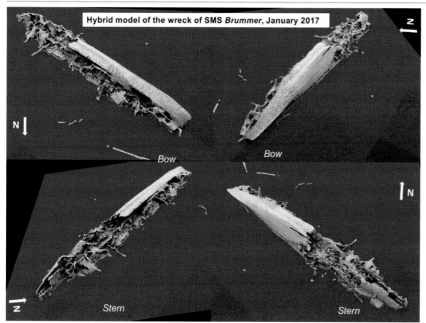

Hybrid model of the wreck of SMS *Brummer*, January 2017

N

Bow

Bow

N

N

Stern

Stern

Figure 13.5. All-round view of the wreck of SMS *Brummer* as scanned in 2017. The wreck's highest point is the bilge keel. Her height has not changed in the last 100 years, despite the wreck steadily degrading at an accelerating rate.

Figures 13.6 to 13.13 feature images of the wreck recorded from 2013, and depict many of the key features one sees when diving SMS *Brummer*. Her historical record makes her perhaps the most important of the light cruiser wrecks, and she is uniquely and noticeably different from the other three. It should be noted that, like the other light cruisers and belying the seemingly unchanged height of the wreck, SMS *Brummer* is now beginning to deteriorate at an accelerating pace. Changes in the wreck are being regularly noticed by divers, and what is depicted in the next few paragraphs may well not be the current state of the wreck by the time this book is published.

The images in Figure 13.6 are of the stern area of the wreck from a video survey in 2013. In Image A the extreme stern of the wreck can be seen. The stern anchor was sitting nicely in its recess with the stock located in the hawsepipe (the chain is snapped off where it runs out onto the deck), with a single bollard situated above it. On the deck behind was the single capstan seen in Image B. The afterdeck was heavily corroded and some time needed to be spent trying to locate evidence of the minelaying apparatus. From the ship's plans it was clear the mines were deployed off the stern of the upper deck along rails.

The mines were stored on the upper deck and on the main deck, where a hoist brought them up to run aft on the upper deck to be dropped over the stern. The rails have all but gone, but a section was found as seen in Image C, close to the seabed under the capstan. The deck is quite rotten here, but the port-side inboard rail can be seen. The outer rail is buried now. Image D shows *Brummer*'s aftermost gun. These 5.9-inch guns were housed in open-backed gun shields.

Moving forward, towards the area of the salvage damage, the photos in Figure 13.7 show some of the next features encountered. In Image A the

Figure 13.6. Images from the stern area of SMS *Brummer*. Image A shows the stern anchor, Image B the stern anchor capstan, devoid of chain, Image C corrosion in the deck and a mine rail, and Image D the aft 5.9-inch gun.

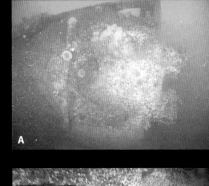

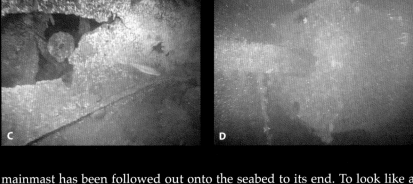

mainmast has been followed out onto the seabed to its end. To look like a British cruiser, the mast was designed to be folded at this point. Returning to the wreck, the state of deterioration is evident because sections of the deck can be seen to have fallen away from the underlying frames. The deck plate seen in the bottom right of the image has had its path to the seabed interrupted by falling across the muzzle of the upper superfiring 5.9-inch gun, which can be seen underneath it. This can be seen in Image C.

These guns can be seen on the drawing in Figure 13.2. The mine rails ran down each side of them, meaning that the guns could only be traversed when there were no mines to interrupt their rotation. But clearly, when in gun action, the presence of mines on board would not be desirable. In fact, it was in this area of the ship that extra bags of coal were stored on the deck during the October 1917 raid on the Shetland convoy.

Moving to the central part of the wreck, the gun mounted on the upper superstructure between the first and second funnels is seen in Image A of Figure 13.8. The drawings of the ship show the gun facing forwards (see Figure 13.2). It in fact faces aft and no explanation for why this appears to have changed in service has so far been found. Either side of this gun on the upper deck, the two torpedo tubes were situated. These were salvaged long ago.

Interestingly, Images B and C show the very nicely preserved (for now) air intakes situated at the base of the funnels and above the boiler rooms. The grates were particularly noteworthy because they appear to have lain

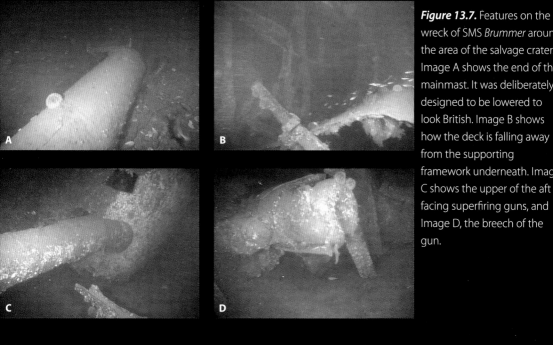

Figure 13.7. Features on the wreck of SMS *Brummer* around the area of the salvage crater. Image A shows the end of the mainmast. It was deliberately designed to be lowered to look British. Image B shows how the deck is falling away from the supporting framework underneath. Image C shows the upper of the aft facing superfiring guns, and Image D, the breech of the gun.

deliberately in differing directions. At least four sets can be seen in the region of the second and third funnels.

Moving forward beyond the gun, one gets to the area of the bridge superstructure. At the top of wreck, right above where the collapsed bridge

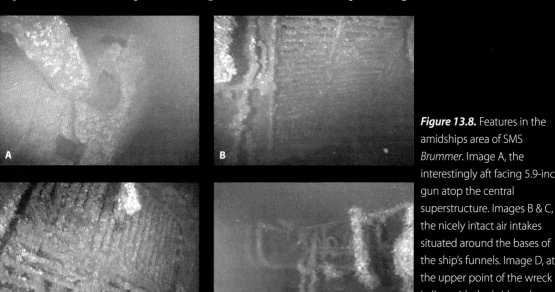

Figure 13.8. Features in the amidships area of SMS *Brummer*. Image A, the interestingly aft facing 5.9-inch gun atop the central superstructure. Images B & C, the nicely intact air intakes situated around the bases of the ship's funnels. Image D, at the upper point of the wreck in line with the bridge, the remains of the stowage rack for the torpedo reload.

Figure 13.9. One of a pair of searchlights situated above the bridge of SMS *Brummer* has corroded to the point where its inner mechanism can be seen. (Gavin Anderson)

Figure 13.10. Images of the better-preserved searchlight, seen from above in A and in close-up with ruler for scale in B.

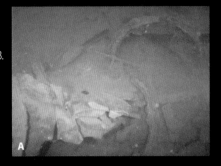

Figure 13.11. SMS *Brummer's* bridge structure is collapsing into the seabed, but it is still a fascinating object. Images A & B show that it has broken away from the base of the foremast. Images C & D show the curved railings at the forward end of the upper bridge.

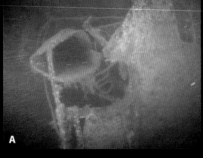
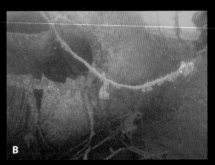

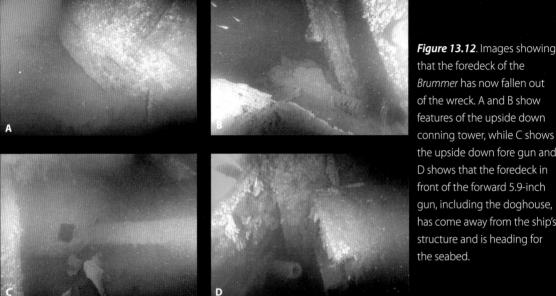

Figure 13.12. Images showing that the foredeck of the *Brummer* has now fallen out of the wreck. A and B show features of the upside down conning tower, while C shows the upside down fore gun and D shows that the foredeck in front of the forward 5.9-inch gun, including the doghouse, has come away from the ship's structure and is heading for the seabed.

now lies, the racking which housed the torpedo reload can be seen, as shown in Image D. This image is from 2017. When filmed in 2013 more of the frames were present. This is one small example of the many changes the wrecks are constantly undergoing.

On the drawing of *Brummer* in Figure 13.2 the searchlights mounted above the bridge can be seen. They were in a pair, mounted side by side. These lights were part of the night fighting system of the ship. The High Seas Fleet proved at the Battle of Jutland that it was better prepared to fight at night. These lights were designed to blind an enemy as much as to illuminate a target. They were not for signalling. The German fleet had unique multi-coloured light trees in each ship which identified them and which could be simply switched on and off when needed, obviating the need for signalling lamps to flash the challenge signals. Signal lamps could temporarily blind the user and observer and also broadcast the challenge signal to anyone watching. German ships at Jutland learned the British challenge signal in this way, simply by observing their signalling.

Figures 13.9 and 13.10 show the more intact of *Brummer*'s searchlights from the bridge position. It is now quite rotten, with the metal casing corroded away long ago. But inside, the ornate mechanism of the iris can be studied. Pieces of these lights can be observed on the other wrecks and on the salvage sites, but this example is a particularly good one. Figure 13.9 gives a good impression of its size with the diver posing behind it. The iris is just like the type seen in an SLR camera, just much larger.

Figure 13.10 shows more of the detail. Image A shows the light seen from above, with the remains of the circular casing on the seabed. In 2014, a one-metre ruler was taken down to the iris, as seen Image B. The diameter of the

Figure 13.13. Images of features at the bow of SMS *Brummer*. A, port side capstan. B, starboard side anchor hawse with anchor inside. C, the port hawse is empty. D, the graceful clipper curve of the bow silhouetted against the light.

iris was 110cm, making it of the standard searchlight type in use in the High Seas Fleet. These lights were rated at 150 amperes and would totally dazzle an opponent. By comparison, signal lamps were rated at only 17 amperes.[17]

Diving on the site reveals that SMS *Brummer*'s bridge is falling apart slowly, but in 2014 it was still in good enough shape to make out many of its constituent parts. Some of these can be seen in Figure 13.11. In Images A and B the main platform can be seen at the point where it has broken away from the base of the foremast. At some point in the past, the foremast was pulled bodily away from the wreck to lie some distance from it, as can be seen on the multibeam images.

Figure 13.14. Features on SMS *Brummer* observed during the diving surveys from 2013 onwards shown on the hybrid model. It is clear that the wreck is changing fast now.

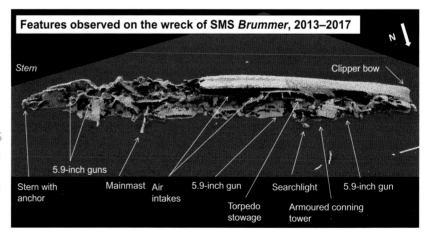

Whether this contributed to the collapse of the bridge is not certain, but it seems the bridge suffered a noticeable collapse around 2010, prior to these images being taken in 2013 and 2014.[18] The collapse has not altered the nice curves of the brass railings around the upper bridge, which can be seen in Images C and D. Below it is the splinter-proof chart house. In Image C the base of the compass binnacle can be seen at the fore-end of the bridge.

In action the ship could be conned and its gunnery controlled from within an armoured conning tower which was situated ahead of the main bridge structure. It had a rangefinder fitted to its roof, which can be seen in Figure 13.2. Today this feature has fallen out of the wreck and lies on the seabed almost completely upside down, its great weight, together with that of the forward gun, contributing greatly to the advanced degradation of the foredeck area of the wreck, as gravity takes charge. The armoured conning tower can be seen in Image A of Figure 13.12. Its slit windows are now at the bottom of the structure. The door at the back of the tower can be seen in Image B. The inside is much collapsed and was stripped by divers many years ago.

The forward gun as seen in Image C is even more upside down than the conning tower, now being totally inverted, opening up the fore part of the wreck. In front of it the deck has now completely fallen away. In 2014, when these images were taken, the muzzle of the forward gun could be seen poking through the upside-down wreckage of the deck. In Image D the muzzle can be seen. In front of it is the forward doghouse entranceway into the ship. This was originally situated on the port side of the gun, which would have to shoot over it in action.

Up at the bow, the wreck is in marginally better condition and the features there are easily recognized on Figure 13.13. The twin capstans are still present. The port one can be seen in Image A, with the rotten frames from the upper side of the wreck in the background. Images B and C show the anchor hawsepipes. The port-side anchor is not present. Finally, the clipper curved bow can be seen in Image D. An attempt was made to get an image of the curve of the bow silhouetted against the sunlight behind to show how it was designed to look British. In fact, though, only the lower portion of the bow was intact in 2013 when the image was taken.

The locations of the features seen in the underwater images are shown together on the hybrid model of the wreck in Figure 13.14. The wreck of SMS *Brummer* has many fine features to find and examine, but it is clear that the wreck is increasingly falling apart. The forward gun, the armoured conning tower and the bridge have all collapsed in recent years, and this has been continuing.

Structural changes observed in the wreck of SMS *Brummer*, 2006–2017

Clearly the first substantial damage all of the surviving wrecks suffered came as a result of the years of commercial salvage. The salvage years in fact offer a baseline upon which to begin to work out what has happened to the wrecks in the subsequent years. On the battleships this was not too difficult to reconcile because the damage was broadly consistent. With some exceptions, their upturned hulls remain largely as they were after the salvage ended.

The case is slightly different with the light cruisers. They lie on their sides and the general state of structural collapse is therefore more evident. Also, it is clear that their slighter-built structures are degrading in a more pronounced manner than the battleships. Figure 13.15 depicts the wreck in 2017 compared with drawings of *Brummer* showing the key items of interest to salvors. In the case of *Brummer* the twin engine rooms with their non-ferrous components and the bronze torpedo tubes were the prized items. Interestingly, the removal of both sets of turbines and condensers created a visible double crater in the wreck still visible in the hybrid model. Moreover, the recovery of the propellers and the torpedo tubes does not, on its own, seem to have caused much damage. The extreme stern has rolled more to the upright, but this is due to other factors, such as time and gravity, affecting the integrity of the hull.

Apart from the occasional verifiable published data, much of what has happened, especially to the light cruiser wrecks, over the years is often based on anecdotal and, indeed, apocryphal stories. This makes it difficult to independently validate. Certainly, one can find very little data of any use prior to 2001.

Although the methodologies employed before then were somewhat limited by more primitive technology than we have today, it was clear that a degree of structural change caused by corrosion was observed in the bow area of SMS *Brummer*. It was noted that there was a general rotting out of the outer skin of the ship and that the bow in particular was collapsing. It was also observed that the forward gun had fallen out of the wreck, with a date of 2004 given.[19] But what happened to the foremast? It was once a prominent feature on the wreck that divers enjoyed.[20]

Anecdotally, John Thornton recalls seeing a freighter anchored close to the *Brummer* one windy winter's evening possibly around 2003. It had moved on by the following day and when he next visited the wreck, the divers reported that the mast had gone and that the area where it had once been had been damaged as a result, in what was probably nothing more than an unfortunate choice of mooring location. But it may well explain how the mast got so obviously pulled clear of the wreck.

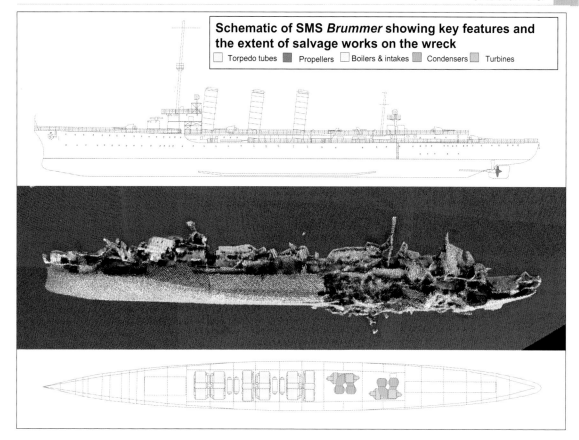

Schematic of SMS *Brummer* showing key features and the extent of salvage works on the wreck

☐ Torpedo tubes ■ Propellers ☐ Boilers & intakes ▦ Condensers ☐ Turbines

As with the battleship wrecks, the ADUS survey of 2006 offers the best baseline data available to make comparisons against, using our data from 2017. The results of comparing both datasets are shown in Figure 13.16. It is very evident just how badly this wreck has deteriorated over the last decade. Highlighted are the most significant areas of change, but there are clearly many others visible too.

In general terms, the upper deck has now largely fallen out of the wreck, taking with it much of the superstructure which was attached. This is particularly noticeable in the area where the upper gun was mounted between the first and second funnels and in the significantly enlarged hole in the bow in line with the forward gun. The gun itself was already on the seabed when the ADUS survey was made. The bridge too looks to have mainly collapsed during this time.

This is genuinely sad to see, but it is inevitable. The degradation is seemingly accelerating. The likelihood is that this will continue and that the life of SMS *Brummer* as a discernible ship-shaped wreck is passing into the stage of old age. The time will come when it will join the many hundreds of World War I–era shipwrecks that are already little more than piles of rusty plates on the sea floor.

Figure 13.15. Clear signs of salvage damage on SMS *Brummer* in the form of a double crater in the region of the ship's two engine rooms. The rest of the damage seen is due to the passage of time.

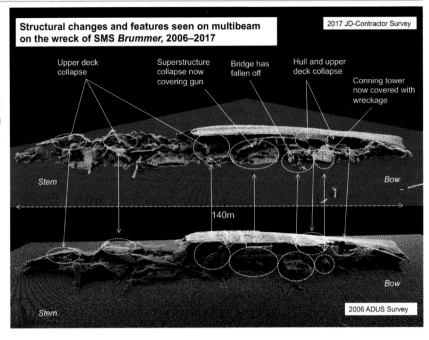

Figure 13.16. The extensive collapse of the wreck of SMS *Brummer* since the 2006 ADUS survey is shown by comparing the data from that survey with our survey of 2017.

Figure 13.17. A diver silhouetted against the light inspecting SMS *Brummer's* armoured conning tower with its rangefinder in place, as it was in 2002. This entire area of the wreck is now unrecognizable. (John Thornton)

Conclusions

Of the four light cruiser wrecks, SMS *Brummer* is the most important historically. It was a revolutionary design of ship. The British did not possess a fast minelaying capability in World War I. By World War II they had developed the 36-knot Abdiel-class minelayer cruiser. These ships gave much valuable service. It is difficult not to think that their design was influenced by SMS *Brummer* and SMS *Bremse*, which were both the subject of keen Admiralty interest during their time in Scapa Flow. Both ships were of course also the successful raiders of a convoy, all but wiping it out.

As a shipwreck, *Brummer* has endured a century of being underwater and has been the subject, successively, of salvage, tourism and archaeological survey – undoubtedly a sign of how things have moved on during that time. What was once a feared weapon became so much junk and then emerged as a protected cultural artefact and an important asset to the local economy. So it is a little sad to see this historic vessel in its dotage. But this is not an isolated case, as the next chapters will show.

1   G. Koop & K.-P. Schmolke (2004), Planmappe: Kleine Kreuzer 1903–1918 BRUMMER- / BREMSE-Klasse (Bonn: Bernard & Graefe Verlag).
2   A. J. Marder (1969), From the Dreadnought to Scapa Flow: The Royal Navy in the Fisher Era, 1904–1919. Volume IV: The Year of Crisis (London: OUP), p. 294.
3   Anon. (1919), 'German Mine-laying Cruisers', *The Engineer*, April, p. 383.
4   N. Friedman (ed.) (1992), *German Warships of World War I: The Royal Navy's*

Official Guide to the Capital Ships, Cruisers, Destroyers, Submarines and Small Craft, 1914–1918 (London: Greenhill), pp. 113–114.

5   N. Friedman (ed.) (1992), *German Warships of World War I: The Royal Navy's Official Guide to the Capital Ships, Cruisers, Destroyers, Submarines and Small Craft, 1914–1918* (London: Greenhill), p. 113.

6   E. Gröner (1990), *German Warships 1815–1945. Volume One: Major Surface Vessels* (London: Conway), pp. 112–113.

7   H. H. Herwig (1980), *'Luxury' Fleet: The Imperial German Navy 1888–1918* (London: George Allen & Unwin), p. 207.

8   N. Novik (1969), 'The Story of the Cruisers Bremse and Brummer', *Warship International*, VI, no. 3, pp. 185–189. Toledo: Naval Records Club.

9   G. P. Halpern (1994), *A Naval History of World War I* (Annapolis: Naval Institute Press, pp. 376–377.

10   H. Newbolt (1931), *History of the Great War Based on Official Documents: Naval Operations. Vol. V* (London: Longmans, Green & Co.), pp. 152–158.

11   A. J. Marder (1969), *From the Dreadnought to Scapa Flow: The Royal Navy in the Fisher Era, 1904–1919. Volume IV: The Year of Crisis* (London: OUP), p. 294.

12   D. Horn (1969), *The German Naval Mutinies of WW1* (New Brunswick: Rutgers University Press), p. 261.

13   D. Woodward (1973), *The Collapse of Power: Mutiny in the High Seas Fleet* (London: Arthur Baker), pp. 165–168.

14   R. Macdonald (2017), *Dive Scapa Flow* (Edinburgh: Mainstream), p. 156.

15   Hydrographic Department of the Admiralty (2017), Record of Wreck No. 1089 SMS *Brummer* (Taunton: Hydrographic Office).

16   Hydrographic Department of the Admiralty (2017), Record of Wreck No. 1089 SMS *Brummer* (Taunton: Hydrographic Office).

17   G. Staff (2014), *German Battlecruisers of World War One: Their Design, Construction and Operations* (Barnsley: Seaforth), p. 71.

18   R. Macdonald (2017), *Dive Scapa Flow* (Edinburgh: Mainstream), p. 160.

19   ScapaMAP 2000–2002 (2003), Report Compiled for Historic Scotland on the Mapping and Management of the Submerged Archaeological Resource in Scapa Flow. Orkney: Scapa Flow Marine Archaeology Project, p. 39. ScapaMAP (2001–2006), Marine Heritage Monitoring with High Resolution Survey Tools: Scapa Flow 2001–2006. Orkney: Scapa Flow Marine Archaeology Project, p. 43.

20   R. Macdonald (2017), *Dive Scapa Flow* (Edinburgh: Mainstream), p. 86.

CHAPTER 14
SMS *KARLSRUHE*

Figure 14.1. SMS *Karlsruhe*, launched 13 January 1916. Design displacement 5,354 tons, length 151m, eight 5.9-inch and three 88mm guns. Four 20-inch torpedo tubes. (Aidan Dodson Collection)

SMS Karlsruhe's unspectacular naval career has done nothing to detract from her popularity as a wreck with visiting divers. She is no longer the spectacular wreck of the 1980s, but she retains a great deal of charm and is still among the most photogenic of the Scapa Flow wrecks. Her degradation in recent years may be a model to show how the other light cruisers will change in the years to come.

Design and service history

SMS *Karlsruhe* was a light cruiser of the four-ship Königsberg class. She was laid down at the Imperial Dockyard, Kiel in 1914 and launched on 31 January 1916, over a month after SMS *Brummer*. Her commissioning took longer and she was not ready until November 1916, too late to take part in the Battle of Jutland. Technically she was *Karlsruhe II*, following a tradition of naming the class after the commerce-raiding cruisers sunk early in the war. The original *Karlsruhe* had been destroyed by an internal explosion in November 1914. Her sister ship, SMS *Emden II*, which functioned as Admiral von Reuter's flag during the Grand Scuttle, carried a distinctive Iron Cross on her bow in tribute to the earlier famous ship of the same name.

The Königsberg class shared design similarities with the earlier Wiesbaden and Magdeburg classes and were good sea boats. They were built with longitudinal framing, with 18 watertight compartments. The double bottom covered 45% of the keel. The ship was powered by twin turbines and shafts with steam from 12 boilers, two of which burned oil. The oil was primarily stored in the double bottom under the engine rooms. Different from *Brummer* and similar to the later-built *Cöln* and *Dresden*, the design placed the engines and condensers in rooms which were side by side.[1]

The Königsberg class was well armoured with a belt of 60mm maximum thickness, 40mm on the sloped portions, fining to 20cm. The armoured conning tower was 100mm thick. The ships of this class were also fitted out as auxiliary minelayers with a mine storage area in the hold for 200 mines. This too received a 20mm (deck) by 30mm (sides) armoured box around it. A 40mm collision bulkhead was also fitted from the hold to the armoured deck just abaft the anchor hawse pipes.

Her complement was nearly half as large again as that serving in SMS *Brummer*. This is accounted for by her significantly more powerful armament. *Karlsruhe* was equipped with twice the number of 5.9-inch guns (eight in all) fitted in pairs, on the foredeck, beside each mast and as a superfiring pair astern. Curiously, British intelligence records state that *Karlsruhe* was only fitted with one gun on the foredeck.[2] However, the construction plans clearly show she was to be built with twin guns forward.[3] This is confirmed by the multibeam hybrid model of the wreck and by diving.

Secondary armament consisted of a pair of 88mm guns sited just forward of the mainmast. She was also equipped with four 20-inch torpedo tubes. Two were fitted below the waterline in line with the bridge and a further pair were mounted on the upper deck alongside the air intakes between the first and second funnels.

SMS *Karlsruhe* in service

SMS *Karlsruhe* joined the Second Scouting Group in December 1916. The ship was not fully ready and had to be docked in February 1917 to be altered. She was back in service to take part in a minesweeping operation in the North Sea on 16 August. The minesweepers were escorted by the light cruiser SMS *Frankfurt* (in command), *Karlsruhe* and three torpedo boats. The operation was aimed at sweeping Route Yellow, a safe passage for U-boats traversing to and from the North Sea. During the afternoon, the minesweepers were attacked by a larger British force of 16 destroyers and three light cruisers.

In very poor visibility, with gunnery ranges of 4,000m or less, the British fell on the minesweepers, which bravely formed a battle line and under sustained fire withdrew behind a smokescreen. The supporting German forces failed to get to grips with the British, leaving the minesweepers to escape unaided. For this perceived lack of resolve, *Frankfurt*'s commander was sacked from his post the following month.[4]

SMS *Karlsruhe* was then transferred to the Baltic to take part in Operation *Albion*, alongside major elements of the High Seas Fleet. The plan was to take the island of Ösel in the Baltic (now part of Estonia) and the protecting batteries on the Sworbe Peninsula. The operation began on 12 October, during which time *Karlsruhe* was involved in the landing of assault troops carried in merchant vessels. The Second Scouting Group also functioned as a screen for the invasion force and conducted an abortive minesweeping operation off the island of Dagö on 19 October. The entire operation was over in little more than a week, with the Russian forces destroyed or retreating.

British intelligence records suggesting she was involved in the Second Battle of Heligoland Bight on 17 November are inaccurate.[5] From German sources it is known she was not present during the action.[6] In fact it was not

Figure 14.2. Captioned as SMS *Karlsruhe* (but possibly SMS *Emden*) interned in Scapa Flow. Note the line of British drifters. (Contemporary postcard, Brotherton Library)

until April 1918 that *Karlsruhe* was involved in another operation. On this occasion she accompanied the fleet on the abortive sortie up the Norway coast which ended when the battlecruiser *Moltke* suffered a breakdown and had to be towed for several hours back to the Bight before power was restored. *Moltke* was subsequently torpedoed by HMS *E42* before making base.

Other than a minelaying operation in the Bight in May, SMS *Karlsruhe* undertook routine duties until October 1918, when she was earmarked to take part in the coastal bombardment of Flanders with two other cruisers. This was part of a broader plan to draw out the British Grand Fleet for a final great naval battle to try to influence the war's outcome and halt Germany's slide to defeat. As described in earlier chapters, this operation was cancelled when at the end of October mutiny broke out among the crews of the capital ships.

Mutiny, internment and scuttling

During the naval mutiny the Second Scouting Group was under the command of Commodore Victor Harder on board SMS *Königsberg*. He had been in command of the ill-fated battlecruiser SMS *Lützow* during the Battle of Jutland. The group seemingly retained enough discipline during this time for SMS *Cöln* and SMS *Königsberg* to reconnaissance the Bight on 10 November in response to reports that British cruisers were out. None were found and the ships returned to base.[7] However, *Karlsruhe* remained in harbour at this time. It seems *Königsberg*'s loyalty could be relied on as she was the ship appointed to carry Admiral Meurer to surrender negotiations with Admiral Beatty in Rosyth on 15 November, four days before the German surrender fleet departed.

As one of the most modern light cruisers in the High Seas Fleet, *Karlsruhe* was named during the armistice negotiations as one of the German warships to be surrendered. The rendezvous at sea off the Firth of Forth took place on

21 November 1918. *Karlsruhe* is depicted at the head of the line of the seven light cruisers which surrendered on that day in the famous 'Der Tag' poster published in Britain. She was flying the broad pennant of Commodore Harder, who had transferred to the ship by this time. The following day the surrendered ships were inspected and then dispatched in groups for Scapa Flow over the next four days.

The seven light cruisers arrived on 26 and 27 November and were berthed off Cava. Touring the newly arrived ships, Admiral Parry found that *Karlsruhe* was 'filthy and couldn't have been cleaned for weeks', such was the state of morale in many elements of the High Seas Fleet by that time.[8] Eight of her 12 boilers were in such poor condition that she was in no state to sail far. Figure 14.2 shows SMS *Karlsruhe* interned, surrounded by drifters.

On the day of the Grand Scuttle *Karlsruhe* was the last of the light cruisers to sink, going under at 1550hrs. Three of the eight light cruisers were saved from sinking to live again as war prizes. By the time she foundered she was the second to last to sink, with only SMS *Markgraf* still afloat, to follow her within the hour.

History as a wreck

SMS *Karlsruhe* sank in a relatively shallow 27 metres of water, so that her masts could be seen at low tide. When originally surveyed in the summer of 1919, the wreck was recorded as being eight metres from the surface. At low tide the foremast dried to six feet and the mainmast to three feet.[9] The original survey shows that the wreck lay at an angle on her starboard side with the masts pointing to the northeast.[10] There she remained undisturbed until 1940, when her masts were removed, presumably as a navigational hazard in the busy wartime naval anchorage.

Her history of salvage began when she was sold outright by the Admiralty in 1955 to Metal Industries. The only light cruiser to have been disposed of prior to this point was SMS *Bremse*, sold to Cox & Danks in 1925. Within a year of acquiring *Karlsruhe*, Metal Industries sold out to Nundy Marine Metals. In 1962 Nundy bought the rights to salvage the other three light cruiser wrecks, but it only ever owned *Karlsruhe* outright. It was Nundy who began the salvage works on the wreck, recovering the valuable components which were relatively easy to reach. Salvage included blasting open her engine room and removing the upper condensers from the port side, the propellers and the external torpedo tubes.

Nundy Marine Metals sold on to Scapa Flow Salvage Ltd in 1970, and it was the latter which extensively salvaged the wreck. Similar to *Brummer*, but unlike *Cöln* and *Dresden*, *Karlsruhe* had been built when Germany's shipyards

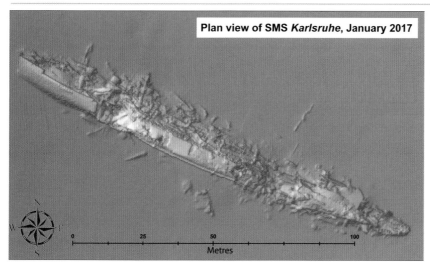

Figure 14.3. DTM model of the wreck of SMS *Karlsruhe*, January 2017.

were not suffering from wartime shortages of non-ferrous metal. Apparently the wreck was very profitable, being the most productive of the wrecks the company worked. Key elements of its work included blasting further down into the wreck to recover the lower condenser and clearing out both engine rooms of anything of value. It also removed the internal torpedo tubes and, in a stroke of good fortune, discovered her bridge to be apparently made of 4.5 tons of solid brass.[11]

The wreck was sold on to Undersea Associates in 1978. As a result of that company going bankrupt the following year, the official receiver sold the wrecks which were not owned by the Ministry of Defence to Clark's Diving

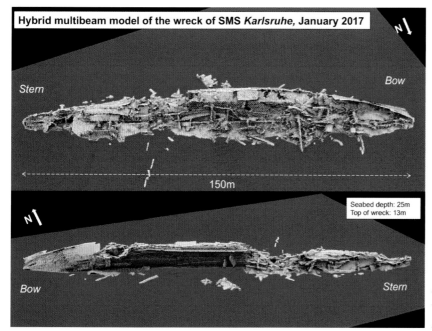

Figure 14.4. Hybrid model of the wreck of SMS *Karlsruhe*, January 2017.

Services Ltd in 1981. Clark's also inherited the salvage leases on the other cruisers. These lapsed in 1986, but Clark's is still *Karlsruhe*'s legal owner. SMS *Karlsruhe* was designated under the Ancient Monuments and Archaeological Areas Act on 17 April 2002.

SMS *Karlsruhe* today

The DTM of SMS *Karlsruhe* as surveyed by us in 2017 is shown in Figure 14.3. The wreck lies on her starboard side and points in the same general direction as all of the surviving wrecks which sank on their moorings during the Grand Scuttle. Unlike the wreck of SMS *Brummer*, it is clear that *Karlsruhe* was blasted open in more than one area. There is a marked hole under the region of the bridge as well as in the engine-room area. A number of features are recognizable when comparing the DTM with the drawing of the ship in Figure 13.2, such as some of the 5.9-inch gun mounts and the armoured conning tower.

Looking at the wreck model in three dimensions when it has been converted into a hybrid model, as seen in Figures 14.4 and 14.5, reveals even more detail. In particular the foremast, bow and stern stand out prominently. Importantly, the wreck can be seen to be much collapsed, lying nearly completely flat on the seabed and with much of it very broken up. In common with *Brummer*, the stern has taken up a different orientation from the rest of the wreck, as a result of it being separated during the salvage operations on the engine room.

One section of the underside of the ship under the bilge keel looks uncannily flat and intact, so much so that we did initially doubt whether it had been covered completely by the multibeam scans. However, from the diving surveys it is known that it is in fact like that. There is dispersed wreckage on that side too, which is unusual, but caused by the way in which the wreck was salvaged.

The overall depth of the seabed is 25 metres and the wreck stood up to 13 metres from the surface when we carried out the multibeam survey. When originally surveyed in 1919, the top of the wreck was recorded as being at 8 metres. The wreck was still showing as 4.5 fathoms (8 metres) from the surface when resurveyed in 1959. The bell was recovered in 1974 by an RAF dive team which reported that the wreck had been blasted open by that time. But despite the blasting, the wreck was still 8 metres from the surface as late as 1977, when the site was surveyed in that year.[12]

The collapse we see now must have begun after that point. By the 2008 survey she was down to 10.5 metres, and by 2010 she had collapsed rapidly to 12.5 metres, which is the depth at which the wreck is currently charted.[13]

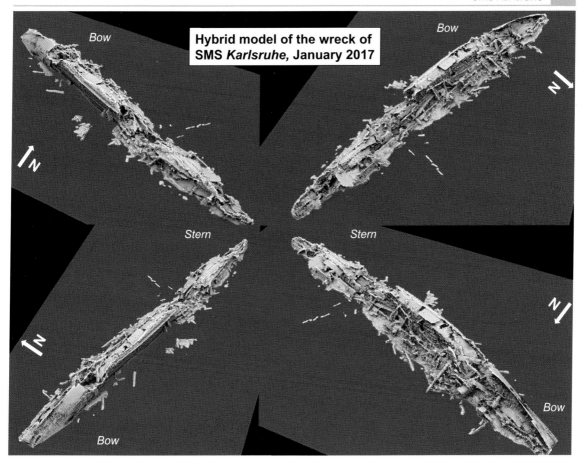

Figure 14.5. All-round view of the hybrid model of the wreck of SMS *Karlsruhe*, January 2017.

The way the central superstructure has slumped almost certainly occurred during the time after 1977. The wreck was being deeply penetrated by divers even after the turn of the millennium, with the boiler rooms being a location regularly explored.

The underwater images which follow were mainly taken in the years 2013–2014, by which time the wreck closely resembled what is seen on the multibeam. There are reports that more collapse has occurred subsequently as the remorseless process of decay continues. Such is the now rapidly changing nature of these elderly wrecks that anything other than a general representation of them can only ever be a snapshot at a specific moment.

Starting at the bow, *Karlsruhe* is noticeably flattened. There is only a little clearance under the bow now and the foredeck has slumped, almost concertinaed as it has slipped towards the seabed. This has created some noteworthy features. Figure 14.6 and 14.7 show what this looks like now. The pair of capstans lie together, where the decking between them has simply folded up with age. This collapse can be traced all the way from further forward, where the anchor hawse pipes are also lying in a similar orientation, as seen in Figure 14.7, Image B. The capstans are an essential feature for

Figure 14.6. The distinctive capstans on the wreck of SMS *Karlsruhe*, looking aft. They give a good impression of how the wreck is collapsing. Both chains are still in situ. (Gavin Anderson)

Figure 14.7. The capstans seen looking forward. Their orientation is similar to the pair of hawse pipes which now also lie side by side. Note how the starboard one is bent upwards.

visiting divers to see and may be the most photographed underwater capstans in the world.

SMS *Karlsruhe* was fitted with a pair of 5.9-inch guns on the foredeck. They too have collapsed in a similar manner to the hawse pipes and capstans, with one almost resting atop the other. These are shown in Figure 14.8. The starboard gun is on the seabed and is particularly interesting because the reinforced mounting is exposed and one can see how the whole arrangement would have originally been built into the ship. The port-side gun has taken a large piece of deck with it when it fell out of the wreck. In Image A the roof of the port gun can be seen in the top right corner. The port gun is depicted in Images B and D. The sliding breeches of both guns are visible and, like all of the German naval guns in Scapa, were partially dismantled before the ships sailed to internment. The wood tampions reported present in the 1980s have long since either rotted or been souvenir hunted.[14]

A little further aft one gets to the armoured conning tower. Unlike the upside-down one on *Brummer* this one is on its side and the roof is visible. In Image A of Figure 14.9 one can see the circular mount which housed a rangefinder of a similar type to the one which used to be visible on *Brummer* before the tower fell off (see Figure 13.15). The hole was large enough to push

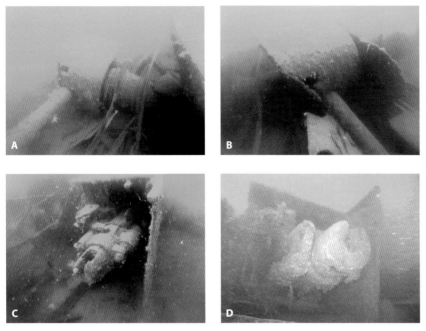

Figure 14.8. SMS *Karlsruhe's* pair of forward guns now also lie side by side. Images A and C show the starboard side one which lies on the seabed. In the upper right-hand corner of Image A the roof of the splinter shield of the port side gun can be seen. It is shown in full in Images B and D.

a video housing through to capture the inside seen in Image B. The doorway can be seen on the left. The inside of the tower is stripped of its contents.

The doorway itself can be seen in Image C. In the 1980s it was still attached, hanging vertically on its hinges. Through the holes in the roof, divers could

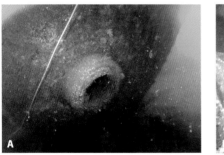

Figure 14.9. SMS *Karlsruhe's* armoured conning tower. Image A shows the roof with the circular hole rangefinder base; B is a view inside through that hole; C shows the rear door which nearly claimed a diver's life; and D is a view inside through the door.

Figure 14.10. Divers by the starboard side gun originally situated aside the foremast. The mast can be seen behind it, lying over the barrel.

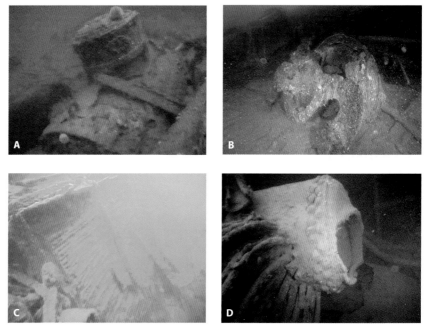

Figure 14.11. Features in the mid part of the wreck. Image A is the boiler of *Karlsruhe*'s steam tender; B is one of the forward searchlights; C is a nice area of intact decking; and D is the end of a Schulz-Thorneycroft type boiler.

only peer at the compass binnacle and telegraphs still housed within it.[15] The allure of sunken brass ultimately proved too strong and the door was gradually opened. At some point during the opening process it fell off, landing on a diver and, according to John Thornton, breaking his leg. His dive buddy was able get him out; very lucky. The door can be seen in the Scapa Flow Visitor Centre and Museum at Lyness. It is armoured and exceedingly heavy. Peering into the doorway today reveals an empty interior, made interesting by being able to see the light streaming in through the armoured slits in the front of the tower. The hole in the roof seen in Image D was probably for a periscope.

Figure 14.12. An atmospheric shot giving a nice impression of the way much of the mid portion of *Karlsruhe* looks today. It has become a sloping mass of collapsing debris, within which large sections of the wooden deck covering can be seen. (Gavin Anderson)

As described, the brass bridge structure was salvaged from the wreck and is not present, so the next major feature to appear is the foremast which lies across the wreck and is broken off at the seabed. It lies across the barrel of the starboard-side 5.9-inch gun which was mounted at this point. The gun, with mast in the background, can be seen in Figure 14.10, with some divers to give scale. The relatively shallow depth of the wreck means that, on a day with sun in the sky and good underwater visibility, the wreck can be quite a serene place.

Some of the myriad items which can be seen in the mid-section of the wreck are shown in Figures 14.11 and 14.12. This area is basically a slope from the top of the wreck to the seabed with the actual superstructure of the ship mostly collapsed. But it nonetheless contains many points of interest. Figure 14.11, Image A shows the remains of a small boiler which is all that now remains of a steam pinnace. This is noteworthy because it seems to signify that it was not used to evacuate the ship during the scuttling and must have gone down with the ship; raising steam would presumably have alerted the British. Scattered on the seabed around it are the remains of the davits for the boats. Just forward of the foremast on the seabed are the remains of the forward

Figure 14.13. Features at the heavily salvaged area of the wreck. Image A shows the starboard side gun. Image B shows what appears to be a turbine casing in the area blasted open.

Figure 14.14. On the less often visited keel side of the wreck a turbine casing with blades can be found, as seen in Images A–C. Image D shows the open frames of the ship in the area where the forward torpedo flat was blasted open. A seal shot by as I was recording it.

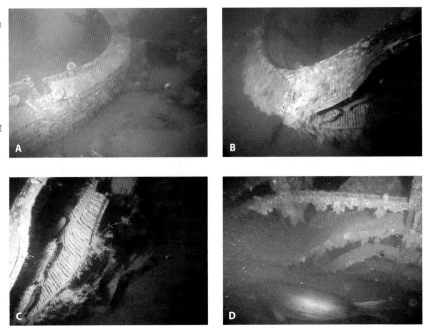

searchlight platform. The platform itself and light mounts can be discerned along with the remains of at least one of the lights, as seen in Image B.

Higher up on the wreck, large sections of the wood deck can be seen in the area between the foremast and the salvage break, as seen in Image C and atmospherically photographed in Figure 14.12. The collapsed framing, cables and timber seen in this image make it so characteristic of the way modern-era shipwrecks degrade. Passing onto the top of the wreck, there are a number of holes in the side of the ship. Upon peering into one of these the view shown in Figure 14.11, Image D can be seen, which shows the steam drum of one of Karlsruhe's 12 boilers. The curved tubes are typical of the Schulz-Thorneycroft patented design which the German 'marine-type' boiler was based on. Interestingly, it looks as if the end has blown out. The boiler rooms used to be a feature of penetrative dives into this wreck. Such is the state of the wreck now that going into them would no longer be recommended.

Moving further aft, one gets to the area of the salvaged engine room. At this point the starboard-side gun originally mounted beside the mainmast can be seen partially buried in the seabed (Image A in Figure 14.13). One has to wonder how it ended up like that and whether it will continue to become more deeply buried, and indeed whether it is indicative of the way the rest of the wreck will go when she surely collapses completely.

The salvage break in the region of the engine room is unmissable. On a day with good visibility one can see the entire area and envisage what was

Figure 14.15. One of Scapa Flow's most iconic images is the stern of SMS *Karlsruhe*, atmospherically captured here. The top portion has now fallen off. (Gavin Anderson)

once there. In Image B the curved remains of what was probably one of the turbine casings can be seen. The valuable non-ferrous blades were key targets for the salvors of the 1970s.

On one dive in 2013 a video recording was made of the 'dark side' of the wreck, a divers' term for the side which is just the hull and therefore not of much interest. On this wreck, however, there were things worth looking at. The main items recorded were the partial remains of the blades of one of the ship's turbine sets. This section still contained the gleaming metal of some of the blades themselves, which must have been accidentally dropped and forgotten about by the salvors. Portions of these blades can be seen elsewhere on the larger wrecks, but only SMS *S54* retains both its turbines intact (see Chapter 17).

Further forward, one comes to a damaged part of the wreck in line with the bridge where the torpedo flat was blasted open. The distorted frames of the ship below the blasted area can be seen in Image D of Figure 14.14. The silvery blur in the bottom of the picture is a passing seal which shot through the gap between myself and the wreck. Divers used to enter the wreck at this point and explore the lower decks. Doing so would appear to be increasingly hazardous, bearing in mind the state of decay today.

SMS *Karlsruhe*'s allure as a shipwreck for divers to explore is completed by its stern. Its angle of orientation coupled with the light at its depth has made it a magnet for photographers, as seen in Gavin Anderson's shot in Figure 14.15. The image shows the hawse pipe at the extreme stern and the unique scalloped cut-outs in the deck.

The exact purpose of these features required archival research to ascertain, starting with the builders' plans. Disappointingly, only a single feature is shown on each side, with doors opening outwards at the main deck level,

Figure 14.16. Images from the stern: A and B show the capstan and its shaft which has been the main support holding the entire structure upright; C shows the locations of what were probably chemical smoke makers; D shows the port side bollard in the collapsed section with the deck hatch behind.

labelled 'H Anlage', probably 'Hinteren Anlage', or, roughly, 'Stern Installation'. But quite what was installed was not described.[16] However, the likely explanation is that they were the housings for chemical smoke generators. This is a feature seen on other German warships, and it is known that the High Seas Fleet made good use of smoke when needed – for example, in the minesweeper action described earlier in this chapter.

Figure 14.16 shows how *Karlsruhe*'s iconic stern looked in 2014. It has since collapsed further so that the upper section had seemingly fallen off during the winter of 2015.[17] The capstan controlling the stern anchor can be seen in Image A. All that remained of the deck when seen end-on is what you see in the image. There was little else holding up the deck at the famously iconic angle seen in Figure 14.15. In fact, the capstan's drive shaft seen from the underside of the deck in Image B was practically all the support the deck had. So collapse was inevitable. Image C shows a close-up of the starboard-side recesses which were for the chemical smoke makers. Finally, Image D shows the port-side mooring bollard at the stern. It lies flat upon wreckage at the seabed level. Behind it is the deck still standing with a rectangular hole where a deck hatch can be seen allowing light through.

The results of the dive surveys, together with the underwater images presented, are shown on the hybrid model of the wreck in Figure 14.17. SMS *Karlsruhe* is without doubt a fascinating shipwreck to examine, belying its initial appearance of being quite broken down now. All of the light cruisers offer almost perfect laboratory conditions for monitoring the way they

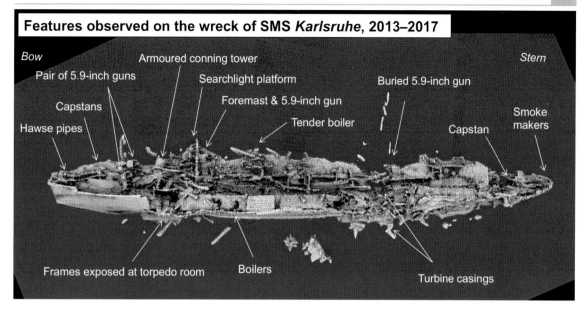

Features observed on the wreck of SMS *Karlsruhe*, 2013–2017

Bow
Armoured conning tower
Stern
Pair of 5.9-inch guns
Searchlight platform
Buried 5.9-inch gun
Capstans
Foremast & 5.9-inch gun
Smoke makers
Hawse pipes
Tender boiler
Capstan
Frames exposed at torpedo room
Boilers
Turbine casings

degrade. Although it is sad to see such a great ship break up, it will unquestionably be an interesting process to observe.

Structural changes observed in the wreck of SMS *Karlsruhe*, 2006–2017

SMS *Karlsruhe* proved to be a rich source of non-ferrous metals during the salvage years. This led inevitably to her being the most damaged by salvage of the four light cruiser wrecks. However, it would be a mistake to assume that her current state as a wreck was due mainly to this activity. Figure 14.18 shows the location of the most desirable components on the plan and elevation drawings of the ship, alongside the hybrid model.

It becomes clear that in addition to the all-too-familiar damage to the engine-room area, blasting her open has affected the wreck in other ways. The extreme stern has been separated from the main body of the wreck, not by blasting in the engine room, but probably by the removal of the propellers and maybe other non-ferrous machinery from the after area of the ship.

It can also clearly be seen that the blasting under the bridge is perfectly in line with the location of the submerged torpedo tubes which were a unique feature of only this light cruiser wreck at Scapa Flow. Also four entire guns are missing from the wreck. These were apparently recovered for scrap in the 1970s.

With the salvage damage as a baseline, the remaining question was how much of the rest of the wreck did the salvage works actually affect? The answer, it seems, is practically none of it. Certainly John Thornton can recall seeing the wreck for the first time in 1981 when the foredeck and afterdeck were still ship-shape, with the salvage areas glaringly obvious standouts in an otherwise intact shipwreck.

Figure 14.17. The location of the key features of the wreck shown in the previous images displayed on the hybrid model. In this case the wreck is seen from top down to allow for the features recorded on the 'dark side' to be shown on the same diagram.

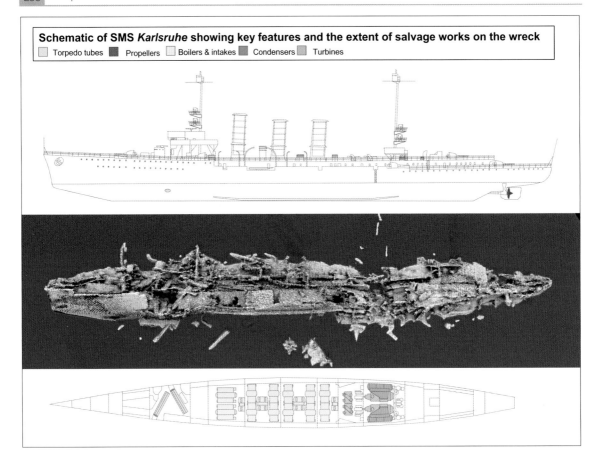

Schematic of SMS *Karlsruhe* showing key features and the extent of salvage works on the wreck

☐ Torpedo tubes ■ Propellers ☐ Boilers & intakes ■ Condensers ☐ Turbines

Figure 14.18. The locations of salvage activity on the wreck of SMS *Karlsruhe* shown by aligning the hybrid model of the wreck in 2017 with drawings showing non-ferrous targets of high priority.

What is for certain is that the wreck of SMS *Karlsruhe* was the first to recognizably deteriorate. This began in the mid-to-late 1980s, when holes began to appear in the upper portion of the wreck, its port side. From then, a general decline has occurred as the wreck has slumped to the seabed. The answer to the question of what caused this wreck to collapse ahead of the other light cruisers is probably related to its depth.

The statistics show that the relatively shallow depth of the wreck has made it the most accessible and therefore the most visited of the German wrecks in Scapa Flow. It was estimated in 2001 that the site had been dived at least 2,160 times in that year.[18] Its fast rate of decay could simply be the result of a relatively high volume of visitors slowly wearing away a monument. This is a feature common on land and a well-understood paradox related to the challenges of providing public access to sites of high cultural significance.

In the years before protection, anecdotally the wreck was a brass bonanza for divers. The incident with the door notwithstanding, divers were able to penetrate the deepest recesses of the wreck and recover an almost endless number of portable artefacts, such as the cage lights the wreck was known for. However, souveniring cannot on its own account for major structural collapse. So what does? Clearly time is a factor, but its effects are not consistent across all of the wrecks, as a recent study has shown.

In 2012 the Ministry of Defence commissioned analysis of the metals from the hulls of a number of shipwrecks in Scapa Flow. SMS *Karlsruhe* was selected as an example from the High Seas Fleet wrecks alongside samples from SS *Prudentia*, HMS *Royal Oak* and HMS *Vanguard*. The metals analysis was carried out using visual, chemical and X-ray techniques. The results were subject to something called Weins numbers analysis.

To summarize, it was found that the rate of corrosion of the metal samples did not follow the usually predictable changes over time which can be calculated using the known factors at work on a specific type of carbon steel. On the samples from *Karlsruhe* (which were the most extensive) the Weins prediction was that the 11–14mm-thick metal would have thinned by 0.3–2.3mm since sinking. The rates of corrosion were in fact seen to be in the region of x7 to x50 faster. The reason for this could not be established with certainty. It was also observed that riveted joints can appear deceptively stable, but in fact be filled with corrosion.[19] By extension, riveted structures may appear visually more stable than they actually are.

One possible theory as to why this accelerated corrosion may be occurring concerns the exhaled gases from divers' scuba equipment. The theory goes that the relatively higher concentration of oxygen in the

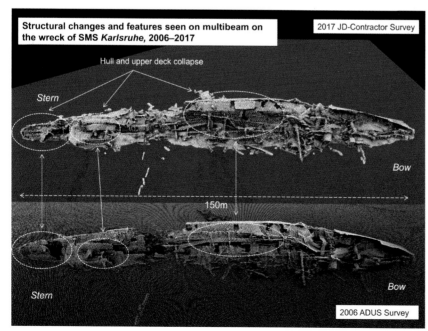

Figure 14.19. Structural changes in the wreck of SMS *Karlsruhe* as seen on multibeam 2006–2017.

compressed air (or the even higher oxygen concentrations in the nitrox mixtures, in increasing use since the 1990s) in use on the wrecks compared with the surrounding seawater is rusting away the wrecks from the inside. Evidence that may support this comes from the fact that it is the upper sides of the wrecks which seem to corrode fastest, being the spot where gases are most likely to accumulate when trapped, causing pitting in the sheets of steel and creating lifting force where the bubbles accumulate. Consistently, the theory goes, it has been the upper sides of the light cruiser wrecks, often in the region of the forecastle, which have corroded first. These areas attracted the artefact-hunting divers in the early days because these were crew accommodation areas. But it should be noted that environmental factors and gravity on their own could also cause degradation of this type, so it is possible it would have occurred this way without visiting divers being a causal factor.

The extent of changes in the wreck over the last decade can be estimated by comparing the 2017 Sea War Museum Jutland survey with the ADUS one from 2006. The results are shown in Figure 14.19. It depicts the ongoing collapse of a shipwreck through time, particularly in the area of the upper sides of the wreck and its attendant superstructure. Of particular note is the falling down of the large davits in the mid-section of the wreck and the very changed nature of the extreme stern, which was described earlier in this chapter. Only the major changes are highlighted in Figure 14.19, but they give a good impression of what seems to be occurring. The wreck has some way to go before it lies completely flat on the seabed, but that outcome is of course inevitable.

Conclusions

Built with the higher-quality materials used on the light cruisers constructed earlier, the ship took time to be commissioned due to manning problems. While her career as a fighting ship may not have been a famous one, SMS *Karlsruhe* has become one of the iconic wrecks of Scapa Flow.

The highest diver visitor numbers are recorded on this wreck, in part because of its attractive depth. The wreck site may well have suffered from collapse as extensively as it has done because of its popularity, but this has not yet been proved beyond doubt. SMS *Karlsruhe* represents one of the most accessible ways for even relatively inexperienced divers to touch a piece of iconic naval history from World War I. Many of its features retain their interest despite the overall declining condition of the site.

1   National Maritime Museum (various dates), constructor's plans of SMS Karlsruhe II. London.

2   N. Friedman (ed.) (1992), German Warships of World War I: The Royal
    Navy's Official Guide to the Capital Ships, Cruisers, Destroyers,
    Submarines and Small Craft, 1914–1918 (London: Greenhill), p. 115.

3   National Maritime Museum (various dates), constructor's plans of
    SMS *Karlsruhe II*. London.

4   G. Staff (2011), *Battle on the Seven Seas: German Cruiser Battles 1914–1918*
    (Barnsley: Pen & Sword), pp. 193–194.

5   H. J. Koerver (ed.) (2009), *Room 40: German Naval Warfare 1914–1918. Volume
    2:   The Fleet in Being* (Steinbach: LIS Reinisch), p. 53.

6   O. Groos (2006), *Der Krieg in der Nordsee Band 7 Vom Sommer 197 bis zum
    Kriegsende 1918 Kritische Edition* (Berlin: Mittler & Sohn), p. 102.

7   T. Philbin (1982), *Admiral von Hipper: The Inconvenient Hero* (Amsterdam:
    Grüner), pp. 172–173.

8   S. C. George (1973), *Jutland to Junkyard: The Raising of the Scuttled German
    High Seas Fleet from Scapa Flow – the greatest salvage operation of all time*
    (Cambridge: Patrick Stephens), p. 23.

9   Hydrographic Department of the Admiralty (2017), Record of Wreck
    No. 1085 SMS *Karlsruhe* (Taunton: Hydrographic Office).

10 Hydrographic Office Archive (various dates), Chart No. C7953 Press 14 H,
    surveyed positions of the sunken German Fleet 1919. Taunton.

11 R. Macdonald (2017), *Dive Scapa Flow* (Edinburgh: Mainstream), p. 191.

12 Hydrographic Department of the Admiralty (2017), Record of Wreck
    No. 1085 SMS *Karlsruhe* (Taunton: Hydrographic Office).

13 Hydrographic Department of the Admiralty (2017), Record of Wreck
    No. 1085 SMS *Karlsruhe* (Taunton: Hydrographic Office).

14 P. L. Smith (1989), *The Naval Wrecks of Scapa Flow* (Kirkwall: Orkney Press),
    p. 56.

15 P. L. Smith (1989), *The Naval Wrecks of Scapa Flow* (Kirkwall: Orkney Press),
    p. 56.

16 National Maritime Museum (various dates), constructor's plans of SMS
    Karlsruhe II. London.

17 R. Macdonald (2017), *Dive Scapa Flow* (Edinburgh: Mainstream), p. 196.

18 ScapaMAP 2000–2002 (2003), Report Compiled for Historic Scotland on the
    Mapping and Management of the Submerged Archaeological Resource in
    Scapa Flow. Orkney: Scapa Flow Marine Archaeology Project, p. 16.

19 Intertek (2014), *Laboratory Analysis of Scapa Flow Ship Wreck Samples and
    Application of the Weins Number Methodology* (Aberdeen: Intertek) (copy
    in author's collection).

CHAPTER 15
SMS *CÖLN*

Figure 15.1. SMS *Cöln,* launched 5 October 1916. Design displacement 5,531 tons, length 156m, eight 5.9-inch and three (two of them in 1918) 88mm guns. Four 60cm torpedo tubes. The larger bridge structure enclosing the armoured conning tower is a distinctive feature of this class, along with four deck mounted torpedo tubes. (Orkney Archive)

SMS Cöln *was a late arrival to the High Seas Fleet and her naval career was largely uneventful. But as a shipwreck she has become the most iconic of the light cruiser wrecks at Scapa Flow, primarily due to the fact that she is now the most intact and visually impressive. A dive on this wreck is truly a remarkable journey back through time. But her current condition is somewhat illusory as her collapse is now beginning to accelerate and her years as an intact wreck are coming to a close.*

Design and service history

The light cruiser SMS *Cöln* was the lead ship of her class, which comprised the last iterations of the light cruiser design of the High Seas Fleet. Only *Cöln* and *Dresden* were completed, and they lie one mile apart on the bottom of Scapa Flow. Her name is often misspelled as *Köln*. While both spellings relate to the city of Cologne, the spelling convention of *Cöln* was in place when the ship was named and that is her official name. Following the tradition of the previous Königsberg class, she was named after the earlier ill-fated SMS *Cöln* which was sunk at the Battle of Heligoland Bight in 1914 with only a single survivor. She is sometimes referred to as *Cöln II* for this reason.

SMS *Cöln* was laid down in 1915 in the Blohm & Voss shipyard, Hamburg, launched in October 1916 and commissioned in January 1918. This extremely long completion period was due in part to personnel shortages in the High Seas Fleet caused by the rapid expansion of the U-boat arm from late 1916. The fleet was stripped of many of its youngest and brightest officers at this time. The shortage of better-quality officers in the fleet is often cited as a reason why morale was allowed to fall so low in 1917 to 1918, undoubtedly a driving factor behind the naval mutiny.

The Cöln class differed slightly from SMS *Karlsruhe*'s Königsberg class, with changes and improvements. As with the earlier light cruisers of this type, they were noted as good sea boats. One source uniquely states, probably erroneously, that SMS *Cöln* was fitted with a roll damping system.[1] The class was built using longitudinal framing with an increased number of watertight compartments – 24 in all. The double bottom covered around 45% of the keel. They were given an increased number of boilers (14, compared with the Königsberg class's 12), of which only eight now burned coal (a reduction of two) and six oil. They powered two marine turbines and two screws. These were laid out in the same fashion as the Königsberg class, side by side. At 27 knots, *Cöln*'s given range was 5,400 nautical miles.[2]

SMS *Cöln* was well armoured with a belt of maximum thickness of 60cm, fining to 18cm below the waterline. The armoured deck was between 20 and 60mm thick, with 40mm on the sloping portions which encapsulated the top of the engine and boiler rooms. She was fitted with a 40mm collision bulkhead of a similar design to that of the Königsberg class. Her armoured conning tower was also the same, with 100cm armour on the vertical face and 20cm on the roof.

The similarities continued with the armament of eight 5.9-inch guns laid out in the same fashion. The Cöln class was originally fitted with an additional third 88mm gun, but this appears to have been removed from them in 1918. The torpedo arrangement was different, with all four tubes being mounted on the upper deck. One pair was as per the Königsberg class, each side of the space between the first two funnels, while the second pair was mounted just aft of the third funnel. The torpedoes were of the more powerful 60cm type as opposed to the earlier 50cm (20-inch) type fitted to the Königsberg class. The Cöln-class ships were designed to carry mines when needed. Sources differ on the actual number, but it was probably similar to the Königsberg class at around 200.

SMS *Cöln* in service

SMS *Cöln* was finally commissioned on 17 January 1918 and joined the Second Scouting Group, consisting entirely of light cruisers, in February. As noted by British intelligence, her career was remarkably uneventful. The Second Scouting Group took part in the last sortie by the High Seas Fleet in April 1918. This was to be a sweep up the Norway coast, with the advanced First Scouting Group of battlecruisers, the Second Scouting Group and accompanying destroyers working 80 miles ahead of the fleet to find and destroy a convoy. The operation was curtailed when the battlecruiser *Moltke* suffered mechanical failure. No convoy was located. Interestingly, from radio intercepts, British intelligence had concluded that SMS *Cöln* was not present as she was exercising at Kiel.[3] This is not mentioned in the German official history, which states that of the light cruisers only *Stralsund* was unavailable.[4]

In May the British recorded that *Cöln* was one of a group of five light cruisers which took part in minelaying operations in the Bight. In 1918, Germany significantly strengthened its defensive minefields around the Bight as a deterrent to British raids. In October *Cöln* was being readied to take part in the fleet sortie into the southern North Sea. She was one of four light cruisers from the Second Scouting Group allocated to attack shipping in the Thames Estuary in an attempt to provoke the British into a major naval confrontation. The raid never took place as open mutiny broke out on 29 October.

Mutiny, internment and scuttling

SMS *Cöln* is noted as one of the few larger warships in the High Seas Fleet that remained at least functional enough for operations during the naval mutiny. The Second Scouting Group was at this time under the command of Commodore Harder, who had been captain of SMS *Lützow* at Jutland. It appears that a number of ships under his command remained loyal, as did many of the torpedo boat formations. In response to an aircraft report of an encroaching British raid, *Cöln* was one of three light cruisers and two torpedo boat flotillas that responded and advanced to meet a threat which was not located. SMS *Königsberg* and SMS *Cöln* were carrying out normal outpost duties at the time.[5]

The surrendered fleet left Germany on 19 November for the Firth of Forth. During the crossing, *Cöln* developed a condenser leak. Von Reuter ordered an escort to tow her if needed, but she managed to struggle on and duly arrived to surrender with the rest of the fleet. Her speed was clearly affected because on her transfer to Scapa on 26–27 November she straggled again. The following weeks saw the arrival of further ships which had departed Germany late. Among them were SMS *König* and SMS *Dresden*, which now keep her company on the seabed of Scapa Flow. On 21 June 1919, the day of the Grand Scuttle, SMS *Cöln* left the surface for her final resting place at 1350hrs, the same time that the famous battlecruiser SMS *Seydlitz* also sank.

History as a wreck

SMS *Cöln* is one of the three remaining light cruiser wrecks in Scapa Flow which was never actually sold to a salvage company. She was, as far as Britain was concerned, legally the property of the Admiralty until sold to Orkney Islands Council on 3 November 1986. But in the years between the Grand Scuttle and her sale, her salvage rights were leased to commercial salvors. This is in fact the way most salvage arrangements with the Admiralty worked. It is the exception rather than the rule for military vessels to be sold outright.

The original salvage lease was taken out by Nundy Marine Metals in 1962. As was usual on the light cruisers, Nundy simply harvested the lowest-hanging and most profitable fruit. This included the easy-to-reach propellers. Nundy sold up to Scapa Flow Salvage Ltd in 1970. This is when the majority of the salvage work took place.

Scapa Flow Salvage Ltd blasted into *Cöln* to recover the condensers and other valuable non-ferrous components, including the upper, easier-to-reach port-side turbine. The other was left in place. It also removed up to three of the torpedo tubes, as one is still in the wreck today. The company soon came to realize that as a late-build warship, her components were not of the quality seen in *Karlsruhe* and *Brummer*. By the time she was completed, even *Cöln*'s portholes were seen to be made of steel. The salvage divers noted that the sailors on board had made a good job of the scuttling, leaving the main sea cocks and the condenser inspection hatches open.[6]

The salvage lease passed next to Undersea Associates in 1978. Bankruptcy followed in 1979 and the lease was then passed by the official receiver to Clark's Diving Services Ltd of Lerwick. When the lease was not renewed by Clark's, control reverted to the Ministry of Defence. The wreck was then sold to Orkney Island Council, which is the current legal owner. SMS *Cöln* was officially designated under the Ancient Monuments and Archaeological Areas Act on 17 April 2002.

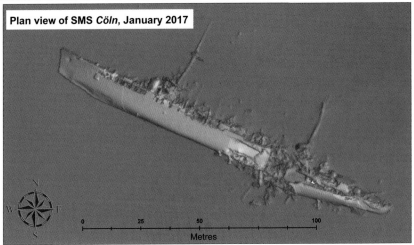

Plan view of SMS *Cöln*, January 2017

Figure 15.2. DTM model of the wreck of SMS *Cöln*, January 2017.

SMS *Cöln* today

The DTM of SMS *Cöln* as scanned in January 2017 is shown in Figure 15.2. The wreck is on her starboard side and is oriented like the rest of the High Seas Fleet wrecks, with the exception of *Markgraf*, which was being moved when she foundered. The salvage area is easily spotted and is minimal compared with that of *Karlsruhe*, supporting the accounts of the salvage work on this wreck being comparatively superficial.

The DTM view shown is directly top down and is sensitive enough to pick out the remains of the funnels of the ship, a rarely seen feature because they are one of the first things to rot away, being made of relatively thin steel. In three dimensions the hybrid model is used to see more detail from any angle viewed, as seen in Figures 15.3 and 15.4.

The wreck is revealed to be the most intact of all the High Seas Fleet shipwrecks. The entire ship's structure is present, and whereas on *Brummer* and *Karlsruhe* the blasting in the engine-room area goes all the way to the seabed, it does not in this case, confirming that only the port-side turbine was removed from the wreck. A good number of features of this ship can be easily spotted on the hybrid model. These include the superfiring pair of guns aft, the still extant davits and the bridge and the armoured conning tower.

As recorded in January 2017, the depth to the seabed was 34 metres and the top of the wreck reached up to 19.5 metres. The original post-scuttling survey carried out in 1919 recorded the top of the wreck to be 11 fathoms (20 metres), and every survey since has confirmed this. So the wreck has not changed in height over the last 100 years[7]. This of course does not mean the wreck hasn't changed during this time. Over the last decade in particular age has taken its toll, as will be shown.

The underwater images which follow were from dives from 2013 to 2017 and they capture some of the interesting features of the wreck recorded while

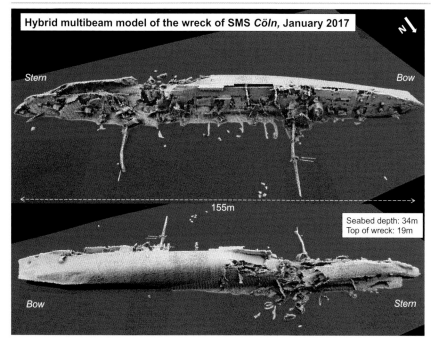

Figure 15.3. Hybrid model
of the wreck of SMS *Cöln*.

surveying the site. The sequence of photographs starts at the bow and works aft. Figure 15.5 shows some of the features of the foredeck. Image A shows one of the pair of capstans present. The chains are still present. Interestingly, the pair of 5.9-inch guns which originally sat side by side on the foredeck have both gone. These were some of a number of items that were recovered in the 1970s by Scapa Flow Salvage Ltd and chopped up for scrap.[8] Images C

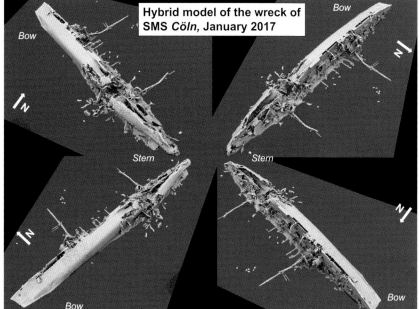

Figure 15.4. All around view
of the wreck of SMS *Cöln*.

Figure 15.5. Features of the foredeck. Image A, one of the pair of capstans. Image B, the lower of the pair of gun mountings. Images C and D, the lower of a pair of skylights.

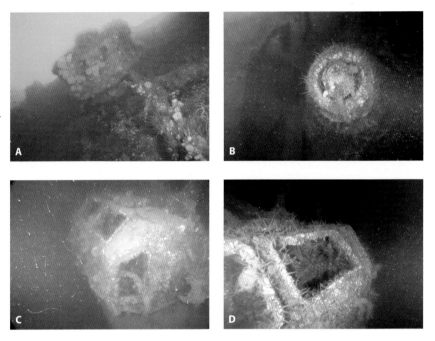

and D show one of a pair of skylights situated aft of the guns, shedding natural light into the crew accommodation area in the deck below.

Figure 15.6 shows images of the armoured conning tower. The type fitted to SMS *Cöln* and to SMS *Dresden* was of a substantially larger type than those

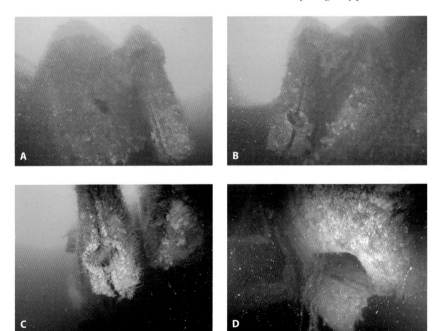

Figure 15.6. The armoured conning tower with its partially broken rangefinder on the roof (Images A–C). Image D shows the open starboard side door seen from above.

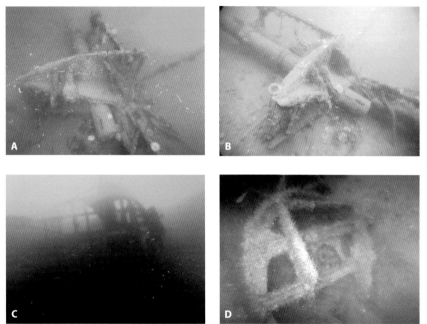

Figure 15.7. The crow's nest of the foremast can be seen in Images A and B; Image C is a view of the bridge from the crow's nest, showing the surviving framework; and Image D shows one of the searchlight platforms upside down on the seabed.

seen on the earlier light cruiser wrecks of *Brummer* and *Karlsruhe*, as can be seen in Figure 13.2. In fact it was effectively two towers in one. The lower forward portion was used to steer the ship. The rear section, which extended higher, was used for gunnery control. Images A and B show the tower from forward (B) and aft (A). The shape of the upper tier can be seen in Image A and the roof of the lower tier can be seen in Image B. Image C shows the lens housing in the surviving arm of the rangefinder fitted atop the upper tier. The upper arm of the rangefinder fell off around the time of the millennium.

Image D is a view of the starboard-side door into the tower. It is an interesting shot because below the doorway it shows the remnants of the bridge structure which was originally built around the armoured tower, incorporating it into the distinctive bridge arrangement seen on the *Cöln* and *Dresden*. The image also shows cables and wires trailing out of the opened door. This seems to indicate that something has been dragged out of there in the past.

By comparison with the armoured tower, the bridge was very lightly built, so it is nice to be able to see a good portion of its structure still currently intact. In Figure 15.7 the framework of beams which made up the floor of the upper bridge structure can be seen silhouetted against the light in Image C. The photo was taken from the seabed, facing the wreck at a location near to where the crow's nest can be seen in Images A and B. The nest itself was enclosed in a metal structure which has rotted now, leaving just the outer frame. On the mast under the crow's nest were a pair of searchlight platforms

Figure 15.8. Image A, the top of the armoured conning tower, showing its tiered design and shut port side door. Image B, one of the iconic extant davits seen from below. Image C, the port side forward wing 5.9-inch gun mounting seen from aft. Image D, a diver swimming through the once intact area of superstructure aft of the bridge.

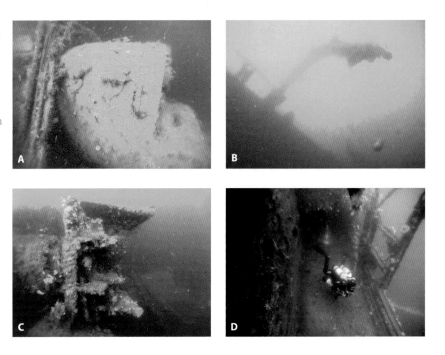

which can be seen in Figure 13.2. The lower of the pair has broken off and lies upside down on the seabed, as seen in Image D.

Up at the top of the wreck the armoured conning tower is seen from above in Image A of Figure 15.8. This shot gives a good view of its two-tiered design.

Figure 15.9. Image A, the surviving high angle AA gun just before the salvage break. Image B, the torpedo loading door at the uppermost point of the vertical torpedo tube seen in Image C. Image D, a large portion of turbine blades left behind by salvors.

It can also be seen that the port-side door is still shut. Just aft of it at the highest point of the wreck is the port-side-wing 5.9-inch gun housing. The roof and gun have been removed, or have fallen off in the past. The gun was reported to be present in 2000.[9] If that is correct, then at some point after that date it must have crashed into the bridge structure below it.

One of the iconic features on the wreck of SMS *Cöln* consists of the remaining overhanging davits, which can be seen in the multibeam images of this wreck

Figure 15.10. The aftermost 5.9-inch gun with diver for perspective. The barrel traversed over the top of the capstan on the quarterdeck. (Gavin Anderson)

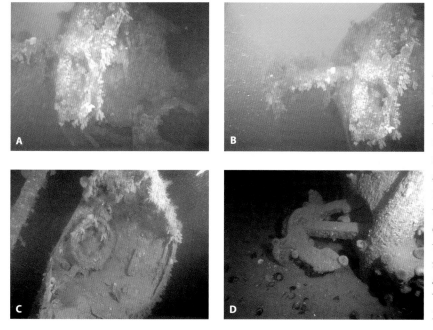

Figure 15.11. Features at the stern. Images A and B show the stern of the quarterdeck with the starboard side smoke making holder and anchor as recorded in 2013. By 2017 this area had completely changed. Image D shows the anchor on the seabed as the stern has collapsed. Image C shows the remains of the port side smoke pot holder, torn open as the wreck has broken up. The starboard one as seen in 2017 is shown in Figure 15.10.

Figure 15.12. The starboard side holder of the chemical smoke making gear as recorded in November 2017. The base on which the smoke pot was located can be seen inside. In this case it has moved to the orientation it would have been in at the point when the pot would have been ejected into the sea. This area of the wreck has recently suffered a major collapse. See Image A in Figure 15.11 to see how it looked in 2013.

and in various artists' impressions made over the years. One of these can be seen silhouetted against the sunlight in Image B. The area shown in Image D was space between the upper deck and the superstructure in the region just under the davit. A diver can be seen swimming aft, having exited from the space behind. As of 2017, this area has now collapsed and is gone for ever.

In the central area of the wreck are the remains of one of the high-angle 88mm AA guns. Some histories say there were originally three on the ship, but that one was removed in 1918. The location of the remaining pair can be seen in the photo of SMS *Cöln* in Figure 15.1. Only one gun remains in place now, but apparently both guns could be seen by divers back in the 1980s.[10] They were reported as pointing forward, as the surviving one still does today. This gun can be seen in Image A of Figure 15.9. Interestingly, these 88mm guns are drawn on the class plans pointing aft, but in reality they point the other way.[11]

With the long history of salvage on these wrecks in mind, it was something of a surprise to come across a torpedo tube on this wreck during the first survey dive in 2013, the presumption being that all had long gone. Made of bronze, these were key salvage targets. In fact, the one seen in Images B and C of Figure 15.9 appears to be the sole survivor anywhere in Scapa Flow. The tube is oriented vertically, with the open end pierced deep into the seabed. The loading door is at the highest point. It is probably the starboard one of the pair situated abaft the third funnel (one each side), roughly where it is found now. It seems it may have swung into the vertical as the ship rolled over and sank. However it got there, it is good to see an example of one of these tubes still visible on the wrecks. They are very substantial when seen up close underwater and always impressive.

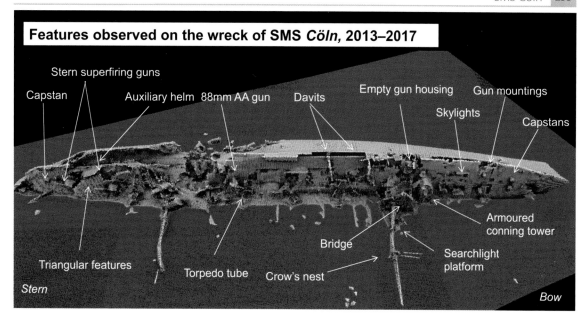

Features observed on the wreck of SMS *Cöln*, 2013–2017

Stern superfiring guns

Capstan   Auxiliary helm 88mm AA gun   Davits   Empty gun housing   Gun mountings

Skylights

Capstans

Armoured conning tower

Bridge

Searchlight platform

Triangular features

Torpedo tube   Crow's nest

Stern

Bow

Figure 15.13. Features seen on the wreck of SMS *Cöln* shown on the hybrid model.

Image D of Figure 15.9 shows a large section of turbine which lies on the seabed near the base of the torpedo tube. This must have been abandoned or forgotten during the salvage operations. Perhaps it and the tube were scheduled for a salvage lift that for whatever reason never took place.

The sternmost area of the wreck, aft of the area opened up by blasting, also contains a number of interesting features. Passing over the superfiring 5.9-inch gun, one comes to one such feature, that shown in Figure 15.10. In this shot Gavin Anderson has nicely captured the aftermost 5.9-inch gun. His dive buddy in the background provides scale and is helping to illuminate the capstan, over which the barrel of the gun traversed.

When recorded in 2013, the stern of the wreck was recognizable as an entire structure. Image A of Figure 15.11 shows the extreme aft end of the quarterdeck as it was then. The circular feature at the bottom of the image looked oddly similar to the double features seen at the same location on the wreck of SMS *Karlsruhe* (see Figures 15.14.and 14.16) and seen again in better condition on the wreck of SMS *Dresden* (see the next chapter).

Similar to the case of *Karlsruhe*, the ship's drawings (of the sister ship *Dresden* in this case) are obscure as to their meaning. The plans show a seaplane sitting on the quarterdeck, although as far as is currently known, neither *Cöln* nor *Dresden* flew aircraft in service, so this feature is probably not related to aviation.[12] It is in fact the holder for the chemical smoke pots which were a feature of German naval design at this location on warships into the 1930s. When in November 2017 the smoke pot holders on port and starboard were scheduled to be recorded on video in the light of this new research, the stern of the wreck was found to have largely collapsed since it was originally recorded in 2013.

The stern of this wreck has altered dramatically in the last few years. The extreme stern of the wreck was characterized in 2013 by the anchor, which had somehow partially fallen out of its hawse and twisted though 90 degrees so that it faced upwards, as shown in Image B of Figure 15.11 But in 2017 it was observed that the stern had collapsed almost entirely and that the anchor now lay on the seabed, as seen in Image D. Image C shows the remains of the port-side smoke pot holder, torn open by the forces at work as the wreck collapses. The pots sat in the circular base seen in the centre of the image. It appears to have been an ejector system by means of which the pot, once set to smoke, could be ejected out through a door in the side of the hull. The starboard-side smoke pot holder is seen in detail in Figure 15.12.

Interestingly, due to the intact nature of this shipwreck most of the features described in the underwater images can actually be seen quite clearly in the hybrid model of the wreck, as shown in Figure 15.13. The artificial illumination given to the point cloud in all of the models in this book is from directly above the wreck. In this instance, even the loading door of the vertical torpedo tube has been illuminated using this process, showing a small circular feature just forward of the 88mm gun.

Structural changes observed in the wreck of SMS *Cöln*, 2006–2017

On SMS *Cöln*, seemingly the most intact of the Scapa Flow wrecks of the High Seas Fleet, it is interesting to see what sorts of changes have occurred in the past. As with the other wrecks, getting an accurate impression of what she looked like going back beyond the time of diver-made videos and marine geophysics is a challenge. Nevertheless, the salvage years give a good baseline for the types of changes which occurred then. The assumption made is that the structures of the wrecks as a whole did not substantively alter until they were blasted open for salvage.

In the case of SMS *Cöln* this primarily occurred after 1972, when the wreck was worked on by Scapa Flow Salvage Ltd. The propellers had been removed before then with minimal damage to the wreck. According to Dougall Campbell of Scapa Flow Salvage Ltd, the wreck yielded profitable metals, but not in anything like the quantities of SMS *Karlsruhe*. The blasting which took place was aimed at the condensers in the ship's engine room, which were successfully recovered. The turbines were in steel housings and had to be broken open to recover the blades. This was hardly worth the effort.[13] This probably explains why a section of the turbine with blades is still seen in the wreck.

Figure 15.14 lines up the hybrid model seen from above with a drawing showing selected internals of *Cöln* in elevation. The area of salvage damage

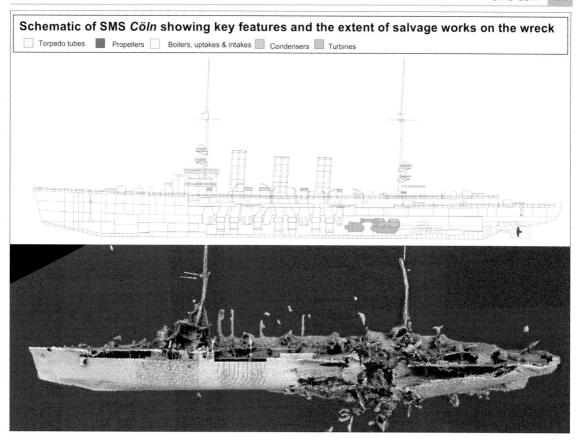

Schematic of SMS *Cöln* showing key features and the extent of salvage works on the wreck

☐ Torpedo tubes ■ Propellers ☐ Boilers, uptakes & intakes ▨ Condensers ▨ Turbines

is easy to pick out, and in fact it can be seen to be limited to the area which lines up perfectly with the condensers, and to an area forward of that which primarily lines up with the high-pressure turbines which have been accessed from the keel of the ship.

Figure 15.14. Diagram showing the key features for salvors in the wreck of SMS *Cöln*. The area of blasting coincides with the condensers and cruising turbines.

Figure 15.15. The upper arm of the rangefinder on SMS *Cöln* in place in 1999. The older recordings of these wrecks are now important resources in helping to understand how they are degrading. (John Thornton)

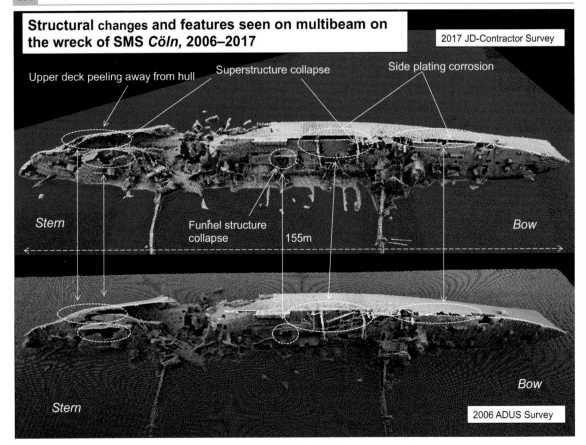

Structural changes and features seen on multibeam on the wreck of SMS *Cöln*, 2006–2017

2017 JD-Contractor Survey

Upper deck peeling away from hull

Superstructure collapse

Side plating corrosion

Stern

Funnel structure collapse

155m

Bow

Stern

Bow

2006 ADUS Survey

Figure 15.16. Changes seen in the wreck by comparing data from the 2006 ADUS survey with data from our own survey in 2017. In a decade the outer skin has begun to significantly corrode in the areas commonly accessed by divers.

Assuming the rest of the changes are not salvage-related means they have occurred since Scapa Flow Salvage ceased work on the wrecks in 1978. There appears to have been no work on this wreck afterwards. Undersea Associates rapidly went bankrupt, and according to Thomas Clark of Clark's Diving Services (the last salvage company to have a salvage lease), no work took place on this wreck.[14]

In reality, then, only the passage of time and the activities of recreational divers who began to visit the wrecks in larger numbers from the 1980s have caused the wreck to degrade further. Corrosion of course has inevitably played its part. Weaker structures such as the funnels are long gone and other less substantial items, such as the rangefinder, have also given way to the ravages of time. The upper arm of the rangefinder was recorded as intact and in place by John Thornton in 1999, but it had gone by 2002 when the area was filmed by him again.

The extent to which the external features of the wreck have changed in the last decade can be measured by comparing our 2017 survey with the 2006 ADUS one. In Figure 15.16 the most obvious changes are highlighted, although others are there which the reader will surely spot. The changes appear to follow a common twofold pattern.

First there is general collapse, as the wreck naturally degrades. In the relatively confined waters of Scapa Flow, compared with sites such as those in the more dynamic marine conditions of the Jutland battlefield, this process has so far been gradual and comparatively benign. The areas around the funnel bases and a portion of the superstructure between the two remaining davits could be interpreted as having collapsed in this way, due to corrosion, gravity and the passage of time.

The second impact on the wreck, which is more difficult to gauge accurately, is the presence of visiting divers. In what appears to be a consistent pattern, it is the upper plating on the sides of the light cruisers, especially in the forecastle area between the main and upper decks, which corrodes away, opening up these areas to the wider marine environment. Reports by divers visiting this wreck since the 1980s show that a popular route was to enter the wreck through the hole on the foredeck, then travel aft along the main deck and frequently pass into the decks below.[15] Another diver guide noted that divers 'rate this wreck extremely high for penetration'.[16] Exploration of shipwrecks motivates many to go diving, but inevitably it seems the wrecks pay a price.

The common pattern of corrosion this seems to cause was, as far as can be researched, first observed during an archaeological survey on the wreck in 2001, when it was noted of the corrosion on the forward side plating 'that the hull was under stress'.[17] Interestingly, it is not detectable on the multibeam results from that year.[18] But by 2006 it could be seen on the ADUS survey, as shown in Figure 15.15. As a result of the archaeological survey by video in the same year, it was merely observed that 'the overall area of corrosion has increased'.[19]

But within a decade almost the entire plating above the main deck from the centre of the ship to the forward capstans has become exposed as the side of the ship in this area has seemingly completely degraded. This is largely identical to the patterns of corrosion seen first on SMS *Karlsruhe* and then on SMS *Brummer* (where the feature is still visible on the multibeam scans) which heralded their more general deterioration and collapse. So it does seem likely that this wreck will inevitably follow the same path in the future.

It is also interesting to observe how the upper deck and superstructure on the area aft of the salvage break have become more separated from the hull over the last decade. It appears that the widening of the gap between them has been caused by the heavier features on the deck side starting to head to the seabed. In a way, this could be seen a precursor to what will inevitably happen to the rest of the wreck. In the cases so far examined this has been a common feature. The heavy decks, aided by gravity and corrosion, have been pulling on the hulls and falling outwards. This is particularly evident on the next wreck site, SMS *Dresden*.

Conclusions

As a classic extant example of the World War I–era light cruiser, SMS *Cöln* is an important shipwreck. Moreover, she is arguably one of the world's great military shipwreck dives. However, as the recent collapse of the extreme stern shows, she too is following a broadly consistent pattern of degradation seen on the other light cruiser wreck sites. Although it is sad to see her go, there will inevitably be an archaeological upside, for as more of the internals of the ship become exposed, they too can then be explored and come to be understood. The drawings and other evidence which survives for these great ships does not provide answers to many features seen, as the example of the smoke pots shows. We know less about the details of these types of ships than many may presume.

1   E. Gröner (1990), German Warships 1815–1945. Volume One: Major Surface Vessels (London: Conway), p. 114.

2   R. Gardiner (ed.) (1985), *Conway's All the World's Fighting Ships 1906–1921* (London: Conway), p. 163.

3   H. J. Koerver (ed.) (2009), *Room 40: German Naval Warfare 1914–1918. Volume 2: The Fleet in Being* (Steinbach: LIS Reinisch), p. 43.

4   O. Groos (2006), *Der Krieg in der Nordsee Band 7 Vom Sommer 197 bis zum Kriegsende 1918 Kritische Edition* (Berlin: Mittler. & Sohn), p. 269.

5   H. J. Koerver (ed.) (2009), *Room 40: German Naval Warfare 1914–1918. Volume 2: The Fleet in Being* (Steinbach: LIS Reinisch), p. 391.

6   R. Macdonald (2017), *Dive Scapa Flow* (Edinburgh: Mainstream), p. 168.

7   Hydrographic Department of the Admiralty (2017), Record of Wreck No. 1090 SMS *Koln* [sic] (Taunton: Hydrographic Office).

8   In telephone conversation with Dougall Campbell of Scapa Flow Salvage Ltd, November 2017.

9   Hydrographic Department of the Admiralty (2017), Record of Wreck No. 1090 SMS *Koln* [sic] (Taunton: Hydrographic Office).

10   P. L. Smith (1989), *The Naval Wrecks of Scapa Flow* (Kirkwall: Orkney Press), p. 65.

11   The Dreadnought Project (dreadnoughtproject.org), constructor's plans of SMS *Dresden II*.

12   The Dreadnought Project (dreadnoughtproject.org), constructor's plans of SMS *Dresden II*.

13   In telephone conversation with Dougall Campbell of Scapa Flow Salvage Ltd, November 2017.

14   In telephone conversation with Thomas Clark of Clark's Diving Services, October 2017.

15 P. L. Smith (1989), *The Naval Wrecks of Scapa Flow* (Kirkwall: Orkney Press), p. 64.

16 L. Wood (2008), *Scapa Flow Dive Guide* (Southend-on-Sea: Aquapress), p. 55.

17 ScapaMAP 2000–2002 (2003), Report Compiled for Historic Scotland on the Mapping and Management of the Submerged Archaeological Resource in Scapa Flow. Orkney: Scapa Flow Marine Archaeology Project, p. 44.

18 ScapaMAP 2000–2002 (2003), Report Compiled for Historic Scotland on the Mapping and Management of the Submerged Archaeological Resource in Scapa Flow. Orkney: Scapa Flow Marine Archaeology Project, p. 34.

19 ScapaMAP (2001–2006), Marine Heritage Monitoring with High Resolution Survey Tools: Scapa Flow 2001–2006. Orkney: Scapa Flow Marine Archaeology Project, p. 38.

CHAPTER 16
SMS *DRESDEN*

Figure 16.1. SMS *Dresden*, launched 25 April 1917. Design displacement 5,531 tons, length 156m, eight 5.9-inch and three (two of them in 1918) 88mm guns. Four 60cm torpedo tubes. The larger bridge structure enclosing the armoured conning tower is a distinctive feature of this class. Note the twin guns on the foredeck. (Aidan Dodson Collection)

SMS Dresden, *like her sister* Cöln, *did not have a noteworthy service career. Ironically, this light cruiser has become far better known since she became a shipwreck. Originally as a salvage target, then as a mecca for wreck divers and latterly as a cultural artefact, the wreck has played many roles. She remains a fascinating example of the German naval architecture of World War I. For those lucky enough to dive on her, she provides an engrossing journey into the past.*

Design and service history

SMS *Dresden* was the second and last to be finished of the Cöln class. She was laid down in the Howaltswerke, Kiel shipyard in 1916 and launched on 25 April 1917. Due to the same personnel issues which affected the commissioning of *Cöln* – primarily the expansion of the U-boat arm – she was not ready for service until 28 March 1918. Technically she was *Dresden II* as, following the convention used to name the other later German light cruisers, she was named after the light cruiser *Dresden* which was scuttled off Robinson Crusoe Island, Chile in March 1915 after a notable career in the southern hemisphere.

Dresden's design particulars were practically identical to SMS *Cöln*'s (see the previous chapter). However, it should be noted that these ships can be identified in photographs by the bridge which encloses the armoured conning tower. German light cruisers of this period were fitted with the armoured conning tower to protect the gunnery control crew. The tower is identifiable on all the light cruisers by the rangefinder on the top. In battle the ship could also be conned from within the tower. The bridge enclosing the armoured conning tower is easy to spot in Figure 16.1.

An anecdote which is worth repeating relates to how British intelligence learned that *Dresden* was being built. So dire was the situation in Germany in 1917 regarding shortages that the superintendent of her construction applied for permission to have his shoes resoled. After a lengthy bureaucratic process the final reply was put in the mail sack for the wrong *Dresden* and sent to Chile, where the crew of the original *Dresden* were interned. There the mails to the crew fell into the hands of the British and were read. Such is the way intelligence is gathered. It is not recorded whether the superintendent's application was successful.[1]

SMS *Dresden* in service

According to British intelligence estimations, once she was commissioned under the command of the Kaiser's son, Prinz Adalbert, SMS *Dresden* spent from April to July 1918 on trials at Kiel and only finally joined the Second Scouting Group on 7 August. On the other hand, the official German history shows her attached to the Second Scouting Group in April.[2] However, she is not listed as partaking in the abortive fleet sweep up the coast of Norway on 23–24 of that month.[3] This is probably because she was still working up.

Her war diary (*Kriegstagebücher*, or KTB) for 1918 shows that her operational career began in late August with a minelaying operation. On 30 August a defect was reported with her port dynamo, which was rectified by 3 September. Sentry duty followed through September. She then operated as an escort of U-boats and minesweepers. These routine operations went without any mishap being recorded right through to when the fleet mutinied.[4] It is one of the more curious inaccuracies to have crept into the literature of the wrecks of the Grand Scuttle that *Dresden* is cited as being torpedoed by a British submarine off Emden in August, with a detailed description of the damage sustained, the battle to save the ship and the extensive repairs needed.[5] From her KTB it seems that this entire event is a fabrication.

Mutiny, internment and scuttling

SMS *Dresden* remained loyal when the initial mutiny broke out and was performing her normal duties. Trouble at Kiel began when the rebellious 3rd Squadron arrived there on 3 November. The following day she was ordered to depart for Eckernförde to operate as a radio relay ship as communications were becoming unreliable. When she attempted to leave harbour, SMS *Markgraf*, the most rebellious of the ships, was moored outside her and would not clear to let her leave. A standoff developed during which time *Markgraf* turned a 12-inch turret on her. It seems that more sober heads prevailed and *Dresden* was allowed to depart.[6]

Later on the same day it seems *Dresden* was ordered to the Baltic to join the 4th Scouting Group. The group arrived at Swinemünde on 7 November. Admiral Karpf, in charge of the group, heard a rumour that evening that the mutinous fleet was sailing to attack him. Without consulting superiors he ordered the entire group to scuttle, destroy confidential books and flood magazines. This was done on board SMS *Brummer*, SMS *Bremse*, SMS *Regensburg* and SMS *Dresden*.

On SMS *Dresden* the magazine flooding appears to have got out of control. The Kingston valves were not shut in time and the entire ship foundered, settling on the harbour floor. The damage to the ship could not be readily repaired until some semblance of order returned to the fleet.[7] Consequently, although named as part of the surrender fleet during the armistice negotiations, the ship did not sail on 19 November because she was in dock receiving temporary repairs. Finally, on December 4 she set sail for Scapa Flow and internment on the same day as SMS *König* and the torpedo boat *V129*, a replacement for SMS *V30*, which had stuck a mine and sunk while in transit with the surrender fleet.

SMS *Dresden* finally arrived at Scapa on the evening of 6 December, too late to be shown to her allocated berth with the rest of the interned fleet. So she was temporarily berthed in Switha Sound overnight alongside a British destroyer and three tugs and was brought into the Flow and inspected the following day.[8] In her final berth, which is her resting place today, she was the most southeastern of the ships moored in the old fleet auxiliary anchorage off Cava.

On the day of the Grand Scuttle SMS *Dresden* departed early for the bottom. Von Reuter recorded the time she sank as 1330hrs, not long after it was realized ashore what was happening and the first attempts were being made to save the ships. In Admiral Fremantle's report of events that day he mentions that, prior to the return of the battle squadron, an attempt was made to save *Dresden*.

Vice Admiral Prendergast organized the saving of several ships and an attempt was made by the trawler *Classin* to beach her. They got the mooring cable free but she foundered while being taken in tow. *Classin* then went on to assist in the successful saving of SMS *Frankfurt*.[9] In his report, Prendergast states: 'An attempt was made to tow *Dresden* but she was sinking too fast.'[10] By the time the battle squadron had returned at 1430hrs, *Dresden* was on the bottom of Scapa Flow. One anchor chain from *Dresden* has been observed to be run out on the seabed, suggesting that *Classin* got that part of her job done before *Dresden* sank.

The report filed by Lt Cdr Fabricius, *Dresden*'s commanding officer, while he was a prisoner seems to confirm that she foundered before she could be shifted off her mooring. It also gives an interesting description of how this process unfolded:

> at about 12.45 p.m. the vessel was abandoned. It was ordered to hoist a white flag in the bow of the vessel which then headed towards the Island of Cava. En route, an armed launch boat approached us and threatening us with their rifles they ordered us to take down the flag. During these negotiations with the helmsman, a tug boat had come alongside the Dresden and pulled down the flag. People climbing on board. Some deployed the anchor chain, and then the second anchor was deployed also. Apparently, the people wanted to slip the chains in order beach the vessel. After a little while, the tug boat took off. Meanwhile the stern of the ship had sunk into the water so deep that water flowed into it through the side windows. The bow was lifted high out of the water [and] capsized to larboard and all 3 funnels broke off upon the impact with the water. A boiler explosion followed, and smoke, water and steam emerged from the floods one last time. Then it was gone. It was 1.32 in the afternoon.[11]

History as a wreck

SMS *Dresden* remained the property of the Ministry of Defence until sold to Orkney Island Council on 3 November 1986. However, before then she had a long history of salvage works carried out on her under licence. These began around 1962 when a salvage lease was obtained for £200 by Nundy Marine

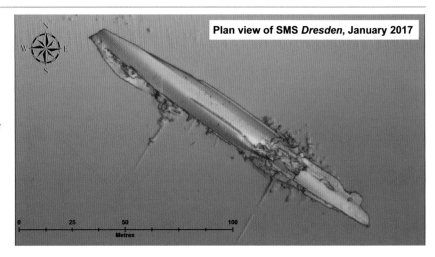

Figure 16.2. DTM model of the wreck of SMS *Dresden*, January 2017. The wreck is lying on its port side, the only light cruiser at Scapa Flow to do so.

Metals, which seems to have removed the propellers and not much else.

The salvage lease passed to Scapa Flow Salvage Ltd in 1970 and it set about liberating the wreck of any metals it could economically recover. Her hull was blasted open and only the upper starboard condensers and pumps were removed. Several other seemingly valuable items were also recovered, but the harvest was a disappointment. Much that seemingly glittered underwater turned to rust when exposed to air.[12] Like her sister SMS *Cöln*, she was built too late in the war to have contained the most valuable of metals seen on the pre-war-built warships. The blockade of Germany affected far more than just foodstuffs. Interestingly, Dougall Campbell of Scapa Flow Salvage Ltd noted that *Dresden* was of a substantially poorer build quality (in terms of profitable metals) than her sister ship SMS *Cöln*.[13]

The salvage rights then passed to Undersea Associates in 1978, with bankruptcy following in 1979. The official receiver then passed the lease on to Clark's Diving Services Ltd of Lerwick. When it let the lease expire in 1985, the Ministry of Defence was then free to sell the wreck to Orkney Islands Council, the current legal owner, which it did, apparently for £1, in 1986. Like the other six surviving warships, she was designated under the Ancient Monuments and Archaeological Areas Act officially on 17 April 2002. It is recorded that the bell was raised from the wreck by Riding Sub-Aqua Club in 1980 and donated to Stromness Museum.[14]

SMS *Dresden* today

The wreck of SMS *Dresden* shown as a DTM can be seen in Figure 16.2. She lies on the port side pointing northwest, an orientation consistent with the other wrecks which were not moved during the scuttling process and consistent with what Fabricius reported. The wreck does not lie truly on her side but is in fact tilted by about 40 degrees past the horizontal. This suggests that when she sank, only her bridges, masts and upper works,

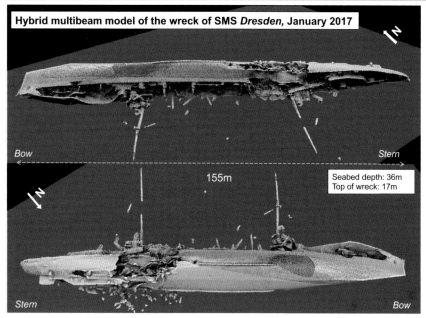

Hybrid multibeam model of the wreck of SMS *Dresden*, January 2017

Bow — Stern

155m

Seabed depth: 36m
Top of wreck: 17m

Stern — Bow

Figure 16.3. Hybrid model of the wreck of SMS *Dresden*, January 2017. The foredeck can be seen to have fallen almost completely out of the wreck.

helped by the relatively short journey to the bottom, prevented the ship from turning turtle completely.

In that regard it seems the dynamics at work when this ship sank were in some way different from those affecting the other three light cruisers, which were more on their sides. This has also affected the way the wreck is degrading. The wreck is also somewhat twisted, so that the stern section does not have quite the same degree of lean towards the seabed as seen at the bow. This suggests that, as with the other light cruisers, the orientation of the stern section has changed over time, as a result of being fully or partially separated from the rest of the body of the hull by blasting.

The blasted remains of the engine-room area attest to the fact that this was the focus of post-scuttling salvage operations. The DTM is sensitive to small changes in height readings and gives a good impression of the dispersed debris around the salvage area. The hybrid model seen in Figures 16.3 and 16.4 shows more detail. In particular, one quite unique aspect of this wreck is the way that the foredeck has fallen out of the wreck. With gravity constantly pulling on them, the joints have failed and the foredeck has unzipped itself from the hull from the hawse pipes to the armoured conning tower and largely lies close to or on the seabed. Internally, the other decks have followed suit. There is also a small blast hole in the keel at the point where the starboard-side propeller shaft exited the hull.

Similar to the wreck of SMS *Cöln*, the blasting in the region of the engine room does not extend to the seabed, as it does with *Brummer* and *Karlsruhe*. The poor quality of materials used in the ship's build ironically saved it from the heavier salvage activity seen on *Brummer* and *Karlsruhe*.

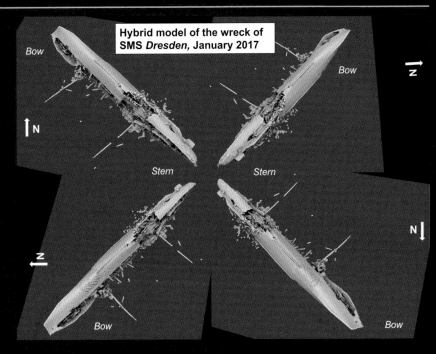

Hybrid model of the wreck of
SMS *Dresden*, January 2017

Figure 16.4. All around view of the wreck of SMS *Dresden*.

The wreck lies on a gradual slope, with the stern at the deepest point of 36 metres. In January 2017 the top of the wreck was recorded to be around 19 metres. It has progressively subsided over the last century as recorded by the UK Hydrographic Office. In the survey carried out immediately after the scuttling, the top of the wreck was recorded as 8 fathoms (14.6 metres). This was still the height of the wreck when she was resurveyed in 1977. In 2010 the height of the wreck was recorded as 16.69 metres.[15] So over the time since 1977 SMS *Dresden* has dropped in height by around five metres. This is most likely due to a combination of structural failure and submergence into the seabed, as the underwater images in this chapter show.

The images of the wreck from Figure 16.5 on begin at the bow and work aft. In Figure 16.5 Gavin Anderson has captured the thrill of exploring shipwrecks as the divers are seen descending to the foredeck region of the wreck, having followed the downline Gavin is on.

In Figure 16.6, Image A an impression of the angle at which the wreck is lying is gained as it shows the deck side pointing down to the seabed at around 40 degrees. Image B shows the light streaming through the starboard-side hawse pipe, with the bow to the left. Image C shows the anchor chain running out of the port-side hawse pipe. This is the chain which

Figure 16.5. Divers making their way down to the foredeck of the *Dresden*. They are around 20 metres deep at this point. (Gavin Anderson)

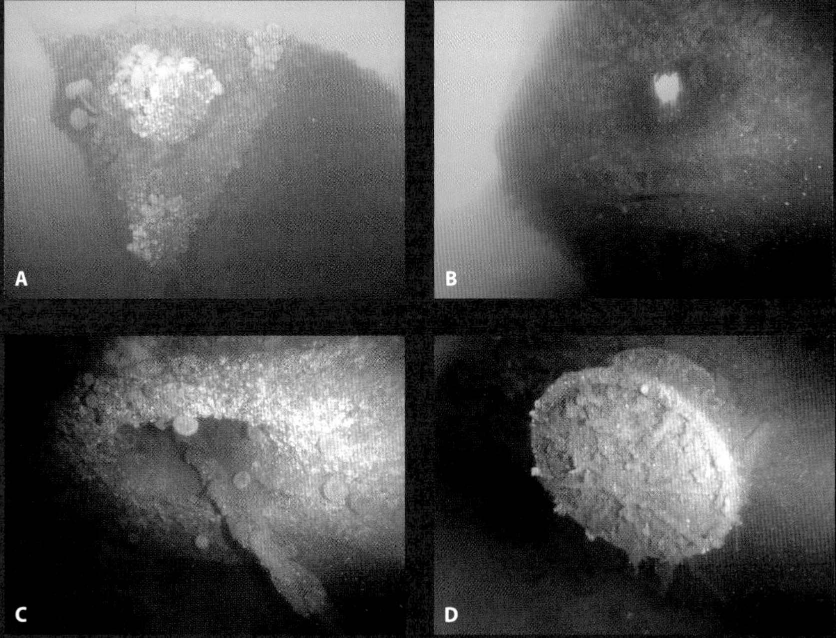

Figure 16.6. Features at the bow of SMS *Dresden*, as described in the text.

lies spread out on the seabed. Image D shows the port-side capstan. To take this image I had to get under the collapsed foredeck.

Interestingly, at the extreme bow of the wreck, the foredeck appears to be in place, but in Image A in Figure 16.7 it is clear that it is not the fixings of the

Figure 16.7. The collapsed foredeck area of SMS *Dresden*, as described in the text. It has now reached the level of the seabed in one area as it continues to fall out of the wreck.

Figure 16.8. The armoured conning tower seen from the front in Image A and from the top in Image B.

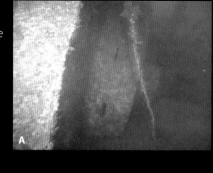

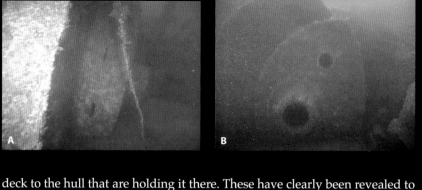

deck to the hull that are holding it there. These have clearly been revealed to have sprung open some time ago. Only the upper hawse pipe is holding the ship together at this point. It was observed during the collapse of this portion of the wreck that further aft the shafts of the capstans had been doing the same job until they finally failed.[16] This is similar to the role played by the after capstan on *Karlsruhe* (see Figure 14.6).

Image B shows the mounting for the port-side 5.9-inch gun now almost completely upside down under the collapsed deck. Interestingly, the gun has been removed, similar to the fore guns on *Cöln*. This most probably happened during the salvage years of the 1970s when Scapa Flow Salvage recovered several examples.[17] Further aft, in Image C the upside-down remains of the deckhouse can be seen. At this point the deck completely falls away and lies in contact with the seabed, as seen in Image D, as a diver equipped with video lighting swims over it.

Figure 16.9. A diver passes the starboard side wing 5.9-inch gun abreast the bridge on the upper side of the wreck. (Gavin Anderson)

The foredeck remains close to the seabed up to the point where it abuts with the forward edge of the armoured conning tower. This is of the same design as that seen on SMS *Cöln*, although now it is in poorer condition. The slit windows looking forwards are seen in Image A of Figure 16.8, and the conning tower's overall shape is seen from the top in Image B, with the now-familiar holes for rangefinder and periscope.

At the top of the wreck the starboard-side-wing 5.9-inch gun survives in situ, as shown with diver in Figure 16.9. Below it the bridge is now collapsed and gives an idea of what will inevitably happen to the same structure on the wreck on SMS *Cöln*. Images A and B in Figure 16.10 were shot on a day with good light and visibility and show how

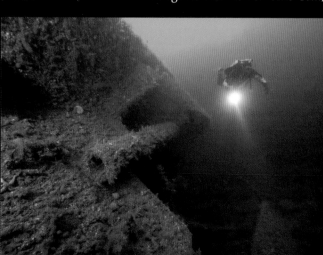

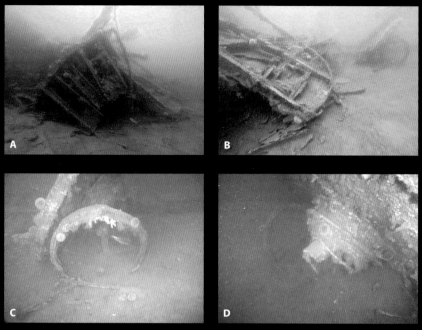

Figure 16.10. The collapsed bridge of SMS *Dresden* looking aft (Images A and B) and the searchlight platform (Images C and D).

the upper portion of the bridge looked in 2014 looking aft. In the distance on the right in Image B a searchlight platform can be seen on its side. This is shown in Images C and D. The body has long corroded away, leaving the outer rim of the light and its base. Where once it was vertical, over the

Figure 16.11. Features around the boiler room area of SMS *Dresden*. Images A and B show fire bricks with the distinctive Kaiserliche Marine 'KMS' marking. Image C shows an opened coal scuttle. In Image D a diver is examining the boiler, which is all that is left of one of *Dresden*'s steam pinnaces.

Figure 16.12. Features on the stern portion of the wreck of SMS *Dresden*. Images A & B show the stern guns. Images C & D show a section of the aft superstructure seen from above in 2014 (C) and in 1999 (D). (A–C, Innes McCartney; D, John Thornton)

last 16 years this feature has been slowly leaning further towards the seabed as time has passed.

Moving aft of the bridge, one enters the area of the boilers. Of all the light cruisers, this wreck offers the best opportunity to see some of the boiler-room

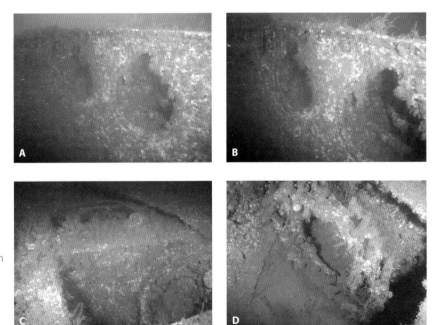

Figure 16.13. A feature originally encountered on SMS *Karlsruhe* is seen again on *Dresden*. In neither case does it appear in any detail on the ship plans. They appear to be apparatus for retaining chemical smoke–making canisters.

features without the need to enter the wrecks. Because of her orientation, some of those features on this wreck are tipped out onto the seabed under the overhanging hull. Images A and B in Figure 16.11 show fire bricks once used inside the boiler housings. The type used by the German navy at this time are very distinctive, being both pale in colour (the British ones are invariably red) and stamped 'KMS', as seen in Image B.

Image C shows what looks to be a coal scuttle which appears to have partially fallen out of the wreck. It is full of large pieces of coal which litter the entire area. Further out on the seabed, similar to the wreck of SMS *Karlsruhe*, there are the remains of a boiler from one of the ship's steam pinnaces which must have gone down with the ship. This can be seen in Image D, being illuminated by the diver's torch.

Moving past the remains of the mainmast, one approaches the stern area of the wreck which features an intact pair of superfiring guns, the upper of which can be seen in Image A of Figure 16.12. The lower gun which was mounted on the quarterdeck can be seen in Image B, with a diver shining a light on the capstan for the aft anchor. The configuration is the same as seen on SMS *Cöln*. It is interesting to observe that the capstan is at the level of the seabed. It was not on the centreline but slightly offset to the port side. It shows that around a third of the width of the wreck at this point is now buried.

Image C shows the aft superstructure seen from above in 2014 at the location of one of the lines which leads to the wreck and is usually tied on to the mooring bollard. The sternmost gun is to the left on the quarterdeck and the upper superfiring gun is on top of the superstructure out of shot. What is particularly noticeable about this image is that the area does not visibly appear too different from when it was recorded in 1999 by John Thornton, as shown in Image D. This is particularly significant because it is an area of the wreck which has been regularly penetrated by visiting divers.

Finally, one reaches the stern of SMS *Dresden*. Figure 16.13 shows images of the well-preserved (in comparison with the others) smoke-making apparatus on the stern of SMS *Dresden*. As seen on SMS *Cöln* and SMS *Karlsruhe*, the smoke-making system was commonly installed in this area on German ships of this period. Unlike *Cöln* but similar to *Karlsruhe* it can be seen that *Dresden* was actually fitted with two pairs of these smoke pot holders. The features are not physically connected, being in separate recesses.

The *Karlsruhe* plans show the best detail of this system and they show that the holders originally had doors in the side of the ship under the quarterdeck. These have now rotted away, but the doorways remain. Similar doorways can be seen in Image C. Inside each feature at the bottom is the holder which, it seems, would eject a primed smoke pot onto the surface of the sea. It turns

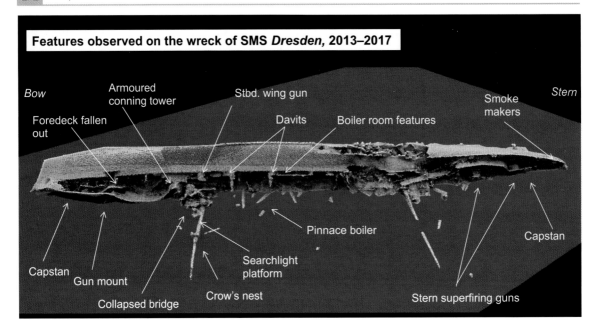

Features observed on the wreck of SMS *Dresden*, 2013–2017

Bow | Armoured conning tower | Stbd. wing gun | Smoke makers | Stern
Foredeck fallen out | | Davits | Boiler room features
Capstan | Gun mount | | Pinnace boiler | Capstan
Collapsed bridge | Crow's nest | Searchlight platform | Stern superfiring guns

Figure 16.14. Features observed during survey dives on SMS *Dresden* highlighted on the hybrid model.

out that this system was very similar to that used by the United States navy and others in the twentieth century.[18]

All of the features shown in the underwater images are drawn together and, along with their locations on the wreck of SMS *Dresden*, shown on the hybrid model in Figure 16.14. SMS *Dresden* is another fascinating Scapa shipwreck with some truly unique features. All of the light cruisers are different, and one learns something new about the archaeology of the High Seas Fleet by studying each individual case.

Structural changes observed in the wreck of SMS *Dresden*, 2006–2017

As noted, there was little appreciable change in the height of the wreck before 1977, which is interesting because it was around that time that salvage work on the site ceased. So it seems that the salvage work created localized damage but did not cause appreciable immediate damage to the rest of the structure of the wreck. The salvage work on *Dresden* was the most minimal that any of the surviving Scapa wrecks were exposed to, and this is evident on the multibeam scans.

Figure 16.15 compares a drawing of *Dresden* in elevation, marking some key salvage targets, with a top-down view of the wreck in the hybrid model. The most attractive material on the wreck was the bronze from which the condensers were invariably made. The blasting on the wreck is centred right over where the condensers were situated. Scapa Flow Salvage also blasted open at least some of the turbine cases to extract the blades, but the effort was not worthwhile, and in salvage terms at least the wreck was considered

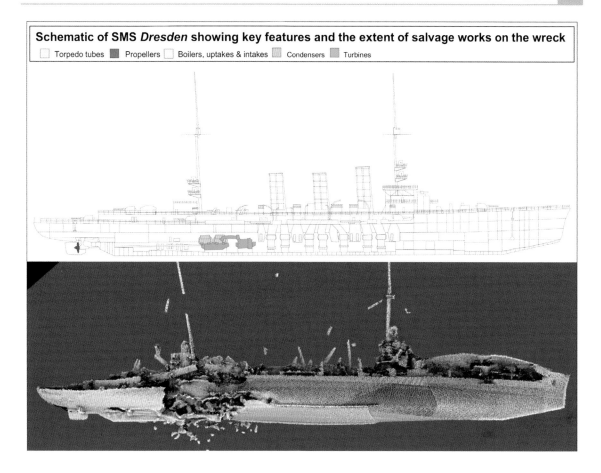

Schematic of SMS *Dresden* showing key features and the extent of salvage works on the wreck

☐ Torpedo tubes ■ Propellers ☐ Boilers, uptakes & intakes ▨ Condensers ▦ Turbines

mainly to be 'rubbish'. [19] The propellers were obviously valuable and salvaged, probably by Nundy. Similarly, the torpedo tubes are not present, so they too must have been salvaged at some point.

Figure 16.15. Potential targets for salvage shown on a drawing of SMS *Dresden* compared with the hybrid model of the wreck.

It is safe to conclude that the remaining degradation of the wreck is down to factors other than the use of explosives. In this case, the wreck of SMS *Dresden* is particularly noteworthy for the manner in which she has broken down over the last 100 years. The very obvious feature is that the foredeck and underlying decks in that area have fallen out. Unlike the other light cruisers, the angle at which the wreck lies would appear to have placed additional stresses on the ship at this point, causing the decks to fail in the way they have done. On all of the light cruisers the foredeck areas have been among the first to give way. And the pattern by which this has happened is notably consistent.

As previously seen on the other light cruisers, the changes in the foredeck began to be noticed when holes appeared in the outer skin of the ship above the foredeck area and collapse followed. Although approximate, the timeline for when this process was observed to begin on the light cruisers is as follows: *Karlsruhe* in the mid-1980s; *Brummer* and *Dresden* in the mid-1990s; and *Cöln* in the years thereafter. In the latter case, the deck is yet to fall out.

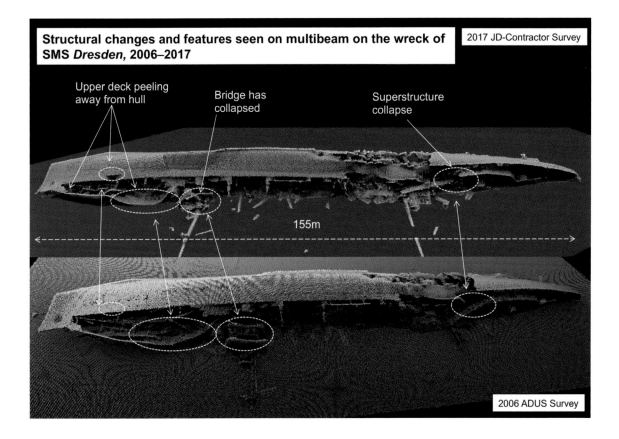

Structural changes and features seen on multibeam on the wreck of SMS *Dresden*, 2006–2017

2017 JD-Contractor Survey

Upper deck peeling away from hull

Bridge has collapsed

Superstructure collapse

155m

2006 ADUS Survey

Figure 16.16. Structural changes in the wreck of SMS *Dresden* as seen by comparing data from the 2006 ADUS survey with data from our own survey of 2017.

The failure of *Dresden*'s foredeck followed a similar path to that of the other light cruiser wrecks. Before it fell out, the outer skin above the foredeck was exhibiting holes caused by corrosion. The area had largely opened up by around 1995 and the deck then began to fall out. An entire strip of steel from the outer hull (very similar to the corroded area still visible on *Cöln*) seemed to have largely corroded away prior to the deck falling out. The fore-end of the strip of steel which originally corroded can be seen on the wreck today and quite clearly on the hybrid model of the multibeam scans in 2017, and even more clearly in the ADUS survey of 2006 (see Figure 16.16). If one was to try to fold the foredeck back into place, a section of the side of the ship approximately one deck wide would be found to be missing. This is particularly noteworthy in relation to the theory that divers' exhaled gas has caused the wrecks to degrade in the way that they have.

There is no doubt that the degradation of *Dresden*'s foredeck makes a compelling case for this theory. But interestingly, a counter argument might be made by looking at the overall condition of the after superstructure on the wreck. As shown in Figure 16.13, Images C and D, not much has changed in this area over the 15 years between the two images being taken. Unsurprisingly, the area from which a photomosaic was made in 2006 looks exactly the same today.[20] This area is still regularly penetrated by divers but it has seemingly not degraded like the bow area. The explanation may lie in the comparative lack of gravitational loading in this area compared with the heavy armoured deck.

As with the other surviving wrecks, we can compare the 2006 ADUS survey with our 2017 one by looking at the differences in the hybrid models. In Figure 16.16 it can be observed that, unsurprisingly, the foredeck area has continued on its journey to the seabed during the decade between the scans. Gravity has bent the deck so that a large portion of it has now reached the seabed. The process was observed in 2014 on the wreck and can be seen in Figure 16.7. It is also noticeable that the bridge collapsed after 2006 and prior to the 2013–2014 survey dives. A portion of the forward end of the superstructure where it had seemingly already been damaged during the salvage operations has now also broken away and collapsed further.

Conclusions

SMS *Dresden*'s career as a warship was uneventful. Arriving at Scapa Flow in a patched-up state, had she not been scuttled, her demise at the end of a blowtorch would have been an ignominious one of no note. But as it is, she has become a cultural artefact, much visited by recreational divers. In this way she is no different from the other late-war light cruisers. As a shipwreck, she was lightly touched by salvage operations and her subsequent degradation through time continues to be a fascinating process to observe.

1   H. J. Koerver (ed.) (2009), Room 40: German Naval Warfare 1914–1918. Volume 2: The Fleet in Being (Steinbach: LIS Reinisch), p. 45.

2   O. Groos (2006), *Der Krieg in der Nordsee Band 7 Vom Sommer 1917 bis zum Kriegsende 1918 Kritische Edition* (Berlin: Mittler & Sohn), p. 222.

3   O. Groos (2006), *Der Krieg in der Nordsee Band 7 Vom Sommer 1917 bis zum Kriegsende 1918 Kritische Edition* (Berlin: Mittler & Sohn), p. 269.

4   National Archives and Records Administration (various dates), microfilmed records of the German Navy, PG64939, Roll T1022-279. Washington, DC.

5   See R. Macdonald (2017), *Dive Scapa Flow* (Edinburgh: Mainstream), pp. 174–175. This was probably repeated from P. L. Smith (1989), *The Naval Wrecks of Scapa Flow* (Kirkwall: Orkney Press), p. 70. The original source of this mythical tale is not known.

6   D. Woodward (1973), *The Collapse of Power: Mutiny in the High Seas Fleet* (London: Arthur Baker), p. 164.

7   D. Woodward (1973), *The Collapse of Power: Mutiny in the High Seas Fleet* (London: Arthur Baker), p. 166.

8   National Archives (various dates), internment of German warships at Scapa Flow, ADM 116/1825. London.

9   National Archives (various dates), sinking of German Fleet at Scapa Flow, ADM 116/2074. London.

10   National Archives (various dates), sinking of German ships at Scapa Flow. Salvage of German ships, ADM 137/2486. London.

11   National Archives and Records Administration (various dates), microfilmed records of the German Navy, PG64939, Roll T1022-1629. Washington, DC.

12   R. Macdonald (2017), *Dive Scapa Flow* (Edinburgh: Mainstream), p. 178.

13   In telephone conversation with Dougall Campbell of Scapa Flow Salvage Ltd, November 2017.

14   Hydrographic Department of the Admiralty (2017), Record of Wreck No. 1080, SMS *Dresden* (Taunton: Hydrographic Office).

15   Hydrographic Department of the Admiralty (2017), Record of Wreck No. 1080, SMS *Dresden* (Taunton: Hydrographic Office).

16   R. Macdonald (2017), *Dive Scapa Flow* (Edinburgh: Mainstream), p. 182.

17   In telephone conversation with Dougall Campbell of Scapa Flow Salvage Ltd, November 2017.

18   US Navy Department, Bureau of Ordnance (1944), Ships' Chemical Smoke Munitions, OP 1042.

19   In telephone conversation with Dougall Campbell of Scapa Flow Salvage Ltd, November 2017.

20   ScapaMAP (2001–2006), Marine Heritage Monitoring with High Resolution Survey Tools: Scapa Flow 2001–2006. Orkney: Scapa Flow Marine Archaeology Project, p. 42.

CHAPTER 17
SMS *S54* AND SMS *V83*

Figure 17.1. The group of torpedo boats hauled ashore off Fara on the day of the Grand Scuttle. In the foreground is probably *V73*, with *S54*, *V82*, *S60* and *V80* behind. (Orkney Archive)

The pair of surviving torpedo boats are both integral to the story of the High Seas Fleet at Scapa Flow. SMS S54 is of significant historical importance, and both wrecks yielded a number of surprises when surveyed. They both also have salvage histories which make them distinct from the other seven surviving wrecks. Even now they remain fascinating examples of the World War I–era torpedo boat.

SMS *S54* service and scuttling

SMS *S54* was part of the large family of V25-class torpedo boats built by Germany from 1913. This was made up of 71 vessels in total. The 'S' prefix means she was built by the F. Schichau company in Elbing. The entire class was oil-fired, but there were design differences between shipyards, making several different sub-classes which can be identified from German and British recognition books. A retractable bow rudder was an interesting feature of the class.

S54 displaced 789 tons and was 83 metres long. Originally she was fitted with three 88mm guns, but was upgraded to three 105mm guns in late 1916. She carried six 50cm torpedo tubes and could also carry a limited number of mines. She was launched on 11 October 1915 and commissioned the following January, when she joined the 3rd Torpedo Boat Flotilla as the lead boat of the 6th Half Flotilla. It was in this capacity that she fought in the Battle of Jutland.

The ship's performance under the command of Lt Cdr Karlowa during the battle is notable. At around the time of the German battle fleet's first turn away, *S54* in company with *V48* found the British destroyer HMS *Shark* disabled and *S54* was able to sink her with a torpedo. *V48* was damaged and sunk as a result of this encounter.[1] Later, during the night phase, *S54* was instrumental in attempting to tow the torpedoed light cruiser and leader of torpedo boats SMS *Rostock* to safety. The attempt had to be abandoned and *Rostock* was scuttled. During this time *S54* had gleaned the first two letters of the British night-time challenge signal, 'UA'. This was repeatedly flashed at approaching British forces, probably giving time to effect the scuttling of the ship.[2]

During 1917 the flotilla was transferred to operate from Zeebrugge with the Flanders force. In November *S54* was mined but towed to safety for repairs. These were carried out in time for her to take part in the evacuation of Flanders in September 1918.[3] By the time of the internment in Scapa Flow, *S54*, under the command of Lt Cdr Steiner, was the lead boat of the entire 3rd Flotilla, which was reduced in size to eight boats and not sub-divided into half flotillas by that time.

On the day of the Grand Scuttle *S54* was prevented from sinking by vessels of the Admiralty port officer acting under Admiral Prendergast's orders and was beached off Fara (see Figure 2.16 for position).[4] According to Admiral Prendergast's account of the scuttling, on hearing of the events unfolding and in order to ascertain whether the torpedo boats could be saved he proceeded to the nearest one to see for himself.

Figure 17.2. SMS *S33*, *34* and *35* on manoeuvres. These were three typical examples of the V25 class. The high and short forecastle with torpedo tubes tucked in aft is characteristic of this class. (Archiv Deutscher Marinebund)

Figure 17.3. Plan view DTM of SMS *S54* showing the wreck to be up against a rocky sea cliff and broken into several pieces.

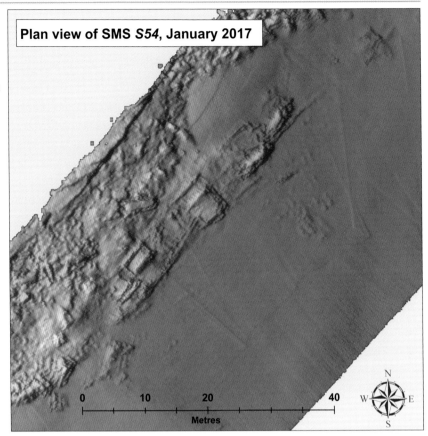

Plan view of SMS *S54*, January 2017

HMS *Victorious* was moored in the centre of Gutter Sound, where, according to the interned fleet berthing plan, she was close to where *S54*'s 3rd Flotilla was moored. So he most probably boarded one of the torpedo boats of this flotilla. Prendergast stated in his report that he was informed by Steiner himself that preparations had been well made. He went on to state that he (Prendergast) personally took down Steiner's German ensign and ordered the other picket boats under his command to do the same.[5] Although not explicitly stated, it is probable that this famous incident during the chaotic scenes of the Grand Scuttle actually took place on the deck of Steiner's own ship, SMS *S54*, giving the ship a unique place in the story of the Grand Scuttle.[6]

Seeing that the ingression of water into the torpedo boats could not be halted because the sea cocks had been deliberately sabotaged, Prendergast ordered them beached. Of the eight ships in the 3rd Flotilla only half (*S53*, *S55*, *G91* and *V70*) were successfully scuttled. The remaining four were beached at Fara, including *S54*, as seen in Figure 17.1. Once the crews had departed the ships of the 3rd Flotilla they had also made for Fara. From there they were ferried to *Victorious*. Steiner later reported that Admiral Prendergast, an officer of the old school, had behaved with courtesy and humanity throughout.[7]

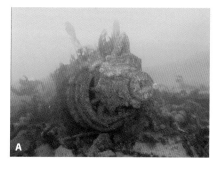 

Figure 17.4. The two main turbines survive on the wreck of SMS *S54*. Images A and B show the aftermost turbine. Images C and D show the foremost. Both are quite intact, with the blades visible in places.

It is all the more remarkable that purely by coincidence the wreck of SMS *S54* survives to this day. The immediate Royal Navy post-scuttling salvage work on the beached torpedo boats was under the command of the 2nd Destroyer Flotilla, which worked fast in recovering the beached craft. By 30 July nine had been floated and then docked, and were then being reconditioned. Another eight were in the process of being recovered.

The recovered torpedo boats then became part of the reparations fleet, to be divided up among the victorious powers. In the case of SMS *S54* this did not matter because she foundered on tow in February 1920 while being transferred. According to the *Orkney Herald*, she was 'let go' in a gale and drifted ashore.[8] The vessel quickly became a complete loss.[9] The *Orcadian* newspaper recorded that she foundered on 13 February.

In another coincidence involving Admiral Prendergast and *S54*, the same edition of the *Orcadian* also recorded that the old pre-dreadnought battleship HMS *Victorious*, which had been Admiral Prendergast's flag during his tenure in command, was being withdrawn to Devonport on the 15th. This was the day that Prendergast officially struck his flag as commander. Scapa Flow was now downgraded to a secondary-ranked navy base and its command fell to captain's rank, based ashore at Lyness.[10]

The Admiralty disposals ledger shows that on 31 December 1927 *S54* was sold to Cox & Danks for £200. She was left untouched throughout 1928, but in 1929 Cox attempted to raise her using cylinders (or camels). This was

Figure 17.5. A closer look at the blades within the sternmost turbine. The easily reachable ones appear to have been pulled out in the past, but enough remain to gain a good impression of the design.

clearly not successful, as the last entry in the ledger states that the wreck had been blown to pieces in 1931, suggesting that ultimately Cox resorted to explosives to salvage the wreck.[11]

SMS *S54* as a wreck

During the multibeam survey, it took time to locate the wreck as she is some distance away from the position given in the Hydrographic record.[12] The DTM can be seen in Figure 17.3. The wreck lies up against a rocky slope with an average depth of around 13m. It was initially tricky to pick it out against the background geology.

The wreckage appeared to point southwest, with at least two sets of boilers being readily identifiable. As our experience had shown at Jutland, these lightly built vessels do not stand up well to the passage of time and the effects of salvage, and in most cases only the boilers remain as easily identifiable extant archaeology. Unlike with the seven larger warships, we had no visual record of the destroyer sites prior to the survey. Both sites were subsequently surveyed by diving in November 2017 and the results from the dive on SMS *S54* are shown in Figures 17.4 to 17.6.

Swimming inshore from the drop-off point in excellent underwater visibility brought us to the stern of the wreck, where the recording began. The first surprise was that both turbine housings are present on the wreck site. It was expected that they would have been recovered during the salvage operations. In Images A and B of Figure 17.4 the aftermost turbine is shown. Images C and D show the foremost turbine, which is still equipped with its propeller shaft, which passes along the port side of the aftermost turbine. In both cases much of the turbine blade assemblies survives, giving a rather unique view of this technology.

Figure 17.6. Features at the forward end of the wreck include the uncanny sight of no. 1 boiler on its side (Images A–C) and the last remaining frames of the bow in Image D.

A closer view of the sternmost turbine's blades can be seen in Figure 17.5. It appears that some of the blades have been removed in the past.

The mid-section of the wreck is dominated by the remains of the three boilers. These were situated in separate compartments, with the forward boiler in room no. 1 being slightly smaller to accommodate it inside the tapering forward section of the ship. Remains of all three boilers are present but have collapsed as the outer structures and water tubes have corroded. However, of particular interest was the forward boiler, which turned out to be in an unusual orientation.

Images A–C in Figure 17.6 show this boiler in detail. It appears to be lying on its side, with what would have been the port-side water trap now the highest point. This is, in my experience, unprecedented. Image A shows the trap from the port side. On the right-hand side, what appears to be the large downcomer pipe used to recirculate cooler water back down to the trap can be seen to be in place. This is a signature feature of the Schulz-Thorneycroft boiler type installed in most units of the High Seas Fleet. It is uncommon to see this feature surviving. This boiler design featured an array of carefully curved water tubes. A near full set can be seen in this example. The view from the underside is unique, as seen in Images A and B, and it would probably only have been seen in this way during manufacture. Image C shows the forward end of the water trap with its pair of locking bars in place over the access hatch.

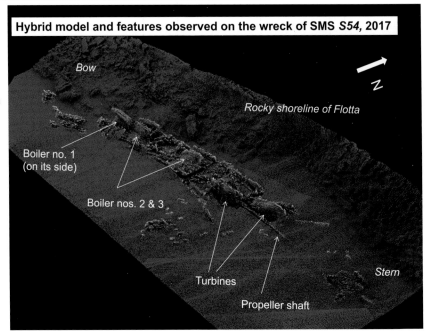

Hybrid model and features observed on the wreck of SMS *S54*, 2017

Figure 17.7. The hybrid model of the wreck of SMS *S54*. The remains are arranged in such a way as to suggest that the wreck may well have been lying on its side after it sank.

One of the primary advantages of being able to survey by video the sites of the torpedo boat wrecks was that it made it possible to more accurately differentiate the actual wreckage from the rocky geology of the seabed. This was essential when it came to creating the hybrid model of the wreck site, shown in Figure 17.7. It would not otherwise have been possible to pick out smaller pieces of the wreck, such as the remains of the bow seen in Image D of Figure 17.6, in any other way. A number of the larger rocks seen in the model could easily have been mistaken for pieces of wreckage. The hybrid model shows that wreck to be broken into several pieces and now largely flattened. The turbines and boilers represent the most obvious remaining features.

In addition to no. 1 boiler being on its side, there is other evidence which suggests that the wreck was initially lying on its starboard side when it sank. One feature seemingly consistent with this, and seen in the design of this and later classes of German destroyer, is the layout of the engine rooms. They are divided in two, fore and aft, with a single turbine and connecting condenser in each room. The plans which are known to survive show that the aftermost engine room housed the port-side turbine and, conversely, the forward engine room would house the starboard turbine.[13] The condensers were mounted in the space next to each turbine.

When studying the destroyers sunk at the Battle of Jutland, a useful schematic was developed which could be overlaid on the plan-view DTMs of the wrecks. It proved extremely useful in helping to identify each wreck.[14] This overlay technique is employed in this case to show how the main

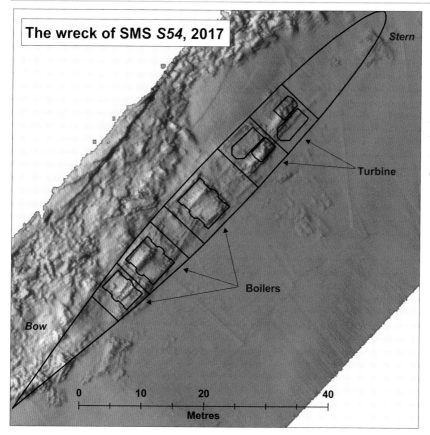

Figure 17.8. Schematic of distribution of heavy machinery according to the general design of German torpedo boats overlaid on the multibeam DTM of the wreck of SMS *S54*.

surviving portions of the wreck of *S54* relate to their original design. This can be seen in Figure 17.8.

In this case it can be seen that the boilers line up well with the general design features, but that the turbines do not. They appear to be situated where one would normally expect to find the condensers. These are not present on the wreck site and would have been the main target of interest for Cox & Danks, having been made of bronze. The use of explosives to open the wreck up could have caused significant distortion to the remaining wreckage, accounting for the seemingly odd dispersal of the remaining turbines.

However, it is also possible that SMS *S54* was built with the engines as they are seen, in a reversal of the normal configuration. This is because at least one published history of German naval vessels states that *S54* was of a class that had an additional cruising turbine fitted to the starboard shaft.[15] This turbine may possibly be one of the ones present, or else it was salvaged from the wreck site, as only two are now seen. In either case it is possible the engine rooms were laid out in a unique way to accommodate this feature only seen on *S54–S66*.

This still leaves the question as to why no. 1 boiler is on its side. Either it sank like that or explosives forced it into that orientation. Unless some account

Figure 17.9. SMS *V83* in the foreground with SMS *G92* behind as beached on the day of the Grand Scuttle at Rysa. *V83* is very low in the water. (Orkney Archive)

of the actual salvage of this wreck can be found, it is likely now that the answer will never be known for certain. The only surviving evidence so far unearthed is a cryptic description given in the *Orcadian* newspaper which stated that the wreck had sunk with the masts 'or parts of them' showing above the water, suggesting that the wreck may have settled at an angle against the slope of the shoreline.[16] This being the case, the wreck could have later settled onto its side.

SMS *V83* service and scuttling

SMS *V83* was also a torpedo boat of the V25 class. The 'V' prefix tells us that the ship was built by A. G. Vulcan, which was building examples of this class in two of its facilities, Stettin and, in *V83*'s case, Hamburg. She was launched in May 1916 and commissioned in July, too late to take part in the Battle of Jutland. She was attached to the 14th Half Flotilla of the 7th Flotilla and served with it until internment at Scapa Flow.

On the day of the Grand Scuttle *V83* was prevented from sinking by vessels under the command of Admiral Prendergast and was beached off Rysa Little (see Figure 2.16 for position).[17] Figure 17.9 shows *V83* ashore with *G92*. Fremantle's report of the scuttling states that the destroyer HMS *Winchelsea*, which had returned with the fleet, beached *G92* in the afternoon, but *V83* is not specifically named.[18] Of the ten ships in her flotilla, four were beached and six were successfully scuttled.

SMS *V83* proved difficult to recover. In July Royal Navy salvage teams abandoned attempts to salve *V83*, *G92* and *G89* as they did not have the means to do so.[19] After better pumps had been supplied, attempts to recover them resumed. By mid-August SMS *G92* had been raised and moved to the floating dock at Lyness, but *V83* remained steadfastly on the bottom off Rysa, despite continued attempts to get her afloat. On 18 August, Prendergast ordered diving operations on *V83* to cease and undertook to salvage the ship without assistance from the divers and ratings from HMS *Resolution* who had been working on her.[20]

The Atlantic Fleet still considered *V83* viable in October when it listed her among the German ships requiring maintenance crews, to be drafted from Chatham.[21] However, by the end of the year it was clear she was going to be written off. Uniquely among the disposals of the German fleet, *V83* and *G89* were sold independently by the Commander in Chief at Rosyth (not by the Admiralty Disposals Board in London, which usually dealt with sales of warships) in 1920, with *V83* being sold to the East Coast Wrecking Company for £150.

The Admiralty disposals ledger shows that *V83* was resold to Mr P. Kerr of Aberdeen on 5 September 1925. The *Orcadian* newspaper reported that Mr Kerr bought the wreck when the former company 'sold out'. It relates how Mr Kerr was a foreman diver with Cox & Danks and knew Scapa well. The wooden steam trawler *Energy* was used for the salvage operations, with the plan to blast off the decks and haul out only the valuable metals below, leaving the hull. However, after a week on site setting up, *Energy* sprung a leak forward on the night of 17 October 1925 and foundered.[22] All five of the crew escaped in the boat.[23]

Attempts to recover the vessel came to naught; however, the Admiralty disposals ledger shows that salvage operations continued through to 1928, presumably by Kerr.[24] Cox was not involved. Of note also is an administrative oversight in January 1924 whereby the wreck was mistakenly sold to Cox & Danks as part of the tranche of other torpedo boats and SMS *Hindenburg* that he purchased at that time. As a consequence, he was given a £200 refund when he purchased the light cruiser SMS *Bremse* the following year.[25]

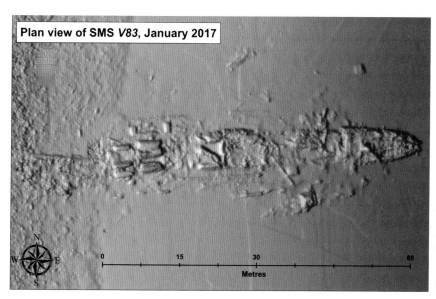

Plan view of SMS *V83*, January 2017

Figure 17.10. Plan view DTM of the wreck of SMS *V83* as scanned in January 2017. The stern is to the east, with the bow of the wreck running up into very shallow water. The wreckage on the south side includes the remains of the steam trawler *Energy*, which foundered there during salvage operations.

SMS *V83* as a wreck

The wreck of SMS *V83* is a popular second dive site with recreational divers. It lies perpendicular to the beach on the east side of the island of Rysa. The multibeam survey had to be carried out in the shallows by *Limbo*, with *Vina* surveying the deeper portion. This allowed us to scan the entire wreck right into very shallow water. The results can be seen in a plan-view DTM in Figure 17.10. The stern is instantly recognizable, as are the three sets of boilers in a similar configuration to those seen on the wreck of SMS *S54*.

The site was carefully recorded on video by diving during November 2017. As with *S54* this was important because, in order to accurately build the hybrid model, it was necessary to be able to accurately distinguish the actual wreckage on site from the underlying geology. Also, it afforded the opportunity to examine the wreck in detail as well as the small salvage vessel to the south. Some of the results of the survey dive conducted in very nice underwater visibility can be seen in Figures 17.11–17.14.

Figure 17.11 shows some of the features observed around the stern of the wreck. The commonly photographed stern gun can be seen in Image A. The stern at the upper deck can be seen in Image B. The dominating feature running over the stern is the heavy fairlead used by the sweeping equipment which is known to have been a feature of the *V67*–*V84* sub-class.[26] Given the function it served, it is a significant structure, looking now slightly over-engineered. However, it was made this way in order to ensure that the sweep gear did not

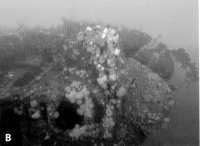

Figure 17.11. Features observed in the stern portion of SMS *V83*. Image A shows the stern gun, Image B the sweeping gear fairlead, Image C the rudder and stern seen from the seabed and Image D one of the fuel storage tanks.

Figure 17.12. The remains of the three boilers dominated the central portion of the wreck of SMS *V83*. Image A shows a collapsed steam drum, Image B the corroded water tubes and Image C a downcomer pipe. Of particular interest were the remains of a built-up wall of furnace lining bricks, seen in image D.

foul the depth-charge chutes, which were also stern-mounted and which have now corroded away but were situated outboard of the fairlead.

Image C shows the stern as seen from the seabed with the sunlight streaming through the wreckage. The frames are exposed now and the rudder is also much corroded. The propellers were removed long ago. Moving inshore along the starboard side of the wreck in an area just abaft of no. 3 boiler, Image D reveals a storage tank with the outer skin now gone. These double-hulled sections were used to store fuel oil and also water.

The areas where the engine rooms were situated are largely devoid of heavy machinery, so it is the three boilers which are the dominant features of the mid-section of the wreck. Features from these boilers are shown in Figure 17.12. The three drum boilers of the German 'marine-type' based on the Schulz-Thorneycroft design are all present but now largely broken down by the

Figure 17.13. Two features in the seaweed at the very shallowest portion of the wreck of SMS *V83*. Image A shows the remains of a porthole and image B a hawse pipe.

Figure 17.14. The boiler of the steam trawler *Energy*, which sank while carrying out salvage work on SMS *V83*.

passage of time and the marine environment. Image A shows the main steam drum of no. 2 boiler collapsed to the seabed to lie inboard of the starboard-side water trap which can be seen on the right of the image. Image B shows how the water tubes have corroded away, showing the starboard-side water trap of no. 1 boiler. This is a causal factor in the collapse of the boilers.

Image C shows the downcomer pipe of the portside water trap of no. 2 boiler, similar to the one seen in Figure 17.6 except in this instance it too has collapsed to the seabed. But even within these quite dilapidated remains there can be surprises. Image D shows a pile of the furnace-lining bricks which were

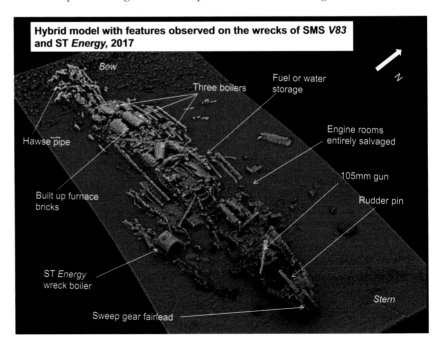

Figure 17.15. The hybrid model of the wrecks of SMS *V83* and the steam trawler *Energy*.

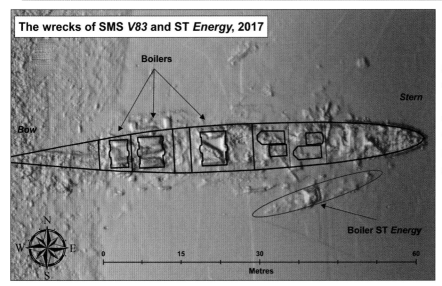

The wrecks of SMS *V83* and ST *Energy*, 2017

Boilers

Stern

Bow

N
W   E
S

Boiler ST *Energy*

0   15   30   60

Metres

Figure 17.16. Schematic of distribution of heavy machinery according to the general design of German torpedo boats, overlaid on the multibeam DTM of the wrecks of SMS *V83* and ST *Energy*.

used to contain heat within the boiler structures. In this case a line of bricks, still built up in its original configuration, can be seen at the aftermost end of no. 2 boiler. It is uncommon to see furnace bricks laid out as originally employed.

Moving forward of no.1 boiler, one begins to enter very shallow water. But among the fronds of kelp are the remains of the forecastle and bow. In Image A of Figure 17.13 the corroded remains of the iron rim of a porthole backing plate can be seen with the dog still present. Image B shows the remains of the port-side anchor hawse pipe. It is now completely separated from any wreckage and lies on the seabed. It was specifically searched for because it appeared to be seen when examining *Limbo*'s detailed survey over the area. Confirming its presence shows just how detailed the multibeam work we conducted turned out to be.

The remains of the steam trawler *Energy* were easily located on the port side of the wreck. They are dominated by the ship's Scotch boiler. This is clearly not of the type seen in the High Seas Fleet, but is of a type commonly used in small steamships. It can be seen in Figure 17.14. The rest of this small wreck is now very broken down but can be seen in the survey data, as shown in the hybrid model in Figure 17.15.

All of the features shown in the underwater images can be seen in the detailed hybrid model. As is usual, the wreckage has been picked out of the underlying geology and coloured grey. But in this case a grading from white to black has been added to highlight how the depth of the wreck changes as it extends off the beach down into deeper water; hence the stern area is generally darker, but the gun is lighter because it is the highest point in that area of the wreck. Combining the images from the underwater video survey with the multibeam data makes for a good representation of the shipwreck and the key features seen.

It is clear in this case that the turbines and condensers were recovered from the wreck, as the area in the region of the engine rooms is the most damaged. Their recovery would have been what *Energy* was planning when it foundered, as it is located aside that area of the wreck. By looking at the hold plan schematic of this type of vessel (i.e. V25 class torpedo boat) when it is overlaid on the DTM, it is revealed that little if anything remains of either the condensers or the turbines, as shown in Figure 17.16.

Interestingly, a linear feature can be seen extending from the area of the port-side condenser out to the wreck of ST *Energy*. It is tempting to imagine that this may represent a crane being used to recover that condenser, but the account of the sinking shows that *Energy* was 'hauled off' the wreck at night when it sprung a leak.[27] This feature is a tube, which can be seen on the video file of the wreck. So although it could be related to the salvage, it is more likely to be one of *V83*'s steam pipes displaced during later salvage operations.

Conclusions

With the large warships of the High Seas Fleet as their neighbours, it is easy to overlook these two torpedo boat wrecks. Although *V83* makes a convenient second dive, being close to the fleet anchorage, *S54* is isolated by her distance from the other wrecks, being off Flotta, as a result of her being lost while on tow away from Orkney. Both are excellent examples of the type of torpedo boat (or small destroyer) being used during World War I. They both have a number of features which are of notable interest and they are also important surviving components of the later story of the salvage of the High Seas Fleet. They in fact constitute unique examples of Royal Navy and locally based salvage initiatives.

SMS *S54* is by any measure an important shipwreck because of her record in wartime and her dramatic role in the chaos of the Grand Scuttle itself. Moreover, as a wreck she is noteworthy because of the rare survival of her turbine sets. Whereas *V83* may not have had such a historic past, the iconic photograph of her beached after the sinking and the story of her salvage and the loss of *Energy* also make her an important shipwreck in a local context.

It is therefore somewhat odd that neither wreck was protected in 2002 when the rest of the surviving wrecks became scheduled monuments. Hopefully this will be rectified at some point and it will be acknowledged that these two important and fascinating little shipwrecks should be regarded as having a similar stature to their larger neighbours. They too were sunk in the service of their nation on that monumental day in June 1919 and are extant witnesses to scuttle and salvage.

1   I. McCartney (2016), *Jutland 1916: The Archaeology of a Naval Battlefield* (London: Bloomsbury), p. 138.

2   I. McCartney (2016), *Jutland 1916: The Archaeology of a Naval Battlefield* (London: Bloomsbury), p. 211.

3   H. J. Koerver (ed.) (2009), *Room 40: German Naval Warfare 1914–1918. Volume 2: The Fleet in Being* (Steinbach: LIS Reinisch), p. 410.

4   National Archives (various dates), sinking of German Fleet at Scapa Flow, ADM 116/2074. London.

5   National Archives (various dates), sinking of German Fleet at Scapa Flow, ADM 116/2074. London.

6   National Archives (various dates), sinking of German Fleet at Scapa Flow, ADM 116/2074. London

7   L. von Reuter (1940), *Scapa Flow: The Account of the Greatest Scuttling of all Time* (London: Hurst & Blackett), p. 144.

8   Orkney Archives (various dates), microfilmed records of the *Orkney Herald*, 1919–1930. Kirkwall, 13 October 1920.

9   Hydrographic Department of the Admiralty (2017), Record of Wreck No. 978 SMS *S54* (Taunton: Hydrographic Office).

10 Orkney Archives (various dates), microfilmed records of the *Orcadian*, 1919–1938. Kirkwall, 19 February 1920.

11 Naval Historical Branch (various dates), *CP 8a Sale Book*, p. 94. Portsmouth.

12 Hydrographic Department of the Admiralty (2017), Record of Wreck No. 978 SMS *S54* (Taunton: Hydrographic Office).

13 There are several surviving sets – for example, the Dreadnought Project (dreadnoughtproject.org) (various dates), constructors' plans of SMS *V170–V177*. Also National Maritime Museum (various dates), ships' plans, SMS *V25–V30*. London.

14 I. McCartney (2016), *Jutland 1916: The Archaeology of a Naval Battlefield* (London: Bloomsbury), p. 25.

15 E. Gröner (1990), *German Warships 1815–1945. Volume One: Major Surface Vessels* (London: Conway), p. 178.

16 Orkney Archives (various dates), microfilmed records of the *Orcadian*. Kirkwall, 26 February 1920.

17 National Archives (various dates), sinking of German Fleet at Scapa Flow, ADM 116/2074. London.

18 National Archives (various dates), sinking of German Fleet at Scapa Flow, ADM 116/2074. London.

19 National Archives (various dates), sinking of German ships at Scapa Flow. Salvage of German ships, ADM 137/2486, p. 132. London.

20   National Archives (various dates), sinking of German ships at Scapa Flow. Salvage of German ships, ADM 137/2486, p. 191. London.

21   National Archives (various dates), sinking of German ships at Scapa Flow. Salvage of German ships, ADM 137/2486, p. 230. London.

22   I. G. Whittaker (1998), *Off Scotland: A Comprehensive Record of Maritime and Aviation Losses in Scottish Waters* (Berwick upon Tweed: C-Anne), p. 81.

23   Orkney Archives (various dates), microfilmed records of the *Orcadian*. Kirkwall, 22 October 1925.

24   Naval Historical Branch (various dates), *CP 8a Sale Book*, p. 20. Portsmouth.

25   Naval Historical Branch (various dates), *CP 8a Sale Book*, pp. 20, 61, 72. Portsmouth.

26   N. Friedman (ed.) (1992), *German Warships of World War I. The Royal Navy's Official Guide to the Capital Ships, Cruisers, Destroyers, Submarines and Small Craft, 1914–1918* (London: Greenhill), p. 230.

27   Orkney Archives (various dates), microfilmed records of the *Orcadian*. Kirkwall, 22 October 1925

PART FOUR
THE GRAND SCUTTLE
100 YEARS ON

John Thornton filling diving cylinders on board MV
Karin. The rugged beauty of Orkney forms a backdrop
for visiting divers. The wrecks have become a new
form of economic resource, visited by thousands each
year. (Gavin Anderson)

CHAPTER 18
CONCLUSIONS: THE CULTURAL LEGACY OF THE GRAND SCUTTLE

Figure 18.1. The Grand Scuttle survivor SMS *G102* as prepared to be sunk in bombing trials in July 1921. Her guns and torpedo tubes have been removed. (US Navy National Museum of Naval Aviation)

One hundred years on, the Scapa wrecks have become a new form of economic resource and a valuable cultural asset. The salvage history contributes to creating a unique underwater industrial landscape. There are now 31 wreck sites in Scapa Flow relating to the Grand Scuttle. Seven are currently protected and it is hoped that this protection can be extended in the future.

To the breakers: the fate of the scuttled fleet

The salvage of whole ships from the greatest scuttling of a fleet in history was carried out over a 20-year period from 1919 to 1939. It was shipwreck recovery on an unprecedented and industrial scale. Only eight ships remain *in situ*, so in all 66 were recovered, to be towed away to a range of differing fates. A total of four salvors and the Royal Navy were responsible for this colossal effort. The tonnage of each ship varied from the largest – the 31,003-ton SMS *Hindenburg* – to the smallest 789-ton early S-class torpedo boats.

Figure 18.2 provides a measure of the effort put into the lifting operations by the Royal Navy and the salvage companies involved. Cox & Danks was the largest contributor by both tonnage and number of ships raised. Metal Industries ranks second by tonnage, but only lifted six heavy warships. The Royal Navy lifted 23 ships, but 19 were torpedo boats of low tonnage.

By the contemporary German measure of 'designed tonnage', 498,989 displacement tons were scuttled on 21 June 1919, of which 401,181 tons were lifted in these efforts. Estimates made by Metal Industries in January 1936 during its salvage operations suggested a recoverable average value per ton per ship of around £5.00.[1] So the entire German fleet as scuttled was worth around £2,000,000 at that time, although this figure is probably slightly optimistic as the designed-tonnage figure used by Germany took into account ships being equipped for speed trials.

Of the 66 ships lifted up to 1939, 48 were broken up by the salvage companies involved or were sold directly to shipbreakers. The rest were sunk on tow (3), reused for experimental purposes in the UK (4) or distributed as prizes of war (11). The 48 ships broken up constituted 343,994 tons, with a total value therefore of around £1,700,000.

The utterly dominant market share controlled by Metal Industries in the breaking of the scuttled fleet is shown in Figure 18.3. It broke up 15 ships, 31% of the total number of ships, but this included all of the large warships

Figure 18.2. Graph showing the number and tonnage of ships lifted from Scapa Flow divided into the five agencies involved, and the number and tonnage of the eight remaining wrecks.

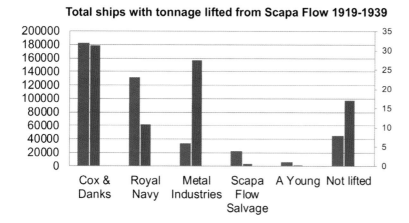

Total ships with tonnage lifted from Scapa Flow 1919-1939

- Tonnage of ships salvaged
- Number of ships salvaged

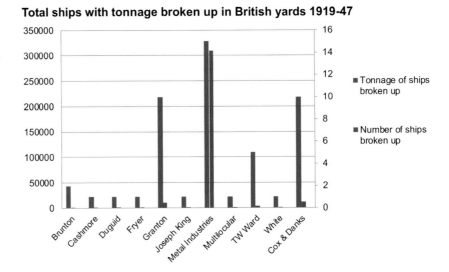

Total ships with tonnage broken up in British yards 1919-47

■ Tonnage of ships broken up

■ Number of ships broken up

Figure 18.3. Graph showing the number and tonnage of ships broken up in British yards divided into the 11 companies involved. Metal Industries effectively held a monopoly.

except SMS *Bremse*, which was broken up at Scapa Flow by Cox & Danks. In fact, the overall tonnage of ships broken up by Metal Industries was 310,174, or 90 per cent of the total tonnage of ships broken. Metal Industries' gross revenue from the breaking of the scuttled fleet is therefore estimated at around £1,550,000 at 1936 prices. From the known prices it paid to Cox & Danks and its own operating records it is known that each large warship broken up made a net profit in the region of £60,000.[2] By comparison, it will be recalled that Cox & Danks barely broke even.

Metal Industries was able to maintain its dominant position because it controlled the main resource needed to break up the large warships – namely, the Admiralty dockyard space at Rosyth. Even when T. W. Ward offered Cox & Danks more money for SMS *Seydlitz* it was debarred from selling to Ward by the Admiralty, which controlled access to its dockyard facilities. Metal Industries appears to have been the Admiralty's favoured dockyard tenant.[3] In effect, this meant that it retained a monopoly over the breaking of the large warships.

By comparison, the Admiralty sales ledger shows that it sold 57 ships of the scuttled fleet for a total of £30,030. It actually sold 58 ships, but the price realized for SMS *Karlsruhe* when it was reputedly sold to Metal Industries in 1955 is not recorded. The Admiralty also sold leases to salvage the light cruisers SMS *Brummer*, SMS *Cöln* and SMS *Dresden*, but the revenue it gained is not known.

The 58 ships the Admiralty sold included five still present, partially salvaged at Scapa Flow: SMS *Karlsruhe*, SMS *V83*, SMS *Markgraf*, SMS *König* and SMS *Kronprinz Wilhelm*. It therefore sold 53 of the 66 ships lifted after the Grand Scuttle. Included in this figure are the two warships which it had initially used for trials, SMS *V44* and SMS *V82*. The balance of 13 is accounted for by 11 ships distributed as war prizes and SMS *Nürnburg* and SMS *Baden*, expended as gunnery targets in the English Channel.

Looking at the price per ton per ship paid to the Admiralty, unsurprisingly it is Metal Industries which struck the best deals. It paid as little as £0.024 per ton for SMS *Derfflinger* and little more for all of the ships it purchased. The highest price paid per ton was by B. Fryer & Sons, which paid over £2.1 per ton for SMS *G92* in 1921. But of course *G92* was already salvaged and simply had to be towed away from Grangemouth, so there was no salvage cost to take into account when bidding for her. The exact details of the sales and fates of all 74 ships are given in Appendix 4.

The scuttled fleet today

The surveying of the wrecks in Scapa Flow has added new data to their long history. In the case of the Grand Scuttle there is a detailed relationship between the archaeology and historical text. The surveys have served to enhance our knowledge of what is there now and what has happened to the wrecks over the last century. The nine extant shipwrecks are very well known, externally at least, although not much has been recorded internally. The recording of the way they are changing is a unique contribution to the text.

The surveys of all the outlying wreck and scrappage sites have also added significantly to the record of the Grand Scuttle and the salvage years. Ultimately, this study is simply part of a continuum of work and doubtless in the future further surveys will show how the wrecks are continuing to change.

Outside of Scapa Flow, six entire ships from the Grand Scuttle still lie on the seabed. All appear to lie below the 60m line and are accessible to only the most experienced and highly trained specialist divers. Four of them are off the coast of the USA. They were expended in bombing and gunnery trials in July 1921. The wreck of SMS *Frankfurt* was surveyed in 2012 with multibeam, as shown in Figure 18.4. At around 120 metres' depth, the wreck lies at the

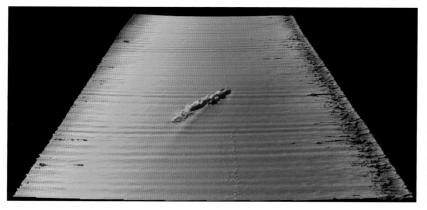

Figure 18.4. Multibeam image of SMS *Frankfurt* as scanned in 2012. The depth of the wreck is at the maximum range for hull-mounted systems. (NOAA)

Figure 18.5. Graph showing the extent of discernible wreckage of specific ships still surviving 100 years after the Grand Scuttle. At least 33 of them have some wreckage remaining on the seabed.

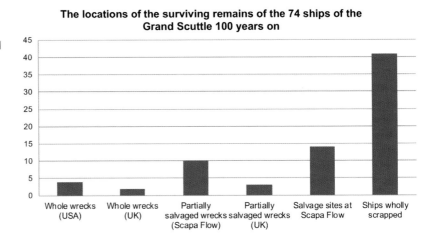

The locations of the surviving remains of the 74 ships of the Grand Scuttle 100 years on

extreme range for hull-mounted multibeam systems, hence the lower resolution compared with the relatively shallower Scapa Flow wrecks.

The three torpedo boats of the Grand Scuttle that sank at the same time, SMS *S132*, SMS *V43* and SMS *G102*, have also been located and surveyed. Figure 18.1 shows *G102* awaiting her fate as a bombing target. It will be recalled that she was the last ship to sink during the Grand Scuttle.

The Royal Navy's gunnery targets SMS *Nürnberg* and SMS *Baden* are known shipwrecks in the English Channel. From the description of the wreck of *Nürnberg* and its current condition, it appears uncannily similar to the way the light cruiser wrecks at Scapa are breaking up.[4] The last surveys carried out on SMS *Baden* suggested that a pair of her turrets may have fallen out when she was deliberately sunk in the Hurd Deep in 1921. The similarity to the way the turrets fell out of her sister *Bayern* during her salvage is evident.[5]

In looking at the case of each of the 74 ships of the Grand Scuttle and ascertaining whether any portions at all of these ships survive, it is surprising to note that remains of 33 of the ships do actually survive, albeit in some cases in quite small fragments. The distribution of these wreck sites is depicted in the graph in Figure 18.5. In addition to the wrecks mentioned above, the remains of three torpedo boats, SMS *V44*, SMS *V81* and SMS *V82*, lie in UK waters outside of Scapa Flow. At Scapa Flow, nine discernible shipwrecks survive, as described in Chapters 10–17, plus the keel of SMS *S36*, as described in Chapter 6.

The salvage sites at Scapa Flow from where 14 of the warships were lifted retain at least some remains, albeit quite small in cases such as SMS *Moltke*. These ships include the seven major warships and the torpedo boat *V78* raised by Cox & Danks, as described in Chapters 6 and 7, and the six major warships raised by Metal Industries, as described in Chapter 8. The scrappage sites, such as the secondary wreck site of SMS *Grosser Kurfürst* and the unidentified torpedo boat wreckage on the *Hindenburg* and *Seydlitz* sites, have been omitted to avoid double counting. In total, 41 of the ships of the Grand Scuttle appear to have been scrapped entirely and have left no discernible trace on the seabed.

Commercial salvage on or of shipwrecks is generally looked on with disdain by archaeologists. Cases of illegal looting, such as those seen on the Battle of Jutland and Java Sea wrecks, are considered heritage crimes, and at least one group of the miscreants involved recently found themselves in an English court of law for looting a wreck in UK waters without a permit.

But what can be said of the salvage of so many wrecks at Scapa Flow? It was, after all, legally sanctioned. The salvaging of the naval graves of *UB116* and HMS *Vanguard* has left a slightly embarrassing legacy. In my view, the work should never have been approved, but it is important to remember that that work was carried out in different times and it would not happen now.

In Orkney the salvage legacy, especially after World War II, may have triggered some degree of remorse. It is important to remember that in the case of the battleship HMS *Royal Oak*, sunk in Scapa Flow by *U47* in 1939 with the loss of 834 men, it was the islanders themselves who protested when plans to raise the wreck were mooted in 1958.[6] It has largely been seen as sacrosanct since that time.

The salvaging of the wrecks of the Grand Scuttle is a different matter. Of course it would be great if all of the wrecks were still there, intact, for divers to enjoy, but we are left with what we have. In fact, what the wrecks of the Grand Scuttle represent today is a unique cultural and industrial underwater landscape with its own character and identity, which this book set out to analyze. The tenacious and innovative Ernest Cox is a character it is difficult not to admire, which is why most of what has been written of him borders on hagiography. The history of Metal Industries is no less interesting for its rapid rise to an industrial giant that was ultimately acquired in an aggressive takeover in 1967 by Thorn Electrical Industries.

It is important to also consider that the Scapa wrecks are easily accessible, being in comparatively benign and protected waters and being close to shore. This makes them ideal candidates for long-term study, especially of site-formation processes. The salvage marks visible on the surviving wrecks can also be seen in this regard. The wrecks are excellent, well-documented comparators of how salvage manifests itself on shipwrecks. For example, the Sea War Museum Jutland's recent survey of the cruiser SMS *Blücher*, sunk at the Battle of Dogger Bank in 1915, shows that the wreck bears the marks of industrial salvage, similar to what is seen in the engine-room areas of the wrecks in Scapa Flow, making it patently obvious what has happened to *Blücher*.

The future of the wrecks

The nine remaining wrecks of the Grand Scuttle at Scapa Flow will never be raised. The sheer cost of conservation alone would be ruinously expensive and is not realistic to consider. So they will remain where they are until time and the marine environment cause their collapse and ultimate disappearance. This is realism and practicality as well as policy and it accords with Rule 1 of the Annex to the 2001 UNESCO Convention on the Protection of Underwater Cultural Heritage, which urges conservation *in situ*.[7]

Accurately predicting what will happen to the wrecks over the next few decades as they continue to degrade is practically impossible due to the myriad forces at work on them. One very useful aspect of the analysis carried out on the wrecks has been the possibility of comparing the 2006 ADUS survey with our own done in 2017. In general terms it can be said that the light cruisers are following a somewhat consistent pattern of degradation, seen at its most advanced state on the shallowest site, that of SMS *Karlsruhe*. The theory that the degradation of the light cruisers by aerobic corrosion has been accelerated by the exhaled gases of recreational divers is compelling.

In Australia the 1976 Historic Shipwrecks Act had a no penetration dive restriction incorporated within it, and it has been used to enhance the protection and preservation of sites such as that of SS *Yongala*. In this case, the damage perceived to be caused by divers was both mechanical, leading to the loss of concretion, and corrosive, due to air pockets forming within the hull of the wreck, as well as being due to unregulated souveniring.[8] This seems logical but is not easy to prove beyond doubt.

The three battleships, having all been subjected to similar salvage activity, could in theory also be expected to degrade in a consistent manner. Certainly, loss of sections of their double bottoms from the tops of the wrecks seems a common feature. It is also suggested that the removal by salvage of their armoured belts may actually have helped lessen the loading on the ships' frames and contributed to extending their lives as extant shipwrecks. This is only a theory, and like so much of the study of shipwreck site-formation processes, it would be hard to validate. It seems that the angle at which *Kronprinz Wilhelm* lies is likely to cause it to break up first, as seen with the loosening of a large section at the top of the wreck.

With the formal protection of seven of the wrecks as monuments in 2002, unregulated souveniring from these sites is officially perceived to have been largely curtailed. In order to have an effect though, laws require enforcement. In 2017 two divers were convicted of looting SMS *Markgraf* and handed heavy fines. The status of the wrecks as monuments is an interesting one because it raises the thorny legal question as to who is ultimately responsible for them, especially when something goes wrong.

A diver has already been seriously injured by falling debris, and it is quite possible that the same or worse will happen again in the future as the wrecks continue to weaken. Who would be liable then? There is also the potential for environmental problems to emerge in the future as they wrecks break up. Who might be liable for any clean-up? One would have to imagine that in the event either was to happen, the Occupiers' Liability (Scotland) Act 1960 would be likely to be tested to its limits by lawyers. In our increasingly litigious world, wreck ownership may not necessarily be a profitable enterprise any more.

There has been the suggestion circulated by the news media in the last few years that Historic Environment Scotland was considering the case for a historic marine protected area for Scapa Flow. The idea promulgated is to widen protection of the seabed to cover all of Scapa Flow under the jurisdiction of the Marine (Scotland) Act 2010, making it a historic marine protected area.[9] As this study has shown, there are at least 30 individual wreck sites in Scapa Flow relating to the Grand Scuttle alone. There are dozens of other wreck sites too, and more could potentially be found in the future.

Indeed, this happened in the summer of 2017 when a diesel motorboat (or pinnace) of German origin was discovered by divers south of the *Bayern* salvage site. The new wreck site was allegedly completely untouched when found and the boat seems likely to have sunk during the Grand Scuttle, becoming the 31st wreck site related to that event on the bottom of Scapa Flow.

A pair of photographs of features from this site can be seen in Figure 18.6, taken when I recorded what is there on video in November 2017. On the top is the Körting maker's plate on the engine and, below, one of the boat's small portholes. The site looked largely untouched. This is because all of the dive boat skippers in Scapa had informally agreed to try and restrict souveniring of items from it. This was a noble gesture, but legislation which automatically protected everything on the seabed would make it unnecessary and it is sincerely hoped protected status for the entirety of Scapa Flow will follow in the future.

Final reflections

A century may have passed since the Grand Scuttle was headline news around the world. It created a unique layer on the ever-changing palimpsest which is the underwater landscape of Scapa Flow. Centuries of history

Figure 18.6. Features seen on the newly found German motor boat discovered in Scapa Flow in 2017. Top, the engine maker's plate, and bottom, a porthole.

preceded it and its imprint has subsequently been partially erased by salvage of the ships and the reuse of the area as a busy naval base, which in turn has left its own traces on the same landscape. It is important to see the Grand Scuttle in context with the myriad other changes to the underwater landscape of Scapa Flow, not least those brought about by barriers and blockships, lost ships and aircraft. Scapa Flow is indeed endowed with a rich shipwreck legacy.

This book has attempted to show that in addition to the seven internationally important protected wrecks, much more of the Grand Scuttle and the salvage years can still be detected 100 years after the event than might be presumed. The wreck sites of Scapa Flow comprise a globally significant historical and cultural artefact, an underwater industrial landscape of unique character to be enjoyed, studied and revered for many decades to come.

Dr Innes McCartney, Leverhulme ECR
Bournemouth University, June 2018
imccartney@bournemouth.ac.uk

1   Orkney Archives (various dates), Diaries of H. Murray Taylor: Notes on Bayern Salvage 1934–1935, D1/59/5. Kirkwall.

2   Naval Historical Branch (various dates), *CP 8a Sale Book*, Portsmouth. I. Buxton, *Metal Industries: Shipbreaking at Rosyth and Charlestown* (Kendal: World Ship Society, 1992), pp. 33–34.

3   I. Buxton (1992), *Metal Industries: Shipbreaking at Rosyth and Charlestown* (Kendal: World Ship Society), pp. 17–18.

4   Hydrographic Department of the Admiralty (2017), Record of Wreck No. 18864 SMS *Nürnberg* (Taunton: Hydrographic Office).

5   Hydrographic Department of the Admiralty (2017), Record of Wreck No. 23354 SMS *Baden* (Taunton: Hydrographic Office).

6   G. S. Snyder (1978), *The Royal Oak Disaster* (London: Presidio), p. 228.

7   UNESCO (2001), Definitions of the 2001 Convention, http://portal.unesco.org/en/ev.php-URL_ID=13520&URL_DO=DO_TOPIC&URL_SECTION=201.html (accessed June 2018).

8   A. Viduka (2011), 'Managing Underwater Cultural Heritage: A Case Study of SS *Yongala*', *Historic Environment*, 23, no. 2, pp. 12–18.

9   A. Munro (2012), 'Marine Survey Uncovers the Hidden Secrets of Scapa Flow Naval Graveyard', *The Scotsman*, 13 July. Edinburgh.

APPENDIX 1:
THE GRAND SCUTTLE, 21 JUNE 1919

SHIPS, COMMANDING OFFICERS, SINKING TIMES AND CASUALTIES		
Flagship – Rear-Admiral von Reuter		
SMS *Emden* (light cruiser)	Lt Cdr Ehlers	
Battleships		
SMS *Baden*	Cdr Zirzow	
SMS *Friedrich der Grosse*	Cdr von Watcher	Sunk at 1216hrs (1)
SMS *Kaiser*	Lt Cdr Wippern	Sunk at 1325hrs (6)
SMS *Prinzregent Luitpold*	Lt Cdr von Reiche	Sunk at 1330hrs (7=)
SMS *Kaiserin*	Cdr Viertel	Sunk at 1400hrs (12=)
SMS *König Albert*	Cdr Böhmer	Sunk at 1254hrs (2)
SMS *Bayern*	Lt Cdr Meissner	Sunk at 1430hrs (15=)
Killed: Yeoman of Signals Hans Hesse		
SMS *Grosser Kurfürst*	Lt Cdr Beer	Sunk at 1330hrs (7=)
SMS *Kronprinz Wilhelm*	Lt Cdr Becker	Sunk at 1315hrs (5)
Killed: Stoker Karl Bauer		
SMS *Markgraf*	Cdr Schumann	Sunk at 1645hrs (19)
Killed: Cdr Walter Schumann, CPO Hermann Dittman		
SMS *König*	Cdr Junkermann	Sunk at 1400hrs (12=)
Battlecruisers		
SMS *Seydlitz*	Lt Cdr Brauer	Sunk at 1350hrs (10=)
SMS *Moltke*	Lt Cdr Erelinger	Sunk at 1310hrs (4)
SMS *Derfflinger*	Cdr Pastuszyk	Sunk at 1445hrs (17)
SMS *Hindenburg*	Cdr Heyden	Sunk at 1700hrs (20)
SMS *Von der Tann*	Lt Cdr Wollanke	Sunk at 1415hrs (14)
Light Cruisers		
SMS *Karlsruhe*	Lt Cdr Ruville	Sunk at 1550hrs (18)
SMS *Nürnberg*	Lt Cdr Georgii	
SMS *Cöln*	Lt Cdr Heinemann	Sunk at 1350hrs (10=)
SMS *Frankfurt*	Lt Cdr Beesel	

Killed: Apprentice Kuno Evertsberg (killed on HMS *Resolution* on night of 23 June)		
SMS *Brummer*	Lt Cdr Prahl	Sunk at 1305hrs (3)
SMS *Bremse*	Lt Schacke	Sunk at 1430hrs (15=)
SMS *Dresden*	Lt Cdr Fabricius	Sunk at 1330hrs (7=)
Torpedo Boats		
1st Torpedo Boat Flotilla		
SMS *G40* (Leader)	Lt Cdr Henrici	Sunk: *G40*
SMS, *G38, G39, G86, V129, S32*		Sunk: *G38, G39, G86, V129, S32*
(the only flotilla entirely sunk)		
2nd Torpedo Boat Flotilla (3rd & 4th Half Flotillas)		
SMS *B110* (Leader)	Lt Cdr Mensche	Sunk: *B110*
3rd Half Flotilla	SMS *G101, G102, G103, G104, V100*	Sunk: *G101, G103, G104*
4th Half Flotilla	SMS *B109, B111, B112*	Sunk: *B109, B111, B112*
3rd Torpedo Boat Flotilla		
SMS *S54* (Leader)	Lt Cdr Steiner	
SMS *S53, S55, G91, V70, V73, V81, V82*	Sunk: *S55, G91, S53, V70*	
6th Torpedo Boat Flotilla (11th & 12th Half Flotillas)		
SMS *V44* (Leader)	Lt Cdr Wehr	
11th Half Flotilla	*V43, V45, V46, S49, S50*	Sunk: *S49, S50, V45*
SMS *S131* (Half Leader)	Lt Cdr von Bonin	Sunk: *S131*
12th Half Flotilla	*V125, V126, V127, V128, S132*	
Killed from *V126*: Warrant Engineer Wilhelm Markgraf, Chief Engine Room Artificers Gustav Funkrath and Friedrich Beicke		
Killed from *V127*: Stoker Karl Funk		
7th Torpedo Boat Flotilla (13th & 14th Half Flotillas)		
SMS *S138* (Leader of Torpedo Boats)	Cdr Cordes	Sunk *S138*
SMS *S56* (Half Leader)	Lt Cdr Roslik	Sunk *S56*
13th Half Flotilla	*S65, V78, V83, G92*	Sunk *V78, S65*
SMS S136 (Half Leader)	Lt Cdr Reimer	Sunk *S136*
14th Half Flotilla	*S137, H145, G89*	Sunk *H145*
9th Torpedo Boat Flotilla (17th Half Flotilla)		
SMS *V80* (Half Leader)	Lt Cdr Ganguin	
S36, S51, S52, S60	Sunk *S52, S36*	

APPENDIX 2:
ADMIRALTY TRANSLATION OF VON REUTER'S ORDER

Commander of Interned Squadron
Order P.39

(Pass) by an Officer   June 17th, 1919. (K).
PERSONAL

To Captain……. F. d. T.

1   The Captains receive the order, "Ships may be ready for sinking", so that on receipt of the order, ships may sink as quickly as possible.

2.   After the disembarkation of the crews as extensive preparations as possible shall be completed. How far co-operation and imparting of knowledge to individual people of the crew without endangering the plans is any way – betrayal to the English – must be for the Commanding Officers to judge.

3.   As preparative measures come into question :- Perpetual keeping open of all inboard valves such as valves in the fore and aft passages along ship's side, valves in bunkers, doors in thwartships and fore and aft bulkheads, hatchway covers, ventilation valves, sideports etc, further estimation of individual ships; freeing of the obstacles blocking torpedo tubes and other such things, lifting of a condenser, opening of valves and shutters in flooding and other pipes &c leaving only one valve closed.

4.   BOATS. If possible only one boat – for removing the crew, is to be cleared away. For that purpose a flag of truce is to be kept ready for taking away in the boat. The boats with their disembarked crews are to make for the land by the shortest route and remain assembled there under their officers.

5.   Sinking is only to take place :-

(a) On case of a forced boarding by the English.

(b) On receipt of explicit orders from me.

6. to 5a.

Commanding Officers must consider thoroughly how they must act independently in case of an attempt by the English to seize them unawares in order to ensure the sinking.

2.   A demand from the English for the ship to be handed over, if not ordered by me, is to be regarded as an interference by force and is to be met by sinking the ships.

to 5b.

The Order may be expressed so that.

The ship is to be sunk immediately.

The ship is to be sunk at a certain hour later on.

SIGNALS

For immediate sinking in accordance with 7a.

"To all Commanding Officers and F.d.T:-

"Paragraph Eleven" Confirm

Chief. I.V.

This signal will be repeated by all methods at our disposal.

The sinking will be immediately commenced.

For sinking at a certain/later hour:- according to 7b :-

1st Example.

"To all Commanding Officers and F.d.T.

"paragraph zero nine one three" Confirm

Chief I.V.

In the case of this signal the first two numbers mean the date, therefore the "ninth", the last two the time at which the sinking is to begin.

The time by clock reckons continuously from noon to noon (Astronomical).

Therefore One three means thirteen

"One O'clock in the night 9/10

2nd Example

One four one one – means ..

14th at 11 O'clock in the evening.

Punctuality at the given time the ship is to begin to sink. Beforehand the attention of the guard (drifters) is not to be attracted to the ship, by the obvious gathering of many men on deck &c.

Confirmation of the receipt of the signal is to take place as follows:-

To Chief of I.V, (Kommendo des Internierungsverbandes)

Paragraphs signal received

Captain of Emden.

10.The coming days will be especially critical as it is a matter of the acceptance or non-acceptance of the peace terms and the outbreak again of hostilities.

Therefore from 18 -6 by day and night increased vigilance is necessary both as regards unusual behaviour of the English and also for signals from "EMDEN".

No extensive reliance can be placed on the personnel anymore; the officers themselves must undertake themselves the observation in the most intense manner.

11. My intention is only to sink the ships if the enemy wishes to take possession of them without approval of our government. If our government has agreed in the treaty to the handing over of the ships, then they will be surrendered, to the lasting shame of those who have placed us in this situation.

12. This document is immediately to be placed securely under lock and key. It must not fall into the hand of the enemy.

Sd. V. Reuter.

This version of von Reuter's order is copied exactly from the version which appears as Appendix F in Admiral Fremantle's report of the 'Sinking of the Interned German Fleet at Scapa' dated 24 June 1919. This can be found in the National Archives in ADM 116/2074.

APPENDIX 3:
ACCOUNT OF THE GRAND SCUTTLE

BY FLEET ENGINEER FAUSTMAN OF SMS *MARKGRAF*

21

10) Preparation for the sinking ship and more

The Gg. order of the J.V. that was received on board on June 18th was at first only brought to the knowledge of the officers and the Obermaschinist [Chief Mechanic].

Some preparations had already been made earlier on. Following communication of the J.V., an illegal occupation of the ship by the Englishmen was thought possible for May 31st, the day of the commemoration of the Battle of the Skagerrak. In this case, the Kommandant [Captain] had already ordered earlier that the ammunition rooms should be flooded so that the ship would sink. For this purpose, the Obermaschinist himself would open all required locks which had also been previously checked for easy functioning, except for the bottom valves. The First Pumpenmeister was the only one on board who could do this in an inconspicuous manner. The Captain only considered a slow and inconspicuous flooding and sinking of the ship while the ship remained in its vertical position. As he did not want the crew to be informed prematurely, the new preparations did not take place yet, however, the ones which had been previously made were repeated.

On June 20th, by order of the J.V., the Kommandant informed the crew about the plan when the men were gathered in the wardroom. The plan was generally met with applause.

22

There were some crewmembers who did not approve of the sinking the ship, but only one had the courage to speak up. It was the Maschinist [Mechanic] Klawe, former Obmann [Chairman] of the S.R. From his political point of view as a U.S. citizen, he did not believe that it was the right thing to do. However, when questioned by the Kommandant, he explained that he would not take any measures against it. From the remaining crew, it was only Oberbootmaat [Senior Maat] Dittmann who, fired up by his love for his country, tried to explain in short words why the sinking of the ship was necessary.

On Saturday, June 21st, the three main condenser pumps were removed, in case that it would be necessary to speed up the sinking of the ship. On this day, the boilers were under steam for the cleaning of the ship, and the Kommandant himself burned the ship's biography and structural drawings in the boiler while I burned the machine's biography, drawings, plans and operating manuals. – At 11.10 a.m. we received a message that communicated the order to sink the ship. The Kommandant let the entire crew report to the middle deck and announced the order. Immediately thereafter, the lifeboats were prepared for launching. First, the launch boat was launched on starboard. Although the Kommandant explicitly explained to the crew that all hands would be needed and the crew had ample time to pack the most important things, many of them tried to shy away from it and wanted to pack up their things. I had to chase them out of the living quarters myself. At this time, the feeding pump in the boiler room broke down. Since the reserve feeding pump did not start up right away,

-23-

the Diesel engine was started up. It worked efficiently and provided the light needed for the launching of the life boats and the lighting throughout the ship. The Kommandant himself gave the order to the Obermaschinist to open the bottom valves and flood the ship. When there was a little hold up on deck during the launch of the life boats, the Kommandant, who was worried about the safety of the crew, had the valves closed again for a short time, as he wanted to avoid any losses of human life during the sinking of the ship. While I was busy below deck chasing the people to get them out for the launching and operating of the boats, and after two boots had been launched, a puffer pulled up starboard and started firing at the middle deck and the launch boat that was towed on this side and on which, by order of the Kommandant, the ship's doctor had hoisted a white flag that was clearly visible. Besides the doctor, the Oberbootsmannsmaat […] Hellwig and the Obermatrose [Leading Seaman] Schmidt were on board of the launch boat. One of the first shots was fired into the back of the head of Oberbootsmannsmaat Dittmann and killed him instantly. The distance to the vessels was approximately 150–250 m. After the Obermaat Dittmann was killed, the Kommandant ordered Signalmaat Arndt to hoist another white flag in the foretop what he did right away. The shelling from the two vessels however did not stop. After about 10 minutes the attention of the two vessels on starboard was drawn

-24-

to the sinking of the light cruiser on the left side and they turned towards the light cruisers. From the puffer on portside the shelling of the speedboat and middle deck continued. By this time, the Kommandant had taken cover behind the C tower on the middle deck. Waving a white handkerchief while observing the puffer through his binoculars, he tried to make the puffer cease fire. However, as soon as he became visible, he was under fire and by the third time he was shot in the head and killed right away. Sanitaetsfeldwebel Sakowski tried to seek shelter for the body of the dead Kommandant, but had to give up because each time he tried to do so they were firing from the puffer at him. When the puffer no longer could locate living targets portside, it turned towards the starboard side. In the meantime, about 50 men, the greater part of the crew, had boarded the launch boat. Since the engine did not start, their boat just drifted away from the ship. After the puffer had been firing at the boat for a short time, it turned towards the battleships in front of the 'Markgraf'. The remaining crew, carrying the two dead men, used this break to climb onboard the speedboat that was portside. As I had not been on deck, I was unaware of the captain's death and the crew leaving the ship. While I was packing up my things, the Obermaschinist, who was also unaware of the captain's death, informed me that the majority of the crew had left the ship

-25-

I was very surprised to hear that because I had expected that the Kommandant would give an order to so. So, I went to the Captain's cabin where I found his bag packed and sitting on the table. From this, I assumed that the Captain was still on board. When the Obermaschinist and I came on deck, the speedboat with the rest of the crew was portside. It was only then, when I asked about the whereabouts of the captain, that I was informed that he and Obermaat Dittrich had been killed in action and that their bodies were on board of the speedboat. I knew that the water was flooding the rooms under deck and that it was no longer possible to close the bottom valves as they were already under water and the rodding already disengaged, so I left the ship along with the Obermaschinist after I had picked up the Captain's bag which I wanted to give to his wife. So, the speedboat steered by Obermaat [Seaman] Grabowski and flying a white flag took off towards the Island of Cava. On our way, a ship from Friedrich the Great was towed to get it out of the firing range of the puffer as quickly as possible, because the puffer made it the target of the attack. When we approached the Island of Cava, we were also fired at from an English outpost and a civilian. The puffer had also followed us and started its shelling again. Shortly thereafter, we were able to convince the outpost to cease fire. As he feared to get shot himself, he was able to cause the puffer to cease fire while fidgeting with his rifle.

-26-

Now the speedboat was ordered to come alongside at the puffer. The tug stayed where it was while the speedboat had to tow the boats near the puffer. During this process, the speedboat was ordered to a second puffer, which had already taken on several boats. It was then towed by the puffer and brought alongside the Ramillies, an English battleship, where our crew had to report on deck right away. We were not allowed to bring any of our luggage. The launch boat with the majority of the crew on it was intentionally hit by a puffer, but it was only slightly damaged. Its crew was taken onboard the puffer and immediately put into the ship's hold. Carrying luggage had been denied by putting a gun to the men's heads. The last men who were sent to the ship's hold could see that a member of the puffer crew (a civilian) was sent to the boat with an axe, put pieces of luggage aside, and smashed the thwart. The Leutnant zur See Bonte von Markgraf who was already on board of the puffer and who had been the Entladeoffizier [Load Control Officer] on the steamship Dollart was called and asked to act as a translator about 10 minutes after the crews had come on board and he could not see anything left of the launch boat. From the puffer the crew was then brought over to the Royal Sovereigns, an English battleship. Not one piece of the luggage that had been in the launch boat was found.

On the Ramillies the luggage left in the life boats was first brought on deck and later below deck by English seamen. We were not permitted access to our luggage although we asked for it several times.

-27-

After the luggage had been moved to another boat that was towed alongside, the speedboat remained alongside with the two dead bodies. We were told that the corpses were supposed to be handed over to an English hospital ship. The crews from the boats which were surrendered to the Ramillies remained on the afterdeck until the early evening, officers and deck officers stayed starboard, the other crews portside, all supervised by guards. At 4.25 a.m. we saw how the Markgraf, after it sunk down up to the galley, tilted portside and capsized. Towards the evening we were accommodated under deck whereas officers, deck officers, and crew were separated. The officers, there were approximately 35 of them, were assigned to an area on the tween deck, the Reserve-Gefechtsverbandplatz, from which everything was removed that could have been used as seating accommodations. For supper, we got a piece of bread with jam and a large jar filled with tea which, in the absence of a drinking cup, we had to drink from a ladle. We were not given any blankets and thus had to sleep on the bare floor. The next morning the officers received a bowl filled with fresh water but there were no towels or soap. Breakfast was served the same way as the supper had been served the day before, it consisted of bread and corned beef. At six in the morning the ship along with the remaining other ships sailed to Murray-Firth where we arrived and disembarked at noon. When we arrived the looted luggage of the officers and crew was spread out on the jetty and beach. After the men had gathered their things, we started to march off to Nigg where we arrived by 5 pm.

-28-

We were given thin woollen blankets and were then accommodated in large empty barracks without any kind of equipment. We received bread and corned beef and because of the good nature of the Scottish guards we received a glass of water when the barracks were closed at 9 pm.

On the morning of June 23rd, the barracks were opened again. For washing and bathing we could use the facilities of the camp, however, we were not given soap or towels. We did not get any breakfast, water, or any other provisions either. At 1:30 pm the first group of men marched off to the Nigg train station where they arrived at 3 pm. After being served corned beef and bread as travel provisions, we climbed into a special train that brought us to Oswestry where we arrived the next morning (June 24th at 10 a.m.) always guarded by Scottish soldiers. We did not receive anything to drink during the trip and were almost dying of thirst so we drank from the water which had been used for washing in the toilets. The officer who was leading the transport and the troops also treated us well, but they were not able to provide us with drinking water. We arrived in Parkhall at 11 a.m. and were subject to a thorough body search during which we had to strip down to our underpants while the Englishmen even had the audacity to ask us for souvenirs. Following the body search, we were assigned to the camps E 3, 4, and 5.

On July 3rd the remnants of our luggage arrived in Oswestry and except for our civilian clothes we were allowed to receive our belongings for which we were issued a receipt. Most of the suitcases had been opened by force and the most precious things were stolen. There were only some suitcases, which had not been opened and most of the luggage was missing.

Faustman

This is a translated excerpt from the reports of officers recorded after the Grand Scuttle. The originals are found in the microfilmed records of the German navy held by the National Archives & Records Administration (NARA), specifically Roll T1022-1629.

APPENDIX 4:
THE ULTIMATE FATES OF THE SHIPS OF THE GRAND SCUTTLE

Battleships

SMS Baden: Saved from sinking and towed to Smoogro Bay on 23 Jun 1919; salved by RN 10 Jul 1919; foundered as target in the Channel 3 Feb 1921; raised 21 May 1921; scuttled in deep water in the Channel on 16 Aug 1921; still a shipwreck today.

SMS Bayern: Sold to MI for £750 on 17 Nov 1933; raised on 1 Sep 1934; towed to MI 26 Apr 1935; arrived 1 May 1935; scrapped from 5 Jun 1935; book closed 11 Mar 1936.

SMS Friedrich der Grosse: Sold to MI for £750 on 9 Jul 1934; raised 29 Apr 1937; towed to MI on 31 Jul 1937; arrived 5 Aug 1937; scrapped from 25 Aug 1937; book closed 18 May 1938.

SMS Grosser Kurfürst: Sold to MI for £750 on 9 Jul 1934; raised on 26 Apr 1938; towed to MI on 23 Jul 1938; arrived 27 Jul 1938; scrapped from 24 Aug 1938; book closed 24 Jan 1940.

SMS Kaiser: Sold to C&D for £1000 on 20 Aug 1928; raised on 20 Mar 1929; resold to AS for £75,000; towed to AS 20 Jul 1929; arrived 24 Jul 1929; scrapped from 11 Sep 1929; book closed 23 Dec 1931.

SMS Kaiserin: Sold to MI for £750 on 9 Nov 1934; raised on 14 May 1936; towed to MI on 27 Aug 1936; arrived 31 Aug 1936; scrapped from 18 Nov 1936; book closed 13 Dec 1937.

SMS König Albert: Sold to MI for £750 on 9 Nov 1934; raised on 31 Jul 1935; towed to Lyness 9 Aug 1935; towed to MI on 29 Apr 1936; arrived 4 May 1936; book closed 1937.

SMS König: Sold to MI for £750 on 20 Apr 1936; sold on to Nundy Marine Metals Ltd c.1956; sold on to Scapa Flow Salvage Ltd in 1970; sold on to Undersea Associates in 1978, bankruptcy 1979; sold by receiver to Clark's Diving Services Ltd in 1981, the current legal owner; designated under the Ancient Monuments and Archaeological Areas Act 17 Apr 2002; still a partially salvaged shipwreck today.

SMS Kronprinz Wilhelm: Sold to MI for £750 on 20 Apr 1936; sold on to Nundy Marine Metals Ltd c.1956; sold on to Scapa Flow Salvage Ltd in 1970; sold on to Undersea Associates in 1978, bankruptcy 1979; sold by receiver to Clark's Diving Services Ltd in 1981, the current legal owner; designated under the Ancient Monuments and Archaeological Areas Act 17 Apr 2002; still a partially salvaged shipwreck today.

SMS Markgraf: Foundered while being pulled off its mooring; sold to MI for £750 on 20 Apr 1936; sold on to Nundy Marine Metals Ltd c.1956; sold on to Scapa Flow Salvage Ltd in 1970; sold on to Undersea Associates in 1978, bankruptcy 1979; sold by receiver to Clark's Diving Services Ltd in 1981, the current legal owner; designated under the Ancient Monuments and Archaeological Areas Act 17 Apr 2002; still a partially salvaged shipwreck today.

SMS Prinzregent Luitpold: Sold to C&D for £1,000 on 15 Aug 1929; raised on 9 Jul 1931; beached 16 Jul 1931; resold to MI for £38,000 14 Mar 1933; towed to MI on 4 May 1933; arrived 11 May 1933; scrapped from 13 Jun 1933; book closed 14 Mar 1934.

Battlecruisers

SMS *Derfflinger*: Sold to MI for £750 on 20 Apr 1936; raised on 25 Jul 1939; towed to Rysa 26 Jul 1939; remained in Scapa throughout WWII; towed to Faslane Nov 1946; completely scrapped by Jun 1948.

SMS *Von der Tann*: Sold to C&D for £1,000 on 15 Aug 1929; raised on 7 Dec 1930; beached at Cava 18 Dec 1930; resold to MI for £30,500 on 14 Mar 1933; towed to MI on 6 Jul 1933; arrived 9 Jul 1933; scrapped from 12 July 1933; book closed 23 May 1934.

SMS *Hindenburg*: Sold to C&D for £3,000 on 10 May 1924; raised on 22 Jul 1930; sold to MI for £75,000 on 18 Aug 1930; towed to MI on 23 Aug 1930; arrived 27 Aug 1930; scrapped from 14 Sep 1930; book closed 23 Dec 1931.

SMS *Moltke*: Sold to C&D for £1,000 on 13 Sep 1926; raised on 9 Jun 1927; next to Cava 29 Jun 1927; moved to Lyness 7 Sep and lightened; resold to AS for £40,000 delivered; left Scapa on tow 18 May 1928; arrived at AS 21 May 1928; scrapped from 16 June 1928; book closed 20 Mar 1929.

SMS *Seydlitz*: Sold to C&D for £3,000 on 10 Oct 1924; raised on 2 Nov 1928; resold to AS Nov 1928 for £65,000; left Scapa on tow 2 May 1929; arrived at AS 11 May 1929; scrapped from 12 June 1929; book closed 30 Dec 1931.

Light Cruisers

SMS *Bremse*: Sold to C&D for £300 on 9 Nov 1925; raised 27 Nov 1929; completely scrapped in Lyness up to May 1931. (SMS Bremse was sold with a £200 discount to compensate C&D, which had bought SMS *V83* when it was considered it could be salvaged. After salvage was abandoned it had already been sold by CinC Rosyth to ECW.)

SMS *Brummer*: Salvage rights (not ownership) bought for £200 by Nundy Marine Metals *c*.1962; sold on to Scapa Flow Salvage Ltd in 1970; sold on to Undersea Associates in 1978, bankruptcy 1979; transferred to Clark's Diving Services Ltd in 1981; lease expired Dec 1982 and ownership reverted to the MOD , ownership sold for £1 to Orkney Islands Council on 3 November 1986, the current legal owner; designated under the Ancient Monuments and Archaeological Areas Act 17 Apr 2002; still a partially salvaged shipwreck today.

SMS *Cöln*: salvage rights (not ownership) bought for £200 by Nundy Marine Metals Ltd *c*.1962; sold on to Scapa Flow Salvage Ltd in 1970; sold on to Undersea Associates in 1978, bankruptcy 1979; transferred to Clark's Diving Services Ltd in 1981; lease expired Dec 1982 and ownership reverted to the MOD, ownership sold for £1 to Orkney Islands Council on 3 November 1986, the current legal owner; designated under the Ancient Monuments and Archaeological Areas Act 17 Apr 2002; still a partially salvaged shipwreck today.

SMS *Dresden*: Salvage rights (not ownership) bought for £200 by Nundy Marine Metals Ltd *c*.1962; sold on to Scapa Flow Salvage Ltd in 1970; sold on to Undersea Associates in 1978, bankruptcy 1979; transferred to Clark's Diving Services Ltd in 1981; lease expired Dec 1982 and ownership reverted to the MOD; ownership sold for £1 to Orkney Islands Council on 3 November 1986, the current legal owner; designated under the Ancient Monuments and Archaeological Areas Act 17 Apr 2002; still a partially salvaged shipwreck today.

SMS *Emden*: Beached in Smoogro Bay; salved by RN 28 Jun 1919; transferred to France 11 Mar 1920; used for explosives tests; scrapped in Caen *c*.1926.

SMS *Frankfurt*: Beached in Smoogro Bay; salved by RN 12 Jul 1919; transferred to USA; sunk as an air target 18 Jul 1921; still a shipwreck today.

SMS *Karlsruhe*: Reported sold to MI in 1955 (amount unknown); sold on to Nundy Marine Metals Ltd *c*.1956; masts removed as navigational hazard Oct 1940; sold on to Scapa Flow Salvage Ltd in 1970; sold on to Undersea Associates in 1978, bankruptcy 1979; sold by official receiver to Clark's Diving Services Ltd in 1981, the current legal owner; designated under the Ancient Monuments and Archaeological Areas Act 17 Apr 2002; still a partially salvaged shipwreck today.

SMS *Nürnberg*: Beached to the west of Cava; salved by RN 3 Jul 1919; sunk as a target in the Channel 7 Jul 1922; still a shipwreck today.

Torpedo Boats and Destroyers

SMS *B109*: Sold to C&D for £200 on 12 Sep 1924; raised on 27 Mar 1926; resold to AS for £600 and towed to AS on 24 Jun 1926; scrapped from 10 Jul 1926; book closed 18 Jun 1929.

SMS *B110*: Sold to C&D for £200 on 12 Sep 1924; raised on 10 Dec 1925 (the 20th torpedo boat C&D lifted); resold to GS on 12 Jan 1926; scrapped *c*.1926.

SMS *B111*: Sold to C&D for £200 on 12 Sep 1924; raised on 8 Mar 1926; resold and towed to GS 8 Apr 1926; scrapped *c*.1926.

SMS *B112*: Sold to C&D for £200 on 12 Sep 1924; raised on 11 Feb 1926; resold and towed to GS 7 Mar 1926; scrapped *c*.1926.

SMS *G38*: Sold to C&D for £200 on 12 Sep 1924; raised on 27 Sep 1924; partially scrapped in Scapa in Jul 1925; hull placed on starboard bilge of *Moltke* in May 1927; completely scrapped in 1929.

SMS *G39*: Sold to C&D for £200 on 12 Sep 1924; raised on 3 Jul 1925; gutted alongside Lyness; completely scrapped by Feb 1927.

SMS *G40*: Sold to C&D for £200 on 12 Sep 1924; raised on 29 Jul 1925; resold and towed to TWW on 18 Aug 1925; scrapped in Inverkeithing in 1926.

SMS *G86*: Sold to C&D for £200 on 12 Sep 1924; raised on 14 Jul 1925; resold to GS; arrived 17 Aug 1925; scrapped *c*.1925.

SMS *G89*: Beached on Fara; RN salvage attempts abandoned on 28 Jun 1919; no attempt made in Jul; wreck sold by CinC Rosyth to A. Young of Stromness for £500 in 1920 while off Fara; raised *c*.Dec 1922 and towed to Stromness and partially broken up; resold to C&D in Aug 1928; towed to Lyness Sep 1928; scrapped by *c*.1931.

SMS *G91*: Sold to C&D for £200 on 10 May 1924; raised on 12 Sep 1924; resold and towed to TWW on 15 Dec 1924; scrapped in Inverkeithing in 1925.

SMS *G92*: Beached on Rysa; raised to Lyness floating dock by 15 Aug 1919; allocated to Britain, towed to Grangemouth; sold by tender to B. Fryer & Sons, along with the surrendered *G95*, for £3,750 the pair on 28 Feb 1921; after arbitration Fryer paid a further £230 in 1925.

SMS *G101*: Sold to C&D for £200 on 12 Sep 1924; raised on 13 Apr 1926 (the 24th C&D lifted); resold to AS for £600 and towed to AS on 17 Jun 1926; scrapped from 26 Jun 1926; book closed 26 Mar 1929.

SMS *G102*: Beached in Mill Bay; salved by RN in Jul–Aug 1919; transferred to USA; sunk as a bombing target 13 Jul 1921; still a shipwreck today.

SMS *G103*: Sold to C&D for £200 on 12 Sep 1924; raised on 30 Sep 1925 (the first of the true destroyer types to be lifted by C&D and the 19th overall); stranded off Lochielair Nov 1925; broken up *c*.1926 (not known if raised or broken up *in situ*).

SMS *G104*: Sold to C&D for £200 on 12 Sep 1924; raised on 30 Apr 1926 (the last of the 25 C&D lifted and the last from the Grand Scuttle); resold to AS for £600 and towed to AS on 11 Jul 1926; scrapped from 4 Aug 1926; book closed 19 Mar 1929.

SMS *H145*: Sold to C&D for £200 on 12 Sep 1924; raised on 14 Mar 1925; gutted and beached in Mill

Bay on 20 Jun 1925; completely scrapped in 1928.

SMS *S32:* Sold to C&D for £200 on 12 Sep 1924; raised on 19 Jun 1925; resold to GS; arrived 8 Jul 1925; scrapped *c.*1925.

SMS *S36:* Sold to C&D for £200 on 12 Sep 1924; raised on 18 Apr 1925 and towed into Mill Bay; re-sunk off Cava to assist in the *Hindenburg* salvage; scrapped *in situ* thereafter; still wreckage present.

SMS *S49:* Sold to SFS&S for £100 on 26 Apr 1923; raised w/c 22 Dec 1924 (SFS&S 4th and last lift); resold to GS on 10 Mar 1925 and scrapped *c.*1925.

SMS *S50:* Sold to SFS&S for £100 on 26 Apr 1923; raised w/c 10 Nov 1924 (SFS&S 3rd lift); resold to MS on 10 Mar 1925 (and towed to Luce Bay, arriving 23 Mar 1925) and scrapped *c.*1925.

SMS *S51:* Beached on Fara; salved by RN in Jul–Aug 1919; allocated to Britain; towed to Grangemouth, sold to James A. White for £750 on 2 March 1921.

SMS *S52:* Sold to C&D for £200 on 12 Sep 1924; raised on 14 Oct 1924; resold and towed to TWW; arrived 16 Dec 1924 and scrapped *c.*1925.

SMS *S53:* Sold to C&D for £200 on 10 May 1924; raised on 14 Aug 1924; hull too buckled for towing; gutted in Scapa 1926; completely scrapped in 1927.

SMS *S54* Beached on Fara; salved by RN in Jul–Aug 1919; lost on tow off Flotta early 1920; sold to C&D for £200 on 31 Dec 1927; lift attempted in Dec 1929; demolished *in situ* in 1931; wreckage still present.

SMS *S55:* Sold to C&D for £200 on 10 May 1924; raised on 29 Aug 1924; resold to GS; arrived 11 Feb 1925; scrapped 1925.

SMS *S56:* Sold to C&D for £200 on 12 Sep 1924; raised on 5 Jun 1925; gutted and beached in Mill Bay 25 Oct 1925; completely scrapped in Mar 1928.

SMS *S60:* Beached on Fara; salved by RN in Jul–Aug 1919; allocated to Japan but sold and scrapped in the UK *c.*1920.

SMS *S65:* Sold to C&D for £200 on 12 Sep 1924; raised on 16 May 1925; resold to GS; arrived 3 Jun 1925; scrapped *c.*1925.

SMS *S131:* Sold to SFS&S for £100 on 26 Apr 1923; raised by 29 Aug 1924 (SFS&S 1st lift); resold to GS on 2 Dec 1924 and scrapped *c.*1925.

SMS *S132:* Saved from sinking on her mooring by **HMS** *Walpole;* transferred to USA; sunk as a gunnery target 15 Jul 1921; still a shipwreck today.

SMS *S136:* Sold to C&D for £200 on 12 Sep 1924; raised on 3 Apr 1925; holed by lifting wires and unable to be towed; gutted and beached in Mill Bay; scrapped in *c.*1928.

SMS *S137:* Beached on Fara; salved by RN to floating dock Lyness 27 Jun 1919; allocated to Britain; towed to Grangemouth, sold to W. Duguid for £920 on 28 Feb 1921.

SMS *S138:* Sold to C&D for £200 on 12 Sep 1924; raised on 1 May 1925; resold and towed to TWW; arrived 16 Jun 1925; scrapped in Inverkeithing in 1926.

SMS *V43:* Beached in Ore Bay; salved by RN in Jul–Aug 1919; transferred to USA; sunk as a gunnery target 15 Jul 1921; still a shipwreck today.

SMS *V44:* Beached on Fara; salved by RN in Jul–Aug 1919; transferred to Britain; used as a target; sold in 1921 while lying in Portsmouth along with *V82* for £900 to TWW; resold to G.W. Pound in 1926 (Admiralty received additional £101); partially scrapped in Portsmouth in 1921 onwards; hull located in Portsmouth harbour in 2016.

SMS *V45:* Sold to SFS&S for £100 on 26 Apr 1923; raised w/c 13 October 1924 (SFS&S 2nd lift); resold to JJK on 2 Dec 1924 and scrapped *c.*1925.

SMS *V46:* Beached in Ore Bay; salved by RN in Jul–Aug 1919; transferred to France; scrapped in Cherbourg *c.*1924.

SMS *V70:* Sold to C&D for £200 on 10 May 1924; raised on 1 Aug 1924 (C&D's 1st successful lift); partially scrapped in Scapa in Sep 1928; remaining part named Salvage Unit No. 3 (and fitted with a crane); cut up in May 1933.

SMS *V73*: Beached on Fara; salved by RN in Jul–Aug 1919; allocated to Britain; towed to Grangemouth; sold to G&W Brunton for £400 on 15 Feb 1921.

SMS *V78*: Sold to C&D for £200 on 12 Sep 1924; raised on 7 Sep 1925 (recovered upside down and righted in Mill Bay before beaching; the 18th and last of the smaller torpedo boats lifted by C&D); resold and towed to GS 7 Oct 1925; scrapped *c*.1926.

SMS *V80*: Beached on Fara; salved by RN in Jul–Aug 1919; transferred to Japan but sold and scrapped in the UK *c*.1922.

SMS *V81*: Beached on Fara; salved by RN in Jul–Aug 1919; lost on tow in Sinclair Bay, Caithness around 1922; wreck sold to J. Mowatt of Stromness for £60 on 23 Sep 1937; 53 tons of scrap metal recovered by end Aug 1938; still wreckage present.

SMS *V82*: Beached on Fara; salved by RN in Jul–Aug 1919; transferred to Britain; used as a target; sold in 1921 while lying in Portsmouth along with *V44* for £900 to TWW; resold to G.W. Pound in 1926 (Admiralty received additional £101); partially scrapped in Portsmouth in 1921 onwards; hull located in Portsmouth harbour in 2016.

SMS *V83*: Beached on Rysa; RN attempts to salvage continued into Oct 1919; sold by CinC Rosyth to ECW for £150 in 1920 while off Rysa; resold to Mr P. Kerr of Aberdeen in 1925; salvaged *in situ* until at least 1928; still wreckage present.

SMS *V100*: Beached in Mill Bay; salved by RN in Jul–Aug 1919; transferred to France; scrapped *c*.1921.

SMS *V125*: Beached in Ore Bay; salved by RN in Jul–Aug 1919; transferred to Britain; sold while at Portsmouth to John Cashmore for £1,010 in Aug 1921.

SMS *V126*: Beached in Ore Bay; salved by RN in Jul–Aug 1919; transferred to France; scrapped in Lorient *c*.1925.

SMS *V127*: Beached in Ore Bay; salved by RN in Jul–Aug 1919; transferred to Japan but sold and scrapped in Dordrecht *c*.1922.

SMS *V128*: Beached in Ore Bay; salved by RN in Jul–Aug 1919; allocated to Britain; towed to Grangemouth; sold to G&W Brunton for £700 on 15 Feb 1921.

SMS *V129*: Sold to C&D for £200 on 12 Sep 1924; raised on 11 Aug 25; resold and towed to TWW on 28 Aug 1925; scrapped in Inverkeithing in 1925.

Notes

Unless stated otherwise, each ship is considered to have sunk on its mooring.

Lists of dates regarding the salvage operations, movements, etc. can vary widely between published sources. Where conflict has been seen to exist, the RN disposals ledger and the accounts books of Metal Industries have been cited as being the most reliable, supported where possible with news pieces from the *Orkney Herald* given in parentheses.

Dates of sales by RN are given as the date of clearance of funds, if known.

Date of scheduling the surviving wrecks as monuments is given as the date the protected zones came into legal effect as recorded by the UK Hydrographic Office.

RN = Royal Navy; D&C = Cox & Danks; ECW = East Coast Wrecking Co.; MI = Metal Industries; SFS&S = Scapa Flow Salvage & Shipbreaking; GS = Granton Shipbreaking Co.; JJK = John Joseph King & Sons; MS = Multilocular Shipbuilding Co.; TWW = Thomas W. Ward; AS = Alloa Shipbreaking Co. (which changed its name to Metal Industries on 22 Nov 1929).

BIBLIOGRAPHY

Admiralty (1912) *Stoker's Manual*. London: HMSO.

Anon. (1919) 'Aboard the German Fleet in Scapa Flow', *The Living Age*, 26 April 1919, pp. 201–203. Boston: Living Age Co.

Anon. (1919) German Mine-laying Cruisers, *The Engineer*, April, p. 383.

Anon. (1925) Scapa Flow Salvage Operations, *The Engineer*, 24 September, pp. 248–249. London.

Anon. (1927) The Salving of the Ex-German Battle-Cruisers 'Moltke' and 'Seydlitz', *The Engineer*, 7 July, pp. 741–745. London.

Anon. (1928) The Salving of the Ex-German Battle-Cruiser 'Moltke'. *The Engineer*, 15 June, p. 737. London.

Anon (1935) Salvage of the König Albert, *Shipbuilding and Shipping Record*, 8 August.

Anon. (1948) The Work of a Shipbreaking Yard, *The Engineer*, 3 December, p. 563. London.

Anon. (1948) The Work of a Shipbreaking Yard, *The Engineer*, 10 December, p. 591. London.

BBC (2015) Letter from Sub Lt Markham of HMS *Revenge* to his mother, 26 June 1919. http://www.bbc.co.uk/news/magazine-33152438

Booth, T. (2011) *Cox's Navy: Salvaging the German High Seas Fleet at Scapa Flow 1924–1931*. Barnsley: Pen & Sword.

Bowman, G. (1964) *The Man Who Bought a Navy*. London: Harrap.

Brotherton Library (various dates) Liddle Collection, Crawford Papers. Leeds.

Brotherton Library (various dates) Liddle Collection, Cunliffe Papers. Leeds.

Brotherton Library (various dates) Liddle Collection, Harkness Papers. Leeds.

Brotherton Library (various dates) Liddle Collection, May Papers. Leeds.

Brotherton Library (various dates) Liddle Collection, Maingay Photographs. Leeds.

Brotherton Library (1972) Liddle Collection, transcript of tape 60, by Peter Liddle. Interview with Miss K. Watt, August 1972. Leeds.

Brown, M. & Meehan, P. (1968) *Scapa Flow: The Story of Britain's Greatest Naval Anchorage in Two World Wars*. London: Alan Lane The Penguin Press.

Bundesarchiv (various dates) Constructor's Plans of SMS *Kronprinz*. Freiburg.

Burrows, C. W. (2007) *Scapa and a Camera*. Penzance: Periscope.

Buxton, I. (1992) *Metal Industries: Shipbreaking at Rosyth and Charlestown*. Kendal: World Ship Society.

Caird Library (various dates) Thursfield account of the scuttle, AGC/10/21. London: National Maritime Museum.

Caird Library (various dates) Correspondence with Charles Madden, BTY/13/29-30. London: National Maritime Museum.

Caird Library (various dates) Photographs of the German Fleet, BTY/23/7. London: National Maritime Museum.

Caird Library (various dates) Junior Officer's Journal, HMS *Royal Sovereign*, JOD/274. London: National Maritime Museum.

Caird Library (various dates) Log of SMS *Nürnburg*, LOG/F8. London: National Maritime Museum.

Campbell, N. J. M. (1986) *Jutland: An Analysis of the Fighting*. London: Conway.

Canmore National Record of the Historic Environment Scotland (various dates) https://canmore.org.uk/site/101973/sms-v81-final-location-sinclairs-bay-north-sea

Cousins, G. (1965) *The Story of Scapa Flow*. London: Muller.

Cox, E. (1932) 'Eight Years' Salvage Work at Scapa Flow', *Proceedings*. London: Institute of Mechanical Engineers.

Davidson Baker, A. (1993) Disposing of the Kaiser's Navy 1918–1920. In J. Sweetman (ed.), *New Interpretations in Naval History*. Annapolis: Naval Institute Press.

Davis, R. H. (1935) *Deep Diving and Submarine Operations: A Manual for Deep Sea Divers and Compressed Air Workers*. London: St Catherine's Press.

Dodson, A. (2016) 'Derfflinger: An Inverted Life', *Warship*, 2016, pp. 175–178.

Dodson, A. (2017) 'After the Kaiser: The Imperial German Navy's Light Cruisers after 1918', *Warship*, 2017, pp. 140–160.

Dorling, Captain Henry Taprell. (1936) *Endless Story: being an account of the work of the destroyers, flotilla-leaders, torpedo-boats and patrol boats in the Great War*. London: Hodder and Stoughton.

Ferguson, D. M. (1985) *The Wrecks of Scapa Flow*. Stromness: Orkney Press.

Ferguson, D. M. (1987) *The Shipwrecks of Hoy Sound*. Stromness: David M. Ferguson.

Freiwald, L. (1932) *The Last Days of the German Fleet*. London: Constable.

Fremantle, Admiral Sir S. R. (1949) *My Naval Career 1880–1928*. London: Hutchinson.

Friedman, N. (ed.) (1992) *German Warships of World War I: The Royal Navy's Official Guide to the Capital Ships, Cruisers, Destroyers, Submarines and Small Craft, 1914–1918*. London: Greenhill.

Friedman, N. (2011) *Naval Weapons of World War One: Guns, Torpedoes, Mines and ASW Weapons of All Nations. An Illustrated Directory*. Barnsley: Seaforth.

Gardiner, R. (ed.) (1985) *Conway's All the World's Fighting Ships 1906–1921*. London: Conway.

George, S. C. (1973) *Jutland to Junkyard: The Raising of the Scuttled German High Seas Fleet from Scapa Flow – the greatest salvage

operation of all time*. Cambridge: Patrick Stephens.

Gordon, A. (1996) *The Rules of the Game: Jutland and British Naval Command*. London: John Murray.

Gores, J. N. (1971) *Marine Salvage*. Newton Abbot: David & Charles.

Gowans Whyte, A. & Hadfield, R. L. (1933) *Deep-Sea Salvage*. London: Sampson Low, Marston & Co.

Gröner, E. (1990) *German Warships 1815–1945. Volume One: Major Surface Vessels*. London: Conway.

Groos, O. (1925) *Der Krieg in der Nordsee Funfer Band Januar bis Juni 1916*. Berlin: Mittler & Sohn.

Groos, O. (2006) *Der Krieg in der Nordsee Band 7 Vom Sommer 1917 bis zum Kriegsende 1918 Kritische Edition*. Berlin: Mittler. & Sohn.

Grosset, H. (1953) *Down to the Ships in the Sea*. London: Hutchinson.

Halpern, G. P. (1994) *A Naval History of World War I*. Annapolis: Naval Institute Press.

Harper, J. E. T. (1927) *Reproduction of the Record of the Battle of Jutland*. London: HMSO.

Henry S., Heath K. & Littlewood M. (2018) *High Sea Fleet Salvage Sites Report*. Edinburgh. Historic Environment Scotland.

Herwig, H. H. (1980) *'Luxury' Fleet: The Imperial German Navy 1888–1918*. London: George Allen & Unwin.

Hewison, W. S. (1990) *This Great Harbour Scapa Flow*. Kirkwall: Orkney Press.

Horn, D. (1969) *The German Naval Mutinies of WW1*. New Brunswick: Rutgers University Press.

Hydrographic Department of the Admiralty (2017) Record of Wreck Nos: 916 SMS *SV81*, 978 SMS *S54*, 1013 SMS *G38*, 1034 SMS *V78*, 1051 SMS *G101*, 1052 SMS *V83*, 1058 SMS *Seydlitz*, 1069 SMS *Hindenburg*, 1073 SMS *S36 (Bow Section)*, 1078 SMS *Kaiser*, 1080 SMS *Dresden*, 1082 SMS *Prinzregent Luitpold*, 1083 SMS *König*, 1084

SMS *Kaiserin*, 1085 SMS *Karlsruhe*, 1087 SMS *Markgraf*, 1088 SMS *Kronprinz Wilhelm*, 1089 SMS *Brummer*, 1090 SMS *Koln*, 1091 SMS *Grosser Kurfürst*, 1094 SMS *Bayern Turrets*, 1114 SMS *B109* (part), 1120 SMS *Bremse*, 1230 *Energy*, 23354 SMS *Baden*, 18864 SMS *Nürnberg*. Taunton: Hydrographic Office.

Hydrographic Department of the Admiralty (various dates) Chart No. 35, Scapa Flow & Approaches. Taunton: Hydrographic Office.

Hydrographic Department of the Admiralty (various dates) Chart No. 2249, Orkney Islands Western Sheet. Taunton: Hydrographic Office.

Hydrographic Department of the Admiralty (various dates) Chart No. 2250, Orkney Islands Eastern Sheet. Taunton: Hydrographic Office.

Hydrographic Department of the Admiralty (various dates) Chart No. 2581, Southern Approaches to Scapa Flow. Taunton: Hydrographic Office.

Hydrographic Office Archive (various dates) Chart No. 2581, Scapa Flow & Approaches, Southern Sheet, 1923. Taunton: Hydrographic Office.

Hydrographic Office Archive (various dates) Chart No. 2581, Scapa Flow & Approaches, Southern Sheet, 1940. Taunton: Hydrographic Office.

Hydrographic Office Archive (various dates) Chart No. 3729, Scapa Flow & Approaches, Northern Sheet, 1923. Taunton: Hydrographic Office.

Hydrographic Office Archive (various dates) Chart No. 3729, Scapa Flow & Approaches, Northern Sheet, 1940. Taunton: Hydrographic Office.

Hydrographic Office Archive (various dates) Chart No. 2578, Scapa Flow South West Portion, 1926. Taunton: Hydrographic Office.

Hydrographic Office Archive (various dates) Chart No. C7954/1, Scapa Flow South West Portion, Survey of the sunken German warships, 1919. Taunton: Hydrographic Office.

Hydrographic Office Archive (various dates) Chart No. C7954/2, Scapa Flow South West Portion, Survey of the Sunken German warships, 1919. Taunton: Hydrographic Office.

Hydrographic Office Archive (various dates) Chart No. C7952/OQ, Berthing Plan for the German Fleet, 1919. Taunton: Hydrographic Office.

Hydrographic Office Archive (various dates) Chart No. C7953, Press 14 H, Surveyed Positions of the Sunken German Fleet, 1919. Taunton: Hydrographic Office.

Hydrographic Office Archive (various dates) Chart No. C7953, Shelf Oq., S.W. portion of Scapa Flow Posns of & depths over wrecks of sunken German Warships and soundings N.W. of Cava I. Taunton: Hydrographic Office.

Imperial War Museum (various dates) Private Papers of Admiral Sir Henry McCall. London.

Intertek (2014) Laboratory Analysis of Scapa Flow Ship Wreck Samples and Application of the Weins Number Methodology. Aberdeen: Intertek (copy in author's collection).

Jackson, B. (2010) *But Not All Men Live! From Scapa to Africa and All Dives in Between. The true tale of a diver who did it all, and lived.* Fareham: Barry Jackson.

Jane's Fighting Ships of World War I (1990) London: Studio Editions.

Judge, J. (2016) *The Imperial German Navy of World War I: A Comprehensive Photographic Study of the Kaiser's Naval Forces. Vol. 1: Warships.* Atglen: Schiffer.

Kenworthy, J. M. (1933) *Sailors, Statesmen – and Others: An Autobiography.* London: Rich & Cowan.

Koerver, H. J. (ed.) (2009) *Room 40: German Naval Warfare 1914–1918. Vol. 1: The Fleet in Action*. Steinbach: LIS Reinisch.

Koerver, H. J. (ed.) (2009) *Room 40: German Naval Warfare 1914–1918. Vol. 2: The Fleet in Being*. Steinbach: LIS Reinisch.

Koop, G. & Schmolke, K.-P. (1995) *Vom Original zum Modell: Die Linienschiffe der BAYERN-Klasse*. Bonn: Bernard & Graefe Verlag.

Koop, G. & Schmolke, K.-P. (1999) *Planmappe: Linienschiffe Ostfriesland und König*. Bonn: Bernard & Graefe Verlag.

Koop, G. & Schmolke, K.-P. (1999) *Vom Original zum Modell: Die Linienschiffe der Nassau bis König-Klasse*. Bonn: Bernard & Graefe Verlag.

Koop, G. & Schmolke, K.-P. (2004) *Planmappe: Kleine Kreuzer 1903–1918 BRUMMER-/BREMSE-Klasse*. Bonn: Bernard &Graefe Verlag.

Lakowski, R. (1993) *Kaiserliche Marine Geheim 1871–1918*. Berlin: Brandenburgisches.

Liddle, P. H. (1985) *The Sailor's War 1914–18*. Poole: Blandford Press.

Lipscomb, F. W. & Davies, J. (1966) *Up She Rises: The History of Naval Salvage*. London: Hutchinson.

Macdonald, R. (1998) *Dive Scapa Flow*. Edinburgh: Mainstream.

Macdonald, R. (2017) *Dive Scapa Flow*. Edinburgh: Mainstream.

Marder, A. J. (1969) *From the Dreadnought to Scapa Flow: The Royal Navy in the Fisher Era, 1904–1919. Vol. IV: The Year of Crisis*. London: OUP.

Marder, A. J. (1970) *From the Dreadnought to Scapa Flow: The Royal Navy in the Fisher Era, 1904–1919. Vol. V: Victory and Aftermath*. London: OUP.

Marder, A. J. (1978) *From the Dreadnought to Scapa Flow: The Royal Navy in the Fisher Era, 1904–1919. Vol. III: Jutland and After*. London: OUP.

Masters, D. (1926) *The Wonders of Salvage*. London: Bodley Head.

Masters, D. (1931) *Salvage Work at Scapa Flow*. London: Cox & Danks.

McCartney, I. (2002) *Lost Patrols: Submarine Wrecks of the English Channel*. Penzance. Periscope.

McCartney, I. (2016) *Jutland 1916: The Archaeology of a Naval Battlefield*. London: Bloomsbury.

McCartney, I. (2017) 'The Opening and Closing Sequences of the Battle of Jutland 1916 Re-examined: Archaeological Investigations of the Wrecks of HMS *Indefatigable* and SMS *V4*', *International Journal of Nautical Archaeology*, 46, no. 2, pp. 317-329.

McCartney, I. (2017) 'The Battle of Jutland's Heritage under Threat: The Extent of Commercial Salvage on the Shipwrecks as Observed 2000–2016', *Mariner's Mirror: The International Quarterly Journal of the Society for Nautical Research*, 103, no. 2, pp. 196–205.

McDermaid, J. (1911) *Shipyard Practice as Applied to Warship Construction*. London: Longmans.

McKenzie, T. (1934) 'How the "Bayern" was Raised', *Shipbuilding and Shipping Record*, 1 November.

McKenzie, T. (1935) 'How the "König Albert" was Raised at Scapa Flow', *Shipbuilding and Shipping Record*, 17 October.

McKenzie, T. (1936) 'How the "Kaiserin" was Raised at Scapa Flow', *Shipbuilding and Shipping Record*, 16 July.

McKenzie, T. (1938) The Salving of the Ex-German Fleet at Scapa', *Minutes Royal Institution of Great Britain*, Friday 28 January.

McKenzie, T. (1949) 'Marine Salvage in Peace and War', *Institution of Engineers and Shipbuilders in Scotland*, 93, Paper 1122, pp. 123–161.

Miller, J. (2000) *Scapa*. Edinburgh: Birlinn.

Ministry of Defence (1986) Certificate of Purchase of SMS *Dresden* to Orkney Islands Council. London: MOD (copy in author's collection).

Ministry of Defence (1986) Certificate of Purchase of SMS *Cöln* to Orkney Islands

Council. London: MOD (copy in author's collection).

Ministry of Defence (1986) Certificate of Purchase of SMS *Brummer* to Orkney Islands Council. London: MOD (copy in author's collection).

Munro, A. (2012) 'Marine Survey Uncovers the Hidden Secrets of Scapa Flow Naval Graveyard', *The Scotsman*, 13 July. Edinburgh.

Murray Taylor, H. (2013) 'The Salvaging of the Ex-German High Seas Fleet at Scapa Flow (1924–1930)', *22nd Proceedings of the Annual Conference 2012*. Gosport: Historical Diving Society.

National Archives (various dates) Scapa Flow: disposal of interned German ships, ADM 1/8562/172. London.

National Archives (various dates) Scapa Flow: Action to be taken re the sinking of German Fleet, ADM 1/8571/296. London.

National Archives (various dates) Scapa Flow: German government's memorandum on scuttling of German warships, ADM 1/8575/331. London.

National Archives (various dates) German ships at Scapa Flow: allocation to Great Britain, ADM 1/8696/43. London.

National Archives (various dates) Account of the salvage and towing to Rosyth of the ex-German battleship *Prinz Regent Luitpold*, ADM 1/8766/77. London.

National Archives (various dates) Return of documents taken from German ships in Scapa Flow, ADM 1/8776/149. London.

National Archives (various dates) FOREIGN COUNTRIES (52): ex-German battle-cruiser DERFFLINGER: efforts to break up for scrap, ADM 1/13330. London.

National Archives (various dates) Admiralty Index 1919, ADM 12/1616A. London.

National Archives (various dates) Admiralty Digest 1919, ADM 12/1622A. London.

National Archives (various dates) Admiralty Index 1920, ADM 12/1632. London.

National Archives (various dates) Admiralty Digest 1920, ADM 12/1638. London.

National Archives (various dates) Internment of German warships at Scapa Flow, ADM 116/1825. London.

National Archives (various dates) Sinking of German Fleet at Scapa Flow, ADM 116/2074. London.

National Archives (various dates) Admiralty salvage agreement with Metal Industries Ltd, ADM 116/4545. London.

National Archives (various dates) Main Fleet base – Scapa Flow: inception, development and history, ADM 116/5790. London.

National Archives (various dates) Sinking of German ships at Scapa Flow: salvage of German ships, ADM 137/2486. London.

National Archives (various dates) Scuttling of German Ships at Scapa Flow and instructions for the internment of such ships, ADM 137/3816. London.

National Archives (various dates) Translation of various German post-war accounts of German naval mutiny, October–November 1918, ADM 137/4186. London.

National Archives (various dates) Requests to allow movement of interned German naval personnel at Scapa Flow, ADM 137/4702. London.

National Archives (various dates) O. Groos, The Battle of Jutland: Official German Account: Admiralty translation, 1926, ADM 186/626. London.

National Archives (various dates) Scuttling of the German ships at Scapa Flow, CAB 24/83/74. London.

National Archives (various dates) Scotland: Orkney Islands. Admiralty chart showing the southern portion of the Orkney Islands, MFQ 1/88. London.

National Archives (various dates) Wrecks of HMS *Vanguard* and German ships *Dresden*, *Brummer* and *Koln* sunk in Scapa Flow: exercise of rights of repossession, TS 68/100. London.

National Archives and Records Administration (various dates) The Microfilmed Records of the German Navy, PG64939, Roll T1022-1629. Washington, DC.

National Archives and Records Administration (various dates) The Microfilmed Records of the German Navy, PG64939, Roll T1022-279. Washington, DC.

National Library of Scotland (various dates) Chart No. 2578, Southwest Portion of Scapa Flow, 1927. Edinburgh.

National Library of Scotland (various dates) Chart No. 2581, Scapa Flow & Approaches (Southern Sheet), 1923. Edinburgh.

National Library of Scotland (various dates) Chart No. 3729, Scapa Flow & Approaches (Northern Sheet), 1923. Edinburgh.

Caird Library (various dates) Charles Peploe Letters, AGC 10/21. London.

National Maritime Museum (various dates) Constructor's Plans of SMS *Karlsruhe II*. London.

National Maritime Museum (various dates) Ship's Plans SMS *V25–V30*. London.

National Maritime Museum (various dates) 'Pumpenplan' SMS *Lützow*. London.

Naval Historical Branch (various dates) *CP 8a Sale Book*. Portsmouth.

New York Times (1919) German Crews Sink Most of Great Scapa Flow Fleet; Ships, with Seacocks Open, Go Down Under German Flag, *New York Times*, 22 June, p. 1.

Newbolt, H. (1931) *History of the Great War Based on Official Documents: Naval Operations, Vol. V*. London: Longmans, Green & Co.

Newcastle University Special Collections (various dates) The Accounts and Minutes of Metal Industries Shipbreaking. Newcastle.

Newton, R. N., RCNC (1941) *Practical Construction of Warships*. London: Longmans.

Novik, N. (1969) 'The Story of the Cruisers *Bremse* and *Brummer*', *Warship International*, VI, no. 3, pp. 185–189. Toledo: Naval Records Club.

Orkney Archives (various dates) Diaries of H. Murray Taylor: Admiralty Work 1934–1946. D1/59. Kirkwall.

Orkney Archives (various dates) Diaries of H. Murray Taylor: *Derfflinger* 1938–1939. D1/59. Kirkwall.

Orkney Archives (various dates) Diaries of H. Murray Taylor: *Kaiserin* 1935–1936. D1/59/1. Kirkwall.

Orkney Archives (various dates) Diaries of H. Murray Taylor: *Friedrich Der Grosse* 1936–1937. D1/59/2. Kirkwall.

Orkney Archives (various dates) Diaries of H. Murray Taylor: *Grosser Kurfürst* 1937–1938. D1/59/3. Kirkwall.

Orkney Archives (various dates) Diaries of H. Murray Taylor: Notes on *Bayern* Salvage 1934–1935. D1/59/5. Kirkwall.

Orkney Archives (various dates) Diaries of H. Murray Taylor: Salvage Logs for *Bayern* and *König Albert* 1934–1935. D1/59/6. Kirkwall.

Orkney Archives (various dates) Diaries of H. Murray Taylor: Salvage Logs for *König Albert* and *Kaiserin* 1935. D1/59/7. Kirkwall.

Orkney Archives (various dates) Diaries of H. Murray Taylor: Salvage Logs for *Kaiserin* and *Friedrich Der Grosse* 1936. D1/59/8. Kirkwall.

Orkney Archives (various dates) Tulloch eyewitness account of the scuttling of the German Fleet. D1/1100. Kirkwall.

Orkney Archives (various dates) Microfilmed records of the *Orkney Herald*, 1919–1931. Kirkwall.

Orkney Archives (various dates) Microfilmed records of the *Orcadian*, 1919–1938. Kirkwall.

Orkney Archives (various dates) Photographic collection of the Scuttle and subsequent salvage of the German Fleet. D1/938. Kirkwall.

Orkney Archives (various dates) Coroner's verdicts of the deaths at work of Cox workers. SC11/7/2/21 to 27. Kirkwall.

Orkney Archives (various dates) Sound recording: Sandy Robertson 1. OSA/340. Kirkwall.

Orkney Archives (various dates) Sound recording: Sandy Robertson 2. OSA/341. Kirkwall.

Orkney Archives (various dates) Sound recording: Sandy Robertson 3. OSA/RCAHMS/014/1. Kirkwall.

Orkney Archives (various dates) Sound recording: Sandy Robertson 4. OSA/RCAHMS/014/2. Kirkwall.

Orkney Archives (various dates) Sound recording: Sandy Robertson 5. OSA/RCAHMS/014/3. Kirkwall.

Orkney Archives (various dates) Sound recording: Harry Taylor 1. OSA/RO5/451. Kirkwall.

Orkney Archives (various dates) Sound recording: Harry Taylor 2. OSA/RO5/452. Kirkwall.

Orkney Archives (various dates) Sound recording: John Rosie 1. OSA/392. Kirkwall.

Orkney Archives (various dates) Sound recording: John Rosie 2. OSA/393. Kirkwall.

Orkney Archives (various dates) Sound recording: John Rosie 3. OSA/394. Kirkwall.

Parkes, O. (1966) *British Battleships: 'Warrior 1860' to 'Vanguard 1950'. A History of Design, Construction and Armament*. London: Seeley Service & Co.

Philbin, T. (1973) *Warship Profile 37: SMS König*. Windsor: Profile Publications.

Philbin, T. (1982) *Admiral von Hipper: The Inconvenient Hero*. Amsterdam: Grüner.

Preston, A. (1972) *Battleships of World War 1: An Illustrated Encyclopaedia of the Battleships of All Nations 1914–1918*. New York: Galahad Books.

Pottinger, J. (1974) *The Salvaging of the German Fleet*. A booklet accompanying the summer exhibition, 1974. Stromness: Stromness Museum.

Roberts, J. (1997) *Battlecruisers*. Annapolis. Naval Institute Press.

Ruge, F. (1972) *Warship Profile 27: SM Torpedo Boat B110*. Windsor: Profile Publications.

Ruge, F. (1973) *Scapa Flow 1919*. London: Ian Allen.

Scapa Flow 1919: With All Flags Flying (1986) Documentary film. London: Channel Four.

ScapaMAP 2000–2002 (2003) Report Compiled for Historic Scotland on the Mapping and Management of the Submerged Archaeological Resource in Scapa Flow, Orkney. Orkney: Scapa Flow Marine Archaeology Project.

ScapaMAP (2001–2006) Marine Heritage Monitoring with High Resolution Survey Tools: Scapa Flow 2001–2006. Orkney: Scapa Flow Marine Archaeology Project.

Scheer, Admiral R. (1920) *Germany's High Sea Fleet in the World War*. London: Cassel.

Schubert, P. & Gibson, L. (1932) *Death of a Fleet 1917–1919*. London: Hutchinson.

Smith, E. C. (1937) *A Short History of Naval and Marine Engineering*. Cambridge: Babcox and Wilcox Ltd.

Smith, P. L. (1989) *The Naval Wrecks of Scapa Flow*. Kirkwall: Orkney Press.

Snyder, G. S. (1978) *The Royal Oak Disaster*. London: Presidio.

Sothern, J. W. M. (1916) *The Marine Steam Turbine: A Practical Description of the Parsons and Curtis Marine Steam Turbines as Presently Constructed, Fitted, and Run*. London: Crosby Lockford & Son.

Staff, G. (2006) *German Battlecruisers 1914–18*. Oxford: Osprey.

Staff, G. (2008) *Battle for the Baltic Islands 1917: Triumph of the Imperial German Navy*. Barnsley: Pen & Sword.

Staff, G. (2010) *German Battleships 1914–18 (1)*. Oxford: Osprey.

Staff, G. (2010) *German Battleships 1914–18 (2)*. Oxford: Osprey.

Staff, G. (2011) *Battle on the Seven Seas: German Cruiser Battles 1914–1918*. Barnsley: Pen & Sword.

Staff, G. (2014) *German Battlecruisers of World War One: Their Design, Construction and Operations*. Barnsley: Seaforth.

Tait, C. (2012) *The Orkney Guide Book*. Orkney: Charles Tait.

Tarrant, V. E. (1995) *Jutland: The German Perspective*. London: Arms and Armour Press.

The Dreadnought Project (dreadnoughtproject.org) Constructor's Plans of SMS *Dresden II*.

The Dreadnought Project (dreadnoughtproject.org) Constructor's Plans of SMS *Friedrich der Grosse*.

The Dreadnought Project (dreadnoughtproject.org) (various dates) Constructor's Plans of SMS *S23*.

The Dreadnought Project (dreadnoughtproject.org) (various dates) Constructors' Plans of SMS *V170–V177*.

Thornton, J. (2003) *The Wrecks of Scapa Flow*. DVD. Scapaflow.com

UNESCO (2001) Definitions of the 2001 Convention. http://portal.unesco.org/en/ev.php-URL_ID=13520&URL_DO=DO_TOPIC&URL_SECTION=201.html (accessed June 2018)

University of California Irvine (various dates) Arthur J. Marder Papers MS.F.002. Correspondence with Cmdr W. M. Phipps Hornby. Irvine, CA.

US Navy Department, Bureau of Ordnance (1944) *Ships' Chemical Smoke Munitions* OP 1042.

van der Vat, D. (1982) *The Grand Scuttle: The Sinking of the German Fleet at Scapa Flow in 1919*. London: Hodder & Stoughton.

Viduka, A. (2011) 'Managing Underwater Cultural Heritage: A Case Study of SS *Yongala*', *Historic Environment*, 23, no. 2, pp. 12–18.

von Hase, G. (1920) *Kiel and Jutland*. London: Skeffington & Son.

von Reuter, L. (1940) *Scapa Flow: The Account of the Greatest Scuttling of all Time*. London: Hurst & Blackett.

von Reuter, L. (2005) *Scapa Flow: The Grave of the German Fleet*. Chesham: Wordsmith.

Wessex Archaeology Coastal & Marine (2012) *Scapa Flow Wreck Surveys. Archaeological Interpretation of Multibeam Data and Desk-based Assessment*. Salisbury: Wessex Archaeology.

Whittaker, I. G. (1998) *Off Scotland: A Comprehensive Record of Maritime and Aviation Losses in Scottish Waters*. Berwick upon Tweed: C-Anne.

Wolfstalt, W. (1939) *Der Seekrieg 1914–1918*. Leipzig: v Hale & Koeler.

Wolz, N. (2013) *From Imperial Splendour to Internment: The German Navy in the First World War*. Annapolis: Naval Institute Press.

Wood, L. (2000) *The Bull & the Barriers: The Wrecks of Scapa Flow*. Stroud: Tempus.

Wood, L. (2008) *Scapa Flow Dive Guide*. Southend-on-Sea: Aquapress.

Woodward, D. (1973) *The Collapse of Power: Mutiny in the High Seas Fleet*. London: Arthur Baker.

INDEX